⦾Harden's

London Restaurants

2015

"Gastronomes' bible"
Evening Standard

Survey driven reviews of nearly 1,600 restaurants

Put us in your client's pocket!

Branded gift books and editions for iPhone
call to discuss the options on 020 7839 4763.

© **Harden's Limited 2014**

ISBN 978-0-9929408-9-8

British Library Cataloguing-in-Publication data:
a catalogue record for this book is available from
the British Library.

Printed in Italy by Legoprint

Research and editorial assistants: Sarah Ashpole, Clare Burnage,
Clodagh Kinsella, Daniel O'Mahony, Wayne Tuckfield

Assistant editor: Karen Moss

Harden's Limited
Golden Cross House, 8 Duncannon Street
London WC2N 4JF

Would restaurateurs (and PRs) please address
communications to 'Editorial' at the above address,
or ideally by email to: editorial@hardens.com

The contents of this book are believed correct at
the time of printing. Nevertheless, the publisher
can accept no responsibility for errors or changes in
or omissions from the details given.

CONTENTS

RATINGS & PRICES

Ratings

Our rating system does not tell you – as most guides do – that expensive restaurants are often better than cheap ones! What we do is compare each restaurant's performance – as judged by the average ratings awarded by reporters in the survey – with other similarly-priced restaurants. This approach has the advantage that it helps you find – whatever your budget for any particular meal – where you will get the best 'bang for your buck'.

The following qualities are assessed:

F — Food
S — Service
A — Ambience

The rating indicates that, *in comparison with other restaurants in the same price-bracket*, performance is…

5 — Exceptional
4 — Very good
3 — Good
2 — Average
1 — Poor

> **NEW IN 2015!**
> Regular readers take note: we've turned our marking system on its head.
> **5** is the new **0**!

Prices

The price shown for each restaurant is the cost for one (1) person of an average three-course dinner with half a bottle of house wine and coffee, any cover charge, service and VAT. Lunch is often cheaper. With BYO restaurants, we have assumed that two people share a £7 bottle of off-licence wine.

Telephone number – all numbers are '020' numbers.

Map reference – shown immediately after the telephone number.

Full postcodes – for non-group restaurants, the first entry in the 'small print' at the end of each listing, so you can set your sat-nav.

Website and Twitter – shown in the small print, where applicable.

Last orders time – listed after the website (if applicable); Sunday may be up to 90 minutes earlier.

Opening hours – unless otherwise stated, restaurants are open for lunch and dinner seven days a week.

Credit and debit cards – unless otherwise stated, Mastercard, Visa, Amex and Maestro are accepted.

Dress – where appropriate, the management's preferences concerning patrons' dress are given.

Special menus – if we know of a particularly good value set menu we note this (e.g. "set weekday L"), together with its formula price (FP), calculated exactly as in 'Prices' above. Details change, so always check ahead.

'Rated on Editors' visit' – indicates ratings have been determined by the Editors personally, based on their visit, rather than derived from the survey.

SRA Star Rating – the sustainability index, as calculated by the Sustainable Restaurant Association – see page 8 for more information.

HOW THIS GUIDE IS WRITTEN

Survey

This guide is based on our 24th annual survey of what 'ordinary' diners-out think of London's restaurants. In 1998, we extended the survey to cover restaurants across the rest of the UK; it is by far the most detailed annual survey of its type. Out-of-town results are published in our UK guide.

This year, the total number of reporters in our combined London/UK survey, conducted mainly online, exceeded 6,250, and, between them, they contributed some 65,000 individual reports.

How we determine the ratings

In the great majority of cases, ratings are arrived at statistically. This essentially involves 'ranking' the average survey rating each restaurant achieves in the survey – for each of food, service and ambience – against the average ratings of the other establishments which fall in the same price-bracket. (This is essentially like football leagues, with the most expensive restaurants going in the top league and the cheaper ones in lower leagues. The restaurant's ranking *within its own particular league* determines its ratings.)

How we write the reviews

The tenor of each review and the ratings are very largely determined by the ranking of the establishment concerned, which we derive as described above. At the margin, we may also pay some regard to the proportion of positive nominations (such as for 'favourite restaurant') compared to negative nominations (such as for 'most overpriced').

To explain why a restaurant has been rated as it has, we extract snippets from survey comments ("enclosed in double quotes"). On larger restaurants, we receive several hundred reports, and a short summary cannot possibly do individual justice to all of them.

What we seek to do – *without any regard to our own personal opinions* – is to illustrate the key themes which have emerged in our analysis of the collective view. The only exception to this is the newest restaurants, where survey views are either few or non-existent, and where we may be obliged to rely on our own opinion. Unless the review carries the small print note "Rated on Editors' visit", however, the ratings awarded are still our best analysis of the survey view, not our own impression.

Richard Harden   **Peter Harden**

If you care about where your food comes from, whether your waiter is paid a fair wage or how the restaurants you eat in are reducing the amount of food they waste, then look out for the Sustainable Restaurant Association's (SRA) ratings next to listings in this guide.

The SRA is a not-for-profit body helping restaurants achieve greater sustainability. Members are scored across three main categories: Sourcing, Environment and Society, so you can easily identify those restaurants doing great things like sourcing seasonably, supporting local producers, using high welfare meat and dairy and ensuring fish stocks aren't endangered.

The One, Two or Three Star rating you'll see at the bottom of a restaurant's listing will also give you a guide as to how well it manages its waste, energy and water and how committed it is to supporting its local community. So when you choose to eat in a restaurant boasting the SRA stars you can rest assured your meal isn't costing the earth. All of the restaurants in the guide with SRA stars have completed the rating in the last 12 months.

"We're proud to support the SRA, and hope that by adding SRA Sustainability Ratings to the restaurants we include, we can help set diners' expectations as to which of their choices will ensure the trade thrives for decades, and hopefully centuries to come." Harden's

Among the winners at the Sustainable Restaurant Awards in February 2014 were:

• cafe-ODE – Sustainable Restaurant of the Year
• Grain Store – London Sustainable Restaurant
• Lussmanns – Sustainable Small Group of the Year
• River Cottage – SRA Award for Sourcing
• Carluccio's – Sustainable Innovation Award
• Belmond Le Manoir aux Quat'Saisons – Sustainable Hotel Restaurant of the Year
• The Gate, Islington – Most Improved Sustainability.

One star – Good Sustainability
Two stars – Excellent Sustainability
Three stars – Exceptional Sustainability

SURVEY FAQs

Q. How do you find your reporters?
A. Anyone can take part. Simply register at www.hardens.com. Actually, we find that many people who complete our survey each year have taken part before. So it's really more a question of a very large and ever-evolving panel, or jury, than a random 'poll'.

Q. Wouldn't a random sample be better?
A. That's really a theoretical question, as there is no obvious way, still less a cost-efficient one, by which one could identify a random sample of the guests at each of, say, 5,000 establishments across the UK, and get them to take part in any sort of survey. And anyway, which is likely to be more useful: a sample of the views of everyone who's been to a particular place, or the views of people who are interested enough in eating-out to have volunteered their feedback?

Q. What sort of people take part?
A. A roughly 60/40 male/female split, from all adult age-groups. As you might expect – as eating out is not the cheapest activity – reporters tend to have white collar jobs (some at very senior levels). By no means, however, is that always the case.

Q. Do people ever try to stuff the ballot?
A. Of course they do! A rising number of efforts are weeded out every year. But stuffing the ballot is not as trivial a task as some people seem to think: the survey results throw up clear natural voting patterns against which 'campaigns' tend to stand out.

Q. Aren't inspections the best way to run a guide?
A. It is often assumed – even by commentators who ought to know better – that inspections are some sort of 'gold standard'. There is no doubt that the inspection model clearly has potential strengths, but one of its prime weaknesses is that it is incredibly expensive. Take the most famous practitioner of the 'inspection model', Michelin. It doesn't claim to visit each and every entry listed in its guide annually. Even once! And who are the inspectors? Often they are catering professionals, whose likes and dislikes may be very different from the establishment's natural customer base. On any restaurant of note, however, Harden's typically has somewhere between dozens and hundreds of reports each and every year from exactly the type of people the restaurant relies upon to stay in business. We believe that such feedback, carefully analysed, is far more revealing and accurate than an occasional 'professional' inspection.

SURVEY MOST MENTIONED

These are the restaurants which were most frequently mentioned by reporters. (Last year's position is given in brackets.) An asterisk* indicates the first appearance in the list of a recently opened restaurant.

1	J Sheekey (1)
2	Scott's (3)
3	Le Gavroche (2)
4	Clos Maggiore (4)
5	The Ledbury (8)
6	The Delaunay (11)
7	Chez Bruce (6)
8	Pollen Street Social (10)
9	Dinner (7)
10	The Wolseley (9)

11	Brasserie Zédel (5)
12	Gymkhana*
13	The Cinnamon Club (17)
14	Galvin La Chapelle (20)
15	The Square (12)
16	Bleeding Heart (16)
17	The River Café (19)
18	Bocca Di Lupo (23)
19	La Trompette (13)
20	Pied à Terre (40)

21	Medlar (13)
22=	La Poule au Pot (21)
22=	Marcus (15)
24=	The Berners Tavern (-)
24=	Benares (23)
26	Galvin Bistrot de Luxe (18)
27	Zucca*
28=	Gauthier Soho (38)
28=	Trinity (28)
30=	Grain Store*

30=	Le Caprice (20)
32	Zuma (34)
33	Gordon Ramsay (30)
34	The Ivy (26)
35	Andrew Edmunds (37)
36=	Tayyabs (35)
36=	The Anchor & Hope (-)
38	Terroirs (33)
39	Yauatcha (-)
40	Amaya (25)

SURVEY NOMINATIONS

Top gastronomic experience

1. The Ledbury (2)
2. Le Gavroche (1)
3. Dinner (3)
4. Chez Bruce (4)
5. Pollen Street Social (5)
6. Pied à Terre (10)
7. Gordon Ramsay (-)
8. The Square (8)
9. Marcus (6)
10. Medlar (9)

Favourite

1. Chez Bruce (1)
2. J Sheekey (5)
3. Clos Maggiore (-)
4. The Ledbury (8)
5. Le Gavroche (2)
6. The River Café (10)
7. The Delaunay (6)
8. Le Caprice (4)
9. Pollen Street Social (9)
10. The Wolseley (3)

Best for business

1. The Wolseley (1)
2. The Delaunay (3)
3. The Square (2)
4. Galvin La Chapelle (4)
5. Bleeding Heart (6)
6. The Don (5)
7. Coq d'Argent (-)
8. Scott's (8)
9. L'Anima (7)
10. Pollen Street Social*

Best for romance

1. Clos Maggiore (1)
2. La Poule au Pot (2)
3. Andrew Edmunds (3)
4. Bleeding Heart (4)
5. Le Gavroche (5)
6. Chez Bruce (7)
7. Galvin at Windows (6)
8. Galvin La Chapelle (-)
9. The Ledbury (-)
10. Gauthier Soho (-)

RANKED BY THE NUMBER OF REPORTERS' VOTES

Best breakfast/brunch

1 The Wolseley (1)
2 The Delaunay (2)
3 Duck & Waffle (8)
4 Riding House Café (5)
5 Roast (3)
6 Colbert*
7 Cecconi's (3)
8 3 South Place*
9 The Pantechnicon (-)
10 Balthazar*

Best bar/pub food

1 The Anchor & Hope (1)
2 Bull & Last (2)
3 Harwood Arms (3)
4 The Jugged Hare*
5 Canton Arms (7)
6 The Gun (8)
7 Ladbroke Arms (10)
8 Pig & Butcher*
9 Truscott Arms*
10 Thomas Cubitt (4)

Most disappointing cooking

1 Oxo Tower (Rest') (1)
2 Dinner (6)
3 Colbert (5)
4 The Ivy (8)
5 Gordon Ramsay (3)
6 Le Gavroche (-)
7 Balthazar (2)
8 Marcus (-)
9 Alain Ducasse (9)
10 Dabbous*

Most overpriced restaurant

1 The River Café (3)
2 Oxo Tower (Rest') (1)
3 Dinner (4)
4 Gordon Ramsay (2)
5 Marcus (7)
6 Alain Ducasse (5)
7 Le Gavroche (8)
8 Cut (6)
9 Balthazar*
10 Pollen Street Social (10)

SURVEY HIGHEST RATINGS

FOOD

SERVICE

£85+

	FOOD		SERVICE
1	The Ledbury	1	Le Gavroche
2	Rasoi	2	The Ledbury
3	Pied à Terre	3	Bubbledogs KT
4	Le Gavroche	4	Fera at Claridge's
5	One-O-One	5	Pied à Terre

£65-£84

	FOOD		SERVICE
1	The Five Fields	1	The Goring Hotel
2	Hedone	2	The Five Fields
3	Chez Bruce	3	Chez Bruce
4	Zuma	4	Trinity
5	HKK	5	Petersham Hotel

£50-£64

	FOOD		SERVICE
1	Sushi Tetsu	1	Sushi Tetsu
2	Moro	2	Oslo Court
3	Dinings	3	Otto's
4	Sukho Fine Thai Cuisine	4	Gauthier Soho
5	Gauthier Soho	5	Clos Maggiore

£40-£49

	FOOD		SERVICE
1	Sushi-Say	1	Lamberts
2	Lamberts	2	Donostia
3	Jin Kichi	3	Pentolina
4	Brawn	4	Sushi-Say
5	Donostia	5	Yming

£39 or less

	FOOD		SERVICE
1	Pitt Cue Co	1	Paradise Hampstead
2	Ragam	2	Boqueria
3	Mangal I	3	Kaffeine
4	Santa Maria	4	Morito
5	Silk Road	5	Blanchette

SURVEY HIGHEST RATINGS

AMBIENCE

1	The Ritz Restaurant
2	Bubbledogs KT
3	Galvin at Windows
4	Oblix
5	Le Gavroche

1	Petersham Hotel
2	The Berners Tavern
3	Rules
4	Criterion
5	The Goring Hotel

1	Clos Maggiore
2	The Wallace
3	L'Aventure
4	La Poule au Pot
5	Randall & Aubin

1	Andrew Edmunds
2	St Johns N19
3	Brawn
4	José
5	The Depot

1	Brasserie Zédel
2	Carom at Meza
3	Churchill Arms
4	Princi
5	The Begging Bowl

OVERALL

1	The Ledbury
2	Bubbledogs KT
3	Le Gavroche
4	Fera at Claridge's
5	Pied à Terre

1	The Five Fields
2	The Goring Hotel
3	Chez Bruce
4	Scott's
5	Galvin La Chapelle

1	Sushi Tetsu
2	Clos Maggiore
3	L'Aventure
4	Randall & Aubin
5	J Sheekey Oyster Bar

1	Lamberts
2	Donostia
3	Brawn
4	Sushi-Say
5	José

1	Carom at Meza
2	The Begging Bowl
3	Pitt Cue Co
4	Paradise Hampstead
5	Meat Mission

SURVEY BEST BY CUISINE

These are the restaurants which received the best average food ratings (excluding establishments with a small or notably local following).

Where the most common types of cuisine are concerned, we present the results in two price-brackets. For less common cuisines, we list the top three, regardless of price.

For further information about restaurants which are particularly notable for their food, see the cuisine lists starting on page 244. These indicate, using an asterisk*, restaurants which offer exceptional or very good food.

British, Modern

£50 and over
1   The Ledbury
2   The Five Fields
3   Hedone
4   Chez Bruce
5   Fera at Claridge's

Under £50
1   Lamberts
2   The Dairy
3   10 Greek Street
4   40 Maltby Street
5   Rochelle Canteen

French

£50 and over
1   Pied à Terre
2   Le Gavroche
3   Pétrus
4   Gauthier Soho
5   The Square

Under £50
1   Brawn
2   Casse-Croute
3   Brula
4   Comptoir Gascon
5   Toasted

Italian/Mediterranean

£50 and over
1   Murano
2   Zucca
3   Al Boccon di'vino
4   Olivomare
5   Theo Randall

Under £50
1   Santore
2   Opera Tavern
3   Pizza Metro
4   Dehesa
5   Le Querce

Indian & Pakistani

£50 and over
1   Rasoi
2   Babur
3   Amaya
4   Gymkhana
5   Benares

Under £50
1   Ragam
2   Indian Rasoi
3   Ganapati
4   Indian Zing
5   Roots at N1

Chinese

£50 and over
1 Kai Mayfair
2 HKK
3 Hunan
4 Min Jiang
5 Royal China Club

Under £50
1 Silk Road
2 A Wong
3 Yipin China
4 Mandarin Kitchen
5 Yming

Japanese

£50 and over
1 Sushi Tetsu
2 Zuma
3 Dinings
4 Chotto Matte
5 Sushisamba

Under £50
1 Sushi-Say
2 Pham Sushi
3 Jin Kichi
4 Koya
5 Bone Daddies

British, Traditional
1 Scott's
2 St John
3 St John Bread & Wine

Vegetarian
1 Ragam
2 Ganapati
3 Mildreds

Burgers, etc
1 Meat Mission
2 Opera Tavern
3 Bar Boulud

Pizza
1 Santa Maria
2 Oliveto
3 Pizza Metro

Fish & Chips
1 Toff's
2 The Fish & Chip Shop
3 The Sea Shell

Thai
1 Sukho Fine Thai Cuisine
2 The Begging Bowl
3 Churchill Arms

Steaks & Grills
1 Carom at Meza
2 The Guinea Grill
3 34

Fish & Seafood
1 One-O-One
2 Scott's
3 J Sheekey

Fusion
1 Bubbledogs KT
2 Eight Over Eight
3 L'Etranger

Spanish
1 Moro
2 Donostia
3 José

Turkish
1 Mangal I
2 Fez Mangal
3 Kazan

Lebanese
1 Maroush
2 Fairuz
3 Yalla Yalla

TOP SPECIAL DEALS

The following menus allow you to eat in the restaurants concerned at a significant discount when compared to their evening à la carte prices.

The prices used are calculated in accordance with our usual formula (i.e. three courses with house wine, coffee and tip).

Special menus are by their nature susceptible to change – please check that they are still available.

Weekday lunch

£95+ Alain Ducasse
Quattro Passi

£85+ Le Gavroche

£70+ The Goring Hotel
Hedone

£65+ L'Atelier de Joel Robuchon
Dinner
The Greenhouse
Hélène Darroze
Marianne
Rib Room

£60+ The Ledbury
Sketch (Lecture Rm)

£55+ Ametsa
Club Gascon
Galvin at Windows
Gordon Ramsay
Hibiscus
Pétrus
Seven Park Place
The Square
Texture

£50+ Alyn Williams
Aqua Shard
Babbo
Bibendum
The Clove Club
Coya
The Ivy
Murano
One-O-One
Pied à Terre
Poissonnerie de l'Avenue
Pollen Street Social
Roast
Savoy Grill
Story
34
Thirty Six
Trinity
Typing Room

£45+ Amaya
L'Autre Pied
Babylon
The Bingham
Cambio de Tercio
The Cinnamon Club
Dabbous

Daphne's
L'Etranger
Franco's
Galvin La Chapelle
Gauthier Soho
The Glasshouse
Hunan
Landmark (Winter Gdn)
Medlar
Quilon
Rules
J Sheekey
Tamarind
La Trompette

£40+ The Abingdon
The Avenue
Bam-Bou
Belvedere
Cheyne Walk Brasserie
Chor Bizarre
Garnier
Hix
Kitchen W8
Lima
Little Social
Le Pont de la Tour
La Poule au Pot
Spice Market
Trishna
Les Trois Garçons

£35+ The Almeida
L'Aventure
Bradley's
Christopher's
The Dock Kitchen
Entrée
Essenza
Frantoio
Frederick's
Galvin Bistrot de Luxe
High Timber
Magdalen
Massimo
Merchants Tavern
Mon Plaisir
Outlaw's Seafood and Grill
Quaglino's
Quantus
Racine
Red Fort
Suk Saran
Sukho Fine Thai Cuisine
Trullo
The Victoria

£30+	The Anchor & Hope		Sonny's Kitchen
	Buen Ayre		
	La Buvette	£25+	Augustine Kitchen
	Chapters		Camino
	City Miyama		Chez Patrick
	Fairuz		Elephant Royale
	Gilgamesh		Mill Lane Bistro
	Hereford Road		The Palmerston
	The Hoxton Grill		Pearl Liang
	Jamie's Diner		Yming
	Joe Allen		
	Kensington Wine Rooms	£20+	Olley's
	The Light House		Le Sacré-Coeur
	Market		
	Mazi	£15+	Apulia
	Odette's		Cellar Gascon
	Orso		El Pirata
	Le P'tit Normand		Sticky Fingers
	Sam's Brasserie		Tentazioni
	Smiths (Dining Rm)		

Pre/post theatre (and early evening)

£80+	The Ritz Restaurant		The Jugged Hare
			Lima
£65+	Atelier de Joel Robuchon		Quaglino's
	Oxo Tower (Rest')		Spice Market
	Tamarind		
		£35+	The Almeida
£55+	Benares		Baltic
			Christopher's
£50+	Bentley's		L'Escargot
	Koffmann's		Franco's
	Oxo Tower (Brass')		Latium
	Wild Honey		Massimo
			Orso
£45+	L'Autre Pied		The Portrait
	Boulestin		Red Fort
	Le Caprice		Sarastro
	Daphne's		
	Gymkhana	£30+	Boulevard
	Homage		Le Garrick
	MASH Steakhouse		Gay Hussar
	Santini		Mon Plaisir
	Savoy Grill		The Noodle House
	Veeraswamy		
		£25+	Café des Amis
£40+	The Avenue		Moti Mahal
	Belvedere		Skylon Grill
	Hix		Yming

Sunday lunch

£85+	Rib Room	£40+	A Cena
			Blueprint Café
£55+	Medlar		The Botanist
	Petersham Hotel		Café Bohème
	Roast		Charlotte's Bistro
	Trinity		Le Cigalon
			Foxlow
£50+	The Glasshouse		Kaifeng
	Kitchen W8		Maggie Jones's
	Odette's		Sam's Brasserie
	Orrery		
	La Trompette	£35+	Babur
			Elephant Royale
£45+	Bradley's		Entrée
	Coq d'Argent		First Floor
	Galvin La Chapelle		The Wharf
	Hix		
	J Sheekey	£30+	Les Associés

THE RESTAURANT SCENE

This year we record a restaurant scene in overdrive. Not only was the openings figure, at 148, very high by historical standards, but the figure for closings, 47, was the lowest this millennium. One should always beware of talk of 'smashing' records, but the level of net openings this year (openings minus closings) – at 98 – is nearly a third higher than the previous record of 75, noted in our 2006 guide.

The ratio of openings to closings tells a similarly robust story. At around 3:1, the ratio is now double what it was at the low point in the cycle, three years ago. Can a 'bull run' like this go on for very much longer? Since our first guide back in 1992, a year-to-year upswing in the ratio has never gone on for more than three consecutive years, so we are very likely now set for some loss of momentum (which is of course a very different thing from an actual reverse).

We are very conscious that the restaurant scene is now getting so big that the bar for registering on the critical appraisal 'radar' has risen in recent years: there are certainly openings which would have seemed of some significance a decade ago which today pass largely unnoticed.

So quickly can the dining out scene change that restaurant years are more like dog years than human ones. Many people who have come to London in the past half-decade think that it is normal and natural for this to be regarded as one of the great dining out cities of the world, not realising just how recently this situation has come to pass – 20 years ago the proposition would rightly have been derided, and even a decade ago it would have sounded very much like boosterism.

It is a paradox that now, in the year when the London restaurant scene can finally and indubitably be said to have 'arrived', Harden's is the only 'comprehensive' guide which has survived long enough to chronicle it, and we lament the apparent passing of the Time Out guide – the only comprehensive London-specific guide in publication longer than this one.

Every year, we choose what to us seem to be the most significant openings of the year. This year, our selection is as follows:

Chiltern Firehouse	City Social
Fera at Claridge's	Kurobuta
Lyle's	Merchants Tavern
The New Angel	The Palomar
The Typing Room	Uni

East – the new West

It is a sign of a new normality that these picks are equally divided between 'East' and 'West' postcodes. Go back a decade, and the East was unrepresented on this list; go back five years, and we would have spotted only a single star there. And it is not just at the top end of the market that an equivalence between East and West is becoming a feature of the market: even Peckham, an historically deprived area in the SE corner of the city, is beginning to show signs of restaurant life!

Interesting restaurants are not only popping up everywhere, they come progressively in every national flavour, and indeed nowadays often a subdivision of a national flavour. A decade ago, we usually described restaurants as, say, 'Italian'. Nowadays they are often Sardinian, Sicilian, Puglian, Neapolitan… And all the (larger) continents, in the last few years including South America, are now represented.

'Trends' do not seem radically to have changed of late. Most obvious is the continuing fetishisation of New York City as the first port of call for anyone looking for so-called inspiration for any 'new' sort of restaurant concept, and the continuing obsession for meat-led restaurants. Perhaps the message that excessive meat consumption is bad both for the individual and the planet will finally get through? One day!

Also imperishable, but over a much longer timescale, seems to be the appeal of some of the fast food classics, and in particular the pizza and the hamburger, both of which are in the process of re-invention by a new generation. It is difficult, though, to say that there is really anything new in this – the first London craze for hamburgers kicked off with the opening of the first Wimpy bar… in 1954.

One area where progressive change definitely is apparent is the continuing move away from the idea that quality dining out is a knife-and-fork activity, usually consisting of three courses – witness the opening of *Fera* at that supposed bastion of the Establishment, Claridge's. If there has been one single decisive shift of recent years, it is that small plates – considered radical a decade ago – now seem very much here to stay.

Prices

The average price of dinner for one at establishments listed in this guide is £49.46 (compared to £47.68 last year). Prices have risen by 2.7% in the past 12 months. This is a little less than last year's rise, and broadly in line with inflation as recorded by the Retail Price Index.

OPENINGS AND CLOSURES

Openings (148)

L'Amorosa
Andina
L'Anima Café
The Ape & Bird
Apulia
Arabica
Artusi
Assunta Madre
Augustine Kitchen
Bar Esteban
Barnyard
Beast
Bibo
Bilbao Berria
Bird
Blackfoot
Blanchette
Blind Pig
Bo Lang
Bobo Social
Bocconcino
Bonnie Gull Seafood Café
The Brackenbury
Bravas
Bubba Gump Shrimp Co.
Buddha Bar London
Bunnychow W1, E1
Café Murano
Café Pistou
The Camberwell Arms
Canvas SW1
Chez Abir
Chicken Shop SW17
Chicken Shop & Dirty
  Burger
The Chiltern Firehouse
Chotto Matte
City Barge
City Social
The Clink
Clutch
Colony Grill Room
Compagnie des Vins
  Surnaturels
Cornish Tiger
DF Mexico
Dip & Flip
Dirty Bones
Dishoom N1

Drakes Tabanco
Dub Jam
East Street
Eat 17
Edwins
Eelbrook
8 Hoxton Square
Ember Yard
Ergon
Er Mei
Fera at Claridge's
Fischer's
Flat Iron WC2
GB Pizza Co.
Gin Joint
Les Gourmets des Ternes
Granger & Co. EC1
Greenberry Cafe
Ham Yard Restaurant
Heddon Street Kitchen
Hill & Szrok
Hixter
Holborn Dining Room
Homeslice
House of Ho
Hubbard & Bell
Ibérica EC1
Ippudo London
Jamaica Patty Co.
Jamie's Diner
Kurobuta
Lima Floral
Linnea
The Lobster House
London House
Lyle's
M
Marani
Margaux
Merchants Tavern
Meza SW17
The New Angel
New Tom's
The Noodle House
Olympic
On the Bab
Pachamama
The Palomar
Parlour

Openings (cont'd)

Patty & Bun EC2
Pavillion
Peckham Bazaar
Penkul & Banks
Peyote
La Polenteria
Pond
Primeur
Q Grill
Quattro Passi
Rabbit
Rabot 1745
Raw Duck
Red Dog SW4
Rextail
Rivea
Rocket WC2
Roka W1, WC2
The Rooftop Café
Rotorino
Rugoletta
Salvation in Noodles
Sea Containers

Shoryu Ramen, Kingly Ct
Source
Spring
Strand Dining Rooms
TED
The Terrace
Ting
Tonkotsu E8
Toto's
Tredwell's
Truscott Arms
21 Bateman Street
Typing Room
Uni
Vapiano SE1
Verden
Villandry SW1
Villiers Coffee Co
Vivo
Whyte & Brown
Wright Bros E1
Yard Sale Pizza
Zest

Closures (47)

Albannach
Anglo Asian Tandoori
Apsleys
L'Art du Fromage
Assiette Anglaise
Automat
Bangalore Express
Beard to Tail
Bincho Yakitori
Bo London
Brompton Bar & Grill
Il Calcio SW5
Cape Town Fish Market
Le Cercle
Chabrot Bistrot des Halles
Chez Marcelle
Choys
Chuen Cheng Ku
Cotidie
Downtown Mayfair
E11even Park Walk
Empress of Sichuan
Fire & Stone E1
Giaconda Dining Rooms
Gran Paradiso

Jenny Lo's Tea House
Ken Lo's Memories
   of China W8
Lola & Simón
Mango & Silk
Mao Tai
Morgan M
Mr Wing
Naamyaa Café
One Blenheim Terrace
Osteria dell'Arancio
The Palm
Pissarro
Porters English
   Restaurant (Jan '15)
Refettorio
Solly's
Thatched House
Toku
Tom Aikens
Tom's Deli
Uli
Verru
Viajant

EATING IN LONDON FAQs

How should I use this guide?

You will often wish to use this guide in a practical way.
At heart, the issue will usually be geographical – where can
we eat near...? To answer such questions, the Maps (from
page 300) and Area Overviews (from page 262) are the
place to start. The latter tell you all the key facts about the
restaurants – perhaps dozens of 'em – in a particular area
in the space of a couple of pages. These Area Overviews are
unique, so please do spend a second to have a look!

This section, though, is about seeking out restaurants for
the joy of it – a few thoughts to lead you to London's best
restaurants for particular types of events, or to lead you
down byways you might not otherwise have considered.

What makes London so special?

London has always been cosmopolitan. In recent years,
however, its emergence as not just a 'world city' but
arguably 'capital of the world' has been marked by an
extraordinary flourishing in the restaurant scene.
Nowadays, good-quality establishments can be found
representing the cuisines of each of the five continents, and
usually in considerable depth. London has also become
perhaps the leading destination for chefs and restaurant
'concepts' from around the world. This very concentration,
of course, draws in more talent and excitement, and thus a
'virtuous" circle is established and reinforced.

This process has been encouraged by an extraordinary
revolution, over the past 20 years, in the attitude of under-
35s to dining out. Two decades ago, food and restaurant-
going was considered very much a minority interest for a
relatively moneyed and relatively old elite. Nowadays, it is
not just the elite which is interested in dining out – indeed,
dining out seems, for many younger Londoners, to have
become an all-consuming interest. The result has been a
much more dynamic restaurant scene, now infinitely
stronger at almost all levels.

Which is London's best restaurant?

'Best' is of course a term that mean different things to
different people, and the top four top-price restaurants at
the moment (see page 15) are all very different in style.
London's original grand Gallic restaurant, *Le Gavroche*, has
had a resurgence in recent times. For a slightly more
modern spin on the traditional restaurant format,
The Ledbury's reign continues unchallenged. But it's a sign
of the vibrant times that the other two top restaurants
are products of the last couple of years – check out the
multi-course menus as *Fera at Claridges*, or sit at the
counter at *Bubbledogs Kitchen Table*.

What about something a little more reasonably priced?

Chez Bruce is now celebrating a decade as Londoners' favourite restaurant, so a trip to this Wandwsworth legend is undoubtedly the obvious choice. Or for something a bit more economical, head a fraction further south to *Lambert's* in Balham – a 'local' restaurant whose consistent high quality is beginning to make a name across south London. Hard-core foodies may also wish to head west to Chiswick (and the far reaches of Chiswick at that), to seek out *Hedone*.

Do all of these suggestions seem a little far out? *The Five Fields*, in Chelsea, is a tip-top destination which is still less well-known than it deserves to be.

What about a big night out?

Dining out is, of course, not all about the quality of the cooking – for many occasions, it's as important to have a striking setting, often right in the heart of town, as it is to have the best cooking.

For a grand all-rounder in the best possible location (next to The Ritz), it's very hard to beat London's original grand brasserie of modern times, the *Wolseley*, whose Edwardian premises are no less impressive once you know they were originally a car showroom. For a slightly less busy, but still glamorous, experience, *Le Caprice*, in a back street a few blocks away, still has many fans.

Other obvious choices, going from West to East, include *Zuma* (Knightsbridge), *Scott's* (Mayfair), *J Sheekey* (Theatreland), the *Delaunay* (Covent Garden) and *Galvin La Chapelle* (Spitalfields).

What about British cooking?

Until recently, the idea of British restaurants (other than simple grill or roast houses) was pretty much unknown. Restaurants properly so called were usually French or (later) Italian in style, and in more recent times Indian or Chinese.

Many of the British restaurants in existence today (still relatively few) can trace their existence back to the Smithfield restaurant *St John*, established in 1994, whose dedication to ancient (and often offal-heavy) English dishes captured the zeitgeist and re-awakened an interest in traditional British food culture that had been quiescent for most of the previous century.

St John is still going strong, and cooking in the same vein can also be seen at *Hereford Road* (Bayswater) and *Magdalen* (South Bank), and also at two Shoreditch restaurants – the new *Lyle's*, and *St John Bread & Wine*.

What about gastropubs?

These are essentially bistros in pub premises, and they come in many styles. What many people still think of as the original gastropub (The Eagle, 1991) still looks very much like a pub with a food counter, but others now look almost indistinguishable from restaurants. Many of the the best gastropubs are found a little way away from the centre – just one of the reasons the relatively central *Anchor & Hope*, on the South Bank, is so wildly popular! Other stars include the *Bull & Last* (Kentish Town), the *Canton Arms* (Stockwell) and the *Harwood Arms* (Fulham). New to the guide this year is the *Camberwell Arms* (Camberwell), sister to the Canton Arms and no less lauded in the early-days reports we have received.

What if I'm in search of tradition and history?

Easy! *Rules*, London's oldest restaurant (1798), could easily have become a tourist trap, but it's a thoroughly good, if not inexpensive, English restaurant, in premises just as charming as anything Paris can offer. Top choice for a traditional dinner in pomp – but without any pomposity – is equally clearly *The Goring*. Or for first rate British seafood served in a wonderfully old-fashioned setting, why not try that bastion of the Establishment, *Wiltons*? Est. 1742, the restaurant was purveyor of oysters to Queen Victoria.

Isn't London supposed to be a top place for curry?

Many visitors come to London wanting to 'try Indian'. The choice of 'Indians' – a term including Pakistani and Bangladeshi restaurants in this context – is so great, however, that you then need to decide what sort of Indian you want to try.

You want value? Two top names in the East End (and hence relatively accessible from central London) are almost legendary 'experiences' – the *Lahore Kebab House* and *Tayyabs*. The predominantly veggie *Rasa* group also includes some very good-value options. Or, for an immersive experience, go down to Tooting, and check out a fixture like *Sree Krishna*.

At the other end of the scale (and, for the most part, right in the heart of town) are the 'nouvelle Indians', where spicy dishes are presented with a heavy European influence. *Amaya, Benares, The Cinnamon Club, The Painted Heron, Quilon, Rasoi, Veeraswamy* and the new *Gymkhana* are all examples of plush restaurants just as suited to business (and in many cases romance) as their European price-equivalents.

In fact, wherever you are in London, you should be in reach of an Indian restaurant of more-than-average note – search out the asterisked restaurants in the Indian and Pakistani lists commencing on page 258.

27

Any money-saving tips?

● If you have the luxury of being in charge of your own timetable, there are some extraordinary bargains to be had simply by lunching rather than dining, and the more reasonably priced menus often available at the lunch service give you the opportunity to check out establishments which might otherwise be simply unattainable. See the spread on pages 18 and 19.

● Think ethnic – for a food 'experience' at modest cost, you're likely to be better off going Indian, Thai, Chinese or Vietnamese (to choose four of the most obvious cuisines) than English, French or Italian. The days when there was any sort of assumption that ethnic restaurants were – in terms of comfort, service and décor – in any way inferior to European ones is long gone, but they are still often somewhat cheaper.

● Don't assume the West End is the obvious destination. It is becoming less and less true anyway that the best and most interesting London restaurants are necessarily to be found within the confines of the Circle Line, so don't be reluctant to explore! Use the maps at the back of this book to identify restaurants near tube stations on a line that's handy for you.

● If you must dine in the West End, try to find either pre-theatre (generally before 7 pm) or post-theatre (generally after 10 pm) menus. You will generally save at least the cost of a cinema ticket, compared to dining à la carte. Many of the more upmarket restaurants in Theatreland do such deals. For some of our top suggestions, see page 19.

● Use this book! Don't take pot luck, when you can benefit from the pre-digested views of thousands of other diners-out. Choose a place with a **5** or **4** for food, and you're very likely to eat much better than if you walk in somewhere 'on spec' – this is good advice anywhere, but is most particularly so in the West End.

● Once you have decided that you want to eat within a particular area, use the Area Overviews (starting on page 262) to identify the restaurants that are offering top value. We have gone to a lot of trouble to boil down a huge amount of data into the results which are handily summarised in such lists. Please use them! You are unlikely to regret it.

● Visit our website, www.hardens.com for the latest reviews, news and offers, and to sign up for our annual spring survey.

DIRECTORY

Comments in "double quotation-marks" were made by reporters.

Establishments which we judge to be particularly notable have their NAME IN CAPITALS.

A Cena TW1 £50 3 3 3
418 Richmond Rd 8288 0108 1–4A
A "better-than-average local", just south of Richmond Bridge in St Margarets, with an "ever-changing Italian menu", and a "top wine list" too. / TW1 2EB; www.acena.co.uk; @acenarestaurant; 10 pm; closed Mon L & Sun D; booking: max 6, Fri & Sat.

A Wong SW1 £34 4 3 3
70-71 Wilton Rd 7828 8931 2–4B
"Extraordinarily good dim sum" are a highlight of the "wacky" and "exciting" dishes on offer at this "canteen-style" Chinese yearling, five minutes' walk from Victoria. / SW1 1DE; www.awong.co.uk; @awongSW1; 10.15 pm; closed Mon L & Sun.

Abbeville Kitchen SW4 £50 3 4 2
47 Abbeville Rd 8772 1110 10–2D
"An amazing neighbourhood spot!" – Clapham locals are delighted with this "welcoming" and "reliable" two-year-old, which offers "generous portions" of "yummy" fare from an "ever-changing" menu; a "delicious brunch" is a highlight. / SW4 9JX; www.abbevillekitchen.com; @abbevillek; 10.30 pm, Sun 9.30 pm; Mon-Thu D only, Fri-Sun open L & D.

Abeno £41 3 3 2
47 Museum St, WC1 7405 3211 2–1C
17-18 Great Newport St, WC2 7379 1160 4–3B
"Interesting", "authentic" and "consistently tasty"; okonomi-yaki – which is to say fancy Japanese omelettes – are the stock-in-trade of these "courteous" West End cafés; all those tabletop barbecues, though, can make the atmosphere rather "smelly". / www.abeno.co.uk; 10 pm-11 pm; WC2 no booking.

The Abingdon W8 £63 3 3 4
54 Abingdon Rd 7937 3339 5–2A
In the sleepy residential backwoods of Kensington, a "great gastropub with reliable food, friendly service and a decent wine list"; it may be no bargain, but it's a "jolly" sort of place, on which feedback is impressively consistent. / W8 6AP; www.theabingdon.co.uk; 10.30 pm, Fri & Sat 11 pm, Sun 10 pm; set weekday L £40 (FP).

Abokado £17 2 4 4
Branches throughout London
"Great for healthy lunches" – this sushi-and-more snack chain inspires consistently upbeat reports. / www.abokado.com; 7.30 pm Mon-Fri, NW1 9 pm, 5 pm Sat & Sun; no Amex; no booking.

About Thyme SW1 £54 3 4 2
82 Wilton Rd 7821 7504 2–4B
"Caring" staff and "satisfying" Spanish-influenced food have made a bit of a name for this "always-buzzy" stalwart of the west-Pimlico wasteland; prices are quite high, though, and some meals this year seemed rather "rough and ready". / SW1V 1DL; www.aboutthyme.co.uk; 10.30 pm; closed Sun.

L'Absinthe NW1 £45 2 3 2
40 Chalcot Rd 7483 4848 8–3B
"An unfailing welcome" helps underpin local support for this "crowded" but "enjoyable" corner bistro, in Primrose Hill; critics, though, say it's "pricey" for food that's "only fair", and feel its "rather static" formula is "in need of a facelift". / NW1 8LS; www.labsinthe.co.uk; @absinthe07jc; 10 pm; closed Mon, Tue L, Wed L & Thu L

Abu Zaad W12 £23 3 3 2
29 Uxbridge Rd 8749 5107 7–1C
"Don't be put off by the location" on a *"drab stretch of the Uxbridge Road"* – there's *"terrific-value, hearty Syrian food"* to be had at this *"elaborately decorated"* café, where *"fantastic, freshly squeezed juices"* compensate for the lack of alcohol. / W12 8LH; www.abuzaad.co.uk; 11 pm; no Amex.

Adams Café W12 £31 2 5 4
77 Askew Rd 8743 0572 7–1B
"Greasy spoon by day, North African grills and tagines by night" – the enduring recipe for success at this *"real"* Shepherd's Bush local, where the personable owners always ensure a *"happy atmosphere"*; licensed nowadays, but you can still BYO. / W12 9AH; www.adamscafe.co.uk; 10 pm; closed Sun.

Addie's Thai Café SW5 £32 3 3 2
121 Earl's Court Rd 7259 2620 5–2A
"Fine Thai street food-style cuisine", with *"authentic flavours"*, helps fuel the buzz at this simple Earl's Court staple. / SW5 9RL; www.addiesthai.co.uk; 11 pm, Sun 10.30 pm; no Amex.

The Admiral Codrington SW3 £53 2 2 2
17 Mossop St 7581 0005 5–2C
This *"enjoyable"* backstreet spot ('The Cod') has long been one of Chelsea's more popular boozers, and it can still get *"very noisy"*; it has a large and airy dining room, where the food is *"generally good"*. / SW3 2LY; www.theadmiralcodrington.co.uk; @TheAdCod; 10 pm, Thu-Sat 11 pm, Sun 9.30 pm.

Afghan Kitchen N1 £26 4 2 1
35 Islington Grn 7359 8019 8–3D
A tiny central Islington café whose mega-cramped, *"spartan"* interior doesn't detract from the appeal of its *"delicious"* and *"interesting"* dishes. / N1 8DU; 11 pm; closed Mon & Sun; no credit cards.

Aglio e Olio SW10 £42 3 3 2
194 Fulham Rd 7351 0070 5–3B
"Loud and proud!"; this *"reverberative"*, *"chaotic"* and *"fun"* canteen, by the Chelsea & Westminster Hospital, offers *"fresh-tasting pasta"* at *"great-value prices"*, and with *"skill and enthusiasm"* too. / SW10 9PN; 11.30 pm.

Akari N1 £39 4 2 3
196 Essex Rd 7226 9943 8–3D
The exterior may look *"just like an old Islington boozer"*, but this is in fact *"a wonderful family-run Japanese"*; don't just order sushi – *"the warm dishes are fantastic"*, and *"they have Asahi on tap"* too. / N1 8LZ; www.akarilondon.co.uk; 11 pm; closed Mon, Tue-Fri D only, Sat & Sun open L & D; no Amex.

Al Duca SW1 £46 2 2 2
4-5 Duke of York St 7839 3090 3–3D
Notably *"unpretentious"* by St James's standards (and *"not overpriced either"*), a *"reliable"* and *"usefully located"* Italian that comes recommended for lunch, business or pre-theatre. / SW1Y 6LA; www.alduca-restaurant.co.uk; 11 pm; closed Sun.

Al Forno £38 2 4 4
349 Upper Richmond Rd, SW15 8878 7522 10–2A
2a King's Rd, SW19 8540 5710 10–2B
*"Your classic friendly local Italian", in "rustic style, circa 1980" –
these "buzzy" joints are "pretty basic", but their "charming" service
and "reasonable prices" make them "good with friends" and family.
/ SW15 11 pm; SW19 11.30 pm, Sun & Mon 10.30 pm.*

Al Hamra W1 £55 3 2 2
31-33 Shepherd Mkt 7493 1954 3–4B
*Three decades in business, this "typically Middle Eastern" Shepherd
Market spot long predates the trendification of Mayfair, but fans
insist it still offers "the best Lebanese food in town"; others aren't
so sure, but the outside tables are certainly a charming sunny day
destination. / W1J 7PT; www.alhamrarestaurant.co.uk; 11.30 pm.*

Al Sultan W1 £46 3 2 1
51-52 Hertford St 7408 1155 3–4B
*"The food is consistently very good", at this long-established
Lebanese, near Shepherd Market; the ambience is "rather sterile"
though, and it's often "let down by sloppy service". / W1J 7ST;
www.alsultan.co.uk; 11 pm.*

Al-Waha W2 £47 3 2 1
75 Westbourne Grove 7229 0806 6–1B
*For fans, this Bayswater Lebanese remains "the best Eastern
Mediterranean place in town", and its "fresh" fare continues to be
a general crowd-pleaser; this year's survey, though, also recorded the
occasional let down. / W2 4UL; www.alwaharestaurant.com; 11 pm;
no Amex.*

Alain Ducasse
Dorchester W1 £121 2 3 2
53 Park Ln 7629 8866 3–3A
*"How this got three Michelin stars, I really don't know!" – the tyre
man's enduring esteem for the Gallic über-chef's "bland foodie
temple" in Mayfair – with its "unchallenging and stratospherically
overpriced" food – is quite unfathomable; on the plus-side, however,
the all-in set lunch is "a steal". / W1K 1QA;
www.alainducasse-dorchester.com; @Chefalinducasse; 9.30 pm; closed Mon,
Sat L & Sun; jacket; set weekday L £96 (FP).*

Albertine W12 £34 2 4 4
1 Wood Ln 8743 9593 7–1C
*"An oasis of calm that deserves our continued support"; this cute old
Shepherd's Bush wine bar "boldly resists the rise of Westfield over the
road", and "continues a tradition of simple but tasty food, with a fine
selection of wines by the glass". / W12 7DP; 10.30 pm; closed
Sat L & Sun; no Amex.*

Albion £45 2 2 2
NEO Bankside, Holland St, SE1 7827 4343 9–3B
2-4 Boundary St, E2 7729 1051 12–1B
*The newer, South Bank, branch of Sir Terence Conran's café duo has
been "a welcome addition to the still underserved area round Tate
Modern" – "ideal for a pre-gallery lunch or brunch"; the "barren but
stylish" Shoreditch original has its fans too, especially for breakfast.
/ 11 pm.*

The Albion N1 £45 2 2 **4**
10 Thornhill Rd 7607 7450 8–3D
An Islington boozer serving "dependable pub fare"; "I visit over and over again, for the great atmosphere, and fantastic beer garden", says one fan. / N1 1HW; www.the-albion.co.uk; @thealbionpub; 10 pm, Sun 9 pm; SRA-2 stars.

Ali Baba NW1 £23 **3** 2 2
32 Ivor Pl 7723 5805 2–1A
"Excellent, if you like the atmosphere of a Cairo café"… this quirky family-run Marylebone BYO (behind a take-away) looks "tired", but it's "faithful" to the real thing, offering decent Middle Eastern cooking. / NW1 6DA; midnight; no credit cards.

Alloro W1 £62 2 **4** 2
19-20 Dover St 7495 4768 3–3C
"Buzzy without being noisy", this "upmarket" Mayfair Italian makes "a great spot for a business lunch"; the food is "solid" too, if "nothing special", given the prices. / W1S 4LU; www.alloro-restaurant.co.uk; 10.30 pm; closed Sat L & Sun.

The Almeida N1 £58 2 2 2
30 Almeida St 7354 4777 8–2D
It's "more than adequate for pre- or post-Almeida Theatre" (opposite), but this large D&D Group venture, in Islington, again incites rather ambivalent commentary – its "noisy" interior can seem "characterless", and its contemporary cooking is "well presented" but a trifle "boring". / N1 1AD; www.almeida-restaurant.co.uk; 10.30 pm; closed Mon L & Sun D; set weekday L & pre-theatre £38 (FP); SRA-2 stars.

Alounak £30 **3** 2 **3**
10 Russell Gdns, W14 7603 1130 7–1D
44 Westbourne Grove, W2 7229 0416 6–1B
"An incredibly cheap, good, authentic and reliable BYO Iranian!" – one reporter neatly captures all the plus points of these "always-buzzing" Bayswater and Olympia cafés. / 11.30 pm; no Amex.

Alquimia SW15 £54 **3** **4** 2
Putney Wharf 8785 0508 10–2B
By the river at Putney Wharf, a sizeable yearling tipped as just the spot for "a wide selection" of "authentic" tapas; lovely al fresco tables in summer. / SW15 2JX; www.alquimiarestaurant.co.uk; @AlquimiaRestUK; 11.30 pm, Sun 10.30 pm.

**Alyn Williams
Westbury Hotel W1** £82 **4** **4** 2
37 Conduit St 7183 6426 3–2C
"A hidden gem!"; with Alyn Williams's "superbly executed" cuisine, "interesting" wines, and service that's "so charming", this "swish" Bond Street hotel dining room deserves a wider following; the catch? – atmosphere is "slightly lacking". / W1S 2YF; www.alynwilliams.com; @Alyn_Williams; 10.30 pm; closed Mon & Sun; jacket; set weekday L £54 (FP).

Amaya SW1 £78 5 4 3
Halkin Arc, 19 Motcomb St 7823 1166 5–1D
"Amazing and free from cliché" – this "unmatchable" Belgravian offers a "refined" tapas-style formula that puts it among the capital's very best subcontinentals; the interior is pleasingly "upscale" too (though "it's best not to sit next to the grill"). / SW1X 8JT; www.amaya.biz; 11.30 pm, Sun 10.30 pm; set weekday L £46 (FP).

Ametsa with Arzak Instruction
Halkin Hotel SW1 £85 2 3 1
5 Halkin St 7333 1234 2–3A
"Why isn't it booked out nightly?", ask fans of Juan Mari Arzak's Basque export to Belgravia, and its "creative, indulgent and beautiful" cuisine; the mega-"bland" interior doesn't help though, and a large minority of reporters just feel that the food is "surprisingly poor, given the pedigree". / SW1X 7DJ; www.comohotels.com/thehalkin/dining/ametsa; @AmetsaArzak; 10 pm; closed Mon L & Sun.

Amico Bio £38 2 2 2
43 New Oxford St, WC1 7836 7509 4–1C
43-44 Cloth Fair, EC1 7600 7778 9–2B
Though they offer potentially "interesting" Italo-veggie fare, these Bloomsbury and Smithfield bistros can fail to live up – "the food sounded so promising, but it was surprisingly dull". / EC1 10.30pm; EC1 closed Sat L & Sun; no booking.

L'Amorosa W6 NEW £42
278 King St 8563 0300 7–2B
Lola & Simon (RIP) was a cute little café on Hammersmith's trafficky main drag; Andy Needham – for 15 years head chef at Belgravia's Zafferano – opened a new neighbourhood Italian on the site as this guide went to press. / W6 0SP; www.lamorosa.co.uk.

Anarkali W6 £34 3 3 2
303-305 King St 8748 1760 7–2B
"Hasn't changed for years" – no bad thing, as this veteran Hammersmith Indian continues to offer "consistently good food and friendly service". / W6 9NH; www.anarkalifinedining.com; midnight, Sun 11.30 pm; no Amex.

The Anchor & Hope SE1 £48 5 3 3
36 The Cut 7928 9898 9–4A
"Number one for pub food in London"; for the 9th year this "convivial" South Bank boozer – with its "hearty" but "superbly precise" British cooking – remains "the benchmark for gastropub eating"; if only it weren't "so horribly hard to get a table" – expect to queue and share tables. / SE1 8LP; www.anchorandhopepub.co.uk; @AnchorHopeCut; 10.30 pm; closed Mon L & Sun D; no Amex; no booking; set weekday L £30 (FP).

Andina E2 NEW £35 4 3 4
1 Redchurch St 7920 6499 12–1B
"Unique flavours focussed on nutritious ingredients from Peru" help win a thumbs-up for this "trendy" Shoreditch newcomer; "the clubby downstairs is the place to sit". / E2 7DJ; www.andinalondon.com; 11 pm.

The Andover Arms W6 £40 2 4 4
57 Aldensey Rd 8748 2155 7–1B
"A solid clientele of male pint-drinkers" only adds to the *"classic friendly local atmosphere"* of this Hammersmith backstreet boozer; *"Sunday roast (book) is a highlight"* of the *"solid"* and *"uncomplicated"* pub grub. / W6 0DL; www.andoverarms.co.uk; @theandoverarms; 11.30 pm; no Amex.

Andrew Edmunds W1 £46 3 4 5
46 Lexington St 7437 5708 3–2D
"Unique" and *"utterly charming"*, this ancient candlelit Soho townhouse remains one of London's most prodigiously popular boltholes; *"squashed"* it may be, and the *"extraordinary"* wine may outshine the cuisine (*"reasonably priced"* as it is)... but *"if you only have eyes for your date, this is the place!"* / W1F 0LW; www.andrewedmunds.com; 10.45 pm, Sun 10.30 pm; no Amex; booking: max 6.

The Angel & Crown WC2 £45 2 2 3
58 St Martin's Ln 7748 5244 4–3B
"A real open fire in the dining room" (rarely found in central London) is a particular feature of this Covent Garden boozer; otherwise, however, by the top standards of the Martin ('Gun' etc) brothers' stable, it's a bit of a damp squib. / WC2N 4EA.

Angels & Gypsies
Church Street Hotel SE5 £42 2 2 3
29-33 Camberwell Church St 7703 5984 1–3C
"Wonderful, wonderful tapas, and a laid-back attitude" have put this *"lively"* modern tapas bar, in Camberwell, firmly on the map; even fans, however, may complain of *"creeping prices"*. / SE5 8TR; www.angelsandgypsies.com; @angelsngypsies; 10.30 pm, Fri & Sat 11 pm.

Angelus W2 £74 3 5 4
4 Bathurst St 7402 0083 6–2D
Thierry Tomassin *"is a great host"*, and he has assembled *"an amazing wine selection"* at this *"cosy"* and *"animated"* pub-conversion, near Lancaster Gate; the prices *"all add up"* though, and while the *"classic"* Gallic cuisine can be *"excellent"*, it can also *"under-deliver"*. / W2 2SD; www.angelusrestaurant.co.uk; 11 pm, Sun 10 pm.

Angler
South Place Hotel EC2 £73 3 3 4
3 South Pl 3215 1260 12–2A
The *"superb view and splendid terrace"* seal the appeal of D&D Group's *"stunning"* top-floor room, over a trendy hotel *"in the heart of the City"*; aside from the *"eye-watering prices"*, it's a *"good all-rounder"*, where fish dishes in particular are *"top-notch"*. / EC2M 2AF; www.anglerrestaurant.com; @southplacehotel; 10 pm; closed Sat L; max 14; set dinner £53 (FP).

The Anglesea Arms W6 £50 4 2 4
35 Wingate Rd 8749 1291 7–1B
Much to the relief of Brackenbury Village regulars, this acclaimed gastropub finally reopened in mid-2014, under the management of the old chef; early reports say its *"ambitious"* food and *"wonderful and welcoming"* ambience are just the same as ever. / W6 0UR; www.angleseaarmspub.co.uk; @_AngleseaArmsW6; 10 pm, Sun 9 pm; closed weekday L.

The Anglesea Arms SW7 £48 2 2 4
15 Selwood Ter 7373 7960 5–2B
"Enjoy a few ales on the terrace first", if you make a summertime visit to this *"charming"* South Kensington pub; the restaurant is *"nothing fantastic, but portions are large. the food's OK, and you can usually get a table"*. / SW7 3QG; www.angleseaarms.com; @angleseaarms; 10 pm, Sun 9.30 pm.

L'Anima EC2 £74 3 3 3
1 Snowden St 7422 7000 12–2B
Undoubtedly *"very classy"*, if also a bit *"cold"* and *"noisy"*, this *"upmarket"* City Italian is an impressive all-rounder, and very popular for business entertaining; some critics, though, do feel it *"lacks the spark it had when it opened"*. / EC2A 2DQ; www.lanima.co.uk; 11 pm, Sat 11.30 pm; closed Sat L & Sun.

L' Anima Café EC2 NEW £45 3 4 3
1 Snowden St 7422 7000 12–2B
Near the grand City-fringe Italian of the same name, a large contemporary-style café-pizzeria-trattoria; some of the food is of very high quality, and some of the prices are very reasonable too. / EC2A 2DQ; Rated on Editors' visit; 10.30 pm, Sat 11 pm; closed Sun.

Annie's £46 2 3 4
162 Thames Rd, W4 8994 9080 1–3A
36-38 White Hart Ln, SW13 8878 2020 10–1A
"Boudoir-chic decor" helps create a *"fantastic"* atmosphere at these Barnes and Strand-on-the-Green family-favourites, where brunch is a highlight of cuisine that's generally rather *"so-so"*. / www.anniesrestaurant.co.uk; 10 pm, Sat 10.30 pm, Sun 9.30 pm.

Antepliler £35 3 2 2
139 Upper St, N1 7226 5441 1–1C
46 Grand Pde, N4 8802 5588 1–1C
"Tasty, plentiful dishes, fast service and decent prices" – such are the virtues of these modern Turkish establishments, in Islington and Newington Green. / www.anteplilerrestaurant.com; 11 pm.

The Anthologist EC2 £42 3 4 3
58 Gresham St 468 0101 9–2C
"A please-all menu, but none the worse for that" – this large and comfortable bar-restaurant, near the Guildhall, is a handy, very versatile standby, and it's open all day too. / EC2V 7BB; www.theanthologistbar.co.uk; @theanthologist; 10 pm; closed Sat & Sun; SRA-3 stars.

Antico SE1 £48 4 4 3
214 Bermondsey St 7407 4682 9–4D
This Bermondsey Italian two-year-old is *"a very laid-back but comfortably romantic venue"*, serving up *"thoughtful"* and *"very well-executed"* cooking; *"the only downside is that it's very noisy"*. / SE1 3TQ; www.antico-london.co.uk; @AnticoLondon; 10.30 pm; closed Mon.

Antidote W1 £57 5 4 3
12a Newburgh St 7287 8488 3–2C
"Astoundingly good" – the food in the upstairs room of this relaunched Soho wine bar can come as a *"surprise"*... until you learn that it is now overseen by Hedone's Mikael Jonsson; on the ground floor, you get *"fantastic biodynamic and natural wines"* too. / W1F 7RR; www.antidotewinebar.com; @AntidoteWineBar; 10.30 pm; closed Sun; max 8.

Antipasto & Pasta SW11   £41   **3 4 2**
511 Battersea Park Rd   7223 9765   10–1C
*"A great local eatery serving no-nonsense Italian food"; this age-old
Battersea fixture never waivers and, as ever, its "half-price nights are
an added bonus". / SW11 3BW; 11.30 pm, Sun 11 pm; need 4+ to book.*

The Ape & Bird WC2 NEW   £46
142 Shaftesbury Ave   7836 3119   4–2B
*In a rare misstep, Russell Norman launched a "very ordinary"
Theatreland gastropub in early-2014; later in the year, however,
it was relaunched in more 'Polpo' style, so we'll hold off on a rating
until next year. / WC2H 8HJ; www.apeandbird.com; @ApeandBird.*

Apollo Banana Leaf SW17   £20   **5 1 1**
190 Tooting High St   8696 1423   10–2C
*This Tooting shop-conversion may look "really grotty" (and "don't
expect service with a smile"), but "it's all about the food here" –
"real" Indian ("not a Korma in sight!") at "unbeatable" prices; BYO.
/ SW17 0SF; www.apollobananaleaf.com; 10.30 pm; no Amex.*

Apostrophe   £18   **3 3 3**
Branches throughout London
*"A bit different" from the sandwich-shop norm – these Gallic-owned
outlets offers sarnies that are "a cut above", plus "excellent" coffee
and "thick hot chocolate to die for". / www.apostropheuk.com;
most branches 6 pm, Sat 5.30 pm; no booking.*

Applebee's Café SE1   £43   **3 2 2**
5 Stoney St   7407 5777   9–4C
*"Brilliant fish straight from the fresh fish counter" (grilled or fried)
is the promise at this "no-nonsense and fun" Borough Market outfit.
/ SE1 9AA; www.applebeesfish.com; @applebeesfish; 10 pm, Fri 10.30 pm;
closed Sun; no Amex.*

Apulia EC1 NEW   £38   **3 3 1**
50 Long Ln   7600 8107   9–2B
*"Genuine", "friendly" and "reasonably-priced", this family-run Italian
newcomer, near Smithfield Market, is quite a hit with most reporters;
the decor is "bare" and "unstyled", though – perhaps to a fault.
/ EC1A 9EJ; www.apuliarestaurant.co.uk; set weekday L £19 (FP).*

aqua kyoto W1   £75   **2 2 2**
240 Regent St (entrance 30 Argyll St)   7478 0540   3–2C
*The Japanese-fusion section of this nightclubby operation, six floors
above Regent Street, wins praise for its views, cocktails and Asian-
inspired cuisine; reports are inconsistent, though, with a minority
noting a "poor" ambience and "ridiculous" prices. / W1B 3BR;
www.aqua-london.com; @aqualondon; 10.30 pm; closed Sun D; booking:
max 6.*

aqua nueva W1   £66   **2 2 2**
240 Regent St (entrance 30 Argyll St)   7478 0540   3–2C
*Near Oxford Circus, a "fancy" nightclub-style Spanish rooftop
operation, with surprisingly striking outside space; the food can
be good but the staff sometimes act "like they're doing you a favour"
– one reason, perhaps, the place inspires little survey commentary.
/ W1B 3BR; www.aqua-london.com; @aqualondon; 10.30 pm; closed Sun.*

Aqua Shard SE1 — £81 — 1 1 4

Level 31, 31 St Thomas St 3011 1256 9–4C
"Go for cocktails, and give the restaurant a miss!" – the Shard's 31st-floor restaurant is a bad case of: "stunning view, shame about the food" (or, to put it another way, the 'Oxo Tower Syndrome' Strikes Again!). / SE1 9RY; www.aquashard.co.uk; @aquashard; 10.30 pm; set weekday L £54 (FP).

Arabica Bar and Kitchen SE1 NEW — £44 — 3 4 3

3 Rochester Walk 3011 5151 9–4C
Unusually stylish by Lebanese restaurant standards, this Borough Market newcomer is a "friendly" and "buzzy" sort of place where the food, on our early-days visit, was always competent, and sometimes better. / SE1 9AF; Rated on Editors' visit; www.arabicabarandkitchen.com; 10.30 pm; closed Sun.

Arbutus W1 — £50 — 4 4 2

63-64 Frith St 7734 4545 4–2A
"Rarely-made classic dishes" (featuring "cheaper cuts and offal") and "interesting wines by the glass and carafe" has won acclaim for this "keenly priced" Soho favourite; its "plain" interior is "not the most comfortable", though, and can get "very noisy" at peak times. / W1D 3JW; www.arbutusrestaurant.co.uk; @artutus; 10.45 pm, Fri & Sat 11.15 pm, Sun 10.30 pm.

Archduke Wine Bar SE1 — £52 — 2 2 2

Concert Hall Approach, South Bank 7928 9370 2–3D
"For meeting up with friends before a South Bank concert", this outpost of the 'Black & Blue' steak 'n' burger chain – under the arches by the Festival Hall – is certainly hyper-convenient; otherwise, though, it's "nothing special", and "expensive for what it is". / SE1 8XU; www.blackandbluerestaurants.com; 10.30 pm, Sun 10 pm.

Ark Fish E18 — £42 — 5 4 2

142 Hermon Hill 8989 5345 1–1D
"Fish 'n' chips, yes, but brilliantly fresh fish superbly cooked" – this no-bookings South Woodford spot is arguably "east London's best fish place", and "worth every penny". / E18 1QH; www.arkfishrestaurant.co.uk; 9.45 pm, Fri & Sat 10.15 pm, Sun 8.45 pm; closed Mon; no Amex.

Artigiano NW3 — £46 — 3 3 3

12a Belsize Ter 7794 4288 8–2A
A "quintessential" neighbourhood Italian, in Belsize Park, where the "solid" cooking includes a "great selection of fish". / NW3 4AX; www.etruscarestaurants.com; @artigianoesp; 10 pm; closed Mon L.

L'Artista NW11 — £35 — 2 4 4

917 Finchley Rd 8731 7501 1–1B
Under the arches by Golders Green tube, this jolly Italian has long been a local favourite, especially for parties – the "obliging" staff "love making a fuss of you", "kids can make as much noise as they like", and the pizza and pasta come "in really good portions". / NW11 7PE; www.lartistapizzeria.com; 11.30 pm.

L'Artiste Musclé W1 — £44 — 2 2 4

1 Shepherd Mkt 7493 6150 3–4B
It's a little bit of a "cliché", but the "Paris-in-London" charms of this pint-sized Shepherd Market bistro still make it an "enjoyable" destination; the cooking may be "unremarkable", but it's "reliable" too. / W1J 7PA; 10 pm, Fri-Sun 10.30 pm.

Artusi SE15 NEW £45 4 3 2
161 Bellenden Rd   3302 8200   1–4D
*"Another excellent Peckham opening!" – this "tiny" Italian may
be "a little overhyped" locally, but it "astonishes" its fans with
an "interesting" menu using "super-fresh ingredients"; shame it can
seem a touch "vibeless". / SE15 4DH; www.artusi.co.uk; @artusipeckham.*

Asadal WC1 £40 3 2 2
227 High Holborn   7430 9006   2–1D
*An implausible dining room to find beneath Holborn tube, offering
"a reliable, traditional Korean dining experience"; shame the service
is rather lacklustre. / WC1V 7DA; www.asadal.co.uk; 10.30 pm; closed
Sun L.*

Asakusa NW1 £36 5 2 2
265 Eversholt St   7388 8533   8–3C
*"A veritable Aladdin's cave of delicious Japanese food", and at
"surprisingly low" prices too; it may look "like a rundown old caff"
and have "chaotic" (if "friendly") service, but this "nondescript" spot,
near Euston Station, is "awesome". / NW1 1BA; 11.30 pm, Sat 11 pm;
D only, closed Sun.*

Ask £41 2 2 2
Branches throughout London
*"Unexciting, but adequate for a basic meal", these "standard" pizza-
and-pasta operations are a paradigm of your "typical chain
restaurant". / www.askcentral.co.uk; most branches 11 pm, Fri & Sat
11.30 pm; some booking restrictions apply.*

Assaggi W2 £75 4 4 2
39 Chepstow Pl   7792 5501   6–1B
*"Some of the best Italian food in London" made "with real love",
plus "terrific" service, has won renown for this "noisy" room above
a Bayswater pub, where "even after so many years, it's still not easy
to get a table"; perhaps it "used to be better value",
but most reporters feel "it still hits the right notes". / W2 4TS; 11 pm;
closed Sun; no Amex.*

Les Associés N8 £46 3 4 2
172 Park Rd   8348 8944   1–1C
*"Tiny, charming and genuine" – it's not much to look at, but this
unassuming Crouch End Gallic stalwart still impresses reporters…
even if it "does need a lick of paint". / N8 8JT; www.lesassocies.co.uk;
@lesassociesn8; 10 pm; closed Mon, Tue L, Sat L & Sun D; 24 hr notice for
L bookings; set Sun L £33 (FP).*

Assunta Madre W1 NEW £83 3 2 2
9-10 Blenheim St   3230 3032   3–2B
*On the former site of Semplice (RIP), a Mayfair offshoot of a
restaurant in Rome; most early-days supporters do praise its
"excellent fresh fish", but not everyone's convinced, and it can seem
"seriously overpriced". / W1S 1LJ; www.assuntamadre.com;
@assuntamadre; 10.30 pm.*

Atari-Ya £32 5 2 1
20 James St, W1   7491 1178   3–1A
1 Station Pde, W5   8896 3175   1–3A
31 Vivian Ave, NW4   8202 2789   1–1B
75 Fairfax Road, NW6   7328 5338   8–2A
The branches are "not the most glamorous", but the cafés run by these Japanese food importers serve "wonderful, expertly prepared sushi" that's some of the best in town ("and that includes the Nobus of the world!"). / www.atariya.co.uk; W1 8 pm, NW4 & NW6 9.30 pm, W9 9 pm; NW4, NW6 closed Mon.

L'Atelier de Joel Robuchon WC2 £86 3 3 3
13-15 West St   7010 8600   4–2B
"Delightful and meticulous" delicacies – eaten on high stools, many beside the open kitchen – help justify the vertiginous prices (the "steal of a set lunch" aside) at this "glamorous" Covent Garden outpost of the Parisian über-chef; as the formula dates, though, reporters find the place increasingly "overrated". / WC2H 9NE; www.joelrobuchon.co.uk; @latelierlondon; midnight, Sun 10 pm; no trainers; set weekday L & pre-theatre £67 (FP).

Athenaeum
Athenaeum Hotel W1 £80 3 3 3
116 Piccadilly   7499 3464   3–4B
"Very good quality, for a hotel restaurant" – this handily-sited dining room ('twixt Hyde Park Corner and The Ritz) is especially worth knowing about for the "great-value set lunch"; "great afternoon teas" too. / W1J 7BJ; www.athenaeumhotel.com; 10.30 pm.

The Atlas SW6 £45 4 4 4
16 Seagrave Rd   7385 9129   5–3A
This "great backstreet pub", near Earl's Court 2, "continues to be a shining light in the desert of north Fulham"; it boasts a "textbook film-set Victorian interior", but "it's the kitchen that continues to draw the crowds", with its "really polished" Mediterranean-inspired cuisine. / SW6 1RX; www.theatlaspub.co.uk; @theatlasfulham; 10 pm.

The Attendant W1 £13 4 4 4
27a, Foley St   7637 3794   2–1B
"How surreal to have London's richest and most flavoursome coffee in an ex-public loo!"; so say fans of this "wonderful conversion" – a year-old café in Fitzrovia. / W1W 6DY; www.the-attendant.com; @Attendantcafe; 6 pm, Sat 5 pm; L only, closed Sun.

Aubaine £58 1 1 1
31 Dover St, W1   7368 0955   3–3C
4 Heddon St, W1   7440 2510   3–2C
Selfridges & Co, 400 Oxford St, W1   7318 3738   3–1A
260-262 Brompton Rd, SW3   7052 0100   5–2C
37-45 Kensington High St, W8   7368 0950   5–1A
Fans insist these Gallic bistro-cafés offer "excellent" breakfasts in a "cosy" but "lively" setting; more generally, though, reporters feel the food is "uninspiring", service "struggling" and prices "scandaludicrous". / www.aubaine.co.uk; @balanslondon; SW3, SW19 10 pm, Sun 9.30 pm; Heddon St 11 pm, Oxford St 9 pm, Sun 6 pm, W8 10 pm, Sun 6 pm, Dover St 10 pm, Sun 9.30 pm; W8 no booking.

Augustine Kitchen SW11 NEW   £45   4 4 1

63 Battersea Bridge Rd   7978 7085   5–4C

"Poorly located in a row of shops", this is a Battersea newcomer
"you could walk straight past"; "it deserves to do well" though – staff
are "fun", and the French cooking is "delicious, and phenomenally
well priced". / SW11 3AU; www.augustine-kitchen.co.uk; @augustinekitchen;
10.30 pm; closed Mon & Sun D; set weekday L £27 (FP).

Aurora W1   £50   3 3 4

49 Lexington St   7494 0514   3–2D

It's a mistake to overlook this "small and cosy" Soho stalwart whose
"romantic" attractions include "a lovely quiet patio offering a few
tables hidden away at the back"; the menu's only short, but "all the
choices are appealing". / W1F 9AP; www.aurorasoho.co.uk; 10 pm, Wed-Sat
10.30 pm, Sun 9 pm.

L'Autre Pied W1   £80   4 4 2

5-7 Blandford St   7486 9696   2–1A

"Colours, tastes and textures are beautifully combined" to create
"exciting and delicious" dishes, at Pied à Terre's Marylebone offshoot;
shame about the interior, though – critics say it has "all the ambience
of a railway café". / W1U 3DB; www.lautrepied.co.uk; 10 pm; closed Sun D;
set weekday L & pre-theatre £49 (FP).

L'Aventure NW8   £60   4 5 5

3 Blenheim Ter   7624 6232   8–3A

Few restaurants can equal the ultra-"cute" charm or longevity of this
St John's Wood "classic", run – "with a high degree of Gallic
authority" – by chef-patronne Catherine Parisot; her cuisine
bourgeoise is "reliably divine" too. / NW8 0EH; 11 pm; closed
Sat L & Sun; set weekday L £36 (FP).

The Avenue SW1   £54   1 3 3

7-9 St James's St   7321 2111   3–4D

"Oh dear, what went wrong?"; the staff may be "charming and hard
working", but the post-relaunch food at this longtime St James's
business favourite is too often "dreadful" – "how can you have
an American place that screws up steak or brownies?" / SW1A 1EE;
www.avenue-restaurant.co.uk; @avenuestjames; 10.30 pm; closed Sat L & Sun;
set weekday L £42 (FP); SRA-2 stars.

Axis

One Aldwych Hotel WC2   £63   2 2 3

1 Aldwych   7300 0300   2–2D

This impressive-looking Covent Garden basement offers a "good-value
pre-theatre set menu", and its film-and-dinner deals attract
"appreciative regulars"; otherwise, however, feedback
is modest in volume, and rather lacklustre. / WC2B 4RH;
www.onealdwych.com; @OneAldwych; 10.30 pm; closed Mon, Sat L & Sun.

Azou W6   £42   4 4 4

375 King St   8563 7266   7–2B

"A real gem, in a forest of competition"; this small, sweet café
on Hammersmith's main drag serves tagines "you will want to eat
time and time again". / W6 9NJ; www.azou.co.uk; @azourestaurant;
11 pm.

Ba Shan W1 £49 4 1 2
24 Romilly St 7287 3266 4–3A
*Just over the road from its famous Soho parent, Bar Shu,
this "not especially friendly" Soho pit stop is nonetheless "worth going
back to" for its "bright, chilli-rich and zingy" dishes, from Hunan.
/ W1D 5AH; www.bashanlondon.com; 11 pm, Fri & Sat 11.30 pm.*

Babbo W1 £79 2 2 2
39 Albermarle St 3205 1099 3–3C
*A small restaurant near The Ritz, hailed by fans as a "true Italian" –
"passionately run" and with "mouthwatering" cuisine; it also has its
critics, though, who say "don't bother going" – "it's too expensive for
what it is!" / W1S 4JQ; www.babborestaurant.co.uk; @BabboRestaurant;
11 pm, Sun 10.30 pm; closed Sun L; set weekday L £51 (FP).*

Babur SE23 £51 5 4 3
119 Brockley Rise 8291 2400 1–4D
*"It's curry Jim, but not as we know it!"; this "fabulously inventive"
Honour Oak Park fixture is "in a different league from your standard
Indian" and – despite a fractional slip in ratings this year – remains
one of SE London's top destinations. / SE23 1JP; www.babur.info;
@BaburRestaurant; 11.30 pm; set Sun L £35 (FP).*

Babylon
Kensington Roof Gardens W8 £72 2 4 4
99 Kensington High St 7368 3993 5–1A
*"Extraordinary to have trees, streams and flamingos, up above
Kensington High Street!" – these "cool" ("blingy") 8th-floor dining
rooms, overlooking the roof gardens, make "such a romantic summer
location"; perhaps best to visit for lunch, when there's a "very good-
value 3-course set option". / W8 5SA; www.virgin.com/roofgardens;
10.30 pm; closed Sun D; set weekday L £46 (FP); SRA-3 stars.*

Il Bacio £43 3 2 2
61 Stoke Newington Church St, N16 7249 3833 1–1C
178-184 Blackstock Rd, N5 7226 3339 8–1D
*A "staple" in both Stoke Newington and Highbury – these "trusted
locals" serve "proper Italian pizza", plus a range of "good-value"
Sardinian dishes. / www.ilbaciohighbury.co.uk; 10 pm-11 pm; Mon-Fri L;
no Amex.*

Baker & Spice £41 2 2 2
54-56 Elizabeth St, SW1 7730 5524 2–4A
47 Denyer St, SW3 7225 3417 5–2D
20 Clifton Rd, W9 7289 2499 8–4A
*Curiously, it's the "lovely" salads (sold by weight) at this chichi
café/bakery chain which have inspired the most commentary of late;
even fans, though, rail at the "exorbitant" prices.
/ www.bakerandspice.uk.com; 7 pm, Sun 6 pm; closed D; no Amex; no booking.*

Balans £48 2 4 3
60-62 Old Compton St, W1 7439 2183 4–3A
Westfield, Ariel Way, W12 8600 3320 7–1C
214 Chiswick High Rd, W4 8742 1435 7–2A
187 Kensington High St, W8 7376 0115 5–1A
Westfield Stratford, E20 8555 5478 1–1D
*"Loud, cheerful, and served up with a little bit of flirtation" (especially
if you're male and gay) – the late-night, heart-of-Soho original of this
small diner chain is "great for breakfast any time". / www.balans.co.uk;
midnight-2 am; 34 Old Compton St 24 hrs, E20 11pm; some booking
restrictions apply.*

The Balcon
Sofitel St James SW1 £59 2 2 **3**
8 Pall Mall 7968 2900 2–3C
Just off Trafalgar Square, this "grand" brasserie, in a "fancy" French hotel, is just the job for a business lunch or "decent pre-theatre" bite; for more serious dining, though, the cuisine can seem rather "ordinary". / SW1Y 5NG; www.thebalconlondon.com; 10.45 pm, Sun 9.45 pm.

Bald Faced Stag N2 £48 **3 3 3**
69 High Rd 8442 1201 1–1B
A popular gastropub that spans the range from "casual eats" – "ideal if you're going to a movie at the Phoenix in East Finchley" – to an "excellent Sunday lunch". / N2 8AB; www.thebaldfacedstagn2.co.uk; @thebaldfacestagn2; 10.30 pm, Sun 9.30 pm.

Balthazar WC2 £64 **1** 2 **4**
4-6 Russell St 3301 1155 4–3D
"Ridiculous prices for ordinary food", and "sloppy" service too – for far too many reporters, Keith McNally's "hyped" and "Disney-esque" NYC-Gallic brasserie import "just doesn't cut the mustard". / WC2E 7BN; www.balthazarlondon.com; @balthazarlondon; Mon-Thu 11.30 pm, Fri & Sat 11.45 pm, Sun 10.30 pm .

Baltic SE1 £53 **3** 2 **3**
74 Blackfriars Rd 7928 1111 9–4A
"So good my eastern European wife got homesick!"; this "beautiful and airy" (but sometimes "very noisy") former warehouse, in Borough, offers some "stylishly executed" (mainly) Polish fare; beware the vodkas though – "they've crushed many an after-work drinker". / SE1 8HA; www.balticrestaurant.co.uk; @BalticLondon; 11 pm, Sun 10.15 pm; closed Mon L; set pre theatre £35 (FP).

Bam-Bou W1 £52 **3** 3 **5**
1 Percy St 7323 9130 2–1C
With its "out-of-this-world" cocktails and "sexy" lighting, this "French colonial-style" Fitzrovia townhouse (rambling over numerous floors) is "a perfect destination for a date", serving French/Vietnamese cuisine of a "high standard". / W1T 1DB; www.bam-bou.co.uk; @CapriceHoldings; midnight; closed Sun D; booking: max 6; set weekday L £41 (FP).

The Banana Tree Canteen £35 2 2 2
103 Wardour St, W1 7437 1351 3–2D
21-23 Westbourne Grove, W2 7221 4085 6–1C
166 Randolph Ave, W9 7286 3869 8–3A
75-79 Battersea Rise, SW11 7228 2828 10–2C
412-416 St John St, EC1 7278 7565 8–3D
As "a good standby for a quick bite", many would tip these Asian-fusion canteens for their "really well-flavoured" dishes at "cheap" prices; they can also seem "nothing special", though, and the branches can get "very noisy". / @bananatree247; 11 pm, Sun 10.30 pm; booking: min 6.

Bangkok SW7 £40 **3** 2 2
9 Bute St 7584 8529 5–2B
"Always busy", but "very unassuming" – this "westernised" South Kensington Thai hasn't changed that much in 40 years in business, and still offers "ever-enjoyable and tasty" fare at "reasonable prices". / SW7 3EY; www.thebankokrestaurant.co.uk; 10.45 pm; no Amex.

Bank Westminster
St James Court Hotel SW1   £61   3 2 2
45 Buckingham Gate   7630 6644   2–4B
"Fine for a business lunch, but a bit unexciting for dinner" –
one reporter neatly captures the spirit of this large brasserie,
near Buckingham Palace, which manages to be a rather colourless
destination, despite its impressive conservatory at the rear.
/ SW1E 6BS; www.bankrestaurants.com; @bank_westmin; 11 pm; closed
Sat L & Sun.

Banners N8   £46   3 4 5
21 Park Rd   8348 2930   1–1C
*An institution for Crouch End folk, this "vibrant" 'world food' diner
is still of note for its "amazing" breakfasts, plus other "reasonably
priced" scoff, usually with a Caribbean slant; "the service has been
good for 20 years now, which is impressive considering how busy they
get!"* / N8 8TE; www.bannersrestaurant.com; 11.30 pm, Fri & Sat midnight,
Sun 11 pm; no Amex.

Baozi Inn WC2   £18   3 2 2
25 Newport Ct   7287 6877   4–3B
*Small, crowded and noisy, this Chinatown café is short on creature
comforts, but it does offer tasty, wallet-friendly Sichuanese staples –
from noodle soups to BBQ pork buns ("so light and fluffy it's like
eating a meaty cloud").* / WC2H 7JS; 10 pm, Fri & Sat 10.30 pm; no credit
cards; no booking.

Bar Boulud
Mandarin Oriental SW1   £69   3 3 4
66 Knightsbridge   7201 3899   5–1D
*"The best burgers anywhere" head up the Franco-American menu
at this NYC super-chef's "slick" and "surprisingly buzzy" brasserie,
in the basement of a grand Knightsbridge hotel; "it's exactly the sort
of place you'd expect to be mediocre, but it's very good indeed!"*
/ SW1X 7LA; www.barboulud.com; 10.45 pm, Sun 9.45 pm; set always
available £27 (FP).

Bar Esteban N8 NEW   £38   5 3 3
29 Park Rd   8340 3090   1–1C
"Livening up Crouch End!" – this "cheerful and bustling" newcomer
is "busy every night", thanks to its "large selection of tapas" that are
"fantastic every time". / N8 8TE; www.baresteban.com; Mon-Sat 10.30 pm,
Sun 9 pm; closed weekday L.

Bar Italia W1   £28   3 4 5
22 Frith St   7437 4520   4–2A
*"The best espresso in London" is to be had at this "iconic" Soho spot,
which – "although a little dented around the edges" – remains
a veritable 24/7 "institution".* / W1D 4RT; www.baritaliasoho.co.uk;
@TheBaristas; open 24 hours, Sun 4 am; no Amex; no booking.

Barbecoa EC4   £64   2 2 3
20 New Change Pas   3005 8555   9–2B
*"Phenomenal" views of St Paul's reward those who get the best seats
at Jamie O's vast City venue; it's "very expensive", though, and while
fans praise its "beautiful" steaks, others decry results as "dreadful".*
/ EC4M 9AG; www.barbecoa.com; @barbecoa; Mon-Sat 10.30 pm,
Sun 9.45 pm .

La Barca SE1 £65 2 2 2

80-81 Lower Marsh 7928 2226 9–4A

This "old-style" Italian veteran, by Waterloo, is certainly "good for business and the Old Vic"; more generally, it divides opinions – to critics it's simply "outdated", but fans argue it's "reliable if pricey". / SE1 7AB; www.labarca-ristorante.com; @labarca1976; 11.15 pm; closed Sat L & Sun.

Il Baretto W1 £63 2 2 2

43 Blandford St 7486 7340 2–1A

Fans say this "buzzy" Marylebone basement Italian is worth seeking out for its "tasty" food and "cheeky" staff; critics, though, find it a "noisy" place that's "too expensive for what it is", where the food is "mediocre" and service "erratic". / W1U 7HF; www.ilbaretto.co.uk; @IlBarettoLondon; 10.15 pm, Sun 9.45 pm.

Barnyard W1 NEW £44 3 3 2

18 Charlotte St 7580 3842 2–1C

Much-hyped wunderkind Ollie Dabbous has gone "democratic and accessible" for his first spin-off – a "cool" rustic-chic Fitzrovia diner, serving comfort food with a twist; critics, however, can see only a "painfully contrived" place, where the food "lacks oomph". / W1T 2LZ.

Barrafina £42 5 5 5

54 Frith St, W1 7813 8016 4–2A
10 Adelaide St, WC2 7440 1456 4–2D

"Our hands-down favourite, even with the nightmare queue!"; the Hart brothers' tiny Soho bar dazzles fans with its "unfailingly exciting" dishes ("especially the seafood and the tortilla"); the new Covent Garden sibling is likewise a wow, serving "the freshest food, with passion". / www.barrafina.co.uk; 11 pm, Sun 10 pm; no booking.

Barrica W1 £40 4 3 4

62 Goodge St 7436 9448 2–1B

Part of "the Goodge St Spanish cluster", this "cosy" venture dishes up "outstandingly delicious tapas", complemented by a wine list "full of things to discover", and all in a great "laid-back" atmosphere – "what's not to like?" / W1T 4NE; www.barrica.co.uk; 10.30 pm; closed Sun.

Bar Shu W1 £52 4 1 2

28 Frith St 7287 6688 4–3A

"You'll blow your socks off", when you sample the "rich and zingy" Sichuan cooking – the "real McCoy" – on offer at this Soho café; "don't go for the ambience", though, or the "patchy" service. / W1D 5LF; www.barshurestaurant.co.uk; 10.30 pm, Fri & Sat 11 pm.

Basilico £36 4 4 1

690 Fulham Rd, SW6 0800 028 3531 10–1B
26 Penton St, N1 0800 093 4224 8–3D
51 Park Rd, N8 8616 0290 1–1C
515 Finchley Rd, NW3 0800 316 2656 1–1B
175 Lavender Hill, SW11 0800 389 9770 10–2C

For take-away pizza, this small chain is, say fans, "the best in town", thanks to its "delicious" thin-crusts and "original" toppings; "dining-in potential is limited". / www.basilico.co.uk; @basilicopizzas; 11 pm; no booking.

Beach Blanket Babylon £63 1️⃣2️⃣3️⃣
45 Ledbury Rd, W11   7229 2907   6–1B
19-23 Bethnal Green Rd, E1   7749 3540   12–1C
As "a great place to socialise", these striking and "atmospheric" Gaudi-esque hangouts, in Notting Hill and Shoreditch, make great party venues... if you can put up with the "appalling overpriced food". / www.beachblanket.co.uk; 10.30 pm; W11 booking advisable Fri-Sat.

Beast W1 NEW £113 3️⃣2️⃣3️⃣
3 Chapel Pl   7495 1816   3–1B
"Surf 'n' turf on steroids"; this rather "pretentious" Goodman-group newcomer, just north of Oxford Street, may offer a menu focussed on "amazing steak and wonderful king crab", but it "hits your wallet hard". / W1G 0BG; @beastrestaurant; 10 pm; closed Mon & Sun.

The Begging Bowl SE15 £39 5️⃣4️⃣5️⃣
168 Bellenden Rd   7635 2627   1–4D
"Best Thai food I've tasted outside Thailand!" – no wonder this "brisk" no-bookings local, in Peckham, is starting to make quite a name for itself. / SE15 4BW; www.thebeggingbowl.co.uk; Mon 9.45 pm, Tue-Sat 9.45 pm, Sun 3.15 pm; closed Sun D.

Beirut Express £43 4️⃣2️⃣2️⃣
65 Old Brompton Rd, SW7   7591 0123   5–2B
112-114 Edgware Rd, W2   7724 2700   6–1D
"Despite the awful neon sign, the food is good!"; for a fast snack, these South Kensington and Bayswater Lebaneses are just the job – "in, shawarma, mezze, out". / www.maroush.com; W2 2 am; SW7 midnight.

Beiteddine SW1 £54 3️⃣3️⃣2️⃣
8 Harriet St   7235 3969   5–1D
"Great food, reasonably priced... despite the area" – just a few yards from Sloane Street, this "friendly" and "reliable" Lebanese of long standing seems ever more like a survivor from another age. / SW1X 9JW; www.beiteddinerestaurant.com; midnight.

Belgo £43 2️⃣4️⃣3️⃣
50 Earlham St, WC2   7813 2233   4–2C
67 Kingsway, WC2   7242 7469   2–2D
72 Chalk Farm Rd, NW1   7267 0718   8–2B
"Especially for groups", these "big", "down-to-earth" and "buzzy" moules and Belgian beer emporia make "good-value" standbys. / www.belgo-restaurants.co.uk; most branches 10.30 pm-11.30 pm; SW4 midnight, Thu 1 am, Fri & Sat 2 am, Sun 12.30 am.

Bellamy's W1 £62 3️⃣4️⃣4️⃣
18-18a Bruton Pl   7491 2727   3–2B
"Genial" owner Gavin Rankin (who used to preside at Annabel's) is much in evidence at his "smart", "old-school" Gallic brasserie, "discreetly located" in a Mayfair mews; NB chaps – "most male customers wear suits". / W1J 6LY; www.bellamysrestaurant.co.uk; 10.30 pm; closed Sat L & Sun.

Bellevue Rendez-Vous SW17   £48   3̶3̶3̶

218 Trinity Rd   8767 5810   10–2C
"Trinity Road is not known for its romantic qualities, but this small French restaurant near Wandsworth Common is an absolute gem" – it has recently come under new ownership, but happily the menu is so far *"much the same"*. / SW17 7HP; www.bellevuerendezvous.com; 10.30 pm; closed Mon L; no Amex.

Belvedere W8   £69   2̶2̶4̶

Holland Pk, off Abbotsbury Rd   7602 1238   7–1D
With its "tranquil and serene" setting in Holland Park, this "beautiful" and "old-fashioned" Art Deco feature is "a lovely restaurant for lunch on a sunny day", particularly on the terrace; you don't go for the service though *("slow" and "inattentive")*, nor the food (often *"unexciting"*). / W8 6LU; www.belvedererestaurant.co.uk; 10.30 pm; closed Sun D; set weekday L & pre-theatre £41 (FP).

Benares W1   £90   3̶3̶3̶

12a Berkeley Square Hs, Berkeley Sq   7629 8886   3–3B
"Atul Kochar is a master of spicing" and *"continues to delight with the innovative interpretation of Indian cuisine"*, at his *"slick and showy"* Mayfair operation; its ratings slipped a notch this year though – perhaps there's just more competition than once there was? / W1J 6BS; www.benaresrestaurant.co.uk; @benaresofficial; 10.30 pm; closed Sun; no trainers; set pre theatre £58 (FP).

Bengal Clipper SE1   £41   3̶3̶3̶

Shad Thames   7357 9001   9–4D
"Reliable" standards make this grand Indian veteran a handy South Bank standby; service is generally *"so helpful"* too, though it can be *"slow"*. / SE1 2YR; www.bengalclipper.co.uk; 11.30 pm, Sun 11 pm.

Benito's Hat   £26   3̶4̶2̶

12 Great Castle St, W1   7636 6560   3–1C
56 Goodge St, W1   7637 3732   2–1B
19 New Row, WC2   7240 5815   4–3C
King's Cross Station, N1   7812 1304   8–3C
12-14 St John St, EC1   7490 4727   9–1B
"Freshly filled burritos at keen prices" – these self-service Mexicans are great for *"food on the run"*; good cocktails and happy hour deals too. / www.benitos-hat.com; 10 pm, Thu-Sat 11 pm; Great Castle St closed Sun.

Bentley's W1   £82   3̶3̶3̶

11-15 Swallow St   7734 4756   3–3D
"Sit downstairs and be entertained by the team of charming oyster shuckers", if you visit this handy veteran fish restaurant, a couple of minutes from Piccadilly Circus; there's also a less interesting dining room upstairs. / W1B 4DG; www.bentleys.org; @bentleys_london; 10.30 pm; no jeans; booking: max 8; set pre theatre £54 (FP).

Bento Café NW1   £37   4̶4̶2̶

9 Parkway   7482 3990   8–3B
Well placed for Camden Town's Jazz Café, this Chinese/Japanese eatery "ought to be better regarded", thanks to its *"vast"* and *"inexpensive"* set menus... and the range of tofu on offer is *"HUGE!"* / NW1 7PG; bentocafe.co.uk; 10.15 pm, Fri & Sat 10.45 pm.

Benugo £36 **2** **3** **4**
Branches throughout London
"The spectacular ambience in the beautiful tea rooms of the V&A"
and the BFI branch's "oasis" on the South Bank are highlights of this
diverse fast-food chain; it still wins praise for "excellent coffee" and
"interesting sandwiches", but it's "not as good as it used to be".
/ www.benugo.com; 4 pm-10 pm; W1 & EC1 branches closed Sat & Sun;
W1 & EC1 branches, no credit cards.

The Berners Tavern
London EDITION W1 £65 **3** **3** **5**
10 Berners St 7908 7979 3–1D
"One of the most impressive dining rooms in London" provides the
"to-die-for" backdrop to a meal at this "glamorous" and "fun"
Marylebone yearling – the food may be "skilfully executed", but it's
"definitely not the main event". / W1T 3NP; 11.45 pm.

Best Mangal £36 **4** **4** **3**
619 Fulham Rd, SW6 7610 0009 5–4A
104 North End Rd, W14 7610 1050 7–2D
66 North End Rd, W14 7602 0212 7–2D
"The best kebabs" plus other "generous and fresh" dishes help make
these "good and cheap" West London charcoal-grill outfits a "great
standby". / www.bestmangal.com; midnight, Sat 1 am; no Amex.

Bevis Marks E1 £64 **2** **2** **2**
3 Middlesex St 7247 5474 9–2D
Kosher restaurants are a rarity, but it's still hard to get excited about
this City spot, which moved from the eponymous synagogue a couple
of years ago; "it means well", but critics say "prices are staggering for
so-so food served in a soulless setting". / E1A 7AA;
www.bevismarkstherestaurant.com; @BMTR_E1; 9 pm; closed Fri D,
Sat & Sun.

Bianco43 £43 **3** **2** **2**
7 Northumberland Ave, WC2 7321 2915 2–3C
43 Greenwich Church St, SE10 8858 2668 1–3D
1-3 Lee Rd, SE3 8318 2700 1–4D
"Tucked away in touristy Greenwich", this three-year-old venture
offers "proper Italian cooking", including some "excellent" pizzas;
it's rather noisy and "cramped", though – why not "leave SE10 to the
visitors and try the Blackheath Village branch"?

Bibendum SW3 £84 **2** **3** **4**
81 Fulham Rd 7581 5817 5–2C
An "amazing" airy dining room, "sophisticated" Gallic cooking,
a "terrific" wine list and "very slick" service lend a great sense
of "classic perfection" to this Brompton Cross landmark, say its fans;
those who remember its glory days, though, may be particularly
prone to thinking it "doesn't sparkle" nowadays. / SW3 6RD;
www.bibendum.co.uk; 11 pm, Sun 10.30 pm; booking: max 12 at L, 10 at
D; set weekday L £52 (FP), set dinner £55 (FP).

Bibendum Oyster Bar SW3 £60 **2** **4** **3**
81 Fulham Rd 7589 1480 5–2C
"For a pop-in lunch or light meal", this luxurious seafood bar, on the
way in to the Chelsea Conran Shop, can be ideal; after a recent
revamp, the odd purist doesn't like the addition of hot dishes to the
menu, but standards remain solid overall. / SW3 6RD;
www.bibendum.co.uk; @bibendumrestaurant; 10 pm; no booking.

Bibimbap Soho W1   £30   3️⃣3️⃣3️⃣
11 Greek St   7287 3434   4–2A
"A gem" – this Soho Korean standby sets itself apart with the preparation of its namesake dish ("a hearty and tasty affair in a hot stone bowl"); "the decor is interesting too – lots of Polaroids of previous happy punters!" / W1D 4DJ; www.bibimbapsoho.com; @bibimbapsoho; 11 pm; closed Sun; no Amex.

Bibo SW15 NEW   £50   4️⃣3️⃣3️⃣
146 Upper Richmond Rd   8780 0592   10–2B
From the Sonny's stable, a Putney newcomer on the site of Wallace & Co (RIP) that "shows real promise" – "OK, the area doesn't need another high-end Italian", but this place is "so well conceived and run that it's very welcome nonetheless". / SW15 2SW; www.biborestaurant.com; @biborestaurant; Mon-Fri 9.45 pm, Fri & Sat 10.45 pm, Sun 8.45 pm.

Big Apple Hot Dogs EC1   £12   4️⃣4️⃣–
239 Old St   387441   12–1B
"The best hot dogs" continue to inspire all who report on this neat little cart, near Old Street. / EC1V 9EY; www.bigapplehotdogs.com; @BigAppleHotdogs.

Big Easy   £51   2️⃣2️⃣2️⃣
12 Maiden Ln, WC2   3728 4888   4–3D
332-334 King's Rd, SW3   7352 4071   5–3C
Chelsea's long-established and "fun" US-style 'crab shack' now has a Covent Garden outpost; the new branch has its fans ("like I was back in New Orleans!"), but expansion seems to have strained standards overall – some "awful" meals have been recorded in both locations of late. / www.bigeasy.co.uk; @bigeasytweet; Mon-Thu 11 pm, Fri-Sat 11.30, Sun 10.30 pm.

Bilbao Berria SW1 NEW   £47   3️⃣4️⃣3️⃣
2 Regent St   7930 8408   3–3D
Newly opened, a stylish tapas bar, with restaurant below; early reports are a little up-and-down, but – by the rather 'anonymous' standards of Theatreland – this struck us as a useful sort of operation, on our early-days visit. / SW1Y 4LR; Rated on Editors' visit.

Bill's   £39   1️⃣2️⃣3️⃣
Branches throughout London
It's still praised for its "quirky" brunch options and "super kid-friendly" style, but this is a chain whose easy-going appeal risks being entirely lost in the dash for growth – increasingly, reporters find it "completely fake", and say the food is "very ordinary", or even plain "grim"! / most branches 11 pm; no booking.

The Bingham TW10   £80   3️⃣3️⃣4️⃣
61-63 Petersham Rd   8940 0902   1–4A
An "elegant" Richmond dining room, in a "sophisticated" boutique hotel, which offers "spectacular" Thames views, "top-class" cooking and a "wonderful" wine list; it's "not cheap", but the set lunch does offer "outstanding value". / TW10 6UT; www.thebingham.co.uk; 10 pm; closed Sun D; no trainers; set weekday L £49 (FP); SRA-1 star.

Bird E2 NEW
£34   4 4 3

42-44 Kingsland Rd   7613 5168   12–1B

Not trying too hard to be hip, this new Shoreditch canteen offers some interesting twists on fried chicken, and – on our early-days visit – a warm welcome too. / E2 8DA; Rated on Editors' visit; www.birdrestaurants.com; @birdrestaurant; Thu-Sat 12.30 am, Sun-Wed 11.30 pm.

Bird in Hand W14
£43   3 4 4

Brook Green   7371 2721   7–1C

"Stick to the pizzas and you can't go wrong", at this "attractive and friendly" Italian, in a former Brook Green boozer. / W14 0LR; www.thebirdinhandlondon.com; @TBIHLondon; Mon-Sat 10 pm, Sun 9.15 pm.

Bird of Smithfield EC1
£67   2 2 3

26 Smithfield St   7559 5100   9–2B

The summer roof terrace is a major attraction at this ex-Ivy chef's solo debut – a sophisticated Smithfield brasserie; fans applaud its comfort food and laud it as an "expensive but impressive" experience, but not all reporters are wowed. / EC1A 9LB; www.birdofsmithfield.com; @BirdoSmithfield; 10 pm; closed Sun; 4+ need to give card details; SRA-1 star.

Bistro 1
£23   2 4 4

27 Frith St, W1   7734 6204   4–3A

75 Beak St, W1   7287 1840   3–2D

33 Southampton St, WC2   7379 7585   4–3D

"Good but not gastronomic food, served cheerfully and quickly" – that's the deal that makes these "terrifically well-located" West End bistros popular with all who comment on them. / www.bistro1.co.uk; @bistro1_london; midnight.

Bistro Aix N8
£53   4 3 3

54 Topsfield Pde, Tottenham Ln   8340 6346   8–1C

"A buzzy local bistro, like a bit of France in the middle of Crouch End" – "decent" cooking, and a "crowded but fun" interior. / N8 8PT; www.bistroaixlondon.co.uk; @bistroaixlondon; 10 pm, Fri & Sat 11 pm; Mon-Thu D only, Fri-Sun open L & D; no Amex.

Bistro Union SW4
£44   2 2 3

40 Abbeville Rd   7042 6400   10–2D

This Clapham bistro "does simple things well", but don't be deceived by its connections to Adam Byatt (of nearby Trinity) – "nothing is earth-shattering". / SW4 9NG; www.bistrounion.co.uk; @BistroUnion; 10 pm, Sun 8 pm.

Bistrot Bruno Loubet
The Zetter EC1
£53   3 3 3

St John's Sq, 86-88 Clerkenwell Rd   7324 4455   9–1A

Bruno Loubet's "impressive" bistro dishes – "with a French touch" plus some "modern flair" – still win plaudits for his relaxed Clerkenwell venture; even some fans feel "standards have slipped a little" of late, though, and critics now find the food "too rich" or "lacking excitement". / EC1M 5RJ; www.bistrotbrunoloubet.com; 10.30 pm, Sun 10 pm; SRA-3 stars.

Bistrotheque E2 £56 3 2 4
23-27 Wadeson St 8983 7900 1–2D
"It's certainly not located to encourage passing trade", but "it's worth the trip to Cambridge Heath" to hang out at this hip, happening and quite "elegant" warehouse-conversion; decent grub too. / E2 9DR; www.bistrotheque.com; @BISTROTHEQUE; 10.30 pm, Fri & Sat 11 pm; closed weekday L; set dinner £34 (FP).

Black & Blue £53 2 2 2
37 Berners St, W1 7436 0451 2–1B
90-92 Wigmore St, W1 7486 1912 3–1A
215-217 Kensington Church St, W8 7727 0004 6–2B
1 Mepham St, SE1 7928 9131 2–3D
1-2 Rochester Walk, SE1 7357 9922 9–4C
"Fantastic" burgers are, on many reports, the highlight of this quite "posh" chain (which offers some comfortable boothed seating); reactions to other aspects of the operations are more muted, but the steaks are generally "reliable" too. / www.blackandbluerestaurant.com; @BlackBlueGroup; most branches 11 pm, Fri & Sat 11.30 pm; W1 closed Sun; no booking.

Blackfoot EC1 NEW £45 3 3 2
46 Exmouth Mkt 7837 4384 9–1A
"Porktastic!"; "it feels like a greasy spoon, and you eat on fairly uncomfortable benches", but this Farringdon newcomer is already winning fans with its ribs and other barbecue treats. / EC1R 4QL; www.blackfootrestaurant.co.uk.

Blanchette W1 NEW £35 3 5 4
9 D'Arblay St 7439 8100 3–1D
Run by three Gallic brothers, this small Soho newcomer is having a "big impact", thanks to its "serious" and "exciting" French "take on tapas"; "very drinkable" wines too, and "service with a smile". / W1F 8DS; www.blanchettesoho.co.uk; @blanchettesoho; closed Sun D.

BLEEDING HEART EC1 £62 3 3 5
Bleeding Heart Yd, Greville St 7242 8238 9–2A
"Well hidden, but what a treasure!"; this age-old City-fringe warren – combining bistro, tavern and restaurant – wows romantics and business diners alike with its "olde-worlde" charm; the "outstanding" wine list, though, is of more note than the Gallic cuisine, which is merely "competent" nowadays. / EC1N 8SJ; www.bleedingheart.co.uk; @bleedingheartyd; 10.30 pm; closed Sun.

The Blind Pig
Social Eating House W1 NEW £36 4 4 4
58 Poland St 7993 3251 3–2D
"A five-star experience" – the new cocktail bar at Jason Atherton's Social Eating House, in Soho is a "relaxed and welcoming" place, serving "fantastic bar snacks". / W1F 7NR; www.socialeatinghouse.com; @BLINDASAPIG; 10.30 pm.

Blue Elephant SW6 £48 3 2 3
The Boulevard 7751 3111 10–1B
Fans say the new location by Chelsea Harbour "works well" ("especially on a sunny day"), but this celebrated Thai (which moved from Fulham Broadway a couple of years ago) is still attracting mixed reports; as ever, the buffet-style Sunday brunch is the top attraction. / SW6 2UB; www.blueelephant.com; @BlueElephantLon; 11.30 pm, Sun 10.30 pm; closed Mon L

Blue Legume   £41   2 2 3
101 Stoke Newington Church St, N16   7923 1303   1–1C
177 Upper St, N1   7226 5858   8–2D
130 Crouch Hill, N8   8442 9282   8–1C
*"For a big brunch and a decent coffee", these "everyday" north
London diners "do the simple things well"; "they're most definitely
family-friendly" too, and "there are always kids and prams".
/ www.thebluelegume.co.uk; 10.30 pm; N8 closed L, N16 closed Sun D.*

Bluebird SW3   £64   1 2 3
350 King's Rd   7559 1000   5–3C
*Fans do praise the "lovely" menu and the "best cocktail list", at this
"hangar-like" younger-scene Chelsea landmark; critics find
it "overpriced", though, and think the food is "particularly poor".
/ SW3 5UU; www.bluebird-restaurant.co.uk; @bluebirdchelsea; 10.30 pm,
Sun 9.30 pm; SRA-2 stars.*

Blueprint Café
Design Museum SE1   £48   3 2 5
28 Shad Thames, Butler's Wharf   7378 7031   9–4D
*"Ask for a window table, to enjoy the great view of the Thames"
(and Tower Bridge) – the main reason to seek out this first-floor
South Bank restaurant; the food is "good, without being great",
and service is on the "poor" side. / SE1 2YD; www.blueprintcafe.co.uk;
@BluePrintCafe; 10.30 pm; closed Sun D; SRA-2 stars.*

Bo Lang SW3 NEW   £67   2 3 3
100 Draycott Ave   7823 7887   5–2C
*We personally have enjoyed visits to this chic (and undoubtedly
"expensive") new dim sum bar, near Brompton Cross, but the limited
early-day survey feedback runs the whole gamut from "great"
to "all style and no substance" – we can sort of understand both
sides! / SW3 3AD; www.bolangrestaurant.co.uk.*

Bob Bob Ricard W1   £63   3 4 5
1 Upper James St   3145 1000   3–2D
*"Subdued light, romantic booths, and quirky touches like a button
to summon champagne" – all conducive to creating a "brilliant"
impression at this madly "luxurious" Soho diner; "you pay for all that
gorgeousness", naturally, but the "high-end comfort food" is generally
very "enjoyable". / W1F 9DF; www.bobbobricard.com; @BobBobRicard;
Mon-Fri 11.15 pm, Sat midnight; closed Sat L & Sun; jacket.*

Bobo Social W1 NEW
95 Charlotte St   7636 9310   2–1C
*'Experimental' burgers and small plates come to Charlotte Street,
as the high-end hamburger craze continues; we didn't have the
chance to check 'em out before this guide went to press. / W1T 4PZ;
www.bobosocial.com.*

BOCCA DI LUPO W1   £64   5 4 4
12 Archer St   7734 2223   3–2D
*"You'd be hard pressed to find better in Italy" – "refreshing" tapas-
style dishes are "enthusiastically served" at this "exciting" backstreet
spot, hidden away near Piccadilly Circus; it's "always jammed",
and can get "too noisy" for some tastes. / W1D 7BB;
www.boccadilupo.com; @boccadilupo; 11 pm, Sun 9.15 pm; booking: max 10.*

Bocconcino W1 NEW
19 Berkeley St   7629 2000   3–3C
Mozzarella via Moscow – a new pizza opening set to consolidate the Russian grip on what we might as well call Mayfair's 'Novikov Quarter'. / W1J 8ED.

Al Boccon di'vino TW9   £67   4 3 5
14 Red Lion St   8940 9060   1–4A
"You get what they decide" ("more food than you can shake a stick at") plus wine (red or white?), at this "wacky, chaotic, and delightfully idiosyncratic" Richmond venue – a "brilliant" experience, "like a party in an Italian home", but "not cheap". / TW9 1RW; www.nonsolovinoltd.co.uk; 8 pm; closed Mon, Tue L & Wed L.

Bodean's   £45   2 2 2
10 Poland St, W1   7287 7575   3–1D
4 Broadway Chambers, SW6   7610 0440   5–4A
169 Clapham High St, SW4   7622 4248   10–2D
16 Byward St, EC3   7488 3883   9–3D
"Nothing special, but it does what it says on the tin"; this US-inspired chain is hailed by fans as a "reliable" (if "unsubtle") choice, but some reports are ambivalent – "if you like your food trendily charred, and covered in BBQ sauce, this is the place for you". / www.bodeansbbq.com; 11 pm, Sun 10.30 pm; 8 or more.

La Bodega Negra W1   £48   2 3 4
13-17 Moor St   7758 4100   4–2B
A "dark" and "very sexy" Mexican that's just the job for "a fun night out"; the food's "OK" too, but even fans note that prices are "hefty". / W1D 5NH; www.labodeganegra.com; 1 am, Sun 11.30 pm.

Boisdale SW1   £64   3 3 4
13-15 Eccleston St   7730 6922   2–4B
With its "plush tartan decor", "meaty Scottish fare" and impressive list of whiskies and wines, this "convivial" Belgravia bastion "oozes a sense of 'male preserve'"; "smokers delight to find somewhere that positively encourages smoking… on the excellent roof terrace". / SW1W 9LX; www.boisdale.co.uk; @boisdaleCW; 11.30 pm; closed Sat L & Sun.

Boisdale of Canary Wharf E14   £62   3 4 3
Cabot Pl   7715 5818   11–1C
A "slightly bizarre" traditional find amongst the shiny towers of Canary Wharf, this "spacious" twin of the famous Belgravia Caledonian wins praise for its "surprisingly good" fare; regular jazz adds to the possibilities for business entertaining. / E14 4QT; www.boisdale.co.uk; 10.30 pm; closed Sun.

The Bolingbroke SW11   £44   3 2 3
174 Northcote Rd   7228 4040   10–2C
"A very good local" – a "buzzy" Battersea boozer, where the menus consist of "a good mix of upmarket pub grub and staples such as burgers". / SW11 6RE; www.renaissancepubs.co.uk; 10.30 pm, Sun 9 pm.

Bombay Brasserie SW7 £59 **4 4 4**
Courtfield Close, Gloucester Rd   7370 4040   5–2B
*"They finally seem to have got it right!"; this South Kensington
institution – London's "original" grand Indian of recent times – has at
last fully recovered from its disastrous refurb, and is now once again
an "exceptional" all-rounder; as ever, get a conservatory table if you
can. / SW7 4QH; www.bombaybrasserielondon.com; @bbsw7; 11.30 pm,
Sun 10.30 pm; closed Mon L.*

Bombay Palace W2 £59 **5 2 1**
50 Connaught St   7723 8855   6–1D
*"Sensational ingredients and spicing, even if the atmosphere is like
an airport" – this grand Bayswater Indian may look "old hat"
(and that's after a recent refurb!), and service is nothing to write
home about, but for many reporters it's "still the best". / W2 2AA;
www.bombay-palace.co.uk; 11.30 pm.*

Bone Daddies W1 £22 **3 4 4**
30-31 Peter St   7287 8581   3–2D
*"Addictive" noodles, "sticky and spicy ribs", "fried chicken to die
for"… – that's the deal making a runaway hit of this "hip" Soho
"ramen-erie", where "aged 40, you feel very old and square";
"the queues, OMG the queues…" / W1F 0AR;
www.bonedaddiesramen.com; @bonedaddiesRbar.*

Bonnie Gull W1 £49 **5 4 4**
21a Foley St   7436 0921   2–1B
*"The sort of place you'd expect to find in a coastal town!";
this "cramped" Fitzrovia bistro serves "a genuine range"
of "outstandingly fresh" fish and seafood, all with "personal" service
and at competitive prices. / W1W 6DS; www.bonniegull.com;
@BonnieGull; 9.45 pm.*

Bonnie Gull Seafood Café EC1 **NEW** £67 **4 3 3**
55-57 Exmouth Mkt   3122 0047   9–1A
*"Amazing" oysters – loyal customers can even win an Oyster Card,
geddit? – head up a menu of "simply prepared and beautifully
presented" fishy dishes at this "seaside-style" café. / EC1R 4QE;
www.bonniegullseafoodcafe.com; @boniegull.*

Boqueria SW2 £34 **4 4 4**
192 Acre Ln   7733 4408   10–2D
*"Vibrant" tapas help win rave reviews for this "fun and laid-back"
(if "noisy") spot, between Clapham and Brixton. / SW2 5UL;
www.boqueriatapas.com; @BoqueriaTapas; 11 pm, Fri & Sat 12 am,
Sun 10 pm; closed weekday L.*

Il Bordello E1 £51 **4 5 4**
81 Wapping High St   7481 9950   11–1A
*This "really buzzing" and "friendly" Wapping fixture is "a great
favourite locally"; "it headlines as a pizzeria, but it's so much more" –
whatever you choose, brace yourself for "large portions". / E1W 2YN;
www.ilbordello.com; 11 pm, Sun 10.30 pm; closed Sat L.*

La Bota N8 £33 **3 4 3**
31 Broadway Pde   8340 3082   1–1C
*A "lovely" Crouch End tapas veteran, praised by the locals for its
"consistently maintained standards of food and service", "generous
portions" and "good prices". / N8 9DB; www.labota.co.uk; 11 pm, Fri-Sun
11.30 pm; closed Mon L; no Amex.*

The Botanist SW1 — £64 — 1 1 1
7 Sloane Sq   7730 0077   5–2D
If certainly offers "great people-watching" (especially for Made In Chelsea fans), and supporters of this ever-throbbing bar-restaurant "don't understand why it gets such a bad rap" – across the board, though, its survey ratings are dire. / SW1W 8EE; www.thebotanistonsloanesquare.com; @TheBotanistSW1; 10.45 pm; set Sun L £41 (FP).

La Bottega — £17 — 3 4 4
20 Ryder St, SW1   7839 5789   3–4C
25 Eccleston St, SW1   7730 2730   2–4B
65 Lower Sloane St, SW1   7730 8844   5–2D
36 Monmouth St, WC2   7836 5255   4–2B **NEW**
97 Old Brompton Rd, SW7   7581 6622   5–2B
"Consistently good coffee", and "simple and fresh" pasta too – all part of the ongoing success of these smart but "casual" and "friendly" café-delis. / www.labottega65.com; Lower Sloane St 8 pm, Sat 6 pm, Sun 5 pm; Eccleston St 7 pm; Old Brompton Rd 8 pm; Ryder St closed Sat & Sun; no booking.

La Bouchée SW7 — £48 — 2 2 4
56 Old Brompton Rd   7589 1929   5–2B
"Very cosy" and "intimate" ("cramped"), this South Kensington spot may be a bit of a "throwback", but it's a charming one, offering "well-presented" Gallic bistro classics, "sometimes rather slowly". / SW7 3DY; 11 pm, Sun 10.30 pm.

Boudin Blanc W1 — £59 — 2 2 3
5 Trebeck St   7499 3292   3–4B
"Prices seem to have increased dramatically over the years", at this Shepherd Market bistro – fans say it's still "worth it", but critics find food and service standards ever more "ordinary", although the al fresco tables are undoubtedly as charming as ever. / W1J 7LT; www.boudinblanc.co.uk; 11 pm.

Boulestin SW1 — £66 — 2 2 2
5 St James's St   7930 2030   3–4D
Joel Kissin's relaunch (under a famous old name) of the "calmly atmospheric" former L'Oranger (RIP) premises in St James's has been rather a curate's egg; even fans may find its "classical French" formula "surprisingly expensive", and critics find the divide between the front café and rear dining area "strange and incoherent" too. / SW1A 1EF; www.boulestin.co.uk; @BoulestinLondon; Mon-Wed 11 pm, Thu-Sat 11.30 pm; closed Sun; set pre theatre £48 (FP).

Boulevard WC2 — £45 — 2 3 3
40 Wellington St   7240 2992   4–3D
Despite its clichéd looks, this Covent Garden brasserie "does what it says on the tin" – "not bad food, reasonable prices, quick service and a buzzing atmosphere"; "try to sit on the first floor if you can". / WC2E 7BD; www.boulevardbrasserie.co.uk; @BoulevardWC2; 11 pm, Fri & Sat 11.30 pm, Sun 10.30 pm; set pre theatre £32 (FP).

The Boundary E2 — £65 — 2 2 2
2-4 Boundary St   7729 1051   12–1B
It's the "magical" rooftop dining area which excites reporters on Sir Terence Conran's "cool-looking" Shoreditch venture (which also has a spacious basement restaurant); portions can be "small", though, and service is on the "sketchy" side. / E2 7DD; www.theboundary.co.uk; 10.30 pm; D only, ex Sun L only.

The Brackenbury W6 NEW £50 4 3 2
129-131 Brackenbury Rd   8741 4928   7–1C
"A welcome return from the dead" – this one-time Hammersmith gem (recently Port of Manila, RIP), relaunched by Ossie Gray (son of River Café founder Ruth), offers "imaginative" Mediterranean-influenced fare that's perhaps on the "pricey" side; the interior configuration, however, remains as "awkward" as ever. / W6 0BQ; www.brackenburyrestaurant.co.uk; @BrackenburyRest.

Bradley's NW3 £57 2 2 2
25 Winchester Rd   7722 3457   8–2A
"Very handy for the Hampstead Theatre", this Swiss Cottage spot perennially wins praise for its "careful cooking", "well-chosen wine" and "classy" decor; as ever, though, there are also critics who insist it's "gone off"! / NW3 3NR; www.bradleysnw3.co.uk; 10 pm; closed Sun D; set weekday L & dinner £37 (FP).

Brady's SW18 £34 3 3 3
Dolphin Hs, Smugglers Way   8877 9599   10–2B
Most reports on the Brady family's stalwart Battersea chippy say it's "even better" in its more "glitzy" new riverside home; it can also seem "less personable" here, though, and some long-term fans have found "delivery short of expectations" of late. / SW18 1DG; www.bradysfish.co.uk; @Bradyfish; 10 pm, Sun 8.30 pm; closed Mon, Tue L, Wed L & Thu L; no Amex; no booking.

La Brasserie SW3 £57 2 2 4
272 Brompton Rd   7581 3089   5–2C
"If you can't get to Paris this is the next best thing" – a "real, French-style brasserie with lots of action", on a prominent Chelsea site; the "very good and very large breakfast" – à l'anglaise – has always been a star weekend attraction. / SW3 2AW; www.labrasserielondon.co.uk; @labrasserie; Mon-Sat 11.30 pm, Sun 11 pm; no booking, Sat L & Sun L.

Brasserie Blanc £53 2 2 3
Branches throughout London
Looking for "reasonably priced food in a pleasant French brasserie-style environment"? – this "upmarket" chain is "worth a try", even if "it can be a bit hit-and-miss"; visitors should especially note the "superbly located" Covent Garden branch, with its first-floor terrace overlooking the Royal Opera House. / www.brasserieblanc.com; most branches close between 10 pm & 11 pm; SE1 closed Sun D, most City branches closed Sat & Sun; SRA-2 stars.

Brasserie Chavot W1 £66 3 3 3
41 Conduit St   7183 6425   3–2C
Fans of Eric Chavot's "elegant" Mayfair chamber do not stint in their praise for his "blisteringly good" brasserie fare; critics find the setting rather "lacking in warmth", though, and may even find the "rich and traditional" cuisine just a touch "passé" – no wonder Michelin approves! / W1S 2YQ; www.brasseriechavot.com; @brasseriechavot; 10.30 pm, Sun 9 pm.

Brasserie Max
Covent Garden Hotel WC2 £72 3 4 3
10 Monmouth St   7806 1000   4–2B
On the intriguing Covent Garden junction which is Seven Dials, a "good-quality hotel restaurant", particularly noted for its "outstanding" breakfasts – choose from "the most extensive menu ever!" / WC2H 9HB; www.coventgardenhotel.co.uk; 11 pm; set always available £44 (FP).

Brasserie Toulouse-Lautrec SE11 £40 **3** **4** **3**
140 Newington Butts 7582 6800 1–3C
"A stalwart of Elephant & Castle", this "charming" and "unpretentious" Gallic restaurant offers a "short but sensible" menu at "good-value" prices; regular musical entertainment "adds zing". / SE11 4RN; www.btlrestaurant.co.uk; @btlrestaurant; 10.30 pm, Sat & Sun 11 pm.

BRASSERIE ZÉDEL W1 £39 **2** **4** **5**
20 Sherwood St 7734 4888 3–2D
Corbin & King's "extravagant" Art Deco-style basement, just seconds from Piccadilly Circus, offers "classic Gallic brasserie fodder" that's "workmanlike" at best – given the "magnificent" gilded decor, "first-class" service, and "unbelievably good prices", however, few reporters really seem to care! / W1F 7ED; www.brasseriezedel.com; @brasseriezedel; 11.45 pm; SRA-3 stars.

Bravas E1 NEW £42 **4** **3** **4**
St Katharine Docks 7481 1464 9–3D
"Overlooking the expensive boats moored in St Katharine Docks", this "lovely" newcomer is "a real find", and offers welcome relief from all the chains hereabouts; attractions include a "flavourful modern take on tapas", a "tasteful" interior and some good outside tables. / E1W 1AT; www.bravastapas.co.uk; @Bravas_Tapas.

Brawn E2 £49 **5** **3** **4**
49 Columbia Rd 7729 5692 12–1C
"Deep flavours and lovely textures" from a "quirky" menu, plus Caves de Pyrène's "glorious" biodynamic wines, decidedly make this "fascinating and characterful" East End bistro the group's star performer nowadays. / E2 7RG; www.brawn.co; @brawn49; 11 pm; closed Mon L & Sun D; no Amex.

Bread Street Kitchen EC4 £62 **2** **3** **2**
1 New Change 3030 4050 9–2B
This "cavernous" and "noisy" venture in a City shopping centre has its attractions for expense-accounters, not least for "power breakfasts"; it's a Gordon Ramsay production, though, and his involvement "has led to inflated prices for some pretty basic fare". / EC4M 9AF; www.breadstreetkitchen.com; @breadstreet; 11 pm, Sun 8 pm.

Briciole W1 £40 **3** **3** **4**
20 Homer St 7723 0040 6–1D
This "buzzy and busy" Italian-accented pub-conversion, in the backwoods of Marylebone, wins consistent praise for its "simple" tapas-sized dishes; some reporters prefer the quieter lunchtimes to "noisy peak times". / W1H 4NA; www.briciole.co.uk; @briciolelondon; 10.15 pm.

Brick Lane Beigel Bake E1 £7 **5** **3** **1**
159 Brick Ln 7729 0616 12–1C
"A London institution"; this "rough and ready" East End bakery offers "incomparable" salt beef beigels 24/7; "I spend more on the cab to get there than I do on the food!" / E1 6SB; open 24 hours; no credit cards; no booking.

Brigade
The Fire Station SE1 £49 3 2 3
139 Tooley St   0844 346 1225   9–4D
In a former fire station near London Bridge, a "comfortable" bistro yearling that's particularly "great for everyday business meetings", even if "poor" service can sometimes be a let down. / SE1 2HZ; www.thebrigade.co.uk; @brigadeSE1; 10 pm.

The Bright Courtyard W1 £59 3 4 2
43-45 Baker St   7486 6998   2–1A
"Clean, modern, fresh Chinese food" – with dim sum the highlight – is winning ever more praise for this airy and coolly decorated Marylebone spot, whose parent establishment is in Shanghai. / W1U 8EW; www.lifefashiongroup.com; @BrightCourtyard; 10.45 pm, Thu-Sat 11.15 pm.

Brilliant UB2 £38 3 3 3
72-76 Western Rd   8574 1928   1–3A
A "legendary" Indian; it's "worth the trek" to seek out its "enjoyable" and "authentic" Punjabi food, deep in the suburban heart of Southall. / UB2 5DZ; www.brilliantrestaurant.com; @BRILLIANTRST; 11 pm, Fri & Sat 11.30 pm; closed Mon, Sat L & Sun L.

Brinkley's SW10 £53 3 3 4
47 Hollywood Rd   7351 1683   5–3B
For the slightly older Chelsea set, a popular destination for a "good local dinner", and one which comes complete with an atmospheric garden; "good-value wine list" too. / SW10 9HX; www.brinkleys.com; 11.30 pm; closed weekday L.

The Brown Cow SW6 £43 4 4 4
676 Fulham Rd   7384 9559   10–1B
A heart-of-Fulham bistro that's really got into its stride in its first full year of operation; all reports praise its "interesting" menu of "well-cooked" gastropub-style fare. / SW6 5SA; www.thebrowncowpub.co.uk; @TheBrownCowPub; 10 pm.

The Brown Dog SW13 £51 3 3 3
28 Cross St   8392 2200   10–1A
"Barnes's secret pleasure" – a cutely "hidden-away" gastropub offering "a short menu of well-cooked favourites"; usually a "relaxed" spot, it gets "a bit more frenetic when the weekend comes". / SW13 0AP; www.thebrowndog.co.uk; @browndogbarnes; 10 pm, Sun 9 pm.

(Hix at Albemarle)
Brown's Hotel W1 £82 2 3 3
Albemarle St   7518 4004   3–3C
With "plenty of space between tables for discreet conversation" (and "surprising original artworks" too), this woody Mayfair hotel dining room makes a "top business breakfast choice"; despite Mark Hix's involvement, though, other fare can be "decidedly average". / W1S 4BP; www.thealbemarlerestaurant.com; 11 pm, Sun 10.30 pm; set always available £60 (FP).

Browns £47 1 1 2
Branches throughout London
"Nice place, shame about the food" – a dreary chain whose only obvious asset is the sometimes grand and historic setting of its branches. / www.browns-restaurants.co.uk; most branches 10 pm-11 pm; EC2 closed Sat D & Sun; W1 closed Sun D.

Brula TW1 £48 **4 4 4**

43 Crown Rd 8892 0602 1–4A

"A little piece of France", in St Margarets; this "enduringly charming and consistent" restaurant dazzles its huge local fan club with its "intimate" style, "friendly" service and "classic" cuisine. / TW1 3EJ; www.brula.co.uk; @brula_tweet; 10.30 pm.

Brunswick House Café SW8 £43 **2 2 5**

30 Wandsworth Rd 7720 2926 10–1D

Set in a vast Georgian house, at Vauxhall Cross, now used as an architectural salvage showroom, this "quirky" restaurant certainly has a "fantastic" atmosphere; the seasonal food's not bad either, and there's a "very decent wine list". / SW8 2LG; www.brunswickhousecafe.co.uk; 10 pm; closed Sun D.

Bubba Gump Shrimp Company W1 NEW

13 Coventry St 3763 5288 4–4A

Now (finally!) open in the former Planet Hollywood premises near Piccadilly Circus, the first UK branch of an American chain loosely based on the characters in 'Forrest Gump'; if successful, more will follow – you have been warned! / W1D 7DH.

Bubbledogs W1 £31 **2 3 4**

70 Charlotte St 7637 7770 2–1C

"Hot dogs and champagne, what's not to love?", say fans of this "fun" and "trendy" Fitzrovia yearling; "a good hot dog is still pretty ordinary", sniff critics – "perhaps I should have drunk more fizz!" / W1T 4QG; www.bubbledogs.co.uk; @bubbledogsUK; 9 pm; closed Sun.

(Kitchen Table)
Bubbledogs W1 £94 **4 5 4**

70 Charlotte St 7637 7770 2–1C

"A unique dining experience"; this "phenomenal" Fitzrovian – a horseshoe-shaped chef's table "secretively curtained" from the adjoining hot dog place – offers "passionate" service and course after course of "astonishingly clever food", "theatrically" prepared "before your very eyes". / W1T 4QG; www.kitchentablelondon.co.uk; @bubbledogsKT; 9.30 pm (6 pm & 7.30 pm seatings only); D only, closed Mon & Sun.

Buddha-Bar London SW1 NEW £70 **1 2 3**

145 Knightsbridge 3667 5222 5–1D

Re-located to Knightsbridge (from WC2), this Parisian-nightclub-style oriental has made remarkably few ripples; it can be "fun", but – given the hefty prices – "the food needs serious improvement". / SW1X 7PA; www.buddhabarlondon.com; @BuddhaBarLondon; 10 pm.

Buen Ayre E8 £51 **4 2 2**

50 Broadway Mkt 7275 9900 1–2D

A packed East End 'parrilla' offering what fans claim is "the best Argentinean steak in London"; only caveat? – "it's impossible to get a booking!" / E8 4QJ; www.buenayre.co.uk; 10.30 pm; no Amex; set weekday L £30 (FP).

Buenos Aires Cafe £52 333
86 Royal Hill, SE10   8488 6764   1–3D
17 Royal Pde, SE3   8318 5333   1–4D
"An independent oasis, standing out in the Blackheath mire"; "run by
a retired Argentinian tango dancer" (who knew?), it's hailed for its
"heavenly steaks" and "good veggie options too"; there is a more
café-like offshoot in Greenwich. / www.buenosairesltd.com; SE3 10.30 pm;
SE10 7 pm, Sat & Sun 6 pm; no Amex.

The Builders Arms SW3 £46 334
13 Britten St   7349 9040   5–2C
"As unpretentious as Chelsea can be, even if everyone still looks
effortlessly loaded" – this lovely boozer, behind Waitrose, wins praise
for "generous helpings" of "simple food done right". / SW3 3TY;
www.geronimo-inns.co.uk; @BuildersChelsea; 10 pm, Thu-Sat 11 pm,
Sun 9 pm; no booking; SRA-2 stars.

The Bull N6 £46 224
13 North Hill   8341 0510   1–1C
Fans of this "lovely" Highgate pub and micro-brewery hail it as
a "superior" local and good all-rounder; it can seem "a bit up itself",
though, and the excellent range of brews is a more reliable attraction
than the sometimes disappointing food. / N6 4AB; thebullhighgate.co.uk;
@Bull_Highgate; 10 pm.

Bull & Last NW5 £60 433
168 Highgate Rd   7267 3641   8–1B
"It's worth braving the crowds" to visit this Kentish Town marvel,
which is "uncontested" as north London's top gastropub; "it just gets
everything right", not least the "creative" comfort food and "fabulous
selection of ales". / NW5 1QS; www.thebullandlast.co.uk; @thebullandlast;
10 pm, Sun 9 pm.

Bumpkin £52 322
119 Sydney St, SW3   3730 9344   5–2B
102 Old Brompton Rd, SW7   7341 0802   5–2B
209 Westbourne Park Rd, W11   7243 9818   6–1B
Westfield Stratford, E20   8221 9900   1–1D
A faux-rustic chain whose "truly British" and "seasonal" menu has
"improved" of late; even fans can still find it "pricey" though, and it
suffers from "hit-and-miss" service and an often-"loud" atmosphere.
/ www.bumpkinuk.com; 11 pm.

Bunnychow £11
74 Wardour St, W1   3697 7762   3–2D NEW
Unit 55 2-4 Bethnal Green Rd, E1   3697 7762   12–2B NEW
After the success of their food truck, and a pop-up at Shoreditch's
Boxpark, these merchants of South African street food are now
coming to Soho with a bricks and mortar operation.
/ www.bunnychow.com.

Buona Sera £39 233
289a King's Rd, SW3   7352 8827   5–3C
22 Northcote Rd, SW11   7228 9925   10–2C
A "useful" and "family-friendly" Battersea local, which remains
a popular (if "very noisy") standby, thanks to its reliable and
affordable pizza and pasta; the Chelsea offshoot benefits from
curious ('70s) double-decker seating. / midnight; SW3 11.30 pm,
Sun 10 pm; SW3 closed Mon L.

Burger & Lobster   £44   **3** **2** **3**

Harvey Nichols, Knightsbridge, SW1   7235 5000   5–1D
29 Clarges St, W1   7409 1699   3–4B
36 Dean St, W1   7432 4800   4–2A
40 St John St, EC1   7490 9230   9–1B
Bow Bells Hs, 1 Bread St, EC4   7248 1789   9–2B

*"A genius idea"; the name says it all about this "fun", "very loud" and
"chaotic" concept, whose smash-hit status is signalled
by "long queues at peak times"; as the chain grows, though, "quality
is not what it was". / www.burgerandlobster.com; @LondonLobster;
10.30 pm; Clarges St closed Sun D, Bread St & St John St closed Sun.*

Busaba Eathai   £39   **2** **2** **4**

35 Panton St, SW1   7930 0088   4–4A
106-110 Wardour St, W1   7255 8686   3–2D
8-13 Bird St, W1   7518 8080   3–1A
44 Floral St, WC2   7759 0088   4–2D
313-319 Old St, EC1   7729 0808   12–1B

*"Buzzy", "friendly" and unusually "stylish" for a chain, these "darkly-
lit" communal Thai canteens are a "reliable" standby for a "quick"
meal; perhaps the cooking is somewhat "Asian-by-numbers",
but most reporters still find it "yummy" and "reasonably priced".
/ www.busaba.co.uk; 11 pm, Fri & Sat 11.30 pm, Sun 10 pm; W1 no booking;
WC1 booking: min 10.*

Bush Dining Hall W12   £43   **1** **2** **3**

304 Uxbridge Rd   8749 0731   7–1B

*"A firm favourite with trendy SheBu locals" – this carefully distressed
hangout (adjacent to a popular music venue) scores well for its
"friendly buzz" and general "cool"; but what is "surprisingly good"
food to fans is, to critics, "trying too hard, and failing". / W12 7LJ;
www.bushhalldining.co.uk; @BushHallDining; 10.30 pm, Fri & Sat 10 pm;
closed Sun D.*

Butcher & Grill SW11   £43   **2** **2** **3**

39-41 Parkgate Rd   7924 3999   5–4C

*For a "lovely brunch", this "attractive" Battersea local (with deli and
butcher attached) is just the job; fans also applaud its "great steaks"
at any time, but not everyone is convinced. / SW11 4NP;
www.thebutcherandgrill.com; @ButcherGrill; 11 pm, Sun 4 pm; closed Sun D.*

Butlers Wharf Chop House SE1   £60   **2** **2** **2**

36e Shad Thames   7403 3403   9–4D

*Despite its impressive location near Tower Bridge, this large
Thameside venue is only "mildly atmospheric"; the few reports
it inspires suggest that its food (traditional British) and service are
similarly middle of the road. / SE1 2YE; www.chophouse.co.uk; 10.45 pm,
Sun 9.45 pm; SRA-2 stars.*

La Buvette TW9   £44   **3** **3** **4**

6 Church Walk   8940 6264   1–4A

*"A delightful location" – by a churchyard in central Richmond –
and "cosy" interior bolster the appeal of this "charming" bistro,
where "classic" ("often rich") dishes are matched with "interesting
regional French wines". / TW9 1SN; www.labuvette.co.uk; @labuvettebistro;
10 pm; set weekday L £33 (FP).*

Byron £36   2 3 3

Branches throughout London

"George Osborne likes them and so do we!"; the survey's second most commented-on multiple (after its former parent, PizzaExpress) cranks out "posh" burgers in "bright and buzzy" branches; despite the group's "relentless expansion", its ratings have held up quite well. / www.byronhamburgers.com; most branches 11 pm; SRA-2 stars.

C London W1 £100   1 1 2

25 Davies St   7399 0500   3–2B

"Eye-wateringly expensive" yet "sorely disappointing", this Mayfair Italian seems to survive mainly on its people-watching possibilities – "do they pay celebs to eat there, to get in the Daily Mail readers?" / W1K 3DE; www.crestaurant.co.uk; 11.45 pm.

C&R Cafe £30   4 2 2

3-4 Rupert Ct, W1   7434 1128   4–3A

52 Westbourne Grove, W2   7221 7979   6–1B

"Perfect for a casual Malaysian meal that's authentic and delicious" – these Chinatown and Bayswater cafés impress all who report on them with their "cheap and cheerful" charms. / www.cnrrestaurant.com; 11 pm.

The Cadogan Arms SW3 £49   3 3 1

298 King's Rd   7352 6500   5–3C

A Chelsea corner boozer, near the UGC cinema, offering "restaurant-quality food in a pub setting"; there are "especially good deals for large groups". / SW3 5UG; www.thecadoganarmschelsea.com; @TheCadoganArms; 10.15 pm, Sun 8.45 pm.

Café 209 SW6 £23   2 3 5

209 Munster Rd   7385 3625   10–1B

With "funny and charming" owner Joy very much in charge, a "brilliant" evening is pretty much guaranteed at this "cheap and cheerful" BYO caff in the depths of Fulham; the Thai fare veers from "pretty average" to "great". / SW6 6BX; 10.30 pm; D only, closed Sun, closed Dec; no Amex.

Le Café Anglais
Whiteley's W2 £59   3 3 4

8 Porchester Gdns   7221 1415   6–1C

This "grand", "bright and airy" Deco-ish brasserie (with oyster bar) – oft-compared to a cruise liner dining room – makes an unlikely find, atop Whiteley's; it's never really seemed to fulfil its potential, and its future is uncertain at the time of writing, as chef-patron Rowley Leigh sold it back to the mall's owners in Sept 2014. / W2 4DB; www.lecafeanglais.co.uk; @LeCafeAnglais; 10.30 pm, Fri & Sat 11 pm, Sun 10 pm.

Café Bohème W1 £46   2 3 4

13 Old Compton St   7734 0623   4–2A

"For an authentic Parisian feel and superb coffee", this "cool" all-hours brasserie, in the very heart of Soho, "takes some beating"; arguably "you don't need to bother with the food", but it's at least "OK". / W1 5JQ; www.cafeboheme.co.uk; @CafeBoheme1; 2.45 am, Sun midnight; no reservations.

Café del Parc N19 £36 444
167 Junction Road 7281 5684 8–1C
"Spectacularly good" food makes this "tiny" spot a big hit up Tuffnell
Park way; its "brilliant experimental Spanish fusion fare" comes
tapas-style – there's no menu, as this is a "le-chef-propose sort
of place". / N19 5PZ; www.delparc.com; 10.30 pm; open D only, Wed-Sun;
no Amex.

Café des Amis WC2 £59 122
11-14 Hanover Pl 7379 3444 4–2D
"Frantic", "noisy", "squashed" – this bistro by the Royal Opera House
doesn't want for custom; some reports, though, are vitriolic about its
standards – "it seems to survive on special offers, pre-purchased
vouchers and never-to-return tourists", says one; the basement bar
is better. / WC2E 9JP; www.cafedesamis.co.uk; @CafedAmis; 11.30 pm,
Sun 7pm; set pre theatre £25 (FP).

Café du Marché EC1 £55 345
22 Charterhouse Sq 7608 1609 9–1B
"Discreetly located in an alley off Charterhouse Square," this City-
fringe "classic" offers food that's "as authentically French as it gets";
it's the "wonderful", "rustic" atmosphere, though, which has long
made it a hugely popular rendezvous for business, and – by night,
when there's jazz – for romance. / EC1M 6DX; www.cafedumarche.co.uk;
@lecafedumarche; 10 pm; closed Sat L & Sun.

Café East SE16 £22 422
100 Redriff Rd 7252 1212 11–2B
"Very authentic" and "delicious" too, the Vietnamese food on offer
at this "very cheap" Bermondsey café pleases all who comment on it;
"service can be brisk, but everything is amazing so it doesn't matter!"
/ SE16 7LH; www.cafeeast.foodkingdom.com; @cafeeastpho; 10.30 pm,
Sun 10 pm; closed Tue.

Café in the Crypt
St Martin's in the Fields WC2 £32 223
Duncannon St 7766 1158 2–2C
With its "handy" location on Trafalgar Square and its "atmospheric"
setting in a huge crypt, this self-service refectory is "always busy"; no-
one would make huge claims for its "nourishing and cheap" fare,
but "at least the profits go to a good cause". / WC2N 4JJ;
stmartin-in-the-fields.org/cafe-in-the-crypt; 8 pm, Thu-Sat 9 pm, Sun 6 pm;
no Amex; no booking.

Café Murano SW1 NEW £52 444
33 St James's St 3371 5559 3–3C
"A new staple in St James's"; Angela Hartnett's "cheaper,
more informal spin-off" is an "unpretentious and charming" venue,
with "genial" service; it serves "proper" Italian dishes at prices that
"don't shock". / SW1A 1HD.

Café Pistou EC1 NEW
8-10 Exmouth Mkt awaiting tel 9–1A
Backed by an ex-Gaucho head honcho, a brand new all-day Provençal
café, in Farringdon's 'little trendy street'; one suspects more will follow.
/ EC1R 4QA; www.cafepistou.co.uk; @CafePistou.

Café Rouge £38 123
Branches throughout London
"Best avoided unless the children really won't wait" – these
"fake French bistros" have their fans as a breakfast destination,
but other meals are sometimes "so badly prepared and served" as to
be simply "dire". / www.caferouge.co.uk; 11 pm, Sun 10.30 pm.

Café Spice Namaste E1 £56 443
16 Prescot St 7488 9242 11–1A
"A gem in a dreary City side street"; Cyrus Todiwala's "interesting
Parsi take on Indian food" – with great game dishes, and "favouring
spicing over heat" – maintains the long-standing acclaim for this
"friendly" stalwart. / E1 8AZ; www.cafespice.co.uk; @cafespicenamast;
10.30 pm; closed Sat L & Sun; SRA-3 stars.

Caffè Caldesi W1 £56 342
118 Marylebone Ln 7487 0754 2–1A
In Marylebone, a "consistent", "reliable" and "friendly"
neighbourhood Italian, with a particular name for its "delicious"
homemade pasta. / W1U 2QF; www.caldesi.com; 10.30 pm, Sun 9.30 pm.

Caffè Nero £13 233
Branches throughout London
"The best mass-produced coffee"; with its "consistent" standards,
this "friendly" multiple manages to seem "a bit less corporate" than
the other major players; it serves "tasty paninis and soups" too.
/ most branches 7 pm; City branches earlier; most City branches closed all
or part of weekend; some branches no credit cards; no booking.

Caffé Vergnano £32 333
Staple Inn, 337-338 High Holborn, WC1 7242 7119 9–2A
62 Charing Cross Rd, WC2 7240 3512 4–3B
Royal Festival Hall, SE1 7921 9339 2–3D
2 New Street Sq, EC4 7936 3404 9–2A
A small group of cafés of note for "simply fantastic coffee"; the SE1
branch, with its "good range of light Italian dishes", is probably the
best place to eat by the RFH. / www.caffevergnano1882.co.uk; EC4 11 pm;
SE1 midnight; WC2 8 pm, Fri & Sat midnight; EC4 Sat & Sun; no Amex.

La Cage Imaginaire NW3 £42 334
16 Flask Walk 7794 6674 8–1A
"In the foodie wasteland of Hampstead", this "cosy" little spot, on a
super-cute lane, is a "reliable" place offering "traditional bistro food
of good quality"; it's "none too expensive", either – "why isn't
it packed?" / NW3 1HE; www.la-cage-imaginaire.co.uk; 11 pm.

Cah-Chi £37 432
394 Garratt Ln, SW18 8946 8811 10–2B
34 Durham Rd, SW20 8947 1081 10–2B
"Healthy and warming", "delicious" and "great value" – there's little
not to like about the Korean scoff on offer at these "unassuming" but
"busy" Korean operations, in Earlsfield and Raynes Park; BYO.
/ www.cahchi.com; SW20 11 pm; SW18 11 pm, Sat & Sun 11.30 pm;
SW20 closed Mon; cash only.

The Camberwell Arms SE5 NEW £55 444

65 Camberwell Church St   7358 4364   1–3C
*"Another fab gastropub from the team behind the Canton Arms" –
this excellent Camberwell newcomer offers some "delicious" food;
"order from the blackboard, then hang out in the cocktail bar
upstairs". / SE5 8TR; www.thecamberwellarms.co.uk; @camberwellarms;
closed Mon L & Sun D.*

Cambio de Tercio SW5 £68 434

161-163 Old Brompton Rd   7244 8970   5–2B
*"Tirelessly energetic owner" Abel Lusa presides over this "special"
Earl's Court venture – thanks to its "exciting and different" cuisine,
"heavenly" wines and positively "Latin" atmosphere, it is often
proclaimed "London's top Spanish restaurant". / SW5 0LJ;
www.cambiodetercio.co.uk; @CambiodTercio; 11.15 pm, Sun 11 pm;
set weekday L £46 (FP).*

Camino N1 £47 233

3 Varnishers Yd, Regent Quarter   7841 7331   8–3C
*"A great place to meet friends near King's Cross" – this handy
hangout serves up tasty tapas washed down with "fabulous sangria".
/ N1 9FD; www.camino.uk.com; @CaminoLondon; Mon-Sat 10.30 pm,
Sun 9.30 pm; set weekday L £26 (FP); SRA-3 stars.*

Cannizaro House SW19 £64 234

West Side, Wimbledon Common   8879 1464   10–2A
*A "beautiful" country house, by Wimbledon Common, with a "divine"
terrace; the food is perhaps a secondary attraction, but no one
disputes that – for a "romantic" setting – this is a hard place to beat;
"good for business and functions" too. / SW19 4UE;
www.cannizarohouse.com; 9.30 pm.*

Canta Napoli £38 332

9 Devonshire Rd, W4   8994 5225   7–2A
136 High St, TW11   8977 3344   1–4A
*"Lively and characterful", these "friendly" Chiswick and Teddington
Italians offers an "excellent selection of basic dishes, including superb
pizza and pasta". / 10.30 pm; no Amex.*

Canteen £42 111

Royal Festival Hall, SE1   0845 686 1122   2–3D
Park Pavilion, 40 Canada Sq, E14   0845 686 1122   11–1C
Crispin Pl, Old Spitalf'ds Mkt, E1   0845 686 1122   12–2B
*Such a shame this perennially promising English-canteen chain
remains so "lacklustre"; it has some "useful" locations (on the South
Bank especially), but too often suffers from "unmotivated" service
and food that "fails to live up to the promise of the menu".
/ www.canteen.co.uk; 11 pm, E14 & W1 Sun 7 pm; no booking weekend L.*

Cantina Laredo WC2 £52 443

10 Upper St Martin's Ln   7420 0630   4–3B
*"I'm from Arizona, so I know an authentic Mexican!"; this grand-US-
diner-style Covent Garden spot attracts consistent praise for "fresh-
tasting" food that's "a cut above", and in "generous portions" too.
/ WC2H 9FB; www.cantinalaredo.co.uk; @CantinaLaredoUK; 11.30 pm,
Sat midnight, Sun 10.30 pm.*

Cantina Vinopolis
Vinopolis SE1   £54   2 2 2
1 Bank End   7940 8333   9–3C
It doesn't fully live up to its cathedral-like setting under South Bank
railway arches, but this café attached to a museum of wine served
some "surprisingly good" meals this year – recommended pre-
theatre, and for Sunday lunch. / SE1 9BU; www.cantinavinopolis.com;
10 pm; closed Sun D.

Canton Arms SW8   £45   3 3 4
177 South Lambeth Rd   7582 8710   10–1D
This "unpretentious" Stockwell gastropub isn't showing quite the
staying power of its sibling, the Anchor & Hope; it can still dish
up some "hearty and homely" dishes, but even some fans note the
formula "doesn't always work". / SW8 1XP; www.cantonarms.com; 10 pm;
closed Mon L & Sun D; no Amex; no booking.

Canvas SW1 NEW
1 Wilbraham Pl   7935 0858   5–2D
Michael Riemenschneider moved his 'design-your-own-menu' fine
dining concept from Marylebone to Chelsea in mid-2014; we think
a proper assessment will sadly have to wait until next year.
/ SW1X 9AE; www.canvaschelsea.com; @CanvasbyMR.

Capote Y Toros SW5   £44   4 3 4
157 Old Brompton Rd   7373 0567   5–2B
"Like being in Seville!"; part of the Cambio de Tercio group,
this "buzzy" and "stylish" South Kensington spot offers "excellent
tapas and a great selection of sherries". / SW5 0LJ;
www.cambiodetercio.co.uk; @CambiodTercio; 11.15 pm; D only, closed
Mon & Sun.

LE CAPRICE SW1   £71   3 4 4
Arlington Hs, Arlington St   7629 2239   3–4C
"Like Ol' Man River, just keeps rolling along!" – this "understated"
'80s brasserie, behind The Ritz, "always make you feel like a million
dollars"; its "robust" comfort food "won't let you down", but it's not
as dazzling as it once was – the "people-watching" is the more
reliable sparkler. / SW1A 1RJ; www.le-caprice.co.uk; @CapriceHoldings;
11.30 pm Mon-Sat, Sun 10.30 pm; set pre theatre £49 (FP).

Caraffini SW1   £51   2 5 3
61-63 Lower Sloane St   7259 0235   5–2D
"The menu hasn't changed in 15 years, nor have the staff!" –
this "very Chelsea" favourite, just a couple of minutes from Sloane
Square, still delights its devoted following with its "polished, old-
school" charm, and "reliable" Italian fare. / SW1W 8DH;
www.caraffini.co.uk; Mon-Fri 11.30 pm, Sat 11 pm; closed Sun.

Caravan   £46   3 2 4
1 Granary Sq, N1   7101 7661   8–3C
11-13 Exmouth Mkt, EC1   7833 8115   9–1A
As "bustling brunch" hangouts go, it's hard to better these "fast and
furious" operations – both the Exmouth Market original, and its
"vast" and "vibey" offshoot by King's Cross – which serve
an "imaginative" tapas-based menu, and coffee roasted in-house.
/ www.caravanonexmouth.co.uk; EC1 10.30 pm, Sun 4 pm; EC1 Sun D.

Carluccio's £42 ▮1▮▮1▮▮2▮
Branches throughout London
"Pleasant" enough to look at, this faux-Italian chain also offers
a "great range of breakfast items" and "makes a big fuss of kids" too
– otherwise, the formula often seems "very stale" nowadays.
/ www.carluccios.com; most branches 11 pm, Sun 10.30 pm; no booking
weekday L; SRA-3 stars.

Carob Tree NW5 £33 ▮4▮▮5▮▮4▮
15 Highgate Rd 7267 9880 8–1B
"Always buzzing", this "terrific-value" Dartmouth Park Greek offers
a menu on which "superb" fish is a particular highlight; great
proprietor too – he "greets every diner like a long-lost cousin".
/ NW5 1QX; 10.30 pm, Sun 9 pm; closed Mon; no Amex.

The Carpenter's Arms W6 £48 ▮3▮▮3▮▮4▮
91 Black Lion Ln 8741 8386 7–2B
In a tucked-away Hammersmith location, a cute neighbourhood pub
with "consistently good" gastro fare; "lovely" garden too. / W6 9BG;
www.carpentersarmssw6.co.uk; 10 pm, Sun 9 pm.

Casa Brindisa SW7 £46 ▮2▮▮2▮▮2▮
7-9 Exhibition Rd 7590 0008 5–2C
A "reliable" tapas stop, handy for South Kensington tube, and with
some nice al fresco tables; it's difficult, though, to disagree with the
suggestion that it's "rather been left behind by a flurry of much better
Spanish places that have subsequently opened". / SW7 2HE;
www.casabrindisa.com; @TapasKitchens; 11 pm, Sun 10 pm.

Casa Malevo W2 £58 ▮4▮▮3▮▮3▮
23 Connaught St 7402 1988 6–1D
"A little gem"; this Bayswater Argentinian serves up some "lovely"
dishes (particularly for carnivores). / W2 2AY; www.casamalevo.com;
@casamalevo; 10.30 pm; D only.

Casse-Croute SE1 £37 ▮4▮▮4▮▮5▮
109 Bermondsey St 7407 2140 9–4D
"Just the sort of place you look for in Paris, and only rarely find" –
this bijou Bermondsey yearling may only have a "limited" menu and
"cramped" interior but it's "perhaps the best of the new-style old-style
bistros!" / SE1 3XB; www.cassecroute.co.uk; @CasseCroute109.

Cattle Grid SW12 £44 ▮3▮▮2▮▮3▮
1 Balham Station Rd 8673 9099 10–2C
Not much to say about this small outfit... but it does offer "perfectly
acceptable burgers and chips, when you're out with the lads".
/ SW12 9SG; www.cattlegridrestaurant.com.

Cây Tre £39 ▮3▮▮3▮▮3▮
42-43 Dean St, W1 7317 9118 4–2A
301 Old St, EC1 7729 8662 12–1B
"Lots of lovely fresh flavours" have won a wide following for this
"buzzy" and "friendly" Vietnamese duo, in Soho and Shoreditch;
at the latter, "arrive early or you may have to queue".
/ www.vietnamesekitchen.co.uk; 11 pm, Fri-Sat 11.30 pm, Sun 10.30 pm.

Cecconi's W1 £75 2 2 4
5a Burlington Gdns 7434 1500 3–3C
"For hedgies and beautiful people", this "sublimely well-heeled" and "buzzy" all-day Italian brasserie is a key Mayfair rendezvous (especially the "superb bar"); "breakfasts are the real deal", but otherwise "standards are average and prices steep" – "the atmosphere's the thing". / W1S 3EP; www.cecconis.co.uk; @SohoHouse; 11.30 pm, Sun 10.30 pm.

Cellar Gascon EC1 £38 3 3 3
59 West Smithfield Rd 7600 7561 9–2B
"Great snacks, such as mini-duck burgers, and good wines, all at reasonable prices" help make for a superior light-bite experience, at this offshoot of Smithfield's famous Club Gascon, a few doors away. / EC1A 9DS; www.cellargascon.com; midnight; closed Sat & Sun; set weekday L £17 (FP), set always available £20 (FP).

Ceviche W1 £46 4 3 3
17 Frith St 7292 2040 4–2A
"Yummy ceviche as the name suggest" and other "tangy, tasty and well-executed" dishes – not to mention "excellent Pisco sours" – "help extend one's sense of what Peruvian food can be", at this "vibrant" and "distinctive" Soho rendezvous. / W1D 4RG; www.cevicheuk.com; @cevicheuk; 11.30 pm, Sun 10.15 pm; SRA-1 star.

Chabrot Bistrot d'Amis SW1 £59 3 4 3
9 Knightsbridge Grn 7225 2238 5–1D
"As French as they get, from the food to the decor" – a "splendid old-style bistro" (which in fact only opened a few years ago), just a short step from Harrods. / SW1X 7QL; www.chabrot.co.uk; 10.30 pm, Sun 9.30 pm; set always available £36 (FP).

Chakra W11 £60 2 1 1
157-159 Notting Hill Gate 7229 2115 6–2B
Some dishes are of "very good quality", so it's a shame this "haute cuisine" Kensington Indian isn't living up to its potential – it offers "small" portions at "high" prices, and service sometimes seems "very slow". / W11 3LF; www.chakralondon.com; @ChakraLondon; 11 pm, Sun 10.30 pm.

Chamberlain's EC3 £70 3 3 2
23-25 Leadenhall Mkt 7648 8690 9–2D
"A strong location" and some "very competent" (if "unadventurous") fish cooking underpin the attractions of this long-established fixture, atmospherically housed in Leadenhall Market; prices, though, can seem "forbidding". / EC3V 1LR; www.chamberlains.org; @chamberlainsldn; 9.15 pm; closed Sat & Sun.

Champor-Champor SE1 £49 3 2 3
62 Weston St 7403 4600 9–4C
"Surprisingly tasty" Thai/Malay dishes and "fabulous", if "bizarre", decor still draws fans to this hidden-away Borough spot; it's not nearly as commented-upon as once it was, however, and some former fans now find it "rather run-of-the-mill". / SE1 3QJ; www.champor-champor.com; @ChamporChampor; 10 pm; D only.

The Chancery EC4   £53   3 4 2
9 Cursitor St   7831 4000   9–2A
A rather "formal" business favourite, "discreetly located" near Chancery Lane; it "maintains its standards", with cooking that's often "first-class", and "helpful" service too. / EC4A 1LL; www.thechancery.co.uk; @chancerylondon; 10.30 pm; closed Sat L & Sun.

Chapters SE3   £52   2 3 2
43-45 Montpelier Vale   8333 2666   1–4D
This "dependable" Blackheath brasserie is, say fans, "a perfect neighbourhood spot", open all day and featuring a "good range of breakfasts"; sceptics, though, say "the food is nothing of note". / SE3 0TJ; www.chaptersrestaurants.com; @Chapters_ADD; 11 pm, Sun 9 pm; set weekday L £31 (FP), set dinner £35 (FP).

Charlotte's Bistro W4   £51   3 4 3
6 Turnham Green Ter   8742 3590   7–2A
"An amazing cocktail list in the tiny gin bar" adds to the appeal of this Chiswick spot as a "good, if slightly pricey, neighbourhood go-to"; it's "cramped" and "noisy", though, and the "brief but sensible menu" is no better than "reliable". / W4 1QP; www.charlottes.co.uk; @CharlottesW4; 10 pm, Fri & Sat 10.30 pm, Sun 9 pm; SRA-1 star.

Charlotte's Place W5   £51   3 4 3
16 St Matthew's Rd   8567 7541   1–3A
"Unexpectedly good for Ealing" – this "homely" bistro, on the Common, pleases all who comment on it with its "simple but flavoursome" food; service is notably "friendly and knowledgeable" too. / W5 3JT; www.charlottes.co.uk; @CharlottesW5; 10.30 pm, Fri & Sat 11 pm, Sun 9 pm; SRA-1 star.

Chelsea Bun Diner SW10   £30   3 2 3
9a Lamont Rd   7352 3635   5–3B
"Perfect, if cholesterol heavy" – a "workmen's caff, Chelsea-style", offering a range of "enormous" breakfasts which will "keep you going all day". / SW10 0HP; www.chelseabun.co.uk; 6 pm; L only; no Amex; no booking, Sat & Sun.

Chettinad W1   £32   3 4 3
16 Percy St   3556 1229   2–1C
"Good, authentic South Indian food" (mainly non-vegetarian) wins many plaudits for this "understated" café-style Fitzrovia two-year-old; "good-value lunchtime set menus". / W1T 1DT; www.chettinadrestaurant.com; @chettinadlondon; Mon-Sat 10.30 pm, Sun 9.30 pm; no Amex.

Cheyne Walk Brasserie SW3   £75   3 3 3
50 Cheyne Walk   7376 8787   5–3C
"Very Chelsea – limited and pricey, but satisfying in an unchallenging way"; this "intimate" Gallic brasserie in a nicely converted pub may be "unjustifiably expensive", but the cooking, largely from the central wood-grill, is "dependable". / SW3 5LR; www.cheynewalkbrasserie.com; 10.30 pm, Sun 9.30 pm; closed Mon L; set weekday L £43 (FP).

Chez Abir W14 NEW   £33   4 3 2
34 Blythe Rd   7603 3241   7–1D
A new owner has taken over at this celebrated Lebanese café, behind Olympia (formerly called Chez Marcelle, but the lady has now retired); foodwise, even the few who feel "the magic is gone" say the cooking's still "perfectly good" and all agree "service is far better!" / W14 0HA.

CHEZ BRUCE SW17 £68 5 5 4
2 Bellevue Rd 8672 0114 10–2C
Bruce Poole's "quintessential neighbourhood restaurant",
by Wandsworth Common, celebrates 10 years as the survey's No.
1 favourite; the secret? – "sublime" and "inspired" cuisine, "brilliant"
wine, "welcoming but unobtrusive" staff... and a cheeseboard "to die
for". / SW17 7EG; www.chezbruce.co.uk; @ChezBruce; 10 pm, Fri & Sat
10.30 pm, Sun 9 pm.

Chez Patrick W8 £47 3 5 4
7 Stratford Rd 7937 6388 5–2A
Host Patrick's "Gallic charm, japes and bonhomie" (and "expert"
service) continue to delight, at this "deceptively slick" stalwart, which
specialises in "fresh, beautifully cooked" fish; its quiet Kensington
backwater location helps make for "a pleasurable escape from the
hurly-burly". / W8 6RF; www.chez-patrick.co.uk; 10.30 pm; closed Sun D;
set weekday L £26 (FP).

Chicken Shop £31 3 4 4
79 Highgate Rd, NW5 3310 2020 8–1B
141 Tooting High St, SW17 8767 5200 10–2B NEW
"Simple but amazing" and "great value too" – this "hip chicken"
chain ("Nandos for grown-ups") "does exactly what it says on the
tin"; the Kentish Town original, though, is much preferred to the
"crowded" and "noisy" Tooting offshoot.

Chicken Shop & Dirty Burger E1 NEW £36
27 Mile End Rd 3310 2010 12–2D
Soho House married their two popular budget brands (see individual
entries), at this Whitechapel newcomer in mid-2014; early-days
reports give their blessing to the union. / E1 4TP; www.chickenshop.com;
@chickenshop; closed weekday L.

Chilango £15 3 2 2
76 Chancery Ln, WC2 7430 1323 2–1D
27 Upper St, N1 7704 2123 8–3D
32 Brushfield St, E1 3246 0086 12–2B
64 London Wall, EC2 7628 7663 9–2C
142 Fleet St, EC4 7353 7353 9–2A
"Spot-on burritos every time" from "very fresh ingredients" inspires
a consistent thumbs-up for this grab-and-go chain. / www.chilango.co.uk;
@Chilango_uk; EC4, EC2, EC1 9 pm; N1 10 pm, Fri & Sat midnight;
EC4, EC2, E1 closed Sat & Sun; no booking.

Chilli Cool WC1 £31 4 1 1
15 Leigh St 7383 3135 2–1D
"Scintillating" Sichuanese cooking ("I've never been served a dish with
30 whole red chillies sitting on it before!") is the draw to this "plain"
Bloomsbury café – it certainly isn't the "poker-faced" and "abrupt"
service. / WC1H 9EW; www.chillicool.com; 10.15 pm.

The Chiltern Firehouse W1 NEW £82 2 2 5
1 Chiltern St 7073 7676 2–1A
"So hard to get a table!" – poseurs and paparazzi abound at Nuno
Mendes's hot Marylebone newcomer... but less starry-eyed reporters
say the food is actually pretty "meh"; "superb fun," though, and the
room itself is "amazing". / W1U 7PA; www.chilternfirehouse.com.

China Tang
Dorchester Hotel W1   £72   2 2 **3**

53 Park Ln   7629 9988   3–3A

Fans of Sir David Tang's '30s-Shanghai Mayfair basement applaud the "wonderful" Art Deco ambience, and say the Peking duck in particular is "amazing"; critics, though, find the whole show monstrously "overrated". / W1K 1QA; www.chinatanglondon.co.uk; @ChinaTangLondon; 11.45 pm; max 14.

Chinese Cricket Club EC4   £55   **4** 2 **1**

19 New Bridge St   7438 8051   9–3A

Despite a setting which "feels like an airport departure lounge", this hotel dining room by Blackfriars Bridge wins plenty of plaudits for its "delightful" oriental fare – "best try the chef's tasting menu"! / EC4V 6DB; www.chinesecricketclub.com; @chinesecclub; 10 pm; closed Sat & Sun L.

Chipotle   £17   **3** **3** 2

101-103 Baker St, W1   7935 9881   2–1A

181-185 Wardour St, W1   7494 4156   3–1D

114-116 Charing Cross Rd, WC2   7836 8491   4–1A

92-93 St Martin's Ln, WC2   7836 7838   4–4B

334 Upper St, N1   7354 3686   8–3D

"Quality meat and flavour-packed salsas" make these "stark" Mexican burrito-stops "a great option for a filling meal on the go"; but something's been lost in its trans-Atlantic translation – "in the US, I would go every time, but here they're not quite there". / www.chipotle.com; 10 pm - 11 pm.

Chisou   £51   **4** 2 2

4 Princes St, W1   7629 3931   3–1C

31 Beauchamp Pl, SW3   3155 0005   5–2D

1-4 Barley Mow Pas, W4   8994 3636   7–2A

"Outstanding sushi" is the culinary standout at this "genuine" Japanese chain (where "a wide range of sakes" is also a feature), both at the "functional" Mayfair original and the "cute" Chiswick offshoot. / www.chisourestaurant.com; Mon-Sat 10.30 pm, Sun 9.30 pm.

Chiswell Street Dining Rooms EC1   £62   2 2 2

56 Chiswell St   7614 0177   12–2A

"Comfortable, smart and wood-panelled", this gastropub-style operation, near the Barbican, is neatly tailored to its local City business market; given the prices, though, standards aren't really much more than "tolerable" all-round. / EC1Y 4SA; www.chiswellstreetdining.com; @chiswelldining; 11 pm; closed Sat & Sun; set always available £36 (FP).

Chor Bizarre W1   £63   **4** **4** **3**

16 Albemarle St   7629 9802   3–3C

A madly antique-festooned Indian that's about as 'alternative' as Mayfair gets; the "honest" cooking is of "surprising quality" too – "not cheap, but not crazy either". / W1S 4HW; www.chorbizarre.com; @ChorBizarreUK; 11.30 pm, Sun 10.30 pm; set weekday L £40 (FP).

Chotto Matte W1   £55   **4** 2 **4**

11-13 Frith St   7042 7171   4–2A

"Is it a nightclub or a restaurant?" – either way, this "achingly trendy and noisy" newcomer, from the ping pong people, is a "welcome new entrant" to the Soho market, offering "fresh" and "zingy" fusion fare that's "more Japanese than Peruvian". / W1D 4RB; www.chotto-matte.com; @ChottoMatteSoho; Mon-Sat 1 am, Sun 11 pm.

Christopher's WC2   £70   **3 2 3**
18 Wellington St   7240 4222   4–3D
*Predating London's current US craze, this "upmarket" surf 'n' turf
venue occupies an "impressive" Covent Garden townhouse (complete
with "buzzy" ground-floor bar); under new owners, it's "just like it was
many years ago" – that's to say "top-quality" but "way overpriced",
and with "patchy" service.* / WC2E 7DD; www.christophersgrill.com;
@christopherswc2; 11.30 pm, Sun 10.30 pm; booking: max 12; set weekday
L & pre-theatre £39 (FP).

Churchill Arms W8   £35   **3 3 5**
119 Kensington Church St   7792 1246   6–2B
*"Fast, furious and full of fun!"; you don't just get "delicious" Thai scoff
at "silly-cheap" prices at this "quirky" pub, off Notting Hill Gate,
but also a "fantastic" setting in a "cute and interesting" flower-filled
conservatory.* / W8 7LN; www.churchillarmskensington.co.uk;
@ChurchilArmsW8; 10 pm, Sun 9.30 pm.

Chutney SW18   £32   **4 4 2**
11 Alma Rd   8870 4588   10–2B
*"Traditional, yet very well done" – a well-established Wandsworth
curry house, consistently rated a cut above the norm.* / SW18 1AA;
www.chutneyrestaurant.co.uk; 11.30 pm; D only.

Chutney Mary SW10   £56   **4 5 4**
535 King's Rd   7351 3113   5–4B
*"If you're looking for an upmarket Indian meal", it's "hard to improve
on" this "glamorous and romantic" stalwart on the border of Chelsea,
with its "beautiful and subtle" dishes, and lovely and
"very professional" service; look out for a change of venue in 2015.*
/ SW10 0SZ; www.realindianfood.com; @RealindianFood; 11.45 pm,
Sun 10.45 pm; closed weekday L; booking: max 8.

Chutneys NW1   £31   **2 2 2**
124 Drummond St   7388 0604   8–4C
*"A stalwart of the 'Little India' South Asian culinary scene" –
a "pleasant enough" café, known for its "astonishingly good-value
lunchtime and Sunday evening buffet".* / NW1 2PA;
www.chutneyseuston.co.uk; 11 pm; no Amex; need 5+ to book.

Ciao Bella WC1   £42   **2 4 3**
86-90 Lamb's Conduit St   7242 4119   2–1D
*"There are some real characters in the waiting team" of this "crazy,
noisy and packed" '70s Italian, in Bloomsbury – a "good-humoured"
place, offering cooking that's affordable but "fairly standard".*
/ WC1N 3LZ; www.ciaobellarestaurant.co.uk; 11.30 pm, Sun 10.30 pm.

Cibo W14   £51   **4 5 3**
3 Russell Gdns   7371 6271   7–1D
*"An old friend" on the Kensington/Olympia border; this "quiet,
spacious and elegant" venue is often overlooked nowadays, but its
"efficient and friendly" staff dish up "true Italian food" – "simply
executed", but of "good quality".* / W14 8EZ; www.ciborestaurant.net;
10.30 pm; closed Sat L & Sun D.

Cigala WC1   £49   **3 3 2**
54 Lamb's Conduit St   7405 1717   2–1D
*In a "not terribly well-served part of town", Bloomsbury, this "busy,
bustling and closely packed" Spanish restaurant serves "a really good
selection of tapas"; the paella's not bad either.* / WC1N 3LW;
www.cigala.co.uk; 10.45 pm, Sun 9.45 pm.

Le Cigalon WC2 £47 3 3 3
115 Chancery Ln 7242 8373 2–2D
"An oasis of calm", near the Law Courts – this "beautiful and light" chamber (once auctioneers' premises) provides a "spacious" setting for this "slightly quirky" Provençal operation; "it's not as good as sibling, Club Gascon", though, and not especially atmospheric at night. / WC2A 1PP; www.cigalon.co.uk; @CIGALON_LONDON; 10 pm; closed Sat & Sun.

THE CINNAMON CLUB SW1 £72 3 3 4
Old Westminster Library, Great Smith St 7222 2555 2–4C
Westminster's "majestic" former library, near the Abbey, may make a "curious" setting for one of London's foremost Indians, but most reporters still acclaim its "thrilling take on contemporary subcontinental cuisine"; standards this year, though, were bit more up-and-down than usual. / SW1P 3BU; www.cinnamonclub.com; @CinnamonClub; 10.30 pm; closed Sun; no trainers; set weekday L & dinner £47 (FP); SRA-2 stars.

Cinnamon Kitchen EC2 £55 4 4 3
9 Devonshire Sq 7626 5000 9–2D
"Smart food with a kick" – from a "different" Indian-fusion menu – makes the Cinnamon Club's "elegant" City cousin a popular standby; some tables occupy an impressive atrium. / EC2M 4YL; www.cinnamon-kitchen.com; @cinnamonkitchen; 11 pm; closed Sat L & Sun; SRA-2 stars.

Cinnamon Soho W1 £44 4 3 2
5 Kingly St 7437 1664 3–2D
"Remarkable quality in a convenient location", just off Regent Street – the promise of this "cheaper member of the famous Cinnamon Club family", where the "fresh" dishes are "so light and tasty". / W1B 5PE; www.cinnamon-kitchen.com/soho-home; @cinnamonsoho; 11 pm, Sun 4.30 pm; closed Sun D.

City Barge W4 NEW £43 4 4 5
27 Strand-on-the-Green 8994 2148 1–3A
A "very good refurbishment" has at last breathed new life into this fine old pub, which has a "great location", by the river at Strand-on-the-Green; "outstanding fish" is – as you'd hope from an ex-Bentley's and ex-Scott's chef – a highlight. / W4 3PH; www.citybargechiswick.com; @citybargew4; 11 pm.

City Càphê EC2 £14 4 3 2
17 Ironmonger St no tel 9–2C
"The daily queue snaking down the street" attests to the charms of this Vietnamese canteen/take-away, near Bank – arrive before noon for "phenomenally good" pho, and "bánh mi that always hit the spot". / EC2V 8EY; www.citycaphe.com; 3 pm; L only, closed Sat & Sun.

City Miyama EC4 £53 3 3 1
17 Godliman St 7489 1937 9–3B
This City stalwart, in a "handy" location not far from St Paul's, draws the lunchtime Japanese crowd with its well-conceived cuisine, with sushi a highlight; well, it can't be the decor. / EC4B 5BD; www.miyama-restaurant.co.uk; 9.30 pm; closed Sat & Sun; set weekday L £34 (FP).

City Social EC2 NEW £79 **4 5 4**
Tower 42 25 Old Broad St 7877 7703 9–2C
*"Views to die for", "fabulous" cooking and "incredibly attentive"
service – Jason Atherton has served up "another hit" with this City
newcomer, "breathing new life" into the 24th-floor premises which
were formerly Rhodes 24 (RIP). / EC2N 1HQ; www.citysociallondon.com.*

Clarke's W8 £69 **3 3 2**
124 Kensington Church St 7221 9225 6–2B
*Sally Clarke's "simple yet adventurous" cuisine has long had many
fans, but but it's impossible to avoid the feeling that her Kensington
restaurant is "not as good as it used to be" – too many meals
"lack inspiration and flair", and the recently refurbished interior can
be "very noisy". / W8 4BH; www.sallyclarke.com; 10 pm; closed Sun;
booking: max 14.*

Claude's Kitchen
Amuse Bouche SW6 £48 **4 4 4**
51 Parsons Green Ln 7371 8517 10–1B
*"A gorgeous little spot, opposite Parson's Green tube", which
is making ripples after a year in business, thanks to its "easygoing"
style and "inventive" cuisine – "have a glass of bubbly in the
downstairs bar, before you head up to the cosy candlelit dining room".
/ SW6 4JA; www.claudeskitchen.co.uk; @AmuseBoucheLDN; 10 pm; closed
weekday L.*

The Clink
HMP Brixton SW2 NEW £30 **2 3 5**
Jebb Ave 7147 6724 10–2D
*"Good luck to the whole project!"; you too can be a – temporary –
guest of Her Majesty at Brixton nick, at this intriguing new
rehabilitation project; "the food's nothing special, but the experience
is quite something". / SW2 5XF; www.theclinkrestaurant.com;
@theclinkcharity; 2 pm; L only; SRA-3 stars.*

The Clissold Arms N2 £49 **3 4 4**
Fortis Grn 8444 4224 1–1C
*"Good honest gastropub cooking" and "a great al fresco eating area"
help win praise for this popular Muswell Hill boozer (famed for its
links to The Kinks). / N2 9HR; www.clissoldarms.co.uk; @ClissoldArms;
10 pm, Sat 10.30 pm, Sun 9 pm.*

CLOS MAGGIORE WC2 £62 **4 5 5**
33 King St 7379 9696 4–3C
*"I don't know how a restaurant could be more romantic!";
the survey's No. 1 trysting spot is an unlikely "oasis" in the tourist hell
that is Covent Garden; but it's not just the "twinkly conservatory" that
sets pheromones pumping – there's a "phenomenal" wine list to back
up "undoubtedly excellent" French cuisine. / WC2E 8JD;
www.closmaggiore.com; @ClosMaggioreWC2; 11 pm, Sun 10 pm; max 7;
set always available £43 (FP).*

The Clove Club EC1 £70 **4 4 4**
Shoreditch Town Hall, 380 Old St 7729 6496 12–1B
*"All the hype is worth it!", say fans of this "foodie hipster heaven" –
a "highly professional" pop-up-turned-permanent, in Shoreditch's
"beautiful" ("if noisy") old town hall; the "eclectic" menu "may look
bizarre, but it works splendidly", though portions are rather "small".
/ EC1V 9LT; www.thecloveclub.com; @thecloveclub; 9.30 pm; closed
Mon L & Sun; set weekday L £53 (FP).*

Club Gascon EC1   £74   **4** **3** **3**
57 West Smithfield   7600 6144   9–2B
"Superbly constructed" SW French regional tapas with "sophistication and imagination" – plus wines "paired with panache" – are the long-running hallmarks of this City-fringe business favourite; prices are on the "astronomical" side, though, and service can sometimes be "very Gallic". / EC1A 9DS; www.clubgascon.com; @club_gascon; 10 pm, Fri & Sat 10.30 pm; closed Sat L & Sun; set weekday L £55 (FP).

Clutch E2 NEW   £30   **4** **4** **4**
4 Ravenscroft St   7729 4402   12–1C
"Calling all fried chicken fans"; this "quirky" but "friendly" Hoxton newcomer serves a "simple but well-executed menu", and "good cocktails" too. / E2 7QG; www.clutchchicken.com.

Coco Di Mama EC4   £10   **4** **3** **2**
90 Fleet St   7583 9277   9–2A
"Superb" pasta "doused in tasty homemade sauce" plus "fantastic" coffee – this small City chain wins nothing but praise. / EC4Y 1DH; cocodimama.co.uk; 5 pm.

Colbert SW1   £60   **1** **2** **3**
51 Sloane Sq   7730 2804   5–2D
"Do they really run The Wolseley too?" – with its "surprisingly poor" food and too often "charmless" service, Corbin & King's year-old successor to Sloane Square's long-running Oriel brasserie is still "terribly disappointing"; come on chaps! / SW1W 8AX; www.colbertchelsea.com; @ColbertChelsea; Sun 10.30 pm, Mon-Thu 11 pm, Fri & Sat 11.30 pm; max 6; SRA-3 stars.

La Collina NW1   £54   **4** **3** **2**
17 Princess Rd   7483 0192   8–3B
"Unusual, high-quality Piedmontese cooking" adds to the "authentic" charm of this gourmet local, hidden away in Primrose Hill; "the small dining room at street level is austere, but the garden is a joy in summer". / NW1 8JR; www.lacollinarestaurant.co.uk; @LacollinaR; 10.15 pm, Sun 9.45 pm, Mon 9.30 pm; closed Mon L.

Le Colombier SW3   £59   **3** **4** **4**
145 Dovehouse St   7351 1155   5–2C
An extremely popular "classic French local", extolled for its "dependable" cooking, "attentive" service and "great backstreet location" (with charming terrace); prices do "reflect the old Chelsea' clientele" (though, paradoxically, top wines "offer real value"). / SW3 6LB; www.le-colombier-restaurant.co.uk; 10.30 pm, Sun 10 pm.

Colony Grill Room
Beaumont Hotel W1 NEW
Brown Hart Gdns   7499 1001   3–2A
As this guide goes to print, London's most respected restaurateurs, Corbin & King of Wolseley fame, open their first hotel (and dining room) in a forgotten corner of Mayfair. / W1K 6TF; www.thebeaumont.com.

Como Lario SW1   £48   **2** **2** **3**
18-22 Holbein Pl   7730 2954   5–2D
"A proper neighbourhood Italian", just five minutes from Sloane Square; it's an "old favourite" for some reporters, even if the food is only "OK". / SW1W 8NL; www.comolario.co.uk; 11.30 pm, Sun 10 pm.

Compagnie des Vins
Surnaturels WC2 NEW   £52   4 2 2
8-10 Neals Yd   7344 7737   4–2C
"Interesting" wines and "delicious" small plates have helped this
"cute" Covent Garden newcomer make waves; it's "hardly cheap",
though, and early-days gripes include "tiny" tables and incidents
of "poor" service. / WC2H 9DP; www.cvssevendials.com.

Comptoir Gascon EC1   £44   3 3 4
63 Charterhouse St   7608 0851   9–1A
"A good, cheap alternative to Club Gascon" – the "attractive" spin-off
from the famous Smithfield tapas bar, nearby, "does a nice line
in duck and other meaty treats", plus "excellent-value" wine.
/ EC1M 6HJ; www.comptoirgascon.com; @ComptoirGascon; 10 pm, Thu & Fri
10.30 pm; closed Mon & Sun.

Comptoir Libanais   £28   2 2 2
59 Broadwick St, W1   7434 4335   3–2C
65 Wigmore St, W1   7935 1110   3–1A
1-5 Exhibition Rd, SW7   7225 5006   5–2C
Westfield, The Balcony, W12   8811 2222   7–1C
Westfield Stratford City, 2 Stratford Pl, E20   8555 6999   1–1D
"Reasonably priced mezze" and "very good juices" are among the
attractions of this colourful and "friendly" Lebanese chain; critics,
though, can find the food rather "variable". / www.lecomptoir.co.uk;
W12 9 pm, Thu & Fri 10 pm, Sun 6 pm; W1 9.30 pm; W12 closed Sun D;
no bookings.

Il Convivio SW1   £58   4 4 3
143 Ebury St   7730 4099   2–4A
"After all these years, Il Convivio still delights"; this "upmarket"
Belgravia "gem" offers "first-rate" Italian cuisine in airy surroundings
supporters find positively "beautiful" – it "deserves to be better
known". / SW1W 9QN; www.etruscarerestaurants.com; 10.45 pm;
closed Sun.

Coopers Restaurant & Bar WC2   £50   3 3 3
49a Lincolns Inn Fields   7831 6211   2–2D
Tucked away in Lincoln's Inn Fields (and with quite a grand dining
room upstairs), a top haunt of local barristers and LSE academics –
lunchtimes "can be noisy", but, by all accounts, "the food is worth it".
/ WC2A 3PF; www.coopers-restaurant.com; @coopers_bistro; 11 pm; closed
Sat & Sun.

Copita W1   £44   3 2 4
27 D'Arblay St   7287 7797   3–1D
"Cramped, noisy and low-lit", this Soho spot is, say fans, a top
example of "quintessential contemporary dining", whose "slightly left-
field" tapas are "up there with Barrafina"; sceptics, however,
feel "some dishes are more successful than others". / W1F 8EP;
www.copita.co.uk; 10.30 pm; closed Sun.

Le Coq N1   £44   3 4 3
292-294 St Paul's Rd   7359 5055   8–2D
"Gorgeous chicken and roast potatoes to die for" – "all served with
a smile" – dazzle fans of this year-old rôtisserie operation,
near Highbury & Islington tube; refuseniks, though, find "the chicken
too ordinary to be the star of the show!" / N1 2LH; www.le-coq.co.uk;
@LeCOQrestaurant; 10.15 pm.

Coq d'Argent EC2 £74 2 2 3
1 Poultry 7395 5000 9–2C
An "impressive" favourite for "power-dining" – this popular City vantage-point owes its fame to its rooftop gardens and "wonderful views"; otherwise, it's a "sterile" sort of operation, and "massively overpriced" for what it is. / EC2R 8EJ; www.coqdargent.co.uk; 9.45 pm; closed Sun D; set always available & Sun L £49 (FP); SRA-2 stars.

Cork & Bottle WC2 £48 2 3 4
44-46 Cranbourn St 7734 7807 4–3B
"Thankfully Leicester Square is not totally lost to chain restaurants", and this "quirky" '70s basement "feels like a step back in time" (even after recent refurb); the food's not the main event, but "you're spoilt for choice for wines". / WC2H 7AN; www.thecorkandbottle.co.uk; @corkbottle1971; 11.30 pm, Sun 10.30 pm; no booking after 6.30 pm.

Cornish Tiger SW11 NEW £48 4 4 3
1 Battersea Rise 7223 7719 10–1C
On a Battersea strip where restaurants rarely have many culinary aspirations, this summer-2014 newcomer boast a chef who trained at the well-known Chapter One (Bromley) – early reports suggest it's a "great local". / SW11 1GH; www.cornishtiger.com; @cornishtiger; 9.45 pm; closed Mon; set dinner £32 (FP).

Corrigan's Mayfair W1 £86 2 2 2
28 Upper Grosvenor St 7499 9943 3–3A
For business dining with "gravitas", fans tip this "dark and staid" Mayfair dining room, and hail its "superbly presented classic dishes"; the more general view, though, is that the food is "nothing special", and "madly overpriced" too. / W1K 7EH; www.corrigansmayfair.com; 10.45 pm, Sun 9.30 pm; closed Sat L; booking: max 10.

Côte £44 2 2 2
Branches throughout London
How sad; though it's still a "default" choice for its army of fans, this brasserie chain is getting ever more "formulaic" under its new (private equity) ownership; critics decry its "joyless" cuisine as "French-by-numbers" – "actually worse than Café Rouge!" / www.cote-restaurants.co.uk; 11 pm.

The Cow W2 £56 3 4 4
89 Westbourne Park Rd 7221 0021 6–1B
"Fresh-as-you-like seafood, among the west London glitterati" – Tom Conran's cramped but "friendly" Oirish boozer, on the Bayswater/Notting Hill border, "is a great pub in its own right", but its Guinness and oysters "make it a pearl!". / W2 5QH; www.thecowlondon.co.uk; 10.30 pm, Sun 10 pm; no Amex.

Coya W1 £76 4 2 3
118 Piccadilly 7042 7118 3–4B
"Ceviches raised to perfection" and other "surprising" flavours have instantly propelled this "vibrant" Mayfair Peruvian into the big league; service can sometimes be a touch "chaotic", though, and critics do fear the place has become "a bit too trendy for its own good". / W1J 7NW; www.coyarestaurant.com; @coyarestaurant; Sun-Wed 10.30 pm, Thu-Sat 11 pm; max party 12; set weekday L £50 (FP).

Crazy Bear W1   £64   2 2 **4**
26-28 Whitfield St   7631 0088   2–1C
"Seductive" decor makes for "a fun night out" at this "funky"
Fitzrovia bar-restaurant; unfortunately, though, "'crazy' describes the
prices too", and the pan-Asian cooking is "not what it was".
/ W1T 2RG; www.crazybeargroup.co.uk; @CrazyBearGroup; 10.30 pm; closed
Mon L & Sun; no shorts.

Criterion W1   £69   2 2 **5**
224 Piccadilly   7930 0488   3–3D
"Possibly the most beautiful restaurant in London", this extraordinary
neo-Byzantine room, right on Piccadilly Circus, is up there with The
Ritz for beauty and romance – what a shame, then, about the
"mediocre" food and sometimes "stilted" service. / W1J 9HP;
www.criterionrestaurant.com; 11.15 pm, Sun 10.30 pm.

The Crooked Well SE5   £49   **3 4 4**
16 Grove Ln   7252 7798   1–3C
In a "classy Camberwell enclave", this "amiable" gastropub is a real
crowd-pleaser, thanks to its "accomplished" British grub (and some
"fabulous" cocktails too). / SE5 8SY; www.thecrookedwell.com;
@crookedwell; 10.30 pm; closed Mon L; no Amex.

Crussh   £17   **4 4** 2
Branches throughout London
"Healthy food on the go" is the promise of this "friendly" small group,
whose smoothies and juices are "a step up"; it also offers good salads
and "filling and very tasty stews". / www.crussh.com; 4.30 pm-8 pm;
many branches closed all or part of weekend; no credit cards in many
branches.

Cumberland Arms W14   £43   **4 4 3**
29 North End Rd   7371 6806   7–2D
"Something of an oasis in the less than salubrious surroundings of the
North End Road" – this handy gastropub, near Olympia, offers
"a fabulous Mediterranean menu"; great music too. / W14 8SZ;
www.thecumberlandarmspub.co.uk; @thecumberland; 10 pm, Sun 9.30 pm.

Cut
45 Park Lane W1   £110   2 2 2
45 Park Ln   7493 4545   3–4A
"The steaks are great", at US über-chef Wolfgang Puck's "corridor-
like" Mayfair dining room; prices (especially wine) are "obscene",
though, service can be "clueless", and the setting is "terrible".
/ W1K 1PN; www.45parklane.com; @the_cut_bar; 10.30 pm; set dinner
£79 (FP).

Cyprus Mangal SW1   £32   **4 3** 1
45 Warwick Way   7828 5940   2–4B
An unremarkable-looking Pimlico fixture, often proclaimed for
"the best kebab in town"; "there's always a line of taxis parked
outside – what better recommendation?" / SW1V 1QS;
cyprusmangal.co.uk/menu; 10.45 pm, Fri & Sat 11.45 pm.

Da Mario SW7   £42   2 **3** 3
15 Gloucester Rd   7584 9078   5–1B
An "always-welcoming" local "institution", near the Royal Albert Hall,
offering a "down-to-earth" menu majoring in pizza; they "dote on
kids". / SW7 4PP; www.damario.co.uk; 11.30 pm.

Da Mario WC2 £46 2 2 3
63 Endell St 7240 3632 4–1C
"A welcome change from all the Covent Garden chains" –
an "idiosyncratic" spot, where the dishes from the "regularly changing
blackboard menu" generally please. / WC2H 9AJ; www.da-mario.co.uk;
11.15 pm; closed Sun.

Dabbous W1 £68 4 3 2
39 Whitfield St 7323 1544 2–1C
Ollie Dabbous is struggling to preserve the wow factor at his concrete-
walled Fitzrovia flagship – most reports still go nuts for his "game-
changing" cuisine, but there was also quite a large minority this year
which just "couldn't see what all the fuss is about". / W1T 2SF;
www.dabbous.co.uk; @dabbous; 9.30 pm (bar open until 11.30 pm); closed
Mon & Sun; set weekday L £46 (FP).

Daddy Donkey EC1 £16 4 3 2
100 Leather Ln 448448 9–2A
"A burrito big enough to serve a small family" is the pay-off for
visitors to this Clerkenwell successor to a legendary van; "join the
queue – it's worth the wait". / EC1N 7TE; www.daddydonkey.co.uk;
@daddydonkey; Mon-Fri 4 pm; L only, closed Sat & Sun.

The Dairy SW4 £40 5 4 4
15 The Pavement 7622 4165 10–2D
"More interesting, more charming and less pretentious than many
a fancy West End eatery" – this "daring" Clapham yearling may be a
bit "cramped", but its "experimental" and "artistic" tapas-style
cuisine really "sparkles". / SW4 0HY; www.the-dairy.co.uk; 9.45 pm; closed
Mon, Tue L & Sun D.

Dalchini SW19 £37 3 4 2
147 Arthur Rd 8947 5966 10–2B
"Pleasing everyone with its mix of Indian and Chinese-influenced
dishes" – this 'Hakka' restaurant, opposite Wimbledon Park tube,
is rated "outstanding" by its fans; even the most sceptical report says
it's "a decent local, and OK value overall". / SW19 8AB;
www.dalchini.co.uk; 10.30 pm, Fri & Sat 11 pm, Sun 10 pm; no Amex.

Daphne's SW3 £68
112 Draycott Ave 7589 4257 5–2C
You're dating yourself if you remember the glory days of this Chelsea
stalwart – once the favourite of Diana, Princess of Wales; after a fire,
it reopened with a tightly packed new look in mid-2014, too late for
survey feedback on the new incarnation. / SW3 3AE;
www.daphnes-restaurant.co.uk; @CapriceHoldings; 11 pm, Sun 10 pm;
set weekday L & pre-theatre £45 (FP).

Daquise SW7 £49 2 3 2
20 Thurloe St 7589 6117 5–2C
There's a "distinct Polish character" to this "shabby-chic" fixture
(est 1947), by South Kensington tube, where the cooking mixes the
"very traditional" (dumplings and so on) with more modern fare.
/ SW7 2LT; www.daquise.co.uk; @GesslerDaquise; 11 pm; no Amex.

The Dartmouth Arms SE23 £38 2 2 3
7 Dartmouth Rd 8488 3117 1–4D
"Lovely design" adds to the charms of this Forest Hill gastroboozer,
acclaimed by fans for its "consistent posh pub grub". / SE23 3HN;
www.thedartmoutharms.com; 10 pm, Sun 9 pm; no Amex.

The Dartmouth Castle W6 £43 **3 4 3**
26 Glenthorne Rd 8748 3614 7–2C
On the fringe of the "concrete jungle that Hammersmith has
become", this "tucked away" Victorian pub serves "reliable gastropub
fare" and "well-kept real ales". / W6 0LS; www.thedartmouthcastle.co.uk;
@DartmouthCastle; 10 pm, Sun 9.30 pm; closed Sat L.

Daylesford Organic £43 **2 2 4**
44b Pimlico Rd, SW1 7881 8060 5–2D
Selfridges & Co, 400 Oxford St, W1 0800 123 400 3–1A
208-212 Westbourne Grove, W11 7313 8050 6–1B
Rather self-consciously stylish Pimlico and Notting Hill cafés to park
your 4x4 outside; they're certainly "not cheap", but as "buzzy"
brunch venues in particular, they have their fans.
/ www.daylesfordorganic.com; SW1 & W11 7 pm, Sun 4 pm; W1 9 pm,
Sun 6.15 pm; W11 no booking L.

Dean Street Townhouse W1 £56 **3 3 4**
69-71 Dean St 7434 1775 4–2A
"Buzzy but relaxed, smart yet casual" – with its slick and clubby
interior, this happening Soho House-group Soho brasserie totally looks
the part; the "simple" menu is "uninspiring" or "well executed",
to taste. / W1D 3SE; www.deanstreettownhouse.com;
@deanstreettownhouse; 11.30 pm, Fri & Sat midnight, Sun 10.30 pm.

Defune W1 £67 **3 2 1**
34 George St 7935 8311 3–1A
An old-school, Marylebone sushi restaurant, where standards are still
"excellent"; the pricing, though, "has gone completely bonkers",
and the "decor doesn't make up for it either". / W1U 7DP;
www.defune.com; 10.45 pm, Sun 10.30 pm.

Dehesa W1 £49 **4 3 4**
25 Ganton St 7494 4170 3–2C
The "enticing" tapas menu is "super-fresh and beautifully presented",
at this Salt Yard spin-off, just off Carnaby Street (though the
occasional reporter does feel portions are "getting smaller"); despite
its "shoe-horned" conditions, it "manages to be both buzzy and
intimate". / W1F 9BP; www.dehesa.co.uk; @SaltYardGroup; 10.45 pm; SRA-2
stars.

THE DELAUNAY WC2 £57 **3 4 5**
55 Aldwych 7499 8558 2–2D
"Wolesley-lite!"; Corbin & King's "classic, European grand café",
on the edge of Covent Garden, is "more intimate" than its sibling,
but otherwise a chip off the old block – the "classy", "feel-good"
ambience, and "reliable" (if "slightly ersatz") Austrian cuisine make
it "a wow for business", especially at breakfast. / WC2B 4BB;
www.thedelaunay.com; @TheDelaunayRest; midnight, Sun 11 pm; SRA-3 stars.

Delfino W1 £51 **3 2 2**
121A Mount St 7499 1256 3–3B
"Superb pizza" – with "lovely thin bases expertly cooked in a wood-
burning oven" – is the draw to this "crowded" Mayfair spot, by the
Connaught. / W1K 3NW; www.finos.co.uk; 10.45 pm; closed Sun.

Delhi Grill N1 £34 **4** **3** **3**

21 Chapel Mkt 7278 8100 8–3D

"Authentic homemade Indian food, like visiting your best auntie's" –
reason to seek out this "innovative" curry shop, which occupies
a "busy café setting", handy for Angel tube. / N1 9EZ;
www.delhigrill.com; 10.30 pm; no credit cards.

La Delizia Limbara SW3 £40 **4** **4** **3**

63-65 Chelsea Manor St 7376 4111 5–3C

"A very simple, but in its own way rather perfect tiny Italian", in a
quiet backstreet off the King's Road; the setting is "cramped" and
minimalist, but it serves "lovely pizza, and a short list of pasta".
/ SW3 5RZ; www.ladelizia.org.uk; @ladelizia; 11 pm, Sun 10.30 pm; no Amex.

Department of Coffee EC1 £15 **3** **3** **4**

14-16 Leather Ln 7419 6906 9–2A

"How a coffee place should be" – "you may not be able to move for
Macbooks and carefully cultivated goatees", but there's no denying
that the coffee at this City spot is "fresh and strong". / EC1N 7SU;
www.departmentofcoffee.co.uk; 6 pm, Sat & Sun 4 pm; L only.

The Depot SW14 £42 **2** **3** **5**

Tideway Yd, Mortlake High St 8878 9462 10–1A

"Lovely views of the Thames", especially from the new riverside
seating area ("definitely a success"), are the main attraction at this
"very popular" Barnes haunt; the food may not be the main point,
but fans insist it's "getting better". / SW14 8SN;
www.depotbrasserie.co.uk; @TheDepotBarnes; 10 pm, Sun 9.30 pm.

Les Deux Salons WC2 £52 **1** **2** **2**

40-42 William IV St 7420 2050 4–4C

Thanks not least to its "top location" (behind the Coliseum),
Will Smith & Anthony Demetre's large faux-Parisian brasserie makes
a great pre-theatre standby; it's "gone downhill since it opened",
though, and too often seems plain "inept" nowadays. / WC2N 4DD;
www.lesdeuxsalons.co.uk; @lesdeuxsalons; 10.45 pm, Sun 5.45 pm; closed
Sun D.

Le Deuxième WC2 £57 **2** **2** **1**

65a Long Acre 7379 0033 4–2D

"A good place for a quick bite before curtain-up"; by the Royal Opera
House, a restaurant that's "always reliable"… even if the menu
"could use changing", and the decor "could do with livening up".
/ WC2E 9JH; www.ledeuxieme.com; @Le_Deuxieme; Mon-Thu 11 pm, Fri &
Sat 11.30 pm, Sun 10 pm; set always available £30 (FP).

DF Mexico
The Old Truman Brewery E1 NEW £31 **3** **3** **4**

Ely's Yd, 15 Hanbury St 3617 6639 12–2C

In Brick Lane's Old Truman Brewery, a casual new diner from the
founders of Wahaca; the food has its moments, but the whole
experience can be somewhat uneven. / E1 6QR; Rated on Editors' visit;
www.dfmexico.co.uk.

dim T £35 2️⃣2️⃣3️⃣

56-62 Wilton Rd, SW1 7834 0507 2–4B
32 Charlotte St, W1 7637 1122 2–1C
1 Hampstead Ln, N6 8340 8800 8–1B
3 Heath St, NW3 7435 0024 8–2A
Tooley St, SE1 7403 7000 9–4D
For a "cheap 'n' cheerful" snack, fans recommend these "buzzy"
canteens, and their "reliable", if rather "predictable", pan-Asian fare.
/ www.dimt.co.uk; @dim_t; most branches 11 pm, Sun 10.30 pm.

Diner £34 1️⃣3️⃣3️⃣

18 Ganton St, W1 7287 8962 3–2C
190 Shaftesbury Ave, WC2 3551 5225 4–1C
105 Gloucester Rd, SW7 7244 7666 5–2B
2 Jamestown Rd, NW1 7485 5223 8–3B
128 Curtain Rd, EC2 7729 4452 12–1B
These buzzy hangouts "pose as American diners", but "actually they
are just bars with bad food", say critics; even fans may concede that
it's "the atmosphere you go for". / www.goodlifediner.com; most branches
11 or 11.30 pm; booking: max 10.

Dinings W1 £57 5️⃣4️⃣1️⃣

22 Harcourt St 7723 0666 8–4A
"Only Tokyo offers fresher, better Japanese!" – Tomonari Chiba (ex-
Nobu) crafts "mind-blowingly good" sushi at his "quirky" Marylebone
den; no prizes for interior design though, and "don't look at the prices
whatever you do". / W1H 4HH; www.dinings.co.uk; @diningslondon;
10.30 pm; closed Sun.

**DINNER
MANDARIN ORIENTAL SW1** £100 3️⃣3️⃣3️⃣

66 Knightsbridge 7201 3833 5–1D
"The definition of occasion dining", say fans of Heston's Knightsbridge
chamber, and its "extremely interesting" Olde English dishes; critics,
though, complain of "dull" food and "silly" prices – the number
of reporters who feel "the weird 15th-century presentation idea is a
con" is on the rise. / SW1X 7LA; www.dinnerbyheston.com; 10.30 pm;
set weekday L £68 (FP).

Dip & Flip SW11 NEW £25 4️⃣3️⃣2️⃣

87 Battersea Rise no tel 10–2C
"The dirtiest burger in London" is hailed by fans of this new dude-
foodish Battersea café, where 'poutine' (cheesy Canadian fries) on the
menu just adds to the "supreme nastiness"; "good value" too.
/ SW11 1HW; www.dipandflip.co.uk; @DipFlippo; Mon-Sat 10 pm, Sun 9 pm;
no booking.

Dirty Bones W8 NEW £39

20 Kensington Church St 7920 6434 6–2B
This Kensington newcomer offers posh hot dogs by day, and by night
a carnivorous menu offering many "simple big flavours", plus "friendly
and relaxed" service and "good music" too; too few reports yet for
a rating, however. / W8 4EP; www.dirty-bones.com; @DirtyBonesLDN;
D only, closed Mon & Sun.

Dirty Burger £14 4 4 4
78 Highgate Rd, NW5   3310 2010   8–2B
Arch 54, 6 South Lambeth Rd, SW8   7074 1444   2–4D
"Dirty brilliance" – the award for "best burger-eating in a shack"
goes to these Kentish Town and Vauxhall phenomena, whose
"gorgeous, drippy burgers" and "fantastic crinkle-cut chips" are the
stuff of urban legend. / www.eatdirtyburger.com; NW5, Mon-Thu midnight,
Fri & Sat 1 am, Sun 11 pm – SW8 Mon-Thu 11 pm, Fri & Sat 2 am,
Sun 8 pm.

Dishoom £41 4 3 4
12 Upper St Martins Ln, WC2   7420 9320   4–3B
Stable St, Granary Sq, N1   7420 9321   8–3C NEW
7 Boundary St, E2   7420 9324   12–1B
"A real buzz" distinguishes these "cool" and "different" – and very
popular – Mumbai-style Parsi cafés, in Covent Garden and
Shoreditch; the food is surprisingly "genuine", and "delicately spiced"
too. / www.dishoom.com; @Dishoom; 11 pm, Sun 10 pm.

Diwana Bhel-Poori House NW1 £31 3 2 1
121-123 Drummond St   7387 5556   8–4C
"Been going since my distant student days… hasn't changed much!"
– critics may say it's "time for a makeover" of the "pine-panelled '70s
interior", but this "very cheap" Little India spot (near Euston) still has
many fans for its "first-rate veggie curries, dosas and breads".
/ NW1 2HL; 11.45 pm, Sun 11 pm; no Amex; need 10+ to book.

The Dock Kitchen
Portobello Dock W10 £58 3 4 5
344 Ladbroke Grove, Portobello Dock   8962 1610   1–2B
The "sublime post-industrial setting", next to a canal, is the high point
of a visit to Stevie Parle's popular venture in deepest Notting Hill;
as to the "eclectic" regular variation of cuisine? – fans love it,
but sceptics find the results "pleasant, but not particularly
interesting". / W10 5BU; www.dockkitchen.co.uk; @TheDockKitchen; 10 pm;
closed Sun D; set weekday L £39 (FP).

The Don EC4 £62 3 4 3
20 St Swithin's Ln   7626 2606   9–3C
"Always a safe bet for business!" – this "slick" fixture near Bank
(with "more atmospheric" basement bistro), remains one of the City's
top lunching spots, thanks to its "surprisingly good" cooking and
"interesting" wines (especially Kiwi and port). / EC4N 8AD;
www.thedonrestaurant.com; @thedonlondon; 10 pm; closed Sat & Sun;
no shorts.

don Fernando's TW9 £44 2 3 2
27f The Quadrant   8948 6447   1–4A
"If you're in Richmond and you need to refuel, look no further than
don Fernando's" – a "happily unchanged place", by the station,
serving "tasty tapas"; it's "a bit dated, but the staff make up for any
shortcomings". / TW9 1DN; www.donfernando.co.uk; 11 pm, Sun 10 pm;
no Amex; no booking.

Donna Margherita SW11 £43 4 3 3
183 Lavender Hill   7228 2660   10–2C
"Well worth quite a trip!" this "lovely" (and "seriously busy")
Battersea Neapolitan inspires 'rave' reports on its "marvellous" pizza,
and its "lively" spirit too. / SW11 5TE; www.donna-margherita.com;
@DMargheritaUK; 10.30 pm, Fri & Sat 11 pm; Mon-Thu D only, Fri-Sun open
L & D.

Donostia W1 £45 **5 4 4**
10 Seymour Pl 3620 1845 2–2A
"Take your taste buds to the very heart of San Sebastian", at this "authentic Basque tapas spot" near Marble Arch, which offers "perfectly executed morsels" and "amicable" service in an "intimate" and "classy" setting. / W1H 7ND; www.donostia.co.uk; @DonostiaW1; 11 pm; closed Mon L.

Dorchester Grill
Dorchester Hotel W1 £98 **2 3 1**
53 Park Ln 7629 8888 3–3A
Hardly anyone has a nice word to say about the "dreary" decor of this (inexplicably) "mock-Scottish" Mayfair grill room; it does make a "good-value lunch destination" but, by night, the food can seem rather "expensive" for what it is. / W1K 1QA; www.thedorchester.com; @TheDorchester; 10.15 pm, Sat 10.45 pm, Sun 10.15 pm; no trainers.

Dose EC1 £13 **4 4 2**
70 Long Ln 7600 0382 9–1B
"Simply fantastic coffee" and a "really good selection of cakes and pastries" earn high praise for this "well-run" Antipodean coffee shop in Smithfield; main problem? – it "could do with bigger premises". / EC1A 9EJ; www.dose-espresso.com; L only, closed Sun; no Amex.

Dotori N4 £28 **4 2 2**
3 Stroud Green Rd 7263 3562 8–1D
"In an unlikely location near Finsbury Park station", a "crowded and very hard to book" South East Asian, offering "superb" (mainly Korean) food; "they should take over the shop next door and make a bit of elbow room!" / N4 2DQ; www.dotorirestaurant.wix.com/dotorirestaurant; 10.30 pm; closed Mon; no Amex.

Dragon Castle SE17 £38 **3 1 1**
100 Walworth Rd 7277 3388 1–3C
"The best dim sum south of the river" has made quite a name for this "keenly priced" fixture, near Elephant & Castle; declining service standards, though, have contributed to a rather "soulless" feel of late. / SE17 1JL; www.dragon-castle.com; @Dragoncastle100; Mon-Sat 11 pm, Sun 10 pm.

Drakes Tabanco W1 **NEW** £45 **3 4 3**
3 Windmill St 7637 9388 2–1C
"Not so much granny's tipple as a whole world of new flavours!" – this Andalusian-inspired Fitzrovia tavern leads on its offer of "interesting sherries direct from the barrel", which is supported by some very decent tapas; the ambience can vary from "quiet" to "shouty". / W1T 2HY; www.drakestabanco.com; 10 pm.

The Drapers Arms N1 £48 **3 2 3**
44 Barnsbury St 7619 0348 8–3D
This "very Farrow & Ball" gastropub is something of an Islington linchpin, with a "great atmosphere", and food that's of "a continually high standard and variety"; it can get "too busy and noisy" at peak times. / N1 1ER; www.thedrapersarms.com; @DrapersArms; 10.30 pm; no Amex.

Dub Jam WC2 NEW £24 4 4 3
20 Bedford St 7836 5876 4–3C
*An "exciting" new Caribbean shack, serving up hot or smokey jerk
BBQ, and rum cocktails; it may be in Covent Garden, but the
"vibrant" decor is "straight off the beach!" / WC2E 9HP;
www.dubjam.co.uk; @dubjambbq; 10 pm.*

Duck & Waffle EC2 £68 2 2 5
110 Bishopsgate, Heron Tower 3640 7310 9–2D
*"Views to die for" and "one of the most interesting breakfast menus
in London" are twin-peak attractions of this 40th-floor City eyrie;
it's open 24/7, but – especially given the "stratospheric" prices –
the performance at other meals can seem "amateurish". / EC2N 4AY;
www.duckandwaffle.com; @DuckandWaffle; open 24 hours.*

Ducksoup W1 £53 2 2 3
41 Dean St 7287 4599 4–2A
*"It can be a bit full of meedjah luvvies", but this "cosy" and bohemian
Soho bistro is acclaimed for its "mix of small plates and quasi-tapas";
some dissenters, though, "just don't understand the hype". / W1D 4PY;
www.ducksoupsoho.co.uk; @ducksoup; 10.30 pm; closed Sun D; Mon-Tue
6+ to book, Wed-Sat 3+ to book.*

The Duke of Cambridge N1 £52 2 3 3
30 St Peter's St 7359 3066 1–2C
*Cooking that's "far above usual pub grub" has helped win a big
following for this Islington backstreet boozer; critics, though, do find
it "overpriced" – "very unspecial, and all in the name of 'Organic'!"
/ N1 8JT; www.dukeorganic.co.uk; @dukeorganic; 10.30 pm, Sun 10 pm;
no Amex.*

Duke of Sussex W4 £46 3 2 4
75 South Pde 8742 8801 7–1A
*"Delicious" food with a "Spanish slant" can come as something of a
surprise at this fine Victorian tavern on the Chiswick/Acton borders,
and it has a lovely garden too; "make sure you allow plenty of time,
though, as the service can be hit-and-miss". / W4 5LF;
www.metropolitanpubcompany.com; @thedukew4; 10.30 pm, Sun 9.30 pm.*

Duke's Brew & Que N1 £44 3 2 3
33 Downham Rd 3006 0795 1–2D
*"The ribs are the thing" ("other items can be hit-and-miss") at this
US-style Dalson barbecue; good beers too. / N1 5AA;
www.dukesbrewandque.com; @DukesJoint; 10.30 pm, Sun 9.30 pm.*

Durbar W2 £33 3 3 3
24 Hereford Rd 7727 1947 6–1B
*Established in Bayswater in 1956, a "reliable and popular Indian",
still hailed by loyal supporters as a "local gem". / W2 4AA;
www.durbartandoori.co.uk; 11.30 pm; closed Fri L.*

The Dysart Petersham TW10 £68 4 4 2
135 Petersham Rd 8940 8005 1–4A
*In a large Arts & Crafts house overlooking Richmond Common,
a year-old restaurant showcasing the skills of "genuinely talented"
chef, Kenneth Culhane; atmosphere can be elusive though,
and reports remain relatively few. / TW10 7AA; www.thedysartarms.co.uk;
9.30 pm; closed Sun D.*

E&O W11 £60 `3` `2` `3`

14 Blenheim Cr 7229 5454 6–1A

"Still does pan-Asian better than anyone else", claim fans, but it's difficult to avoid the conclusion that this "vibrant" Notting Hill celeb-magnet has "gone downhill" of late – service is a touch "aloof", and the food "not quite as exciting". / W11 1NN; www.rickerrestaurants.com; 11 pm, Sun 10.30 pm; booking: max 6.

The Eagle EC1 £33 `4` `3` `4`

159 Farringdon Rd 7837 1353 9–1A

"The original gastropub and still one of the best"; this "fun" Farringdon watering hole has held true to its "unpretentious" formula over many years, and still offers "well-seasoned, honest, seasonal, posh-peasant food, plus very reasonable wine". / EC1R 3AL; www.theeaglefarringdon.co.uk; @eaglefarringdon; 10.30 pm; closed Sun D; no Amex; no booking.

Earl Spencer SW18 £46 `3` `2` `3`

260-262 Merton Rd 8870 9244 10–2B

Next to a trafficky stretch of highway, this Wandsworth gastropub makes a handy pit stop, with "consistently high standards". / SW18 5JL; www.theearlspencer.co.uk; @TheEarlSpencer; 11 pm; Mon-Thu D only, Fri-Sun open L & D; no booking Sun.

East Street W1 NEW £36 `3` `3` `4`

3-5 Rathbone Pl 7323 0860 3–1C

"Be transported to the food markets of SE Asia!" – that's the shtick at this colourful and "interesting" diner-style operation, just north of Oxford Street; it certainly makes "an interesting alternative to Wagamama!" / W1T 1HJ; www.eaststreetrestaurant.com; @EastStreetEats; 11 pm, Sun 10 pm.

Eat £14 `2` `2` `2`

Branches throughout London

"They don't seem as well organised as Pret but the food seems healthier!" – especially when it comes to "the best soups", some reporters prefer this sandwich-and-snack chain to its better-known competitor. / www.eat.co.uk; 4 pm-8 pm; most City branches closed all or part of weekend; no credit cards; no booking.

Eat 17 E17 NEW £39 `3` `4` `5`

28-30 Orford Rd 8521 5279 1–1D

"Delicious British food and value for money, in a great and buzzy, if slightly chaotic, atmosphere" – the formula that's proved a hit for this "casual" Walthamstow operation, which now has an offshoot in Hackney. / E17 9NJ; www.eat17.co.uk.

Eat Tokyo £23 `4` `2` `2`

50 Red Lion St, WC1 7242 3490 2–1D
15 Whitcomb St, WC2 7930 6117 4–4B
169 King St, W6 8741 7916 7–2B
18 Hillgate St, W8 7792 9313 6–2B
14 North End Rd, NW11 8209 0079 1–1B

"Spankingly fresh sushi" at "very reasonable prices" wins a major thumbs-up for these busy Japanese outfits; service is "prompt"… but "more focussed on getting the job done than wooing customers!"

Ebury Restaurant & Wine Bar SW1   £53   2 2 3
139 Ebury St   7730 5447   2–4A
"You wouldn't go here for gastronomic fireworks", but this "stress-free" Belgravia old-timer offers "decent value", and is "hard to beat for a relaxing evening". / SW1W 9QU; www.eburyrestaurant.co.uk; 10.15 pm.

Eco SW4   £35   3 3 4
162 Clapham High St   7978 1108   10–2D
"Excellent pizzas" (other dishes "can be a bit hit-and-miss") win many fans for this perennially trendy Clapham fixture. / SW4 7UG; www.ecorestaurants.com; @ecopizzaLDN; 11 pm, Fri & Sat 11.30 pm.

Ed's Easy Diner   £32   1 2 3
12 Moor St, W1   7434 4439   4–2A
Trocadero, 19 Rupert St, W1   7287 1951   3–3D
Sedley Pl, 14 Woodstock St, W1   7493 9916   3–2B
Euston Station, NW1   7388 6967   8–3C
Southside Shopping Centre, SW18   8874 5634   10–2B
These Happy Days-style diners seem rather "formulaic" nowadays; they can still be "fun for all the family", but even some fans would concede that "the burgers can be bettered", and critics just say they're "ghastly". / www.edseasydiner.co.uk; Rupert St 10.30 pm, Fri & Sat 11.30 pm, Sun 10 pm; Moor St 11.30 pm, Thu-Sat midnight, Sun 10 pm, Sedley Place 9 pm, Thu-Sat 10 pm, NW1 Mon-Sat 10 pm, Sun 9 pm; Moor St no booking.

Edera W11   £61   3 4 3
148 Holland Park Ave   7221 6090   6–2A
"Very fine" Sardinian cooking makes it well worth checking out this upscale and "reliable" Holland Park fixture; not too often, though – "please change the menu!" / W11 4UE; www.atoz.co.uk; 11 pm, Sun 10 pm.

Edwins SE1 NEW   £48   3 3 4
202-206 Borough High St   7403 9913   9–4B
A small and "romantic" new Borough Market bistro, from a chef who formerly worked at the trendy Riding House Café; on some accounts, it's an "inventive" and "classy" sort of joint, but early-days feedback is far from unanimous. / SE1 1JX; www.edwinsborough.co.uk; @edwinsborough; 9.30 pm; closed Sun D.

Eelbrook SW6 NEW
Eel Brook Common, New King's Rd   3417 0287   10–1B
A new spot, by Eel Brook Common, with Brett Barnes (previously of Ducksoup, Arbutus, and Hix) in the kitchen; it focuses on small plates with British, European and North African ingredients. / SW6 4SE; @EelbrookTweets.

8 Hoxton Square N1 NEW   £49   3 3 2
8-9 Hoxton Sq   7729 4232   12–1B
"A brilliant follow-up to 10 Greek St"; the "simple" new Hoxton sibling to the Soho spot has "the same winning formula" – "well-designed and well-executed food", complemented by "fantastic, regularly changing wines". / N1 6NU; www.8hoxtonsquare.com; @8HoxtonSquare.

Eight Over Eight SW3 £57 3 3 3
392 King's Rd 7349 9934 5–3B
For "a fantastic evening with friends", Will Ricker's "buzzing and vibey" haunt, near World's End, remains a "fun" destination, offering "well-presented" Asian-fusion fare that's "always reliable". / SW3 5UZ; www.rickerrestaurants.com; 11 pm, Sun 10.30 pm.

Electric Diner W11 £43 2 4 4
191 Portobello Rd 7908 9696 6–1A
If you're looking for "a classic, cool and vibey destination" that epitomises Notting Hill, you won't do much better than this well-established brasserie; top tip – a "cracking" brunch. / W11 2ED; www.electricdiner.com; @ElectricDiner; 11 pm, Sun 10 pm.

Elena's L'Etoile W1 £53 1 1 1
30 Charlotte St 7636 7189 2–1C
In Fitzrovia, an "old-fashioned and very traditional French restaurant" (est 1896) serving "solid Gallic fare"; since Elena retired, "it's faded remarkably from its former glories" – "with a bit of effort, it could be so much better". / W1T 2NG; www.elenasletoile.co.uk; @elenasletoile; 10.30 pm; closed Sat L & Sun.

Elephant Royale
Locke's Wharf E14 £50 2 2 2
Westferry Rd 7987 7999 11–2C
Rather up-and-down reports of late on this riverside Thai (whose terrace offers stunning views of Greenwich); one thing is certain, though – "the fixed price lunch is much better value than the evening menu". / E14 3WA; www.elephantroyale.com; 10.30 pm, Fri & Sat 11 pm, Sun 10 pm; set weekday L £25 (FP), set Sun L £37 (FP).

Elliot's Café SE1 £52 4 3 3
12 Stoney St 7403 7436 9–4C
"Quite ambitious cooking" and "funky natural wines" ("you might need advice") have helped make a hit of this convivial "bare-brick" café, which "truly takes on the atmosphere of Borough Market". / SE1 9AD; www.elliotscafe.com; @elliotscafe; 9.30 pm; closed Sun; 8 max.

Ember Yard W1 NEW £51 3 3 3
60 Berwick St 7439 8057 3–1D
A Salt Yard spin-off which cooks over wood in an effort to differentiate itself from the tapas herd; results can be "interesting", but "edgy decor and friendly service don't make up for the feeling it's all been done better before… by the same people!" / W1F 8SU; www.emberyard.co.uk; @emberyard; SRA-2 stars.

Emile's SW15 £44 4 4 2
96-98 Felsham Rd 8789 3323 10–2B
"Hidden away from passing trade", in a "quiet Putney backwater", this "cosy" stalwart has long survived by "pleasing the locals" – highlights include the signature Beef Wellington, and some "superb" wines. / SW15 1DQ; www.emilesrestaurant.co.uk; 11 pm; D only, closed Sun; no Amex.

The Empress E9 £47 3 4 3
130 Lauriston Rd 8533 5123 1–2D
"Ticking all the boxes for a great local" – a "friendly" gastroboozer, near Victoria Park , which continues to impress with its all-round quality. / E9 7LH; www.empresse9.co.uk; @elliottlidstone; 10 pm, Sun 9.30 pm; closed Mon L; no Amex.

The Engineer NW1 £58 2 2 3
65 Gloucester Ave   7483 1890   8–3B
With its "lovely" terrace, this Primrose Hill gastropub is still a "little gem"; feedback is limited nowadays though – given its glamorous past, it's hard not to find the current performance rather plodding. / NW1 8JH; www.theengineerprimrosehill.co.uk; @TheEngineerPub; 10 pm.

Enoteca Turi SW15 £59 4 4 3
28 Putney High St   8785 4449   10–2B
"Always a bit under the radar, owing to its less than perfect location", Giuseppe and Pamela Turi's "very accomplished" and "welcoming" Putney Bridge-side stalwart dependably offers "first-class Italian regional cooking" plus "a massive selection of carefully chosen Italian wines". / SW15 1SQ; www.enotecaturi.com; @enoteca_turi; 10.30 pm, Fri & Sat 11 pm; closed Sun.

The Enterprise SW3 £58 2 3 3
35 Walton St   7584 3148   5–2C
The food may be perfectly "wholesome and tasty", but it's the the "club"-like ambience which makes this "buzzing" corner bistro a true Chelsea "classic". / SW3 2HU; www.theenterprise.co.uk; 10 pm, Sat 10.30 pm; no booking, except weekday L.

Entrée SW11 £58 4 4 3
2 Battersea Rise   7223 5147   10–2C
With its "interesting but not pretentious" food, this Battersea venture is a "local favourite that never fails to please"; NB: "under-advertised BYO Tuesdays are a bonus". / SW11 1ED; www.entreebattersea.co.uk; @entreebattersea; 10.30 pm; closed Mon, Tue L, Wed L, Thu L, Fri L, Sat D & Sun D; set weekday L £35 (FP), set Sun L £39 (FP).

Er Mei WC2 NEW £37 4 4 3
6 Lisle St   7734 8128   4–3A
"A great find"; there's "no compromise" on the "challenging" and "wonderfully spicy" cooking at this "proper" Sichuanese newcomer, on the former Chinatown site of the Empress of Sichuan (RIP); service is "not what you'd expect" – it's "completely charming"! / WC2H 7BG.

Ergon W1 £48 4 4 3
16 Picton Pl   8899 6595   3–1A
"Finally, some good Greek food in the West End..."; this "interesting" newcomer, near Selfridges, serves "contemporary" cooking in a "cool and informal setting" – "my Greek friends were as impressed as I was!" / W1U 1BP; www.ergonproducts.co.uk; @ErgonLondon.

Eriki NW3 £40 4 3 2
4-6 Northways Pde, Finchley Rd   7722 0606   8–2A
"Very decent Indian food in a less than inspiring ambience" – the appeal of this Swiss Cottage spot changes little from year to year; "as a carnivore, I decided to go veggie here... and I was not disappointed". / NW3 5EN; www.eriki.co.uk; 10.45 pm; closed Sat L.

Esarn Kheaw W12 £34 4 3 1
314 Uxbridge Rd   8743 8930   7–1B
"The most authentic north eastern Thai cooking" – "bursting with strong hearty flavours" – is served by an "ebullient" long-time proprietor, at this Shepherd's Bush "gem"; "don't be put off by the slightly down-at-heel feel!" / W12 7LJ; www.esarnkheaw.co.uk; @esarn_kheaw; 11 pm; closed Sat L & Sun L; no Amex.

L'Escargot W1 £60
48 Greek St   7439 7474   4–2A
*Under new ownership, this venerable Gallic classic, in the heart
of Soho, has been transformed into a temple of theatricality (or, if you
prefer, high camp); a full assessment will have to wait until next year's
survey. / W1D 4EF; lescargotrestaurant.co.uk; @EscargotLondon; 11.15 pm;
closed Sun D; set pre theatre £35 (FP).*

Essenza W11 £58   3 3 3
210 Kensington Park Rd   7792 1066   6–1A
*"Solid" and "friendly", this modest Notting Hill Italian never makes
many waves; its small fan club, though, say it's "a winner every time".
/ W11 1NR; www.essenza.co.uk; 11.30 pm; set weekday L £37 (FP).*

L'Etranger SW7 £71   3 4 2
36 Gloucester Rd   7584 1118   5–1B
*"Huge and comprehensive", the wine list at this "slightly anodyne"
South Kensington venture is "spectacular" (if "frankly overpriced")...
perhaps to the extent of eclipsing the Asian/French cuisine,
"imaginative" as it is. / SW7 4QT; www.etranger.co.uk; 11 pm,
Sun 10.30 pm; set weekday L £46 (FP).*

Everest Inn SE3 £35   4 4 4
41 Montpelier Vale   8852 7872   1–4D
*"Nepalese food with flair", "sweet service" and "low prices" come
together to create a winning combination at this "cosy" fixture, which
is "probably the best restaurant in Blackheath". / SE3 0TJ;
www.everestinn.co.uk; midnight, Sun 11 pm.*

Eyre Brothers EC2 £57   4 3 4
70 Leonard St   7613 5346   12–1B
*An "elegant, modern, dark-wood sanctuary", near Silicon Roundabout,
offering "clean and sophisticated" Hispanic cooking backed up by
a "recherché list of Iberian wines"; its popularity with the business
market long predates the 'emergence' of the area around it.
/ EC2A 4QX; www.eyrebrothers.co.uk; 10 pm; closed Sat L & Sun.*

Faanoos £27   3 2 4
472 Chiswick High Rd, W4   8994 4217   7–2A
481 Richmond Road, SW14   8878 5738   1–4A
*"Excellent flatbread cooked before your very eyes" is a highlight
of the "great Persian fare" on offer at this duo of "reasonably-priced"
local restaurants, in Chiswick. / SW14 11 pm; W4 11 pm; Fri & Sat
midnight.*

Fabrizio EC1 £53   4 4 2
30 Saint Cross St   7430 1503   9–1A
*A handy little haunt, near Hatton Garden, where Fabrizio himself
"is as charming as ever", and where the Sicilian dishes, using the
"freshest produce", are "always exceptional". / EC1N 8UH;
www.fabriziorestaurant.co.uk; 10 pm; closed Sat L & Sun.*

Fabrizio N19 £32   3 4 2
34 Highgate Hill   7561 9073   8–1C
*"A real gem on Highgate Hill"; this "wonderful neighbourhood
trattoria" serves up "delicious pasta and pizza", and "with a smile"
too; only downside? – it can prove "incredibly noisy". / N19 5NL;
www.fabriziolondon.co.uk; 10 pm.*

Fairuz W1 £50 4 3 3
3 Blandford St 7486 8108 2–1A
*"People say it's a hidden gem and they are right" – it may
be somewhat "cramped", but this Marylebone Lebanese is a
"very reliable" destination, and "reasonably priced" too.* / W1H 3DA;
www.fairuz.uk.com; 11 pm, Sun 10.30 pm; set weekday L £30 (FP).

La Famiglia SW10 £62 2 2 2
7 Langton St 7351 0761 5–3B
*This perennially fashionable '60s trattoria, at World's End, is a real
"golden oldie", say fans – "just how an Italian ought to be"; those
who look at the telescope from the other end, however, may perceive
a "dinosaur" that's "subsiding into expensive mediocrity".* / SW10 0JL;
www.lafamiglia.co.uk; 11.45 pm.

Fat Boy's £35 2 3 3
10a-10b Edensor Rd, W4 8994 8089 10–1A
33 Haven Grn, W5 8998 5868 1–2A
201 Upper Richmond Rd, SW14 8876 0644 1–4A
431 Richmond Rd, TW1 8892 7657 1–4A
68 High St, TW8 8569 8481 1–3A
*"Charming" staff serve "straightforward but fresh" Thai dishes
at these "reliable" neighbourhood cafés; a "great-value set lunch" is a
highlight.* / www.fatboysthai.co.uk; 11 pm.

Faulkner's E8 £30 4 3 2
424-426 Kingsland Rd 7254 6152 1–1D
*An old-school chippy that has remained impervious to Dalston's
trendification; all reports agree, though, that it still knocks out "great"
fish and chips.* / E8 4AA; 10 pm, Fri-Sun 11 pm; no Amex; need 8+ to book.

The Fellow N1 £46 3 3 3
24 York Way 7833 4395 8–3C
*"In an upcoming area handy for King's Cross and St Pancras",
a gastropub that offers an "interesting and varied" menu (including
"excellent skin-on chips"); the roof terrace is an unexpected boon
in summer months.* / N1 9AA; www.thefellow.co.uk; @24yorkway; 9.45 pm.

Fera at Claridge's
Claridge's Hotel W1 NEW £141 4 5 5
55 Brook St 7107 8888 3–2B
*"Hats off" to Simon Rogan, for the relaunch of this landmark
Mayfair Art Deco chamber, where "gloriously attentive" service only
adds to the enjoyment of the "phenomenal" meals – up to
17 courses that are "so different" (and, for those who so opt,
come with some "exceptionally well-matched wines").* / W1K 4HR;
www.claridges.co.uk/fera.

Fernandez & Wells £34 3 2 4
16a, St Anne's Ct, W1 7494 4242 3–1D
43 Lexington St, W1 7734 1546 3–2D
73 Beak St, W1 7287 8124 3–2D
Somerset Hs, Strand, WC2 7420 9408 2–2D
*A "faintly chaotic" small chain, which offers "delicious bits and bobs",
as well as "decent-value wines" and excellent coffee; the "magical"
Somerset House location, with its high-ceilinged setting, is perhaps the
one most actively worth seeking out.* / www.fernandezandwells.com;
Lexington St & St Anne's court 10 pm; Beak St 6 pm, Somerset House 11 pm;
St Anne's Court closed Sun.

Fez Mangal W11 £22 **5 4 3**
104 Ladbroke Grove 7229 3010 6–1A
It may be "more of a take-away", but you can still have a "fantastic" time at this "very popular" Turkish grill in Notting Hill, where the menu – with "absolutely fresh grilled lamb" a highlight – offers "exceptional value"; BYO. / W11 1PY; www.fezmangal.co.uk; 11.30 pm; no Amex.

Ffiona's W8 £54 **2 3 3**
51 Kensington Church St 7937 4152 5–1A
"I went for brunch, and wanted to stay to dinner too!" – Ffiona's quirky dinner-party-style Kensington bistro seems especially popular for Sunday brunch nowadays, but her "home-cooking" can go down well at any time. / W8 4BA; www.ffionas.com; @ffionasnotes; 11 pm, Sun 10 pm; closed Mon; no Amex.

Fifteen N1 £61 **1 1 1**
15 Westland Pl 3375 1515 12–1A
"You pay for the celeb associations, rather than the calibre of the cooking", at this "seriously overpriced" and "ordinary" Hoxton trattoria – it "trades on Jamie Oliver's name alone". / N1 7LP; www.fifteen.net; @JamiesFifteen; 10 pm; booking: max 12.

The Fifth Floor Restaurant
Harvey Nichols SW1 £62 **3 3 3**
109-125 Knightsbridge 7235 5250 5–1D
Still vanishingly few comments on the top-floor dining room at this famous Knightsbridge department store which, in its '90s heyday, was the talk of the town; no serious complaints though, and the occasional fan insists the cooking is "top-class". / SW1X 7RJ; www.harveynichols.com; 10.45 pm; closed Sun D; SRA-2 stars.

La Figa E14 £41 **3 3 3**
45 Narrow St 7790 0077 11–1B
"A lovely Limehouse Italian", serving up "enormous portions" – all part of what fans say is its "excellent value for money". / E14 8DN; www.lafigarestaurant.co.uk; 11 pm, Sun 10.30 pm.

Fino W1 £53 **4 4 4**
33 Charlotte St 7813 8010 2–1C
An "airy" basement provides a surprisingly "atmospheric" setting for the Hart brothers' Fitzrovia favourite; the appeal is very straightforward – "top-notch" tapas and a splendid selection of wines and sherries. / W1T 1RR; www.finorestaurant.com; 10.30 pm; closed Sat L & Sun; booking: max 12; SRA-1 star.

Fire & Stone £42 **2 2 2**
31-32 Maiden Ln, WC2 0844 371 2550 4–3D
Westfield, Ariel Way, W12 0844 371 2551 7–1C
"If you fancy a curry or roast on your pizza", this "smart" chain – with its "unique toppings" – is the place to start; rather too often, however, it's a case of "high expectations, but low delivery". / www.fireandstone.com; WC2 11 pm; W12 11.15 pm; E1 11pm, Sun 8 pm.

First Floor W11 £47 **3 2 5**
186 Portobello Rd 7243 0072 6–1A
A "beautiful" upper-floor high-ceilinged dining room makes this Portobello fixture a top spot for a special night out; the food "never fails to please", either (particularly the "very good-value fixed menu"). / W11 1LA; www.firstfloorportobello.co.uk; 10.30 pm; set Sun L £38 (FP).

Fischer's W1 NEW   £58   2 3 3
50 Marylebone High St   7466 5501   2–1A
*Corbin & King's debuts are often surprisingly shaky, and their new
"Austrian-themed café", in Marylebone, is no exception; to fans,
its "interesting" menu (and, of course, yummy Viennoiserie) helps
make it "a joy"; for critics, though, the whole show is just too "fake".
/ W1U 5HN; www.fischers.co.uk; @fischers.*

The Fish & Chip Shop N1   £44   4 4 4
189 Upper St   3227 0979   8–2D
*"Thriving, and deservedly so", this "posh" but "jolly" chippy has been
"a very welcome addition to Islington", though even fans can find
it "expensive"; as this guide goes to press, we hear a new branch is to
open in the City. / N1 1RQ; www.thefishandchipshop.uk.com;
@TheFishChipShop; 11 pm, Sun 10 pm; SRA-1 star.*

Fish Central EC1   £30   3 3 2
149-155 Central St   7253 4970   12–1A
*"Unbelievably fresh fish at reasonable prices" keeps the customers
happy at this "fab" and "buzzy" chippy, 'twixt Old Street and
Islington; – "a great choice for those visiting the Barbican". / EC1V 8AP;
www.fishcentral.co.uk; 10.30 pm, Fri & Sat 11 pm; closed Sun.*

Fish Club   £39   4 4 2
189 St John's Hill, SW11   7978 7115   10–2C
57 Clapham High St, SW4   7720 5853   10–2D
*"Really exciting" dishes impress all who report on these "trusty" south
London chippies – "it's all in the quality of the sourcing".
/ www.thefishclub.com; 10 pm; closed Mon L; no bookings.*

Fish in a Tie SW11   £37   3 4 4
105 Falcon Rd   7924 1913   10–1C
*"Mad crazy-busy on a Friday night" – this "fun" and "very friendly"
bistro, behind Clapham Junction, offers inexpensive "Mediterranean-
inspired" fare that's "consistently good", and which comes "at very
reasonable prices". / SW11 2PF; www.fishinatie.co.uk; midnight, Sun 11 pm;
no Amex.*

Fish Market EC2   £53   3 4 3
16B New St   3503 0790   9–2D
*"Very near, but seeming far from the bustle of Bishopsgate" –
this "relaxed" operation, in an "interesting" converted warehouse,
deserves to be better known for its "well-prepared fish dishes" and its
"super staff". / EC2M 4TR; www.fishmarket-restaurant.co.uk;
@FishMarketNS; 10.30 pm; closed Sun; SRA-3 stars.*

fish! SE1   £57   2 2 2
Cathedral St   7407 3803   9–4C
*On a good day, you find "plain" fish dishes of "good quality" in this
"noisy" and "crowded" glazed shed, by Borough Market;
some visitors, though, find standards "very average all-round", and at
prices which can seem "ridiculous". / SE1 9AL; www.fishkitchen.com;
@fishborough; 10.45 pm, Sun 10.30 pm.*

Fishworks   £51   3 2 2
7-9 Swallow St, W1   7734 5813   3–3D
89 Marylebone High St, W1   7935 9796   2–1A
*"Fresh fish simply but expertly prepared" – that's really the whole
story at these "predictable" bistros; neither service nor ambience,
though, is anything to write home about. / www.fishworks.co.uk;
10.30 pm.*

Fitou's Thai Restaurant W10 £26 `4` `3` `2`
1 Dalgarno Gdns 8968 0558 6–1A
*"A great-value BYO Thai", by Little Wormwood Scrubs, offering food
that's "good and fresh". / W10 5LL; www.fitourestaurant.co.uk; 10.30 pm;
closed Sun L.*

The Five Fields SW3 £74 `5` `5` `4`
8-9 Blacklands Ter 7838 1082 5–2D
*"A gem in the heart of Chelsea"; this "brilliant" yearling is a
formidable all-rounder, combining "sensational" and "clever" cooking
with a "stunning and intimate" interior, plus service that "perfectly
balances formality with being welcoming". / SW3 2SP;
www.fivefieldsrestaurant.com; @The5Fields; 10 pm; D only, closed Mon & Sun.*

Five Guys WC2 £13 `3` `2` `2`
1-3 Long Acre 0833 005 4–3C
*"You need two hands, and three Hail Marys", say fans, to handle one
of the "proper, sloppy burgers" at these "very American" joints,
now in Islington as well as Covent Garden; overall, though, reporters
aren't quite convinced that the transition over the Pond has been
totally successful. / WC2E 9LH; www.fiveguys.co.uk.*

500 N19 £44 `3` `4` `2`
782 Holloway Rd 7272 3406 8–1C
*A "poky" but "personal" Archway Sicilian, where the cooking
is "unusual", "generous" and "good value"; some customers, though,
do find enjoyment limited by the "cramped and noisy" premises.
/ N19 3JH; www.500restaurant.co.uk; @500restaurant; 10.30 pm,
Sun 9.30 pm; Mon-Thu D only, Fri-Sun open L & D.*

Flat Iron £22 `4` `5` `4`
17 Beak St, W1 no tel 3–2D
9 Denmark St, WC2 no tel 4–1A **NEW**
*"The best value-for-money steak and chips" make these trendy "no-
frills" diners, in Soho and by Centrepoint "a perfect example of doing
one simple thing well"; they're "cramped" mind, and there's "always
a big queue, so get there early".*

Flat White W1 £11 `4` `4` `4`
17 Berwick St 7734 0370 3–2D
*"Great flat whites every time", plus a few choice snacks, keep 'em
packing in to this "lovely little boutique coffee joint", in Soho.
/ W1F 0PT; www.flat-white.co.uk; L only; no credit cards; no booking.*

Fleet River Bakery WC2 £20 `3` `2` `3`
71 Lincolns Inn Fields 7691 1457 2–1D
*Tucked away in Holborn, a "very busy" café that offers "unusual
breakfast choices", "delicious sandwiches" and excellent Monmouth
Coffee... but where service can sometimes be "infuriatingly slow".
/ WC2A 3JF; www.fleetriverbakery.com; @Fleetriver; 5 pm, Sat 3 pm; L only,
closed Sun.*

Flesh and Buns WC2 £50 `3` `2` `2`
41 Earlham St 7632 9500 4–2C
*"Plates of steamed buns with delicious fillings, and lots of little nibbles
such as sushi" offer some "good Asian flavours" at this "industrial-
style" Covent Garden basement yearling – a sibling to Bone Daddies;
at the peak, though, the atmosphere can be "mad". / WC2H 9LX;
www.fleshandbuns.com; @FleshandBuns; Mon-Tue 10.30 pm, Wed-Sat
9.30 pm, Sun 9.30 pm.*

Food for Thought WC2　　　　　£23　　4 4 2
31 Neal St　7836 0239　4–2C
"Cramped" but adored – this rambling Covent Garden basement has long offered "some of the best vegetarian food in town" at "good-value" prices; BYO. / WC2H 9PR; www.foodforthought-london.co.uk; 8 pm, Sun 5 pm; closed Sun D; no credit cards; no booking.

Forman's E3　　　　　　　£54　　4 3 3
Stour Rd, Fish Island　8525 2365　1–1D
It's not just the "lovely view of the Olympic Stadium" which make it worth a trip to this dining room inside the East End's famous producer of 'London-smoke' salmon – the food is relatively simple, but "top-notch". / E3 2NT; www.formans.co.uk/restaurant; @formanslondon; 9 pm; Closed Mon-Wed, Thu & Fri D only, Sat open L & D, closed Sun D.

(The Fountain)
Fortnum & Mason W1　　　　£61　　2 3 2
181 Piccadilly　7734 8040　3–3D
"Ideal for aunts, grannies or godchildren" – the buttery of HM's grocer remains "a nice spot for a traditional British experience"; highlights include "first-class" breakfasts, "excellent" afternoon teas and "legendary" knickerbocker glories. / W1A 1ER; www.fortnumandmason.com; @fortnumandmason; 7.45 pm; closed Sun D; Smart / formal dresswear.

(1707)
Fortnum & Mason W1　　　　£46　　3 4 3
181 Piccadilly　7734 8040　3–3D
"Take the wine flight", if you visit the famous grocer's basement wine bar, where you can "sample a huge variety of very good wines" – their whole list is available, plus £10 corkage; the tapas-style platters also make it a decent "snack lunch" option. / W1A 1ER; www.fortnumandmason.co.uk; @fortnumandmason; 8 pm, Sun 6 pm; closed Sun D.

(The Diamond Jubilee Tea Salon)
Fortnum & Mason W1　　　　£56　　3 5 5
181 Piccadilly　7734 8040　3–3D
"A totally extravagant experience, especially if you go for the champagne version" – afternoon tea at Fortnum's most recently-opened dining room is an "extremely restful" experience, "with a piano tinkling in the background", and one which usually satisfies all-round. / W1A 1ER; www.fortnumandmason.com; @fortnumandmason; 7 pm, Sun 6 pm; Deposit for 11+.

40 Maltby Street SE1　　　　£41　　4 4 4
40 Maltby St　7237 9247　9–4D
This "under-the-arches foodie destination" – in the 'new' Borough Market – offers a "most interesting selection of bio and small producer wines", complemented by "outstanding" small-plate dishes; "get there early as it's full by 8 pm". / SE1 3PA; www.40maltbystreet.com; @40maltbystreet; 9.30 pm; closed Mon, Tue, Wed L, Thu L, Sat D & Sun; no Amex; no bookings.

Four Regions TW9　　　　　£44　　3 3 2
102-104 Kew Rd　8940 9044　1–4A
The definition of a "good local", this "friendly" and "efficient" Richmond Chinese "never disappoints", thanks not least to its "consistently good" cooking; lunch and pre-theatre menus come especially recommended. / TW9 2PQ; www.fourregions.co.uk; @fourregions; 11.30 pm, Sun 11 pm.

The Four Seasons £32 **4 1 1**
12 Gerrard St, W1   7494 0870   4–3A
23 Wardour St, W1   7287 9995   4–3A
84 Queensway, W2   7229 4320   6–2C
"Unbelievable" roast duck is the special attraction of these "down-at-heel" diners in Bayswater and Chinatown; "curt service and a complete lack of ambience" are all part of the package. / www.fs-restaurants.co.uk; Queensway 11 pm, Sun 10h45 pm; Gerrard St 1 am; Wardour St 1am, Fri-Sat 3.30 am.

Fox & Grapes SW19 £55 **2 2 2**
9 Camp Rd   8619 1300   10–2A
Most reporters like this "lovely fresh and vibrant local restaurant", in a large former boozer, right by Wimbledon Common; there are still quite a few doubters, though, for whom this is a "slightly oddball" place that's "expensive for what it is". / SW19 4UN; www.foxandgrapeswimbledon.co.uk; 9.30 pm, Sun 8.15 pm; no Amex.

The Fox & Hounds SW11 £47 **4 4 4**
66 Latchmere Rd   7924 5483   10–1C
A Battersea gastroboozer "belonging to the team that operate the Atlas... and it shows!"; indeed, such is the quality of its "sympathetic interpretations of Mediterranean classics" that "it's getting harder and harder just to drop in and grab a table". / SW11 2JU; www.thefoxandhoundspub.co.uk; @thefoxbattersea; 10 pm; Mon-Thu D only, Fri-Sun open L & D.

The Fox and Anchor EC1 £49 **3 3 5**
115 Charterhouse St   7250 1300   9–1B
"When you've had enough of east London trendiness", head for this "legendary" Clerkenwell pub, where "simple" British food is cooked with "lightness of touch" in perfect "olde worlde" splendour; breakfast with a pint is an institution. / EC1M 6AA; www.foxandanchor.com; @MeetMeAtTheFox; 11 pm.

Foxlow EC1 £49 **3 3 3**
St John St   7014 8070   9–2A
"Hawksmoor-lite"; this "democratic" Clerkenwell spin-off from the famous group is extolled by fans for its "really chilled" style and "impossibly tender" meat; critics do say it "lacks a certain zing", though, and can find it "a bit expensive" too. / EC1M 4AN; www.foxlow.co.uk; @Foxlow(EC1); SRA-3 stars.

Foxtrot Oscar SW3 £55 **2 2 2**
79 Royal Hospital Rd   7352 4448   5–3D
Oddly divided views on Gordon Ramsay's tenure at this age-old Chelsea bolthole, a few doors from his flagship; fans say it's a "friendly" place serving "classy" fare – there are almost as many critics, though, for whom this is "just a poorly run local bistro, charging top prices". / SW3 4HN; www.gordonramsay.com/foxtrotoscar; @foxtrot_oscar; 10 pm, Sun 9 pm.

Franco Manca £22 **4** **3** **3**
144 Chiswick High Rd, W4 8747 4822 7–2A
76 Northcote Rd, SW11 7924 3110 10–2D
53 Bedford Hill, SW12 8772 0489 10–2C **NEW**
Unit 4 Market Row, SW9 7738 3021 10–2D
Westfield Stratford, E20 8522 6669 1–1D
"Outstanding" sourdough crusts (an "ideal combo between chewy
and crispy") and "keen" prices win many supporters for this
mushrooming Neapolitan chain; in a quest for "unbelievably good"
pizza, however, there's still no substitute for a visit to the the
"carefree" Brixton original. / www.francomanca.co.uk; SW9 10.30,
Mon 5 pm; W4 11 pm; E20 9 pm, Thu-Sat 10 pm, Sun 6 pm;
SW9 no bookings.

Franco's SW1 £74 **3** **4** **3**
61 Jermyn St 7499 2211 3–3C
"Good enough, without being spectacular"; this "efficient" St James's
Italian certainly has a handy location, especially for business, and it
rarely positively disappoints; it can can seem rather "crowded",
though, and prices are "high". / SW1Y 6LX; www.francoslondon.com;
10.30 pm; closed Sun; set pre-theatre £39 (FP), set weekday L £46 (FP).

Franklins SE22 £49 **3** **3** **3**
157 Lordship Ln 8299 9598 1–4D
"Assuredly good comfort cooking" continues to win plaudits for this
"lovely East Dulwich local" – a converted pub, where there are
"always new dishes on the notably seasonal menu". / SE22 8HX;
www.franklinsrestaurant.com; @frankinsse22; 10.30 pm; no Amex.

Frantoio SW10 £56 **2** **2** **3**
397 King's Rd 7352 4146 5–3B
"A fun spot where the food is OK, but not the point" – that's the
traditional view on this World's End Italian; it suffered from a couple
of very 'down' reports though this year, and a feeling it's "lost its vim".
/ SW10 0LR; 11.15 pm, Sun 10.15 pm; set weekday L £36 (FP).

Frederick's N1 £62 **2** **3** **4**
106 Islington High St 7359 2888 8–3D
A surprisingly grand and spacious, and rather "pricey", Islington old-
timer, which is a "lovely place to eat", especially if you nab a seat
in the conservatory or garden; the rather "samey" cuisine, though,
"has not really kept up with the times". / N1 8EG; www.fredericks.co.uk;
11 pm; closed Sun; set weekday L & dinner £36 (FP).

La Fromagerie Café W1 £39 **3** **2** **4**
2-6 Moxon St 7935 0341 3–1A
"Unusual, beautifully prepared, fresh and simple" dishes and
"fabulous coffee" are to be had at this "relaxed" café, adjacent
to Marylebone's famous cheese shop – a "great place for brunch",
in particular. / W1U 4EW; www.lafromagerie.co.uk; @lafromagerieuk;
6.30 pm, Sat 6 pm, Sun 5 pm; L only; no booking.

The Frontline Club W2 £58 **3** **3** **3**
13 Norfolk Pl 7479 8960 6–1D
"Interesting photos" and "affordable, honest food" (plus, to be
perfectly frank, a "lack of nearby competition") combine to make this
comfy dining room – part of a war reporters' club –
"the best restaurant near Paddington". / W2 1QJ; www.frontlineclub.com;
10.30 pm; closed Sat L & Sun.

Fujiyama SW9 £28 **4** **3** **2**
5-7 Vining St 7737 2369 10–2D
A "buzzy" Brixton canteen serving "excellent sushi (including
selection/sharing plates) and decent Katsu and tempura"; "quick"
service too. / SW9 8QA; www.newfujiyama.com; 11 pm.

Fulham Wine Rooms SW6 £52 **2** **3** **4**
871-873 Fulham Rd 7042 9440 10–1B
"The perfect place to entertain all wine buffs!" – a lively bar, offering
a "very large assortment" of wines by the glass; the food is "probably
of secondary interest". / SW6 5HP; www.greatwinesbytheglass.com;
@winerooms; 11 pm; closed weekday L.

Fuzzy's Grub £14 **3** **2** **2**
6 Crown Pas, SW1 7925 2791 3–4D
15 Basinghall St, EC2 7726 6771 9–2C
58 Houdsditch, EC3 7929 1400 9–2D
10 Well Ct, EC4 7236 8400 9–2B
62 Fleet St, EC4 7583 6060 9–2A
"Roast in a bap – awesome!"; these British-themed diners are
best known for their huge sarnies stuffed with roast meats.
/ www.fuzzysgrub.co.uk; most branches between 3 pm and 5 pm; closed
Sat & Sun; no Amex; no booking.

Gaby's WC2 £35 **3** **3** **2**
30 Charing Cross Rd 7836 4233 4–3B
"Still defying the developers" – this '60s "time warp", by Leicester
Square tube, is a Theatreland "institution", thanks to its "super salt
beef", "top falafel" and "amazing latkes", and "Gaby himself
brightens up the dingy, claustrophobic space". / WC2H 0DE; midnight,
Sun 10 pm; no Amex.

Gail's Bread £27 **3** **3** **4**
Branches throughout London
"For a pastry and to rest your feet", these "buzzy and friendly" cafés
make an excellent standby. / www.gailsbread.co.uk; W11 & WC1 7 pm;
NW3 & NW6 8 pm, W1 10 pm, SW7 9 pm, Sun 8 pm; no booking.

Gallery Mess
Saatchi Gallery SW3 £52 **2** **2** **2**
Duke of Yorks HQ, Kings Rd 7730 8135 5–2D
"For a break from shopping" ("or an agreeable venue to talk
business)", this "stylish attachment" to the gallery near Sloane
Square is a "buzzy" sort of place with very pretty views; sadly,
though, neither food nor service rises to the location. / SW3 4RY;
www.saatchigallery.com/gallerymess; @gallerymess; 9.30 pm, Sun 6 pm; closed
Sun D; set dinner £34 (FP).

Gallipoli £36 **3** **4** **3**
102 Upper St, N1 7359 0630 8–3D
107 Upper St, N1 7226 5333 8–3D
120 Upper St, N1 7226 8099 8–3D
They may look "cramped" and slightly "clapped out", but these
"retro" Turkish bistros, in Islington, offer "deliciously filling" mezze
at "bargain" prices, in a "cheerful" and "friendly" setting.
/ www.cafegallipoli.com; 11 pm, Fri & Sat midnight.

Galvin at Windows
Park Lane London Hilton Hotel W1   £99   2 3 5
22 Park Ln   7208 4021   3–4A
"Keen to impress foreign visitors" (or a date)? – head for this Mayfair
chamber, where the panorama from the 28th floor includes
"stunning" view over Buckingham Palace and its gardens; you need
a "large wallet", though, and the food is much less memorable than
the view. / W1K 1BE; www.galvinatwindows.com; @GalvinatWindows; 10 pm,
Sat & Sun 10.30 pm; closed Sat L & Sun D; no shorts; set weekday L £56 (FP).

Galvin Bistrot de Luxe W1   £65   3 4 4
66 Baker St   7935 4007   2–1A
With its "unpretentiously professional" service and "staunchly
traditional" styling, the Galvin brothers' original Gallic bistro,
in Marylebone, remains many reporters' favourite; the "classy"
cuisine, though, has sometimes seemed to be "resting on its laurels"
of late. / W1U 7DJ; www.galvinrestaurants.com; @galvin_brothers; Mon-Wed
10.30 pm, Thu-Sat 10.45 pm, Sun 9.30 pm; set weekday L £37 (FP), set
dinner £39 (FP).

GALVIN LA CHAPELLE E1   £74   4 4 5
35 Spital Sq   7299 0400   12–2B
"A simply spectacular experience"; the Galvin brothers' "superlative"
venture occupies a "stunning" cathedral-like Spitalfields hall;
its "superb" Gallic dishes and "smooth" service make it a splendid
choice for a business or romantic occasion. / E1 6DY;
www.galvinrestaurants.com; 10.30 pm, Sun 9.30 pm; set weekday L, dinner &
Sun L £48 (FP).

Ganapati SE15   £43   5 4 4
38 Holly Grove   7277 2928   1–4C
"Exquisite Keralan food" at "great-value" prices again inspires
ecstatic reports on this "tiny and basic" neighbourhood "diamond"
in "an unlikely corner of Peckham"; it's "rather cramped", but "always
fun". / SE15 5DF; www.ganapatirestaurant.com; 10.30 pm, Sun 10 pm; closed
Mon; no Amex.

Garnier SW5   £56   3 4 2
314 Earl's Court Rd   7370 4536   5–2A
The Garnier brothers' "classic" Gallic yearling, in Earl's Court, offers
bourgeois cooking "of a generally high standard", and "fairly priced"
wines too; the decor is "very boring", though, and "being on a busy
road doesn't boost the ambience". / SW5 9BQ; www.garnierestaurant.com;
Mon-Sat 10.30 pm, Sun 10 pm; set weekday L £43 (FP).

Le Garrick WC2   £42   2 2 3
10-12 Garrick St   7240 7649   4–3C
A veteran Covent Garden wine bar, offering "authentic" French
staples at "quite sensible prices", which fans proclaim a "fabulous
oasis"... but "it's the atmosphere downstairs, especially when there
is live music, that sets the place apart". / WC2E 9BH;
www.frenchrestaurantlondon.co.uk; @le_garrick; 10.30 pm; closed Sun.

Garrison SE1   £48   3 3 3
99-101 Bermondsey St   7089 9355   9–4D
A "charming" Bermondsey corner boozer that's "a bit cramped,
but has a buzz about it" – for anything "from a great breakfast to an
evening meal", it rarely fails to hit the spot. / SE1 3XB;
www.thegarrison.co.uk; @TheGarrisonSE1; 10 pm, Fri & Sat 10.30 pm,
Sun 9.30 pm.

Gastro SW4 £43 2 1 5
67 Venn St 7627 0222 10–2D
"Toujours français!" – it may offer a rather "limited" menu, but this notably "pleasant" bistro, by the Clapham Picture House, is "a great choice for a quick bite" (or breakfast); nice al fresco tables too.
/ SW4 0BD; midnight; no Amex.

The Gate £44 3 2 2
51 Queen Caroline St, W6 8748 6932 7–2C
370 St John St, EC1 7278 5483 8–3D
"Serious, thoughtful and imaginative" veggie cooking has carved out a big name for this Hammersmith fixture, and its newer sibling near Sadler's Wells; they've lost their mojo a bit in recent years, though, and W6 seems more "densely packed" and "café-like" since its recent refurbishment. / www.thegaterestaurants.com; @gaterestaurant; EC1 10.30 pm, W6 10.30, Sat 11 pm.

Gaucho £72 2 1 1
25 Swallow St, W1 7734 4040 3–3D
60a, Charlotte St, W1 7580 6252 2–1C
89 Sloane Ave, SW3 7584 9901 5–2C
Tooley St, SE1 7407 5222 9–4D
93a Charterhouse St, EC1 7490 1676 9–1B
"Did they fly the meat in from Argentina on a private jet?" – this "opulent" and business-friendly chain offers "beautiful" steaks and a "fabulously diverse Argentinian wine list", but its "exploitative" prices are becoming a major turn-off for some reporters. / www.gaucho-restaurants.co.uk; 11 pm, Fri & Sat 11.30 pm, SE10, Piccadilly midnight, Sun 11 pm; EC3 & EC1 closed Sat & Sun; WC2 & EC2 closed Sat L & Sun.

Gauthier Soho W1 £63 5 5 4
21 Romilly St 7494 3111 4–3A
Ring the bell for entry to Alexis Gauthier's "wonderfully quirky" Soho townhouse – a perfect venue "for a luxurious date"; the "dreamy" Gallic cuisine (with much emphasis on vegetables) and "impeccable" service are far from secondary attractions, however, and the "superb" wine list includes "some real curiosities". / W1D 5AF; www.gauthiersoho.co.uk; 10.30 pm; closed Mon L & Sun; set weekday L £46 (FP).

LE GAVROCHE W1 £136 5 5 5
43 Upper Brook St 7408 0881 3–2A
"Steeped in classic Gallic tradition", this "formal" Mayfair basement is "immune from trends and fashion", and – with Michel Roux Jr often very much in evidence – "unsurpassed" for those looking for a "majestic" old-school meal; "the bill makes you cry", though, so "book months ahead for the fantastic lunch deal". / W1K 7QR; www.le-gavroche.co.uk; @legavroche_; 10 pm; closed Sat L & Sun; jacket required; set weekday L £86 (FP).

Gay Hussar W1 £48 2 3 4
2 Greek St 7437 0973 4–2A
This Soho "stalwart" (famed for its socialist-intelligentsia associations) is an "unchanging" and "comforting" favourite for fans of its "hearty" middle European cooking; some reporters, though, are less starry-eyed – "it may be an icon, but it's mediocre and cramped". / W1D 4NB; www.gayhussar.co.uk; 10.45 pm; closed Sun; set pre theatre £33 (FP).

Gaylord W1 £56 **3** **3** **2**
79-81 Mortimer St   7580 3615   2–1B
*"Delicious" food ("if a little pricey and rather creamy") still wins
a following for this "bizarrely old-fashioned" grand subcontinental,
just north of Oxford Street; critics, though, find it "unmemorable,
given the prices". / W1W 7SJ; www.gaylordlondon.com; 10.45 pm,
Sun 10.30 pm.*

Gazette £39 **2** **2** **4**
79 Sherwood Ct, Chatfield Rd, SW11   7223 0999   10–1C
100 Balham High St, SW12   8772 1232   10–2C
147 Upper Richmond Rd, SW15   8789 6996   10–2B **NEW**
*Despite sometimes "pedestrian" cooking and service "infused with
Gallic indifference", this small chain generally wins praise for its
"classic bistro style" and affordable prices; they must be doing
something right, as a new branch has just opened, in Putney.
/ www.gazettebrasserie.co.uk; 11 pm.*

GB Pizza EC1 £29 **4** **4** **3**
50 Exmouth Mkt   7278 6252   9–1A
*"Delicious thin and crispy pizza in a pared-down setting and at very
good-value prices" – this new Farringdon pizzeria (which has
an acclaimed Margate sibling) gets an instant thumbs-up from
reporters. / EC1R 4QD; www.greatbritishpizzacompany.wordpress.com.*

Geales £48 **2** **1** **2**
1 Cale St, SW3   7965 0555   5–2C
2 Farmer St, W8   7727 7528   6–2B
*Of this duo of posh chippys, it's the Notting Hill original which is more
often praised for "properly cooked" (if "not cheap") fresh fish than
the Chelsea offshoot; service impresses at neither branch.
/ www.geales.com; @geales1; 10.30 pm, Sun 9.30 pm; Mon L.*

Gelupo W1 £10 **5** **2** **3**
7 Archer St   7287 5555   3–2D
*"The best ice cream outside Italy", "magnificent" granitas,
and superb coffee are all reasons to seek out this tiny Soho café,
opposite Bocca di Lupo (same owners); "skip dessert wherever you
are dining, and go here!" / W1D 7AU; www.gelupo.com; 11 pm, Fri & Sat
12.30 am; no Amex; no booking.*

Gem N1 £31 **3** **4** **4**
265 Upper St   7359 0405   8–2D
*A "buzzy old Islington favourite" – a "friendly" sort of place which
always "gets the staples right"; these include "great-value Turkish
mezze". / N1 2UQ; www.gemrestaurant.org.uk; @Gum_restaurant; 11 pm,
Fri & Sat midnight, Sun 10.30 pm; no Amex.*

La Genova W1 £60 **2** **2** **2**
32 North Audley St   7629 5916   3–2A
*If you regard "old-style" as a compliment, this veteran Mayfair Italian
may suit you – "good for a business lunch", and "expensive, but so
reliable". / W1K 6ZG; www.lagenovarestaurant.com; 11 pm; closed Sun.*

George & Vulture EC3 £49 **2** **3** **5**
3 Castle Ct   7626 9710   9–3C
*These "unique" dining rooms – frequently visited by Dickens –
can make "a wonderful place for an indulgent old-fashioned City
lunch"; perhaps more for chaps, though – "you don't find many
women". / EC3V 9DL; 2.15 pm; L only, closed Sat & Sun.*

Gifto's Lahore Karahi UB1 £18 3 2 2
162-164 The Broadway 8813 8669 1–3A
*This Formica-topped canteen may be "brisk and brusque", but it
remains a Southall linchpin with its "authentic" spicing and its "great
value" food ("especially the grills"). / UB1 1NN; www.gifto.com; 11.30 pm,
Sat-Sun midnight.*

Gilak N19 £36 3 3 2
663 Holloway Rd 7272 1692 8–1C
*At the "unprepossessing end of Holloway Road", this "friendly"
Archway Iranian is a staple for local students, thanks to its "lovely
food and flavours" – think stews, kebabs, salads… / N19 5SE;
www.gilakrestaurant.co.uk; @Gilakrestaurant; 11 pm; no Amex.*

Gilbert Scott
St Pancras Renaissance NW1 £61 2 2 4
Euston Rd 7278 3888 8–3C
*"A very bad first impression for visitors off the Eurostar!";
the "beautifully restored" Neo-Gothic interior of Marcus Wareing's
St Pancras dining room may be "extraordinary"… but everything else
about it is decidedly run-of-the-mill. / NW1 2AR; www.thegilbertscott.co.uk;
@Thegilbertscott; 10.45 pm.*

Gilgamesh NW1 £71 2 2 3
The Stables, Camden Mkt, Chalk Farm Rd 7428 4922 8–3B
*"For a special occasion", this huge pan-Asian venue in Camden Lock,
with its barmily lavish wood carving, makes a "stunning" impression
on first-timers; the style can ultimately seem rather "tacky", though,
and critics find the whole performance rather "tired". / NW1 8AH;
www.gilgameshbar.com; 11 pm, Fri & Sat 11.30 pm; set weekday L £33 (FP).*

Gin Joint EC2 NEW £51 2 3 3
Barbican Centre, Silk St 7588 3008 12–2A
*Searcy's relaunched (and renamed) brasserie within the Barbican
Centre has all the hallmarks of the predecessors on this site –
a "useful" and "pleasant" standby, where the food is sometimes
"surprisingly good". / EC2Y 8DS; www.searcys.co.uk/venues/gin-joint;
@ginjoint_london.*

Ginger & White £17 3 3 4
2 England's Ln, NW3 7722 9944 8–2A
4a-5a, Perrins Ct, NW3 7431 9098 8–2A
*These chic Hampstead and Belsize Park cafés have quite a name,
not just for "brilliant" coffee, but for "great food" too – brunch
a speciality. / www.gingerandwhite.com; 5.30 pm, W1 6 pm; W1 closed Sun.*

Giraffe £42 1 2 1
Branches throughout London
*"Don't go without kids… but with them it's perfect!" – this "buzzy"
Tesco-owned 'world food' chain is generally "unspectacular" foodwise,
but its "varied brunch menu" is a big draw and the "free balloons,
plastic giraffes and so on" ensure "children love it". / www.giraffe.net;
10.45 pm, Sun 10.30 pm; no booking, Sat & Sun 9 am-5 pm.*

The Glasshouse TW9 £65 **5 5 3**
14 Station Pde 8940 6777 1–3A
"A good runner-up to Chez Bruce"; this "first-class" Kew sibling
to London's favourite restaurant is a "very-good-value" destination,
where the food is "always fabulous and seasonal" and staff "always
go the extra mile"; if there's a weakness, it's the light but "noisy"
interior. / TW9 3PZ; www.glasshouserestaurant.co.uk; @The_Glasshouse;
10.15 pm, Sun 9.45 pm; set weekday L £47 (FP).

Gold Mine W2 £34 **3 2 1**
102 Queensway 7792 8331 6–2C
"The best Cantonese roast duck in London" is the star attraction
at this "crowded" Bayswater spot; "just don't expect 5* service!"
/ W2 3RR; 11 pm.

Golden Dragon W1 £34 **3 2 2**
28-29 Gerrard St 7734 1073 4–3A
Some of "the best dim sum in Chinatown", say fans, is to be had
at this prominent establishment – a top 'plain vanilla' choice in these
parts, complete with traditionally "indifferent" service. / W1 6JW;
Mon-Thu 11.15 pm, Fri & Sat 11.30 pm, Sun 11 pm Sun.

Golden Hind W1 £26 **3 4 2**
73 Marylebone Ln 7486 3644 2–1A
"Premier League fish and chips" served by "friendly and efficient
staff" have won a big fan club for this "exemplary", if "functional",
Marylebone institution; BYO. / W1U 2PN; 10 pm; closed Sat L & Sun.

Good Earth £57 **3 3 2**
233 Brompton Rd, SW3 7584 3658 5–2C
143-145 The Broadway, NW7 8959 7011 1–1B
11 Bellevue Rd, SW17 8682 9230 10–2C
"Consistency" and "very good quality" have long made it "worth
paying the money" for these comfortable Chinese stalwarts,
in Knightsbridge and Mill Hill; but the sentiment that it "doesn't quite
hit the high notes it did" was more in evidence this year.
/ www.goodearthgroup.co.uk; 11 pm, Sun 10.30 pm.

Goodman £65 **3 3 3**
24-26 Maddox St, W1 7499 3776 3–2C
3 South Quay, E14 7531 0300 11–1C
11 Old Jewry, EC2 7600 8220 9–2C
"Testosterone-fuelled" and often "noisy", these "stylish" Mayfair,
City and Canary Wharf steakhouses are natural "power-lunching"
spots par excellence; "go hungry" – "the choice of cuts
is almost overwhelming" and the quality of the meat is, for a chain,
"stunning" (and – "a nudge ahead of Hawksmoor").
/ www.goodmanrestaurants.com; 10.30 pm; W1 & E14 closed Sun; EC2 closed
Sat & Sun.

Gordon Ramsay SW3 £127 **3 4 3**
68-69 Royal Hospital Rd 7352 4441 5–3D
Critics of GR's Chelsea flagship still decry it as "lacking innovation
or interest", and even fans warn of "hysterical laughter at the prices";
its ratings recovered somewhat this year, though, supported by more
praise for a "class act", and in particular Clare Smyth's cuisine that's
"amazing from start to finish". / SW3 4HP; www.gordonramsay.com;
@GordonRamsey; 10.15 pm; closed Sat & Sun; no jeans or trainers; booking:
max 8; set weekday L £58 (FP).

Gordon's Wine Bar WC2 £33 2 3 5
47 Villiers St 7930 1408 4–4D
"Get a seat in the cave – it's about as interesting a place to get drunk as there is!"; by Embankment tube, this cellar wine bar, which also boasts a huge terrace, is a "fun" spot, with an "excellent and varied" wine list; "you don't really go for the food". / WC2N 6NE; www.gordonswinebar.com; 11 pm; no booking.

The Goring Hotel SW1 £82 3 5 5
15 Beeston Pl 7396 9000 2–4B
"Class personified"; this "very grown-up" dining room, in a "luxurious" family-run hotel near Victoria, is perhaps the last redoubt of "classically English" virtues – its "superb" staff dish up such "safe" staples as "perfect" breakfasts, "unbeatable" beef Wellington and, obviously, the "best ever afternoon tea". / SW1W 0JW; www.thegoring.com; 10 pm; closed Sat L; no jeans or trainers; table of 8 max.

Gourmet Burger Kitchen £30 2 2 2
Branches throughout London
For an "honest, proper burger and trimmings", many fans still tip these "no-nonsense" cafés; this year, however, ratings slipped noticeably behind younger rival Byron, and a growing band of critics perceive a "former favourite" that's now "nothing special". / www.gbkinfo.com; most branches close 10.30 pm; no booking.

Gourmet Pizza Company
Gabriels Wharf SE1 £31 2 2 3
56 Upper Ground 7928 3188 9–3A
"Very busy and buzzy", this PizzaExpress in disguise boasts a great South Bank location (with terrace and City views); "at weekends, be prepared to wait if you haven't booked". / SE1 9PP; www.gourmetpizzacompany.co.uk; 11.30 pm.

Gourmet San E2 £25 4 2 1
261 Bethnal Green Rd 7729 8388 12–1D
It's not much to look at, but that's nothing to do with the real appeal of this Bethnal Green Sichuanese – "outstanding and varied food at great prices". / E2 6AH; www.oldplace.co.uk; 11 pm; D only.

Les Gourmets des Ternes W9 NEW £58
18 Formosa St 7286 3742 8–4A
A pocket-sized new Maida Vale outpost of a bistro in Paris's 8ème; one initial report suggests it's "not nearly as good as the original", but it's too early for a verdict – more reports please… / W9 1EE; www.lesgourmetslondon.com; closed Mon & Sun D.

The Gowlett SE15 £32 4 3 4
62 Gowlett Rd 7635 7048 1–4C
"Superb crispy pizzas" are the speciality at this "friendly local", in Peckham Rye, which also boasts a handsome wood-panelled interior and an ever-changing range of draft beers. / SE15 4HY; www.thegowlett.com; @theGowlettArms; 10.30 pm, Sun 9 pm; no credit cards.

Goya SW1 £46 2 3 2
34 Lupus St 7976 5309 2–4C
A useful destination in thinly-provided Pimlico; even some fans of this "solid local" may concede its tapas are "not the best in town", but the "buzzy" ground-floor bar is a "friendly" sort of standby. / SW1V 3EB; www.goyarestaurant.co.uk; 11.30 pm, Sun 11 pm.

Grain Store N1 £53 3 2 3
1-3 Stable St, Granary Sq   7324 4466   8–3C
Bruno Loubet's "industrial chic" yearling divides opinions; fans hail "a real boon to the rejuvenation of King's Cross", and praise the "must-try" meat-lite cooking and "fun" vibe – critics sense a degree of "hype", though, about an "echoey" place with "tame" food, "high" prices and "misdirected" service. / N1C 4AB; www.grainstore.com; @GrainStoreKX; 10.30 pm; closed Sun D; booking: max 14; SRA-3 stars.

The Grand Imperial
Guoman Grosvenor Hotel SW1 £60 3 2 2
101 Buckingham Palace Rd   7821 8898   2–4B
Excellent lunchtime dim sum is the top reason to seek out this cavernous dining room, adjacent to Victoria Station; at other times it can seem "a touch pricey for what it is.". / SW1W 0SJ; www.grandimperiallondon.com; 10.30 pm.

Granger & Co £49 2 3 4
175 Westbourne Grove, W11   7229 9111   6–1B
Buckley Building, 49 Clerkenwell Grn, EC1   7251 9032   9–1A
"For an easy meal with a stylish crowd in a fun setting", these "chilled" Antipodean diners, in Notting Hill and Clerkenwell, fit the bill, especially for brunch; fans say the "uncomplicated" Asian-influenced food is "appealing" too, but critics say it's "inconsistent" and "overpriced".

The Grapes E14 £43 1 2 5
76 Narrow St   7987 4396   11–1B
A Limehouse relic majoring in fish 'n' chips and Sunday roast – no culinary haunt this, but fans insist that's "not an issue for a 500-year-old pub in a famous street, on the bank of the Thames". / E14 8BP; www.thegrapes.co.uk; @TheGrapesLondon; 9.30 pm; closed Sat L & Sun D; no Amex.

Grazing Goat W1 £57 3 2 3
6 New Quebec St   7724 7243   2–2A
Quietly located near Marble Arch, a gastropub which can make a "surprisingly good" central standby; the food is "well presented and tasty", if perhaps "a bit pricey" for what it is. / W1H 7RQ; www.thegrazinggoat.co.uk; @TheGrazingGoat; 10 pm, Sun 9.30 pm; ; SRA-3 stars.

Great Nepalese NW1 £34 3 4 2
48 Eversholt St   7388 6737   8–3C
"The location in a scruffy Euston side street doesn't promise much", but the menu at this Nepalese stalwart "delivers in spades", offering "interesting" national dishes, as well as the usual north Indian suspects. / NW1 1DA; www.great-nepalese.co.uk; 11.30 pm, Sun 10 pm.

Great Queen Street WC2 £45 3 3 3
32 Great Queen St   7242 0622   4–1D
"Hearty" and "well-cooked" British seasonal fare from an ever-changing menu has made a big name for this "casual", "cramped" and "very noisy" Covent Garden fixture; some former fans, though, do fear it's slipping. / WC2B 5AA; www.greatqueenstreetrestaurant.co.uk; @greatqueenstreet; 10.30 pm; closed Sun D; no Amex.

The Greedy Buddha SW6   £33   3 2 2
144 Wandsworth Bridge Rd   7751 3311   10–1B
A Fulham Indian where some "brilliant" meals are recorded; service, though, can be rather "amateur". / SW6 2UH; www.thegreedybuddha.com; @thegreedybuddha; 10.30 pm, Fri & Sat 11.30 pm; no Amex.

Green Cottage NW3   £41   3 1 1
9 New College Pde   7722 5305   8–2A
Still "much loved by the regulars", a generally "reliable" Swiss Cottage Cantonese; the setting "is not inspiring", though, and the service can seem "weary". / NW3 5EP; 10.30 pm, Sun 9.30 pm; no Amex.

Green Man & French Horn WC2   £45   3 4 4
54 St Martin's Ln   7836 2645   4–4C
An "idiosyncratic" bistro menu complements "a brilliant selection of Loire wines" (favouring biodynamic vintages) at this "squashed" but "lively" ex-pub, in the heart of Theatreland – it's now better rated than its nearby parent, Terroirs. / WC2N 4EA; www.greenmanfrenchhorn.co; @gm_fh.

Green's SW1   £75   3 4 4
36 Duke St   7930 4566   3–3D
Simon Parker Bowles's "clubby" bastion of the St James's Establishment "remains absolutely as it always has been", and its loyal clientele – who enjoy its unhurried meals of "unadventurous" English fare – wouldn't have it any other way; a move, possibly to Mayfair, is on the cards for late-2015. / SW1Y 6DF; www.greens.org.uk; 10.30 pm; closed Sun; no jeans or trainers.

Greenberry Café NW1 NEW   £40   3 3 3
101 Regent's Park Rd   7483 3765   8–2B
"Everything a neighbourhood café should be"; this "light and airy" glass-fronted spot, in Primrose Hill, is "a great improvement on its predecessor Troika" (RIP), offering good coffee, cakes, brunches and light meals, and "sweet" service too. / NW1 8UR; greenberrycafe.co.uk; 10 pm; closed Sun D; no Amex; set always available £25 (FP).

The Greenhouse W1   £128   4 4 4
27a Hays Mews   7499 3331   3–3B
"An oasis of peace", "tucked away" in a Mayfair mews with "discreet" service, where Arnaud Bignon's "inventive but un-gimmicky" cuisine is the counterpoint to an "enormous", "connoisseur's" wine list; apart from the fact it's "cripplingly expensive", what's not to like? / W1J 5NY; www.greenhouserestaurant.co.uk; 10.15 pm; closed Sat L & Sun; booking: max 8; set weekday L £65 (FP).

Grumbles SW1   £43   2 3 3
35 Churton St   7834 0149   2–4B
"Not glamorous" but still a "great local eatery" – this prehistoric Pimlico bistro may offer "very simple" cuisine, but it's "good value, especially at lunch". / SW1V 2LT; www.grumblesrestaurant.co.uk; 10.45 pm.

Guglee   £33   3 4 4
7 New College Pde, NW3   7317 8555   8–2A
279 West End Ln, NW6   7317 8555   1–1B
With their "deliciously light, but not insubstantial" dishes and "fresh, modern ambience", these West Hampstead and Swiss Cottage Indians are "a cut above your average local curry house". / www.guglee.co.uk; 11 pm.

The Guinea Grill W1 £67 3 3 3
30 Bruton Pl 7499 1210 3–3B
Tucked away in a mews, attached to a quaint pub, this "old-school" dining room serves "solid" steak and pies in quaint (slightly "tired") comfort; this is Mayfair, though, and prices are "hardly pub prices!" / W1J 6NL; www.theguinea.co.uk; @guineagrill; 10.30 pm; closed Sat L & Sun; booking: max 8.

The Gun E14 £59 3 3 5
27 Coldharbour 7515 5222 11–1C
"A refuge from the sterility of Canary Wharf" – this "atmospheric and tastefully refurbished" tavern "could not have a better riverside location", with stunning views over to the O2; the food "doesn't disappoint" either, if at prices which reflect the local market. / E14 9NS; www.thegundocklands.com; @thegundocklands; 10.30 pm, Sun 9.30 pm.

Gung-Ho NW6 £40 3 4 2
328-332 West End Ln 7794 1444 1–1B
"Situated in the 'burbs, but the food is anything but 'local'", say fans of this West Hampstead stalwart, whose reputation for "always helpful" service and "delicious" cooking is recovering after last year's change of ownership. / NW6 1LN; www.stir-fry.co.uk; 11.30 pm; no Amex.

Gustoso Ristorante & Enoteca SW1 £43 3 5 3
33 Willow Pl 7834 5778 2–4B
"Tucked away in a quiet Westminster backstreet, but known by those in the know", this Sardinian yearling is becoming "a firm favourite" – it's run by "very welcoming" people, and its "simple" food is "authentic" and "affordable". / SW1P 1JH; ristorantegustoso.co.uk; @GustosoRist; 10.30 pm, Fri & Sat 11 pm, Sun 9.30 pm.

GYMKHANA W1 £63 5 4 4
42 Albemarle St 3011 5900 3–3C
Straight into the super-league of London's nouvelle Indians, this "unstuffy" yearling, near The Ritz, offers a "sensationally subtle" cuisine, including some "wonderfully original game and other dishes" – it's "worth the hassle to get a table". / W1S 4JH; www.gymkhanalondon.com; @GymkhanaLondon; 10.30 pm; closed Sun.

Haché £37 3 3 4
329-331 Fulham Rd, SW10 7823 3515 5–3B
24 Inverness St, NW1 7485 9100 8–3B
153 Clapham High St, SW4 7738 8760 10–2D
147-149 Curtain Rd, EC2 7739 8396 12–1B
"The place to go if you're after a juicy patty!" – this "small and friendly" group "continues to set the standards for high-grade burgers"; survey ratings support those who say it "definitely outperforms the bigger operators". / www.hacheburgers.com; 10.30 pm, Fri-Sat 11 pm, Sun 10 pm.

Hakkasan £89 4 2 4
17 Bruton St, W1 7907 1888 3–2C
8 Hanway Pl, W1 7927 7000 4–1A
These "dark and brooding" nightclub-style haunts "elevate westernised Chinese food to a new level" – despite their crowds, noise, "snotty" service and "out-of-this-world" prices, they are the bedrock for what's now a growing global brand; "to avoid a second mortgage, check out the extraordinary dim sum at lunchtime". / www.hakkasan.com; midnight, Sun 11 pm.

Halepi W2 £44 **3 4 2**
18 Leinster Ter 7262 1070 6–2C
*Just north of Hyde Park, an "old-fashioned" taverna still worth
seeking out for its "well-cooked" Greek dishes; even supporters,
though, can find it "expensive, for what's on offer". / W2 3ET;
www.halepi.co.uk; midnight.*

Ham Yard Restaurant
Ham Yard Hotel W1 NEW £51 **2 2 2**
1 Ham Yd 3642 2000 3–2D
*All credit to Firmdale Hotels for developing this unbelievably central
site, whose courtyard feels a million miles from Soho; shame there's
still so much to do, though – our early-days visit found a menu
seemingly extracted from a late-'90s time-capsule, and reporters
found the atmosphere remarkably "lacklustre". / W1D 7DT; Rated
on Editors' visit; www.hamyardhotel.com; @ham_yard.*

The Hampshire Hog W6 £50 **2 2 3**
227 King St 8748 3391 7–2B
*"Bright and cheerful", this pub near Hammersmith Town Hall
benefits not only from a "lovely" interior, but also from a "large and
very attractive garden"; foodwise it had great early-days promise,
but some more "ordinary" meals were reported this year. / W6 9JT;
www.thehampshirehog.com; @TheHampshireHog; 11 pm; closed Sun D;
SRA-2 stars.*

Harbour City W1 £40 **2 1 1**
46 Gerrard St 7439 7859 4–3B
*"Incredibly cheap, impeccable dim sum" – the main reason to visit
this Gerrard Street stalwart, which is "otherwise very
undistinguished". / W1D 5QH; www.harbourcity.com.hk; 11.30 pm, Fri & Sat
midnight, Sun 10.30 pm.*

Hard Rock Café W1 £49 **3 2 4**
150 Old Park Ln 7629 0382 3–4B
*"Still rocking!"; the world's first Hard Rock is "still buzzing after
40 years", and you do get "a good burger"; brace yourself, though,
for the noise. / W1K 1QZ; www.hardrock.com/london; @HardRockLondon;
midnight; need 20+ to book.*

Hardy's Brasserie W1 £49 **2 2 4**
53 Dorset St 7935 5929 2–1A
*"Largely unchanged over the years", this "pleasant" Marylebone
haunt is a "great place to spend a quiet evening"; the fact that it's
"now open for weekend breakfasts" is a "real bonus" too.
/ W1U 7NH; www.hardysbrasserie.com; @hardys_W1; 10 pm; closed
Sat & Sun.*

Hare & Tortoise £30 **3 2 3**
11-13 The Brunswick, WC1 7278 9799 2–1D
373 Kensington High St, W14 7603 8887 7–1D
38 Haven Grn, W5 8810 7066 1–2A
296-298 Upper Richmond Rd, SW15 8394 7666 10–2B
90 New Bridge St, EC4 7651 0266 9–2A
*"A great place to grab a meal" – this "fuss-free" pan-Asian chain
"knocks Wagamama into a cocked hat", offering great sushi, noodles
and "tasty Asian dishes" at "impressively low prices".
/ www.hareandtortoise-restaurants.co.uk; 10.45 pm, Fri & Sat 11.15 pm;
EC4 10 pm; EC4 closed Sun; W14 no bookings.*

Harry Morgan's NW8 £40 2 2 2

31 St John's Wood High St   7722 1869   8–3A

"Not beautiful, or gourmet, but dependable"; this classic Jewish deli, in St John's Wood, is arguably a bit "pricey" and "tired", but it still inspires a high degree of loyalty, especially for the "really good salt beef" which is its trademark. / NW8 7NH; www.harrys.co.uk; 10.30 pm.

Harwood Arms SW6 £59 4 3 3

Walham Grove   7386 1847   5–3A

"Don't be fooled, this ain't pub grub!" – "top-quality" dishes (especially game) are cooked "with flair" at this esteemed boozer in the backwoods of Fulham; from a very high starting point, though, standards have "slipped" a bit in recent times. / SW6 1QP; www.harwoodarms.com; 9.15 pm, Sun 9 pm; closed Mon L.

Hashi SW20 £36 4 4 3

54 Durham Rd   8944 1888   10–2A

A "charming and intimate" local, "tucked away in Raynes Park"; its "beautiful" sushi and sashimi, say fans, are "as good as at any Japanese you'd find in Mayfair". / SW20 0TW; www.hashicooking.co.uk; 10.30 pm; closed Mon; no Amex.

The Havelock Tavern W14 £44 3 2 3

57 Masbro Rd   7603 5374   7–1C

"This archetypal Olympia gastropub has mellowed in recent years" – the sullen service of old has mercifully been ditched, but so has the former promise of excitement, though the food is still "of good quality". / W14 0LS; www.havelocktavern.com; @HavelockTavern; 10 pm, Sun 9.30 pm; no booking.

The Haven N20 £50 2 2 2

1363 High Rd   8445 7419   1–1B

"West End quality on the edge of London" – the optimistic view on this popular (and sometimes "very noisy") local; not everyone's convinced, though, and sceptics say "standards have dropped" in recent times. / N20 9LN; www.haven-bistro.co.uk; 11 pm.

Hawksmoor £64 4 4 3

5a, Air St, W1   7406 3980   3–3D
11 Langley St, WC2   7420 9390   4–2C
3 Yeoman's Row, SW3   7590 9290   5–2C **NEW**
157 Commercial St, E1   7426 4850   12–2B
10-12 Basinghall St, EC2   7397 8120   9–2C

"Absurdly juicy" steaks and "first-class cocktails" underpin huge acclaim for Huw Gott & Will Beckett's "casual and laid-back" temples to meat; even fans admit prices are "eye-watering", though, and ratings are beginning to fall some way behind those of its main rival, Goodman. / www.thehawksmoor.com; all branches between 10 pm & 11 pm; EC2 closed Sat-Sun.

Haz £37 2 3 3

9 Cutler St, E1   7929 7923   9–2D
34 Foster Ln, EC2   7600 4172   9–2B
112 Houndsditch, EC3   7623 8180   9–2D
6 Mincing Ln, EC3   7929 3173   9–3D

For a "relatively cheap and cheerful" bite in the City, these "very buzzy and busy" Turkish outlets make a "slightly different" choice, and the fare is generally pretty "decent". / www.hazrestaurant.co.uk; 11.30 pm; EC3 closed Sun.

Hazuki WC2 £41 2 2 2
43 Chandos Pl   7240 2530   4–4C
This really handily located Japanese, by the Coliseum, seems to risk losing its way; the set lunch menus may still be worth seeking out, but a worrying number of reports have found the whole performance rather "tired" of late. / WC2M 4HS; www.hazukilondon.co.uk; 10.30 pm, Sun 9.30 pm.

Heddon Street Kitchen W1 NEW
3-9 Heddon St   7592 1212   3–2C
Gordon Ramsay makes his first leap into the heart of the West End with this new restaurant just off Regent Street, modelled on his City venture Bread Street Kitchen. / W1B 4BE; www.gordonramsay.com/heddon-street.

Hedone W4 £80 5 4 3
301-303 Chiswick High Rd   8747 0377   7–2A
"Truly staggering!"; after three years in operation, Mikael Jonsson's "unsung" open-kitchen venture, in outer Chiswick, has finally got properly into its stride – his "incredibly clever" modern Scandi dishes deliver "small bites of perfection and amazement". / W4 4HH; www.hedonerestaurant.com; 9.30 pm; closed Mon, Tue L, Wed L & Sun; set weekday L £74 (FP).

Hélène Darroze
The Connaught Hotel W1 £125 2 3 4
Carlos Pl   3147 7200   3–3B
"Beautiful, decadent and extravagant", this Mayfair dining room certainly looks the part to host some "stunning" fine dining experiences, and fans do indeed say it offers "perfection"; there are, though, too many reports of "very average" experiences too… and all at "ferocious" prices! / W1K 2AL; www.the-connaught.co.uk; @TheConnaught; 9.30 pm; closed Mon & Sun; jacket & tie; set weekday L £65 (FP).

The Henry Root SW10 £56 2 2 3
9 Park Walk   7352 7040   5–3B
"A very flexible format", accommodating anything from a bar snack to a slap-up meal, helps make this "warm and now well-established" Chelsea hangout "a good neighbourhood all-rounder" – "not fine food, but reliable". / SW10 0AJ; www.thehenryroot.com; @thehenryroot; 10.45 pm, Sun 8.45 pm.

Hereford Road W2 £49 3 3 2
3 Hereford Rd   7727 1144   6–1B
"For nose-to-tail eating without the price tag", Tom Pemberton's "noisy" Bayswater fixture wins praise for his "well-cooked", notably "seasonal" dishes (with "less offal and more fish and veg of late"); however, it does not achieve ratings quite as stellar as its foodie renown would imply. / W2 4AB; www.herefordroad.org; @3HerefordRoad; 10.30 pm, Sun 10 pm; set weekday L £32 (FP).

Hibiscus W1 £122 3 3 2
29 Maddox St   7629 2999   3–2C
As usual, Claude Bosi's low-key foodie temple, in Mayfair, polarises reporters – fans extol an "outstanding" venture serving "truly memorable" dishes, but a large minority of critics complain of "overwrought" dishes at "extortionate" prices. / W1S 2PA; www.hibiscusrestaurant.co.uk; @HibiscusLondon; 11 pm; closed Mon & Sun; set weekday L £56 (FP).

High Road Brasserie W4　　　　£54　　2 2 3
162-166 Chiswick High Rd　8742 7474　7–2A
*As a venue for an "excellent breakfast" or "family brunch",
this prominently sited Soho House group brasserie offers a handy
perch for the Chiswick Set to see and be seen – al fresco tables are
particularly prized. / W4 1PR; www.brasserie.highroadhouse.co.uk;
@sohohouse; 10.45 pm, Fri & Sat 11.45 pm, Sun 10 pm.*

High Timber EC4　　　　£56　　3 4 4
8 High Timber　7248 1777　9–3B
*"A hidden gem, only 100m from the Millennium Bridge", and offering
"stunning" views from the outside tables; its culinary appeal
is "straight down the line" – "excellent steak" plus "amazing South
African wines", so "be sure to walk through the temperature-
controlled cellars". / EC4V 3PA; www.hightimber.com; @HTimber; 10 pm;
closed Sat & Sun; set weekday L £39 (FP).*

Hill & Szrok E8 NEW　　　　£40
60 Broadway Mkt　7833 1933　1–2D
*"Affordable treats for carnivores" – that's the key attraction
of Broadway Market's new "butcher by day, restaurant by night";
early-days survey feedback, though, was too limited to justify a rating.
/ E8 4QJ; www.hillandszrok.co.uk.*

Hilliard EC4　　　　£28　　4 2 2
26a Tudor St　7353 8150　9–3A
*"Queues of affluent lawyers" attest to the quality of the "first-class"
sandwiches – and a "good selection of hot dishes" too – at this
cramped all-day operation, by the Temple. / EC4Y 0AY;
www.hilliardfood.co.uk; 6 pm; L only, closed Sat & Sun; no booking.*

Hix W1　　　　£65　　2 2 2
66-70 Brewer St　7292 3518　3–2D
*Fans hail Mark Hix's discreet Soho dining room as a "very cool"
urban haunt, where "top ingredients" are "flawlessly prepared";
even fans can find it "overpriced", though, and harsher critics say it's
"heavy weather" all-round – "best bet is to remain in the excellent
basement bar!" / W1F 9UP; www.hixsoho.co.uk; @HixRestaurants;
11.30 pm, Sun 10.30 pm; set weekday L & pre-theatre £43 (FP).*

Hix Oyster & Chop House EC1　　　£58　　3 2 2
36-37 Greenhill Rents, Cowcross St　7017 1930　9–1A
*Mark Hix's "busy" but decidedly "basic" Smithfield dining room offers
a "great range of surf 'n' turf", generally quite well realised; it's pricey
though, and the "friendly" service can be "slow". / EC1M 6BN;
www.restaurantsetcltd.com; @HixRestaurants; 11 pm, Sun 10 pm; closed
Sat L.*

Hixter EC2 NEW　　　　£81　　3 3 3
9a Devonshire Sq　7220 9498　9–2D
*"Great meat" features in reports on Mark Hix's trendy (son of
Tramshed) steak 'n' chicken joints, near Liverpool Street – "cramped
and noisy, but always fun"; now open on the South Bank too.
/ EC2M 4AE; www.hixter.co.uk; @hixtercity; closed Sat & Sun.*

HKK EC2 £70 5 5 3
Broadgate Quarter, 88 Worship St 3535 1888 12–2B
*"An amazing realm of taste sensations" rewards those who explore
the "superb, bite-sized Cantonese banquet menu" on offer at this
"reliably incredible" City-fringe yearling; the contemporary interior,
though, is rather "austere".* / EC2A 2BE; www.hkklondon.com;
@HKKlondon; 10 pm; closed Sun.

Hoi Polloi
Ace Hotel E1 £57 2 3 3
100 Shoreditch High St 8880 6100 12–1B
*"A fun addition to Shoreditch" – this "large dining space" scores well
for its "hip" style and "in-crowd buzz", even if the cooking can
be "a touch underwhelming".* / E1 6JQ; hoi-polloi.co.uk; @wearehoipolloi;
Sun-Wed midnight, Thu-Sat 1am; up to 6, 7-12 alacarte credit card details
cancellation within 48 hours set menu 13-20.

Holborn Dining Room
Rosewood London WC1 NEW £58 2 2 3
252 High Holborn 3747 8633 2–1D
*"A vast barn of a room" – sheer size often seems to be the main
impression of this impressive new Midtown space; food and service
are rated "merely average", but this certainly makes a "good business
lunch option" nonetheless.* / WC1V 7EN; www.holborndiningroom.com;
@HolbornDining; 11.15pm, Sun 10.30 pm.

Hole in the Wall W4 £41 2 3 3
12 Sutton Lane North 8742 7185 7–2A
*For Chiswick folk, an "excellent local gastropub", of particular note
for a "grassy back garden, big enough for kids to roam in"; the food's
quite 'gastro' too.* / W4 4LD; www.holeinthewallchiswickco.uk;
@HoleInTheWallW4; 9.45 pm, Sun 9.15 pm; closed Mon L & Tue L.

Holy Cow SW11 £25 4 3 3
166 Battersea Pk Rd 7498 2000 10–1C
*A "really top Indian take-away", offering "cheap and very authentic"
curries (which is why, exceptionally, we list it here); of its numerous
branches, the Battersea operation listed is "definitely a cut above".*
/ SW11 4ND; www.holycowfineindianfood.com; 11 pm, Sun 10.30 pm; D only.

Homage
Waldorf Hilton WC2 £75 1 1 2
22 Aldwych 7836 2400 2–2D
*A "lovely" former ballroom, with "an excellent location" on the fringe
of Covent Garden; sadly, though, the experience of dining here is too
often characterised as "shambolic" – what a waste!* / WC2B 4DD;
www.waldorfhilton.co.uk/dining-bars/homage-grand-s; Mon-Wed 10 pm,
Thu-Sat 10.30 pm, Sun 9.30 pm; D only; set pre theatre £48 (FP).

Homeslice WC2 NEW £23 5 3 2
13 Neal's Yd 7836 4604 4–2C
*"They know how to make pizza exciting again", at this "rammed"
Covent Garden yearling, where servings are "ENORMOUS" – "you'll
think you can't finish, but you'll find a way!"; "staff are cheerful in the
face of the queue, but it's too noisy a place to linger".* / WC2H 9DP;
www.homeslicepizza.co.uk; @homesliceLDN; Mon-Sat 10 pm, Sun 7.15 pm.

Honest Burgers £38 **4 4 4**
4 Meard St, W1   3609 9524   4–2A
159 Portobello Rd, W11   awaiting tel   6–1B
54-56 Camden Lock Pl, NW1   8617 3949   8–2B
72 Tooting High St, SW17   3601 5700   10–2B **NEW**
Brixton Village, Coldharbour Ln, SW9   7733 7963   10–2D
*"A leading light in London's burger explosion!"; "for quick and tasty
food, you'll be hard pressed to better" this "brilliant" chain, with its
Ginger Pig-sourced meat and "lusciously addictive" chips; "plan ahead
to beat the queues" though – at weekends, they're "dreadful".
/ www.honestburgers.co.uk; @honestburgers; 10 pm - 11 pm; SW9 closed
Mon D.*

Honey & Co W1 £32 **4 4 3**
25a, Warren St   7388 6175   2–1B
*"You have to squeeze in, go with the flow, and not stand
on ceremony", but the pay-off at this "tiny" but "committed" café,
near Warren Street tube, is "superb" and "zesty" modern Israeli food
prepared "with real flair". / W1T 5JZ; www.honeyandco.co.uk;
@Honeyandco; closed Sun.*

The Horseshoe NW3 £48 **3 2 3**
28 Heath St   7431 7206   8–2A
*Two things make this Hampstead pub "very popular" – an "ever-
changing" menu, and "sensational beer from Camden Brewery"
(which was formerly produced on-site); oh, and the dearth of local
competition probably helps too! / NW3 6TE;
www.thehorseshoehampstead.com; @getluckyatthehorseshoe; 10 pm, Fri & Sat
11 pm.*

Hot Stuff SW8 £20 **3 3 2**
23 Wilcox Rd   7720 1480   10–1D
*"Tasty, deeply flavoured curries, with lots of interesting specials" –
reason to seek out this "unassuming" Indian BYO, deep in Vauxhall.
/ SW8 2XA; www.eathotstuff.com; 9.30 pm; closed Mon; no Amex.*

House of Ho W1 NEW £59 **4 3 2**
57-59 Old Compton St   7287 0770   4–3A
*"Creative" and "tasty" fare has helped this Vietnamese newcomer
make quite a splash; located on Soho's main drag, it's aiming to be
a "cool venue for a young crowd", but can suffer from "a lack
of atmosphere". / W1D 6HP; www.houseofho.co.uk; @houseofho; Mon-Fri
10.30 pm, Thu-Sun 11.30 pm.*

The Hoxton Grill EC2 £52 **2 2 4**
81 Great Eastern St   7739 9111   12–1B
*The "NYC warehouse-y" style makes for a "funky" vibe, at this
"buzzing" Shoreditch venue, tipped by fans for its diner-style fare –
the odd "really bad" experience was reported this year,
but breakfasts and burgers are usually praised. / EC2A 3HU;
www.hoxtongrill.co.uk; @hoxtongrill; 11.45 pm; set weekday L £34 (FP).*

Hubbard & Bell
Hoxton Hotel WC1 NEW
199-206 High Holborn   7661 3030   2–1D
*From Soho House, a new 'Brooklyn-style' all-day restaurant
in London's newest Midtown hotel. / WC1V 7BD;
www.hubbardandbell.com.*

Hudsons SW15 £42 2 2 3
113 Lower Richmond Rd 8785 4522 10–1A
"They have everything covered when it comes to breakfast", at this "cheap and cheerful" Putney bistro – a perennially popular hang out for local thirty-somethings. / SW15 1EX; www.hudsonsrestaurant.co.uk; @hudsonsw15; 10 pm, Sun 9.30 pm; closed Tue L.

Hummus Bros £17 3 3 2
88 Wardour St, W1 7734 1311 3–2D
37-63 Southampton Row, WC1 7404 7079 2–1D
62 Exmouth Mkt, EC1 7812 1177 9–1A
128 Cheapside, EC2 7726 8011 9–2B
"Upbeat and friendly", these "quick-snack" spots "do exactly what you'd expect, quickly, freshly, efficiently and at a good price"; "you leave feeling healthy too". / www.hbros.co.uk; W1 10 pm, Thu-Sat 11 pm; WC1 9 pm, EC1 10 pm, Thu-Sat 11 pm, Sun 4 pm; WC1, EC2 closed Sat & Sun; no booking.

Hunan SW1 £65 5 3 1
51 Pimlico Rd 7730 5712 5–2D
"The best Chinese in town" – Michael Peng "continues the traditions set by his father", at this "delightfully odd" and "cramped" Pimlico stalwart; there's no menu – "tell them what you like, and mouthwatering little plates from heaven just keep on coming". / SW1W 8NE; www.hunanlondon.com; 9.30 pm; closed Sun; set weekday L £48 (FP).

Huong-Viet
An Viet House N1 £35 3 2 2
12-14 Englefield Rd 7249 0877 1–1C
"After two decades, I'm still a fan"; this Vietnamese fixture, in a community centre – built as De Beauvoir's public baths – remains pretty much as it ever was; BYO. / N1 4LS; 11 pm; closed Sun; no Amex.

Hush £58 2 2 3
8 Lancashire Ct, W1 7659 1500 3–2B
95-97 High Holborn, WC1 7242 4580 2–1D
"One of the best outdoor terraces in central London" helps make the tucked-away Mayfair branch of this small group a "lovely place to meet"; the "comfort food" is "all a bit bland", with the EC4 and WC1 branches more likely to be judged "underwhelming". / www.hush.co.uk; @Hush_Restaurant; W1 10.45 pm; WC1 10.30 pm, Sun 9.30 pm; WC1 closed Sun.

Hutong
The Shard SE1 £77 2 2 4
31 St Thomas St 3011 1257 9–4C
"A view to die for" rewards those who ascend to this "exciting" Chinese dining room on the 33rd floor of London's great new landmark – "you certainly pay for it", though, and reporters are split between those who think this is an "expensive but impressive" destination, and those who just find standards "very average". / SE1 9RY; www.hutong.co.uk; @HutongShard; 11 pm.

Ibérica £46 3 2 3
195 Great Portland St, W1 7636 8650 2–1B
12 Cabot Sq, E14 7636 8650 11–1C
89 Turnmill St, EC1 7636 8650 9–1A **NEW**
Fans are "very impressed" by these modern tapas joints – the "airy"
Gt Portland St original is the best, and the E14 branch is "one of the
Wharf's better restaurants"; drifting survey ratings, however,
suggest the food is not what it once was. / 11 pm; W1 closed Sun D.

Imli Street W1 £38 3 4 4
167-169 Wardour St 7287 4243 3–1D
A "very busy" Soho operation, where "flavoursome and interesting"
Indian street food comes in "small dishes", encouraging "lots of
sampling", and at prices which "won't break the bank". / W1F 8WR;
www.imlistreet.com; 11 pm, Sun 10 pm.

Inaho W2 £40 4 3 2
4 Hereford Rd 7221 8495 6–1B
"Top-quality Japanese in a charming chalet!" – imagine having "lovely
sushi in someone's front room", and you have a pretty good picture
of this tiny Bayswater shack. / W2 4AA; 10.30 pm; closed Sat L & Sun;
no Amex or Maestro.

Inamo £45 2 2 2
4-12 Regent St, SW1 7484 0500 3–3D
134-136 Wardour St, W1 7851 7051 3–1D
"A gimmick, yes, but fun to go once" – using your table as a
touchscreen to order your oriental lunch or dinner is, obviously,
something "kids love", but most adults seem to enjoy it too;
everything else is a bit incidental. / www.inamo-restaurant.com;
@InamoRestaurant; 11 pm, SW1 12 am.

India Club
Strand Continental Hotel WC2 £25 3 2 1
143 Strand 7836 0650 2–2D
"Hopefully, it will never change!"; with its "decent" subcontinental
food and "oddly compelling" ambience, this "down-at-heel" canteen,
near the Indian High Commission, retains a devoted fan club; BYO.
/ WC2R 1JA; www.strand-continental.co.uk; 10.50 pm; no credit cards; booking:
max 6.

Indian Moment SW11 £35 3 4 3
44 Northcote Rd 7223 6575 10–2C
"A slightly healthier curry option" – this Battersea spot wins praise for
its non-traditional food preparation, and "attractive" modern design
too. / SW11 1NZ; www.indianmoment.co.uk; @indianmoment; 11.30 pm,
Fri & Sat midnight; no Amex.

Indian Ocean SW17 £30 4 4 3
214 Trinity Rd 8672 7740 10–2C
"A local indian that never disappoints"; with its "fresh and well-
cooked dishes" and its "very good" service, this Wandsworth
institution continues to achieve "surprisingly good" standards.
/ SW17 7HP; www.indianoceanrestaurant.com; 11.30 pm.

Indian Rasoi N2 £38 443
7 Denmark Ter 8883 9093 1–1B
"Really unusual Indian fare" with *"clear flavours, subtle spicing,
and little resort to creamy sauces"* wins acclaim for this *"tiny"* but
"brilliant" Muswell Hill spot; it's *"always full"*. / N2 9HG;
www.indian-rasoi.co.uk; 10.30 pm; no Amex.

Indian Zilla SW13 £44 553
2-3 Rocks Ln 8878 3989 10–1A
Manoj Vasaikar's *"subtly spiced and creative"* dishes attract rave
reviews for this *"posh"* Barnes curry house (an offshoot of Indian
Zing) – *"factor in the price, and it's one of the best Indians in town"*.
/ SW13 0DB; www.indianzilla.co.uk; 11 pm, Sun 10.30 pm; closed weekday L.

Indian Zing W6 £48 543
236 King St 8748 5959 7–2B
"Bursts of gorgeous flavours" characterise Manoj Vasaikar's *"lovely
and light"* modern Indian cooking, which has won a gigantic fan club
for this *"always-busy"* little place, near Ravenscourt Park; *"closely-
packed tables"* are the only real gripe. / W6 0RS; www.indianzing.co.uk;
@IndianZing; 11 pm, Sun 10 pm; set always available £30 (FP).

Indigo
One Aldwych WC2 £65 233
1 Aldwych 7300 0400 2–2D
"A good view of the bar from the balcony" adds to the buzz at this
Theatreland mezzanine dining room; its affordable set deals make
it an *"excellent pre-theatre venue"*, and handy for business too.
/ WC2B 4BZ; www.onealdwych.com; 10.15 pm.

Inn the Park SW1 £50 224
St James's Pk 7451 9999 2–3C
*"A beautiful location in the heart of St James's Park, but the food
is average"* – that's always been the trade-off at this striking all-day
café, which celebrated its 10th year with a refurb in 2014.
/ SW1A 2BJ; www.peytonandbyrne.co.uk; @PeytonandByrne; 8.30 pm; closed
Sun D; no Amex.

Inside SE10 £43 441
19 Greenwich South St 8265 5060 1–3D
*"Well worth putting up with the disappointing ambience for the sake
of the delicious food"* – Guy Awford is a *"chef-patron who cares"*,
and the cooking at his *"cramped"* and *"unpretentious"* side street
restaurant is *"still the best in Greenwich"*. / SE10 8NW;
www.insiderestaurant.co.uk; @insideandgreenwich; 10.30 pm, Fri & Sat
11 pm; closed Mon & Sun D.

Ippudo London WC2 NEW
Central St Giles Piazza 7240 4469 4–1B
This globally popular ramen bar opens its first European
outpost in Central St Giles. / WC2H 8AG; ippudo.co.uk; @IppudoLondon.

Isarn N1 £46 432
119 Upper St 7424 5153 8–3D
An *"understated"* Islington spot where the *"unstereotypical"* Thai
cuisine is *"a cut above"* the norm. / N1 1QP; www.isarn.co.uk; 11 pm,
Sun 10.30 pm.

Ishtar W1
£45 **3**4**3**

10-12 Crawford St 7224 2446 2–1A

"A great little Turkish restaurant in Marylebone", and world-famous thereabouts for *"the best-value set lunch in town"*. / W1U 6AZ; www.ishtarrestaurant.com; 11 pm, Sun 10.30 pm.

Itsu
£33 **2**3**2**

Branches throughout London

"Guilt-free" fast food – *"healthy and fresh"* soups, sushi and other Asian-inspired snacks – win praise for this *"exploding"* cafeteria chain. / www.itsu.co.uk; 11 pm; E14 10 pm; some are closed Sat & Sun; no booking.

The Ivy WC2
£72 **2**3**3**

1-5 West St 7836 4751 4–3B

This former Theatreland idol still wows fans with its *"slick and polished"* style and *"predictable"* nursery fare; those who remember the glory days when this was London's favourite restaurant, though, may find its current performance *"embarrassing"* – time, they say, *"for a complete overhaul"*. / WC2H 9NQ; www.the-ivy.co.uk; @CapriceHoldings; 11 pm, Sun 10 pm; no shorts; booking: max 6; set weekday L & dinner £50 (FP).

Izgara N3
£34 **3**2**1**

11 Hendon Lane 8371 8282 1–1B

"Great mezze" and a *"sensible choice of charcoal- or oven-cooked meats"* – the attractions which ensure this Turkish venture, in North Finchley, is always *"busy and cramped"*. / N3 1RT; www.izgararestaurant.net; 11.30 pm; no Amex.

Jackson & Rye W1
£40 **1**1**2**

56 Wardour St 7437 8338 3–2D

A *"NYC-wannabe"*, this smartly turned out new Soho diner does have a *"nice bar"* and it can turn out a decent brunch too; service, though, can be *"truly awful"*, and the cooking is *"by numbers"*. / W1D 4JG; www.jacksonrye.com; @jacksonrye.

Jai Krishna N4
£19 **4**3**2**

161 Stroud Green Rd 7272 1680 8–1D

"Nearly 30 years on, still excellent value for money"; this *"very welcoming"* South Indian veggie, in Stroud Green, *"always delivers exceptional food"*… *"and it's BYO too"*. / N4 3PZ; 10.30 pm; closed Sun; no credit cards.

Jamaica Patty Co. WC2 NEW
£10 **3**2**2**

26 New Row 7836 3334 4–3C

"Great Jamaican patties… in central London!" – not much to add about this brightly lit Covent Garden pit stop, where the fuel is *"cheap"* and *"tasty"*. / WC2N 4LA; www.jamaicapatty.co.uk.

Jamie's Diner W1 NEW
£50 **2**1**2**

32a, Shaftsbury Ave 3697 4117 3–3D

Jamie Oliver's *"family-friendly"* new Soho diner is *"billed as a 'pop-up'*, but has all the hallmarks of a chain roll-out to come"; fans say its classic US diner dishes are *"done well"*, but true to past form, critics just see *"style over substance"*. / W1D 7EF; www.jamieoliversdiner.com; @jamiesdiner; Mon-Fri 11pm, Sat & Sun 10.30 pm; set weekday L & dinner £30 (FP).

Jamie's Italian £44 | 1 | 1 | 2 |
Branches throughout London
"How does he get away with it?"; although these cult-of-Jamie diners do have have their fans (especially 'en famille'), few chains incite as much harsh criticism as this one, with many reporters finding them "completely overrated", "lamentable", "the most disappointing ever"... / www.jamiesitalian.com; @JamiesItalianUK; 11.30 pm, Sun 10.30 pm; over 6.

Jin Kichi NW3 £42 | 5 | 4 | 3 |
73 Heath St 7794 6158 8–1A
"I come all the way from Surrey to my favourite restaurant!"; how does this "tiny" and "cramped" Hampstead old-timer justify such a trek? – "expert" Japanese cooking, with "fantastic" teriyaki a highlight. / NW3 6UG; www.jinkichi.com; 11 pm, Sun 10 pm; closed Mon L.

Joanna's SE19 £44 | 3 | 4 | 4 |
56 Westow Hill 8670 4052 1–4D
Still a "longstanding favourite"; thanks to its "very pleasant" food and "good house cocktails", this "old-school" Crystal Palace brasserie continues to elicit very positive reports from locals. / SE19 1RX; www.joannas.uk.com; @JoannasRest; 10.45 pm, Sun 10.15 pm.

Joe Allen WC2 £53 | 1 | 2 | 4 |
13 Exeter St 7836 0651 4–3D
Fortunately, the "buzzy" atmosphere has long been the "whole point" of this late-night Theatreland basement (est NYC '65, London '77), where the best bet foodwise is the "authentic" (and famously off-menu) burger; despite new owners in recent times though, its performance generally remains "tired". / WC2E 7DT; www.joeallen.co.uk; Sun-Thu 11.45 pm, Fri & Sat 12.45 am; set weekday L & dinner £34 (FP).

Joe's Brasserie SW6 £43 | 2 | 4 | 3 |
130 Wandsworth Bridge Rd 7731 7835 10–1B
"Average food is strongly supported by a very reasonable wine list", at John Brinkley's ever-"popular", deepest Fulham stalwart; "good terrace" too. / SW6 2UL; www.brinkleys.com; 11 pm.

José SE1 £41 | 5 | 4 | 5 |
104 Bermondsey St 7403 4902 9–4D
There's no let-up in the superlatives for José Pizarro's "tiny", "intimate" and "packed" Bermondsey corner bar; waiting for a table "can be a bore", but it's well worth it for tapas that are "light years ahead" of most rivals, plus "fantastic" wines. / SE1 3UB; www.josepizarro.com; @Jose_Pizarro; 10.30 pm, Sun 5.30; closed Fri D, Sat D & Sun D.

Joy King Lau WC2 £35 | 3 | 2 | 2 |
3 Leicester St 7437 1132 4–3A
"Tremendous" old-school Cantonese food makes this three-floor venture, off Leicester Square, "a very much better-than-average Chinatown destination"; its "not the best ambience or service, but it's the food and prices you go for". / WC2H 7BL; www.joykinglau.com; 11.30 pm, Sun 10.30 pm.

The Jugged Hare EC1 £64 ⓷⓷⓷
49 Chiswell St 7614 0134 12–2A
"Great hearty British food" – majoring in *"meat, meat and more meat, plus a little fish"* – makes this *"fantastic and buzzy"* gastroboozer a very popular City standby, even if at times it's *"so noisy it's impossible to chat"*. / EC1Y 4SA; www.juggedhare.com; @juggedhare; 11 pm, Sun 10 pm; set pre theatre £44 (FP).

Julie's W11 £66 ⓵⓵⓹
135 Portland Rd 7229 8331 6–2A
"Very special" and *"unfailingly romantic"*, this deeply '70s Holland Park labyrinth undoubtedly is... but when will someone put a rocket under the kitchen – *"it's bad enough that the cooking is so poor, but at these prices?"* / W11 4LW; www.juliesrestaurant.com; 11 pm.

The Junction Tavern NW5 £45 ⓷⓸⓸
101 Fortess Rd 7485 9400 8–2B
"Just what you want from a local gastropub" – this Kentish Town spot continues to generate impressively consistent ratings. / NW5 1AG; www.junctiontavern.co.uk; @Junction Tavern; 10.15 pm, Sun 9.15 pm; Mon-Thu D only, Fri-Sun open L & D; no Amex.

Juniper Dining N5 £46 ⓷⓷⓶
100 Highbury Pk 7288 8716 8–1D
A *"very good local"*, in Highbury, offering simple yet *"excellent"* seasonal British dishes (many gluten-free); early-evening set price menus offer *"extremely good value for money"*. / N5 2XE; www.juniperdining.co.uk; @Juniperdining; 9.30 pm; closed Mon & Sun D.

JW Steakhouse
Grosvenor House Hotel W1 £77 ⓶⓶⓶
86 Park Ln 7399 8460 3–3A
The steaks at the vast, characterless and pricey Mayfair dining room *"can disappoint"*, but the puds are *"awesome"* – the cheesecake, in particular, is *"superb, and big enough for two!"* / W1K 7TN; www.jwsteakhouse.co.uk; 10.30 pm, Fri & Sat 11 pm.

K10 £37 ⓸⓷⓶
20 Copthall Ave, EC2 7562 8510 9–2C
3 Appold St, EC2 7539 9209 12–2B
"Well above average for a fastish food experience", these City operations do a good line in *"reasonably-priced"* sushi, plus some non-Japanese fare (including hot dishes), which you grab from the passing conveyor; thumbs up for the lively new Appold/Sun St branch. / www.k10.com; Appold 9 pm, Wed-Fri 9.30 pm; both branches Sat & Sun, Copthall closed Mon-Fri D.

Kadiri's NW10 £23 ⓸⓷⓶
26 High Rd 8459 0936 1–1A
"A true taste of India!"; this '70s spot, in Willesden, is *"cramped, but well worth it"* – the food's *"fabulous"* and the menu *"much more varied than usual"*. / NW10 2QD; www.kadiris.com.

Kaffeine W1 £12 ⓷⓸⓹
66 Great Titchfield St 7580 6755 3–1C
"Outstanding coffee made with care and consideration", *"amazingly inventive sandwiches and salads"* plus *"cakes to die for"* – no wonder this *"great independent"* has a following out of step with its modest size. / W1W 7QJ; www.kaffeine.co.uk; @kaffeinelondon; L only; no Amex; no bookings.

Kai Mayfair W1 £97 **4 4 2**
65 South Audley St   7493 8988   3–3A
Some "exemplary and exquisite" meals won stellar ratings this year
for this Mayfair Chinese "classic"; the interior can "lack atmosphere",
though, and prices are "off the scale". / W1K 2QU; www.kaimayfair.co.uk;
@kaimayfair; 10.45 pm, Sun 10.15 pm.

Kaifeng NW4 £62 **3 2 2**
51 Church Rd   8203 7888   1–1B
A Hendon stalwart that's still, say fans, "the best Chinese-kosher
restaurant in town" (and coeliac- and allergy-friendly too); it's the kind
of place where "standards never drop… but then again nor do the
prices!" / NW4 4DU; www.kaifeng.co.uk; 10 pm; closed Fri & Sat; set Sun L
£44 (FP).

Kaosarn £26 **4 3 4**
110 St Johns Hill, SW11   7223 7888   10–2C
Brixton Village, Coldharbour Ln, SW9   7095 8922   10–2D
"Delicious", "spicy'" and "fragrant" – the Thai food at these BYO
cafés, in Brixton Village and Battersea, is an "amazing bargain";
no wonder they're "always hopping"! / SW9 10 pm, Sun 9 pm;
sw11 closed Mon L.

Karma W14 £40 **4 4 2**
44 Blythe Rd   7602 9333   7–1D
"Tucked away in a place you wouldn't expect to find much life",
this Olympia backwoods Indian is of note for its "unusually authentic"
curries; "atmosphere can be lacking", though – "perhaps why the
delivery service is so popular!" / W14 0HA; www.k-a-r-m-a.co.uk;
@KarmaKensington; 11 pm; no Amex.

Karpo NW1 £49 **3 2 1**
23 Euston Rd   7843 2221   8–3C
With its "interesting" and "tasty" fare, this dining room opposite
St Pancras can sometimes seem quite a "find"; the setting is "stark",
though, and service can come "with attitude". / NW1 2SD;
www.karpo.co.uk; @karporestaurants; 10.30 pm.

**Kaspar's Seafood and Grill
The Savoy Hotel WC2** £74 **3 3 3**
100 The Strand   7836 4343   4–3D
Critics may say it "lacks imagination", but the Savoy's former River
Restaurant wins a solid thumbs-up from reporters for its
"very acceptable" fish and fruits de mer, and "lovely" setting
(especially if you get one of the few window tables); "excellent"
breakfast too. / WC2R 0EU; www.kaspars.co.uk; 11 pm; set always available
£42 (FP); SRA-3 stars.

Kateh W9 £43 **5 4 3**
5 Warwick Pl   7289 3393   8–4A
A "treasure near Little Venice", offering "top-drawer" dishes which
"reflect the diversity and depth of Persian food"; "it may
be cramped", but otherwise it's "hard to fault". / W9 2PX;
www.katehrestaurant.co.uk; 11 pm, Sun 9.30 pm; closed weekday L.

Kazan £46 **3 3 3**
77 Wilton Rd, SW1   7233 8298   2–4B
93-94 Wilton Rd, SW1   7233 7100   2–4B
*"We went as it was handy, but I'd go back as the food was a cut
above!"; this Pimlico spot – which has a spin-off café on the other
side of the road – serves "fine and subtle" mezze and grills.
/ www.kazan-restaurant.com; 10 pm.*

The Keeper's House
Royal Academy W1 £60 **3 2 3**
Royal Academy Of Arts, Piccadilly   7300 5881   3–3D
*"Tucked away" in the basement of the Royal Academy,
an "interesting" year-old restaurant (restricted to 'Friends'
at lunchtime) – fans find it "lovely" all-round, but critics decry "style
over substance". / W1J 0BD; www.keepershouse.org.uk; 8.30 pm; D only,
closed Sun.*

Ken Lo's Memories SW1 £60 **3 4 3**
65-69 Ebury St   7730 7734   2–4B
*A grand Belgravia Chinese veteran, sometimes accused of "resting
on its old reputation"; what's almost more striking, though, is the
ongoing enthusiasm of the fans, for whom it's still "top-notch" and
"always reliable". / SW1W 0NZ; www.memoriesofchina.co.uk; 10.45 pm,
Sun 10 pm.*

Kennington Tandoori SE11 £48 **4 4 3**
313 Kennington Rd   7735 9247   1–3C
*"Wonderful Indian food" with "superb flavours" wins nothing but
praise for this "busy" local fixture, whose "very varied clientele"
includes a good number of politicos. / SE11 4QE;
www.kenningtontandoori.com; @TheKTL; 11.30 pm; no Amex.*

Kensington Place W8 £54 **4 5 3**
201-209 Kensington Church St   7727 3184   6–2B
*"They seem to have found their feet again at last!" – this "incredibly
noisy" '90s 'goldfish bowl', just off Notting Hill Gate, has notably
"friendly" service, and offers "comforting, classy and nourishing"
dishes, majoring in "fish from their own fish shop" next door.
/ W8 7LX; www.kensingtonplace-restaurant.co.uk; @kprestaurantW8;
10.30 pm; closed Mon L & Sun D; SRA-2 stars.*

Kensington Square Kitchen W8 £33 **3 4 4**
9 Kensington Sq   7938 2598   5–1A
*A "refreshingly one-off café", on a scenic square off bustling
Kensington High Street, which is particularly attractive as a
breakfast option, cramped as it is. / W8 5EP;
www.kensingtonsquarekitchen.co.uk; @KSKRestaurant; 3.30 pm; L only;
no Amex.*

The Kensington Wine Rooms W8 £50 **2 2 3**
127-129 Kensington Church St   7727 8142   6–2B
*A "huge range of wines by the glass" garners plenty of praise for this
pub-conversion near Notting Hill Gate – the food is rather incidental.
/ W8 7LP; www.greatwinesbytheglass.com; @wine_rooms; 10.45 pm;
set weekday L £30 (FP).*

Kentish Canteen NW5 £44 243
300 Kentish Town Rd 7485 7331 8–2C
*"Every area should have one", say fans of this "pleasant" and
"friendly" Kentish Town spot, praising its "small but well judged
menu"; sceptics though say that the cooking "strives to be a cut
above, and doesn't quite make it".* / NW5 2TG; www.kentishcanteen.co.uk;
@kentishcanteen; 10.30 pm.

(Brew House)
Kenwood House NW3 £33 225
Hampstead Heath 8341 5384 8–1A
*"A delicious breakfast, with fresh ingredients, on the edge
of Hampstead Heath" is one of the headline attractions – along with
afternoon tea – at Kenwood House's relaunched café, whose garden
tables, in particular, are "perfect on a sunny day".* / NW3 7JR;
www.companyofcooks.com; @EHKenwood; 6 pm (summer), 4 pm (winter);
L only.

Kerbisher & Malt £19 332
53 New Broadway, W5 8840 4418 1–2A
164 Shepherd's Bush Rd, W6 3556 0228 7–1C
170 Upper Richmond Rd West, SW14 8876 3404 1–4A NEW
50 Abbeville Rd, SW4 3417 4350 10–2D NEW
*"Exceptionally fresh fish, lightly prepared" wins praise for this
modern-day reinvention of the chippy; there's some feeling
it "promises more than it delivers", though, and critics find the
cooking no more than "OK".* / www.kerbisher.co.uk; 10 pm - 10.30pm,
Sun 9 pm - 9.30 pm; W6 Closed Mon; no booking.

Kettners W1 £60 223
29 Romilly St 7734 6112 4–2A
*With its "very traditionally-styled dining room", and a champagne bar
for pre-prandials, this Soho "old favourite" (originally established
1867) still has its fans, especially pre-theatre; critics are pretty
strident, though – "this is the most overpriced rubbish I've ever had!"*
/ W1D 5HP; www.kettners.com; 11 pm, Fri & Sat 11.30 pm, Sun 9.30 pm.

Khan's W2 £23 422
13-15 Westbourne Grove 7727 5420 6–1C
*"Still a standard-bearer for Indian food"; this authentic (no-booze)
Bayswater veteran has a style and ambience sometimes compared,
not always favourably, to a subcontinental railway station.* / W2 4UA;
www.khansrestaurant.com; 11.30 pm, Sat-Sun midnight.

Kiku W1 £55 542
17 Half Moon St 7499 4208 3–4B
*With its "delicious" and "authentic" cuisine, it's perhaps no wonder
this Mayfair fixture is "full of Japanese from the consulate";
only quibble – the "cold" ambience of the room.* / W1J 7BE;
www.kikurestaurant.co.uk; 10.15 pm, Sun 9.45 pm; closed Sun L.

Kikuchi W1 £52 521
14 Hanway St 7637 7720 4–1A
*"Just for the sushi – nothing else"; this hard-to-find spot,
off Tottenham Court Road, serves "excellent" food, but the
surroundings are "basic", and service – though some find
it "endearing" – can be "below par".* / W1T 1UD; 10.30 pm; closed Sun.

Kimchee WC1 £39 4 2 3
71 High Holborn 7430 0956 2–1D
This "very busy" Midtown Korean "Wagamama lookalike" offers "a great intro to Asian food", and is "a useful, quick place" for "a fun and affordable lunch"; service though can be amateur. / WC1V 6EA; www.kimchee.uk.com; @kimcheerest; 10.30 pm.

Kings Road Steakhouse & Grill
Marco Pierre White SW3 £56 2 1 1
386 King's Rd 7351 9997 5–3B
This Chelsea steakhouse does have its fans who praise its "consistently excellent steak and other dishes"; equally passionate are its foes – "I've eaten in countless places in the 12 years I've lived in London, and none has felt as overpriced and cynical as this". / SW3 5UZ; www.londonsteakhousecompanies.com; 10.30 pm, Sun 10 pm.

Kipferl N1 £43 3 3 3
20 Camden Pas 77041 555 8–3D
"Something a bit different!" – "unfussy yet sophisticated", this Islington deli-restaurant offers such Austrian delights as "hearty" soups and "outstanding" strudel. / N1 8ED; www.kipferl.co.uk; @KipferlCafe; 9.30 pm; closed Mon.

Kiraku W5 £35 5 3 2
8 Station Pde 8992 2848 1–3A
"It's easy to find a more expensive Japanese, but harder to find a better one", say fans of this "canteen-like" outfit, near Ealing Common tube; "everything tastes so very fresh" – "for value, it can't be beaten". / W5 3LD; www.kiraku.co.uk; @kirakulondon; 10 pm; closed Mon; no Amex.

Kitchen W8 W8 £65 5 4 3
11-13 Abingdon Road 7937 0120 5–1A
Offering "very complex" dishes at "amazing value-for-money" prices, and "courteous" service too, this "grown-up" Kensington spot, part-owned by Phil (The Square) Howard, has a large and devoted following. / W8 6AH; www.kitchenw8.com; @KitchenW8; 10.15 pm, Sun 9.15 pm; set weekday L £43 (FP), set Sun L £53 (FP).

Koba W1 £44 3 2 3
11 Rathbone St 7580 8825 2–1C
"One of the best Korean restaurants in town"; this Fitzrovia spot generally hits the spot, although the occasional critic can find the cuisine "somewhat muted"… "but the Soju and the table cooking make up for it!" / W1T 1NA; 10.30 pm; closed Sun L.

Koffmann's
The Berkeley SW1 £82 5 5 3
The Berkeley, Wilton Pl 7107 8844 5–1D
"Masterful chef" Pierre Koffmann – the man who made La Tante Claire London's best restaurant of the '90s – is truly back with a vengeance at this Knightsbridge venue, though nowadays his "faultless" Gallic gastronomy seems more "gutsy" than of old; the deep-basement setting, though, will never truly sparkle. / SW1X 7RL; www.the-berkeley.co.uk/top_restaurants.aspx; 10.30 pm; set pre theatre £52 (FP).

123

Kolossi Grill EC1   £33   3 4 4
56-60 Rosebery Ave   7278 5758   9–1A
A Farringdon veteran that its devotees have enjoyed for more than three decades; they say that, for value, its bargain-basement Greek Cypriot meze just "can't be beaten". / EC1R 4RR; www.kolossigrill.com; 11 pm; closed Sat L & Sun.

Konditor & Cook   £27   3 4 2
Curzon Soho, 99 Shaftesbury Ave, W1   0844 854 9367   4–3A
46 Gray's Inn Rd, WC1   0844 854 9365   9–1A
10 Stoney St, SE1   0844 854 9363   9–4C
22 Cornwall Road, SE1   0844 854 9361   9–4A
30 St Mary Axe, EC3   0844 854 9369   9–2D
"Dark, dense, fudgey, squishy, incredible"… and that's just the Boston Brownies – there's a "vast selection" of "fatally tempting" cakes on offer at this "enthusiastic" small group; "great coffee" and "tasty hot food" too. / www.konditorandcook.com; 6 pm; W1 11 pm; WC1 & EC3 closed Sat & Sun; SE1 closed Sun; no booking.

Kopapa WC2   £58   2 2 2
32-34 Monmouth St   7240 6076   4–2B
Peter Gordon is a chef with pedigree (Sugar Club, Providores), and his "excellent and interesting" Pacific-fusion dishes please many visitors to this "crowded" Theatreland café; reports are very up-and-down, though, and doubters "just can't see what the excitement is about". / WC2H 9HA; www.kopapa.co.uk; @Kopapacafe; 10.45 pm, Sun 9.45 pm.

Koya W1   £35   4 4 3
49 Frith St   7434 4463   4–2A
"No faff, just incredible food"; this "tiny" and "simple" Soho Japanese is ferociously popular, especially for its udon noodles. / W1D 4SG; www.koya.co.uk; @KoyaUdon; 10.30 pm; no booking.

Koya-Bar W1   £34   4 4 4
50 Frith St   7434 4463   4–2A
A "better space than the original Koya" (next door), this "pleasingly functional noodle bar" feels "more like Tokyo than any of the other recent similar openings"; good breakfasts too. / W1D 4SQ; www.koyabar.co.uk; Mon-Wed 10 pm, Thu-Sat 10.30 pm, Sun 9.30 pm.

Kulu Kulu   £32   3 1 1
76 Brewer St, W1   7734 7316   3–2D
51-53 Shelton St, WC2   7240 5687   4–2C
39 Thurloe Pl, SW7   7589 2225   5–2C
"Don't go if you want posh surroundings" but, "for a cheap sushi-fix", these "run down and scruffy" conveyor-cafés do the job; their "generous" portions are "freshly made", and "prices are good". / 10 pm; SW7 10.30 pm; closed Sun; no Amex; no booking.

Kurobuta W2 NEW   £55   4 2 3
17-20 Kendal St   3475 4158   6–1D
After his King's Road pop-up, Nobu's former head chef opened this "welcome addition to London's rock 'n' roll Asian dining scene" – a "very casual" and "buzzy" izakaya-style spot, in Bayswater, serving "all sorts of funky Japanese dishes" which deliver "incredible and unusual" flavours. / W2 2AW; www.kurobuta-london.com; @KurobutaLondon; 10.30 pm; groups of 6+ cancelling less than 48hrs in advance are charged £25pp.

The Ladbroke Arms W11 £50 3 1 4
54 Ladbroke Rd 7727 6648 6–2B
A "smart" gastropub, with "idyllic" outside tables, whose "dependable" cooking has helped make this quite a Notting Hill stalwart; of late, however, some reporters have formed the view that the service "stinks" – what a shame! / W11 3NW;
www.capitalpubcompany.com; @ladbrokearms; 9.30 pm; no booking after 8 pm.

Ladurée £62 2 2 2
Harrods, 87-135 Brompton Rd, SW1 3155 0111 5–1D
71-72 Burlington Arc, Piccadilly, W1 7491 9155 3–3C
1 Covent Garden Mkt, WC2 7240 0706 4–3D
14 Cornhill, EC3 7283 5727 9–2C
"Exquisite macaroons and other mouthwateringly delicious pastries" win fans for these bijoux and pricey outposts of the Parisian pâtisserie; larger branches also offer a more extensive grand-café menu. / www.laduree.com; SW1 8.45 pm, Sun 5.45 pm; W1 6.30 pm, Sun 5 pm, EC3 8 pm; EC3 closed Sat-Sun; W1 no booking, SW1 no booking 3 pm-6 pm.

The Lady Ottoline WC1 £50 2 2 3
11a, Northington St 7831 0008 2–1D
"In an area where the choice is limited" (Bloomsbury), this beautifully restored Victorian pub makes a "happy" sort of destination; middling survey ratings though, suggest it's not quite living up to its potential. / WC1N 2JF; www.theladyottoline.com; @theladyottoline; 10 pm, Sun 8 pm.

Lahore Karahi SW17 £23 4 2 2
1 Tooting High Street, London 8767 2477 10–2C
"Great-value, no-nonsense food" is the winning formula behind this bustling, canteen-style Tooting Pakistani; don't forget to BYO. / SW17 0SN; www.lahorekarahi.co.uk; midnight; no Amex.

Lahore Kebab House £26 5 2 2
668 Streatham High Rd, SW16 8765 0771 10–2D
2-10 Umberston St, E1 7488 2551 11–1A
"Still the gold standard, despite its expansion", this "noisy" and "vibrant" Pakistani canteen in Whitechapel (with spin-offs) has a massive fan club for its "divine" lamb chops, and "great curries" too – who cares if the "Formica-tabled" ambience is "not the nicest"?; BYO. / midnight.

Lamberts SW12 £47 5 5 4
2 Station Pde 8675 2233 10–2C
"Excels in every way"; this "enterprising" and "pleasant" favourite, near Balham station, is a "wonderful" and "sensibly priced" operation – "more relaxed than Chez Bruce, but snapping at its heels in terms of quality". / SW12 9AZ; www.lambertsrestaurant.com; @lamberts_balham; 10 pm, Sun 5 pm; closed Mon & Sun D; no Amex; SRA-3 stars.

(Winter Garden)
The Landmark NW1 £82 2 3 4
222 Marylebone Rd 7631 8000 8–4A
"Free-flowing champagne and an extensive array of wonderful dishes" make for an "excellent Sunday brunch" in the "beautiful" atrium of this Marylebone hotel; its afternoon teas and so on also have their fans. / NW1 6JQ; www.landmarklondon.co.uk; @landmarklondon; 10.30 pm; no trainers; booking: max 12; set weekday L £49 (FP).

Langan's Brasserie W1 £64 2 2 4
Stratton St   7491 8822   3–3C
*For its (older) fan club, this famous brasserie veteran near the Ritz
"fits like an old slipper" – it's "always fun", and still "always buzzing";
the uninitiated, however, may merely find standards "no better than
average". / W1J 8LB; www.langansrestaurants.co.uk; @langanslondon;
11 pm, Fri & Sat 11.30 pm, Sun 10 pm.*

Lantana Cafe £35 3 3 4
13-14 Charlotte Pl, W1   7323 6601   2–1C
Unit 2, 1 Oliver's Yd, 55 City Rd, EC1   7253 5273   12–1A
*"Tucked away down a Fitzrovia side street", this Oz café
is "THE chilled place for coffee and brunch with friends"; we receive
little feedback on its spin-offs in Shoreditch and Camden Town.*

Lardo E8 £39 3 2 4
Richmond Rd   8533 8229   1–2D
*It helps to be "25, skinny and wearing a checked shirt", but all are
welcome to enjoy this "buzzy" Hackney two-year-old, where the
"well-sourced" Italian small plates "hit all the right notes". / E8 3NJ;
www.lardo.co.uk; @lardolondon; 10.30 pm, Sun 9.30 pm.*

Latium W1 £54 4 5 3
21 Berners St   7323 9123   3–1D
*Maurizio Morelli's "subtle" venture remains "one of the best Italians
in central London"; it stars "terrific" Roman cooking ("magnificent
ravioli"), "courteous and respectful" service, and a wine list "that's
an attraction in itself". / W1T 3LP; www.latiumrestaurant.com;
@LatiumLondon; 10.30 pm, Sat 11 pm; closed Sat L & Sun L.*

Launceston Place W8 £75 3 4 4
1a Launceston Pl   7937 6912   5–1B
*"Tucked away in the backstreets of Kensington", this "calm,
comfortable and intimate" townhouse is picture book-perfect for
a "discreet, romantic dinner"; fans applaud its "elegant" cuisine too
(although it can sometimes seem rather "safe"). / W8 5RL;
www.launcestonplace-restaurant.co.uk; 10 pm; closed Mon & Tue L; SRA-2
stars.*

The Lawn Bistro SW19 £61 2 2 2
67 High St   8947 8278   10–2B
*A "French-themed" bistro of two years' standing that's been
"very welcome in Wimbledon Village"; indeed, "on a good day, it's the
best place in the area", but results can 'miss', and even fans can feel
that "portions are too small and prices too high"! / SW19 5EE;
www.thelawnbistro.co.uk; @thelawnbistro; 9.30 pm, Sat 10 pm; closed
Mon & Sun D.*

THE LEDBURY W11 £135 5 5 4
127 Ledbury Rd   7792 9090   6–1B
*"Superb meals seem natural", at Brett Graham's "flawless" Notting
Hill stand-out: yet again London's No. 1 restaurant; there's
"no pomp" – staff are "so naturally courteous and efficient" –
and his "inspired" cuisine is "as close to perfect as you can get".
/ W11 2AQ; www.theledbury.com; @theledbury; 10.15 pm; closed
Mon L & Tue L; set weekday L £62 (FP).*

Lemonia NW1 £45 2 3 4
89 Regent's Park Rd   7586 7454   8–3B
"Always packed, even on Mondays", this "unchanging" Primrose Hill mega-taverna is a north London "phenomenon"; doubtless its straightforward old-favourite dishes "could be improved", but staff are "unflappable" and the atmosphere is "always cheerful". / NW1 8UY; www.lemonia.co.uk; @Lemonia_Greek; 11 pm; closed Sun D; no Amex.

Leon £26 3 3 3
Branches throughout London
"I just wish there were more branches!" – this "superbly innovative" chain went "from strength to strength" this year, consistently applauded for "very wholesome" dishes that are "healthy, tasty and fresh" and, "very attractively presented" too. / www.leonrestaurants.co.uk; 10 pm; W1 8.45 pm; E14 8 pm; EC4 closed Sun; W1 closed Sat & Sun; no booking L.

Leong's Legends W1 £37 3 2 3
3 Macclesfield St   7287 0288   4–3A
"A lovely, atmospheric tucked-away location" ("like a private club") adds to the charms of this budget Chinatown diner, which specialises in soup dumplings (Xiao Long Baou); the cooking has been rather "up and down" of late, "but the best is very good". / W1D 6AX; www.leongslegend.com; 11 pm, Sat 11.30 pm; no booking.

Levant W1 £54 2 2 3
Jason Ct, 76 Wigmore St   7224 1111   3–1A
Some fans still find this "expensive" party-Lebanese, near Selfridges, a "fun" destination (especially "in a group"); the food rarely excites, though, and the music can seem "painfully loud". / W1U 2SJ; www.levant.co.uk; 9.45pm, Fri & Sat midnight.

The Lido Café
Brockwell Lido SE24 £45 2 2 3
Dulwich Rd   7737 8183   10–2D
"It's great to sit overlooking the swimming pool" – the special attraction of eating at this "lovely" south London lido, which is a "fun destination for all ages"; the food's generally "not bad" either. / SE24 0PA; www.thelidocafe.co.uk; @thelidocafe; 9.30 pm; closed Sun D; no Amex.

The Light House SW19 £56 2 3 3
75-77 Ridgway   8944 6338   10–2B
Something of a "flagship for Wimbledon dining", this "airy" and "accommodating" local favourite dishes up food that "certainly does not want for creativity" – the realisation, however, "doesn't always nail it". / SW19 4ST; www.lighthousewimbledon.com; 10.30 pm; closed Sun D; set weekday L £34 (FP), set always available £38 (FP).

Lima W1 £56 4 2 2
31 Rathbone Pl   3002 2640   2–1C
"Taste bud-reviving" Peruvian dishes (with "outstanding ceviches" and "delicious" pisco sours) win ongoing acclaim for this Fitzrovia yearling (which recently added a Covent Garden offshoot); service can be "inefficient", though, and the interior is "cramped and noisy". / W1T 1JH; www.limalondon.com; @lima_london; 10.30 pm; closed Sun; set weekday L & pre-theatre £40 (FP); SRA-1 star.

Lima Floral WC2 NEW £57
14 Garrick St   7240 5778   4–3C
*Newly established in re-emerging Covent Garden, an offshoot
of Fitzrovia's Lima; too few reports yet for a rating, but they tend
to suggest it's a satisfactory destination for Peruvian fare, rather than
an earth-shattering one. / WC2E 9BJ; www.limafloral.com; @Lima_london;
11.30 pm; closed Sun D.*

Linnea TW9 £48   5 4 3
Kew Green   8940 5696   1–3A
*"Would be 3x the price in Knightsbridge or Soho"; Jonas Karlsson's
newcomer on the Green may be "a bit clinical" ambience-wise,
but some locals are already tipping his cooking ("a Scandi take
on modern European") as "better even than the nearby Glasshouse".
/ TW9 3BH; www.linneakew.co.uk; 10.30 pm; closed Mon & Sun.*

Lisboa Pâtisserie W10 £8   4 4 2
57 Golborne Rd   8968 5242   6–1A
*"Great coffee, and perhaps the best pastries in London!" win ongoing
acclaim for this "stalwart" Portuguese café in North Kensington;
it's "always busy". / W10 5NR; 7 pm; L & early evening only; no booking.*

Little Bay £32   2 3 4
228 Belsize Rd, NW6   7372 4699   1–2B
228 York Rd, SW11   7223 4080   10–2B
171 Farringdon Rd, EC1   7278 1234   9–1A
*"How do they offer such good value?" – that's always the question
at these "eccentric and outlandishly themed" budget bistros, where
the "food is uninspiring, but hard to fault at the price".
/ www.little-bay.co.uk; @TheLittleBay; 11.30 pm, Sun 11 pm; no Amex,
NW6 no credit cards.*

Little Georgia Café £39   3 2 3
14 Barnsbury Rd, N1   7278 6100   8–3D
87 Goldsmiths Row, E2   7739 8154   1–2D
*They weren't joking about the "little", when they named this
reasonably priced Hackney café (which now has an offshoot
in Islington); "interesting and tasty brunch dishes" are a highlight.
/ www.littlegeorgia.co.uk.*

Little Social W1 £74   3 3 3
5 Pollen St   7870 3730   3–2C
*"Small", "cosy" and "comforting" – this Mayfair mews bistro can
seem "a nicer and less pretentious place that its famous sibling,
Pollen Street Social, just across the road"; since last year, however,
survey satisfaction has notably headed south – has it been overlooked
as the Atherton empire explodes? / W1S 1NE; www.littlesocial.co.uk;
@_littlesocial; 10.30 pm; closed Sun; set weekday L £42 (FP).*

LMNT E8 £37   2 3 5
316 Queensbridge Rd   7249 6727   1–2D
*"You just have to go with the whole weird experience!", at this
bonkers, pharaoh-kitsch Dalston pub-conversion; not everyone loves
the food, but it's mostly rated well. / E8 3NH; www.lmnt.co.uk; 10.30 pm;
Mon-Thu D only, Fri-Sun open L & D; no Amex.*

The Lobster House SW18 NEW £55 2 2 3
94 Point Pleasant 8871 1226 10–2B
This "chilled" new 'pontoon bar' has a "lovely location", on the river by Wandsworth Park; foodwise the clue is in the name, and though not all reporters are wowed, fans say its surf 'n' turf offering is "awesome". / SW18 1PP; www.thelobster-house.co.uk.

Lobster Pot SE11 £62 4 3 2
3 Kennington Ln 7582 5556 1–3C
"Real" Breton seafood "of the highest quality" is a surprise find at this "tiny" family-run stalwart; that's not just because of its lost-in-Kennington location, but also in view of the surreal nautical decor – listen out for the seagulls! / SE11 4RG; www.lobsterpotrestaurant.co.uk; 10.30 pm; closed Mon & Sun; booking: max 8.

Locanda Locatelli
Hyatt Regency W1 £77 3 3 4
8 Seymour St 7935 9088 2–2A
A "perennial favourite" for most reporters, Giorgio Locatelli's "great-looking" (and "calm") Marylebone Italian offers "very accomplished" cuisine and "amazing" wines; service can be "snooty", though, and a few refuseniks say the food's "not really up to the hype and prices". / W1H 7JZ; www.locandalocatelli.com; 11 pm, Thu-Sat 11.30 pm, Sun 10.15 pm; booking: max 8.

Locanda Ottomezzo W8 £66 3 4 3
2-4 Thackeray St 7937 2200 5–1B
"An always-appealing menu of beautifully cooked Italian food served with charm and passion" has won this Kensington venture a strong neighbourhood following; "for easy eats and good coffee", visit the café. / W8 5ET; www.locandaottoemezzo.co.uk; 10.30 pm, Fri & Sat 10.45 pm; closed Mon L, Sat L & Sun.

Loch Fyne £45 2 2 2
2-4 Catherine St, WC2 7240 4999 2–2D
77-78 Gracechurch St, EC3 7929 8380 9–3C
"Never a wow, but fairly reliable" – one reporter nicely captures the slight ambivalence that envelopes many reports on this national fish-and-seafood chain; it undoubtedly has its fans, though, and some "good locations" too. / www.lochfyne-restaurants.com; 10 pm; WC2 10.30 pm.

The Lockhart W1 £54 2 2 2
24 Seymour Pl 3011 5400 2–2A
Critics of this southern-USA yearling attack its "alarmingly uneven standards" and "surprisingly unatmospheric" interior; fans, though, love its "down-home, sinfully delicious and calorific" treats, which include "the best fried chicken" and "amazing cornbread". / W1H 7NL; www.lockhartlondon.com; @LockhartLondon; 10.30 pm; closed Mon.

Lola Rojo SW11 £43 3 2 3
78 Northcote Rd 7350 2262 10–2C
"Dependable and inventive Spanish food" that's "priced so that you don't feel guilty about going regularly" wins praise for this modern Hispanic venue, in Battersea. / SW11 6QL; www.lolarojo.net; 10.30 pm, Sat & Sun 11 pm; no Amex.

London House SW11 NEW £57 454
7-9 Battersea Sq 7592 8545 10–1C
*"Ramsay does it right!" – his "slick" Battersea newcomer debuts
as one of the highest-rated in the GR empire, winning praise for
accomplished cooking and often-"excellent" value; good wine list too.
/ SW11 3RA; www.gordonramsay.com/london-house; @londonhouse; Mon-Fri
10 pm; closed Mon, Tue L, Wed L & Thu L.*

Look Mum No Hands! EC1 £30 334
49 Old St 7253 1025 9–1B
*"Worth pulling on the Lycra for" – this bike-themed Clerkenwell café
(part of a cycle shop) offers "wholesome, if slightly cranky, fare" and
"the best filter coffee in town"; "they show all the major cycling races
too". / EC1V 9HX; www.lookmumnohands.co.uk; @1ookmumnohands;
10 pm.*

The Lord Northbrook SE12 £36 344
116 Burnt Ash Rd 8318 1127 1–4D
*"A great pub, in an area lacking great pubs!" – this "large" and
"handsome" Lea Green hostelry serves "very enjoyable" and "varied"
cooking alongside "an ever-changing roster of interesting real ales".
/ SE12 8PU; www.thelordnorthbrook.co.uk; 9 pm, Fri & Sat 10 pm.*

Lorenzo SE19 £42 343
73 Westow Hill 8761 7485 1–4D
*Thanks to its "authentic Italian food", this Upper Norwood fixture
is always "very busy"; "book on the ground floor", though –
the "basement can be slightly overpowering and cramped".
/ SE19 1TX; www.lorenzo.uk.com; 10.30 pm.*

Lotus Chinese Floating Restaurant E14 £43 322
9 Oakland Quay 7515 6445 11–2C
*"The prices seem to keep going up, but the quality of the dim sum
is still very good", at this boat permanently moored near Canary
Wharf; it's particularly "popular and bustling" at lunch – "be sure
to arrive early". / E14 9EA; www.lotusfloating.co.uk; 10.30 pm; closed Mon.*

Lucio SW3 £63 222
257 Fulham Rd 7823 3007 5–3B
*Many locals still love this Chelsea Italian, hailing its "professionalism"
and "superb home-cooking"; even fans note it's "expensive", though,
and critics sense it's become "arrogant" to boot. / SW3 6HY;
www.luciorestaurant.com; 10.45 pm.*

Lucky Seven W2 £40 333
127 Westbourne Park Rd 7727 6771 6–1B
*"Back to the USA in the '50s" – Tom Conran's authentic-looking
diner, on the fringe of Notting Hill, is a top spot for burger and
shakes; "you really do feel like you're back in America". / W2 5QL;
www.lucky7london.co.uk; 10.15 pm, Sun 10 pm; no Amex; no booking.*

Lupita WC2 £39 323
13-15 Villiers St 7930 5355 4–4D
*A "really tasty Mexican", by Charing Cross – it makes "a handy no-
reservations option when you need a tasty bite on a budget".
/ WC2N 6ND; www.lupita.co.uk; @LupitaUK; 11 pm, Fri & Sat 11.30 pm,
Sun 10 pm.*

Lutyens EC4   £74   2 2 2
85 Fleet St   7583 8385   9–2A
*Sir Terence Conran's deadly-dull but "convenient" City-fringe brasserie
offers a "bland" (but "pricey") menu that's "easy for business" –
"the food comes and goes without notice, so you can get on with
work!" / EC4Y IAE; www.lutyens-restaurant.com; 9.45 pm; closed Sat & Sun;
set dinner £49 (FP).*

Lyle's EI NEW   £66   4 4 2
The Tea Building, 56 Shoreditch High St   3011 5911   12–IB
*"Sparse" the decor may be, but this Shoreditch newcomer surprises
with its "very intelligent and interesting dishes, with a real light touch"
(in the school of St John), and "excellent" service too. / EI 6JJ;
www.lyleslondon.com; @lyleslondon; 10 pm; closed Sat L & Sun.*

M EC2 NEW
2-3 Threadneedle Walk   3327 7770   9–2C
*From former Gaucho head honcho, Martin Williams, comes this big
City opening; boasting two restaurants in one – M Grill and M Raw –
the menu maxes out on beef. / EC2 8HP; www.mrestaurants.co.uk;
@mrestaurants_.*

Ma Cuisine TW9   £42   3 4 3
9 Station Approach   8332 1923   I–3A
*"A petite venue with lots of charm", near Kew Gardens station;
its traditional bistro fare is "very reliable", and "cheap" too, "if you
stick to the set menus". / TW9 3QB; www.macuisinekew.co.uk; 10 pm,
Fri & Sat 10.30 pm; no Amex.*

Ma Goa SW15   £40   4 4 2
242-244 Upper Richmond Rd   8780 1767   10–2B
*"Never disappointing!"; this family-run Putney "old favourite" has won
local adulation with its "interesting" Goan home-cooking and "smiley"
service; oh, and great value too. / SW15 6TG; www.ma-goa.com;
@magoarestaurant; 10.30 pm, Fri & Sat 11 pm.*

Made In Camden
Roundhouse NWI   £39   3 3 3
Chalk Farm Rd   7424 8495   8–2B
*An attractive bar-dining room that manages not to play total second
fiddle to Camden Town's hip Roundhouse, which it's part of;
the "excellent selection of small plate-style light dishes" are "perfect
for lunch". / NWI 8EH; www.madeincamden.com; 10.15 pm.*

Made in Italy   £42   3 3 4
14a, Old Compton St, WI   0011 1214   4–2B
50 James St, WI   7224 0182   3–IA
249 King's Rd, SW3   7352 1880   5–3C
*"Excellent pizza" served by-the-metre retains a loyal fan club for the
buzzy Chelsea original; the other offshoots inspire little feedback.
/ www.madeinitalygroup.co.uk; 11 pm, Sun 10 pm; SW3 closed Mon L.*

Madhu's UBI   £35   4 3 3
39 South Rd   8574 1897   I–3A
*With its "superb" cuisine, and smart interior, this celebrated Indian,
is "probably marginally the best in Southall"; they also do the
subcontinental catering for some top West End hotels. / UBI ISW;
www.madhus.co.uk; 11.30 pm; closed Tue, Sat L & Sun L.*

The Magazine Restaurant
Serpentine Gallery W2 £50 ② ③ ⑤

Kensington Gdns 7298 7552 6–2D
Zaha Hadid's "seductive" architecture lends a "lively cosmopolitan" vibe to this "beautiful" new structure, in Hyde Park; there's "nothing much wrong with the food", and "the walk to and fro is good for the digestion". / W2 3XA; www.magazine-restaurant.co.uk; @TheMagazineLDN; Tue & Sun 6 pm, Wed-Sat 10.45 pm; closed Mon, Tue D & Sun D.

Magdalen SE1 £55 ④ ④ ③

152 Tooley St 7403 1342 9–4D
"Lots of offal" and unusual "carnivorous" dishes appear on the "creative" seasonal menu of this "hidden gem" in the still-thin environs of City Hall – a very "honest" and "pleasingly low-key" venture that's ideal for "a discreet business lunch". / SE1 2TU; www.magdalenrestaurant.co.uk; @Magdalense1; 10 pm; closed Sat L & Sun; set weekday L £35 (FP).

Maggie Jones's W8 £55 ② ③ ⑤

6 Old Court Pl 7937 6462 5–1A
"It was better in the '70s" – apparently – but this rustic (if "very cramped") stalwart, near Kensington Palace, retains a "special", romantic allure, and remains "very popular" for its solid Anglo-French fare. / W8 4PL; www.maggie-jones.co.uk; 11 pm, Sun 10.30 pm; set Sun L £42 (FP).

Maguro W9 £38 ④ ④ ③

5 Lanark Pl 7289 4353 8–4A
This very small Maida Vale Japanese was once a local secret... but "has now become so popular it can sometimes be difficult to get a table"; it serves "really good" food, but "without the stellar prices". / W9 1BT; www.maguro-restaurant.com; 10.30 pm; no Amex.

Maison Bertaux W1 £16 ④ ② ③

28 Greek St 7437 6007 4–2A
"Shabby", "cramped", "chaotic"... "please don't change!" – this most "quirky" of Soho cafés (est 1871) continues to delights fans with its "epic" croissants and "delicious" cakes. / W1D 5DQ; www.maisonbertaux.com; @Maison_Bertaux; 10.15 pm, Sun 8 pm.

Malabar W8 £44 ④ ④ ②

27 Uxbridge St 7727 8800 6–2B
"It just keeps going!"; "always-reliable", this elegantly understated Notting Hill Indian veteran "has maintained high standards over many years". / W8 7TQ; www.malabar-restaurant.co.uk; 11 pm, Sun 10.30 pm; set Sun L £25 (FP).

Malabar Junction WC1 £41 ③ ② ③

107 Gt Russell St 7580 5230 2–1C
A spacious and "charming" Keralan venue, near the British Museum; it can be quiet... "which is surprising as it's really good and reasonably priced". / WC1B 3NA; www.malabarjunction.com; 11 pm.

The Mall Tavern W8 £46 ② ② ③

71-73 Palace Gardens Ter 7229 3374 6–2B
Near Notting Hill Gate, an attractive gastropub which has made quite a name for its "impressive menu and wine list"; some "fantastic" meals are recorded, but reports have become much less consistent than they once were. / W8 4RU; www.themalltavern.com; @themalltavern; 10 pm; no Amex.

The Malt House SW6 £58 4 4 3
17 Vanston Pl 7084 6888 5–3A
Even those "apprehensive about its Made in Chelsea connections"
applaud this Fulham gastroboozer for its "interesting" food;
"very good service" too. / SW6 1AY; www.malthousefulham.co.uk;
@MalthouseFulham; 10 pm, Sun 9 pm.

Mandalay W2 £27 3 3 1
444 Edgware Rd 7258 3696 8–4A
It may be "very basic" and "at the run-down end of the Edgware
Road", but this "friendly" family-run operation offers "different"
Burmese dishes that are "cheap" and "tasty"; "always book to avoid
disappointment – even on a Monday night!" / W2 1EG;
www.mandalayway.com; 10.30 pm; closed Sun.

Mandarin Kitchen W2 £41 4 1 1
14-16 Queensway 7727 9012 6–2C
"Still the place for lobster noodles" (and "so many other interesting
dishes" too), this "densely packed" Bayswater Chinese may be a bit
of a "dump", but it remains as "reliable" a destination as you'll find.
/ W2 3RX; 11.15 pm.

Mangal I E8 £31 5 3 2
10 Arcola St 7275 8981 1–1C
"The best Turkish grill in London" is to be found at this "sparsely
decorated" and "brilliant-value" BYO café; "there are quite a few
similarly named establishments in Dalston – accept no imitations!"
/ E8 2DJ; www.mangal1.com; @Mangalone; midnight, Sat & Sun 1 am;
no credit cards.

Mangal II N16 £37 3 3 2
4 Stoke Newington Rd 7254 7888 1–1C
Famously Gilbert & George's nightly supper haunt – a "cheap and
cheerful" Ockabasi offering some of the "best grilled meats
in Dalston". / N16 8BH; www.mangal2.com; 1 am.

Mango Food of India SE1 £46 3 2 2
5-6 Cromwell Buildings, Redcross Way 7407 0333 9–4C
Mainly of interest to Borough Market visitors who find themselves
craving an Indian meal – a "cramped" operation offering
"some innovative takes on your standard offerings". / SE1 9HR;
www.lovemango.co.uk; 11 pm.

Mango Room NW1 £45 3 3 2
10-12 Kentish Town Rd 7482 5065 8–3B
"One of the best in Camden Town!" – a popular and laid-back haunt
which "after all these years, is still serving interesting and very good
Caribbean food". / NW1 8NH; www.mangoroom.co.uk; 11 pm.

Mango Tree SW1 £54 1 1 2
46 Grosvenor Pl 7823 1888 2–4B
This Belgravia outpost of an international Thai operation inspires
deeply mixed reports, too many of them very disappointing; they're
"always rammed though, thanks to the coupon-dining crowd".
/ SW1X 7EQ; www.mangotree.org.uk; 11 pm, Thu-Sat 11.30 pm,
Sun 10.30 pm.

Manicomio £61 323
85 Duke of York Sq, SW3 7730 3366 5–2D
6 Gutter Ln, EC2 7726 5010 9–2B
"Glorious al fresco seating" adds lustre to both of these Chelsea and
City Italians – *"efficient"*, if somewhat *"perfunctory"*, operations
serving food that's *"competent, if a little overpriced"*.
/ www.manicomio.co.uk; SW3 10.30 pm, Sun 10 pm; EC2 10 pm; EC2 closed
Sat & Sun.

Manna NW3 £57 232
4 Erskine Rd 7722 8028 8–3B
*The UK's longest-established veggie, in Primrose Hill, is mainly
of interest as an historical footnote nowadays – it's not without (local)
fans, but pricey and perennially inconsistent.* / NW3 3AJ;
www.mannav.com; @mannacuisine; 10 pm; closed Mon.

Marani W1 NEW £68 332
54-55 Curzon St 7495 1260 3–3B
*Implausibly located in a charming townhouse in the heart of Mayfair
(on the former site of Tempo, RIP), an "interesting" family-run
Georgian newcomer – "charming, albeit a little amateur at times".*
/ W1J 8PG; www.maranilondon.co.uk; 11 pm.

**MARCUS
THE BERKELEY SW1** £116 333
Wilton Pl 7235 1200 5–1D
*"Marcus Wareing seems to have taken his eye off the ball";
an allegedly informalising refurbishment (plus snappier name) has
somehow succeeded in making his Knightsbridge dining room even
stuffier than before, and its "good, not amazing" cuisine is struggling
to justify prices some reporters find "ridiculous".* / SW1X 7RL;
www.marcuswareing.com; @marcuswareing; 10.45 pm; closed Sun; no jeans
or trainers; booking: max 8.

Margaux SW5 NEW £64 333
152 Old Brompton Rd 7373 5753 5–2B
*A "local bistro", newly opened in Earl's Court, where "good-rather-
than-amazing" Gallic fare vies for attention with the thoughtful wine
selection.* / SW5 0BE; www.barmargaux.co.uk.

Marianne W2 £91 443
104 Chepstow Rd 3675 7750 6–1B
*"A joyous experience"; Marianne Lumb' serves "astonishing, delicate
and wonderful" dishes in the "small and most delightful" dining room
of this "intimate" Bayswater yearling – a "very romantic" location,
where "the focus is on your food and your partner".* / W2 5QS;
www.mariannerestaurant.com; @Marianne_W2; 9.15 pm; closed Mon;
set weekday L £65 (FP).

Market NW1 £50 432
43 Parkway 7267 9700 8–3B
*A Camden Town "treasure" that's "worth seeking out" –
a "welcoming" bare-bricked bistro offering a menu of updated
"classic" dishes that are "well-cooked and well-served".* / NW1 7PN;
www.marketrestaurant.co.uk; @MarketCamden; 10.30 pm, Sun 3 pm; closed
Sun D; set weekday L £32 (FP).

Maroush £48 4 2 2
I) 21 Edgware Rd, W2 7723 0773 6–1D
II) 38 Beauchamp Pl, SW3 7581 5434 5–1C
V) 3-4 Vere St, W1 7493 5050 3–1B
VI) 68 Edgware Rd, W2 7224 9339 6–1D
'Garden') 1 Connaught St, W2 7262 0222 6–1D
The "fresh bright flavours" of the Lebanese cuisine leap off the plates
of this long-established chain; a "top shawarma" in the bustling
café/take-aways (I and II) offers a budget-friendly alternative to the
grander adjoining dining rooms. / www.maroush.com; most branches close
between 12.30 am-5 am.

Masala Zone £33 3 4 3
9 Marshall St, W1 7287 9966 3–2D
48 Floral St, WC2 7379 0101 4–2D
147 Earl's Court Rd, SW5 7373 0220 5–2A
75 Bishop's Bridge Rd, W2 7221 0055 6–1C
80 Upper St, N1 7359 3399 8–3D
"Surprised at how good this chain was!" – these "cheerful and lively"
Indian pit stops deliver a "highly professional" package of "fresh and
distinctive street food" at "reasonable prices", and in "very convenient
locations" too. / www.realindianfood.com; 11 pm, Sun 10.30 pm; no Amex;
booking: min 10.

MASH Steakhouse W1 £83 3 3 2
77 Brewer St 7734 2608 3–2D
"Not cheap, but it's a great space with great steaks", says one fan
of this "beautiful" subterranean Art Deco chamber, hidden away near
Piccadilly Circus; critics find prices high, though, and complain of a
"lack of any real atmosphere". / W1F 9ZN;
www.mashsteak.dk/restaurants/london; 11.30 pm, Sun 11 pm; closed Sun L;
set pre theatre £46 (FP).

Massimo
Corinthia Hotel SW1 £76 2 4 4
10 Northumberland Ave 7998 0555 2–3D
The "opulent" setting may be "amazing", but this Italian dining room,
near Trafalgar Square, has put in a mixed performance since its
launch a few years ago; of late, however, it has begun to garner more
praise, especially for the "excellent-value" set lunch, and "charming"
service too. / SW1A 2BD; www.massimo-restaurant.co.uk; @massimorest;
10.45 pm; closed Sun; set weekday L & pre-theatre £38 (FP).

Masters Super Fish SE1 £30 4 1 1
191 Waterloo Rd 7928 6924 9–4A
"Very popular with cabbies" – this, "basic no-frills chippy" is "just as
advertised, which is to say, pretty super"; sadly, though, "it's being
discovered by tourists – damn those TripAdvisor reviews!" / SE1 8UX;
10.30 pm; closed Sun, Mon L; no Amex; no booking Fri D.

Matsuba TW9 £44 4 3 2
10 Red Lion St 8605 3513 1–4A
"Outstanding quality for Richmond" – this very "competent" Japanese
café serves "beautifully cooked and presented dishes" (including some
Korean options); sushi is of a "high standard". / TW9 1RW;
www.matsuba-restaurant.com; @matsuba; 10.30 pm; closed Sun.

Matsuri SW1   £86   **3 3 1**
15 Bury St   7839 1101   3–3D
For "authentic teppan-yaki exquisitely done", this long-established
St James's basement is just the job, even if the "ambience could
be better"; "the sushi bar is a secret gem". / SW1Y 6AL;
www.matsuri-restaurant.com; 10.30 pm, Sun 10 pm.

Maxela SW7   £46   **4 3 3**
84 Old Brompton Rd   7589 5834   5–2B
"The butcher cuts the meat in front of you", at this "known-only-to-
the-cognoscenti" South Kensington yearling, whose "wonderful cuts
of Italian beef" are "the most flavoursome ever". / SW7 3LQ;
www.maxela.co.uk; @MaxelaUk; 11 pm.

maze W1   £80   **2 2 2**
10-13 Grosvenor Sq   7107 0000   3–2A
The food is "first-rate", say fans of this Gordon Ramsay production
in Mayfair, where dishes are served tapas-style; critics, though,
just find the whole operation "haphazard" and "confused" – at the
prices, it "just doesn't make sense". / W1K 6JP;
www.gordonramsay.com/maze; 10.30 pm.

maze Grill W1   £76   **1 1 1**
10-13 Grosvenor Sq   7495 2211   3–2A
Gordon Ramsay's "utterly forgettable" Mayfair grill restaurant is often
just "a total embarrassment" nowadays – "like an upmarket
McDonalds" but "with prices off the Richter scale"; "the bill stunned
my wife into silence, a feat I've failed to achieve for some years…"
/ W1K 6JP; www.gordonramsay.com; 11 pm; no shorts.

Mazi W8   £59   **3 2 2**
12-14 Hillgate St   7229 3794   6–2B
"Innovative modern Greek cuisine" wins plenty of plaudits for this
"busy" yearling, off Notting Hill Gate; the dining room, though,
is undoubtedly rather "cramped". / W8 7SR; www.mazi.co.uk;
@mazinottinghill; 10.30 pm; closed Mon L & Tue L; set weekday L £33 (FP).

Meat Mission N1   £33   **4 3 3**
14-15 Hoxton Mkt   7739 8212   12–1B
"Burger to die for, lethal cocktails, fantastic decor… what more could
you want?" – this "buzzy" ("extremely noisy") Hoxton Square outlet
of the 'Meat' franchise is, say fans, "incredibly cheap for the quality".
/ N1 6HG; www.meatmission.com; @MEATmission; midnight, Sun 10 pm.

MEATLiquor W1   £36   **3 2 3**
74 Welbeck St   7224 4239   3–1B
"Dingy" and deafening, this dive off Oxford Street has quite a name
for its "dirty, luscious burgers"; ratings are slipping though – "the rock
'n' roll grunge act doesn't seem quite as new any more". / W1G 0BA;
www.meatliquor.com; @MEATliquor; 11 pm, Fri & Sat 1 am, Sun 9.30 pm;
closed Sun; no booking.

MEATmarket WC2   £31   **4 2 2**
Jubilee Market Hall, 1 Tavistock Ct   7836 2139   4–3D
"If you like greasy burgers with just the right slip-factor", this "über-
trendy" burger joint – overlooking Covent Garden's Jubilee Market,
and with its "grouchy, too-cool-for-school" service – may be just the
ticket. / WC2E 8BD; www.themeatmarket.co.uk; 11 pm, Sun 10 pm; no Amex.

We've turned our ratings system upside down!

As always Harden's will assess:

F – **Food**
S – **Service**
A – **Ambience**

But now <u>high</u> numbers are <u>better</u>…

5 – **Exceptional**

4 – **Very good**

3 – **Good**

2 – **Average**

1 – **Poor**

Mediterraneo W11 £59 **3** **3** **3**

37 Kensington Park Rd 7792 3131 6–1A

It "feels like the real deal", sitting at a table in this "good simple Italian, by Portobello Market" – quite a local favourite, and still, say fans, serving the "best tiramisù" in town. / W11 2EU; www.mediterraneo-restaurant.co.uk; 11.30 pm, Sun 10.30 pm; booking: max 10.

MEDLAR SW10 £67 **5** **4** **3**

438 King's Rd 7349 1900 5–3B

"Ambitious", "meticulously executed" cuisine and "an interesting and varied wine list" (presided over by an award-winning sommelier) make this Chelsea spot "more than just a neighbourhood gem"; fans say the ambience is "lovely" too, though critics find it "unremarkable". / SW10 0LJ; @medlarchelsea; 10.30 pm; set weekday L £49 (FP).

Mele e Pere W1 £50 **2** **2** **2**

46 Brewer St 7096 2096 3–2D

"It deserves more recognition", say fans of this "buzzy" Italian basement, in Soho, who laud its "well priced small plates and interesting wines"; it can be "extremely noisy", though, and sceptics feel it "promises more than it delivers". / W1F 9TF; www.meleepere.co.uk; @meleEpere; 11 pm.

Menier Chocolate Factory SE1 £52 **1** **2** **3**

51-53 Southwark St 7234 9610 9–4B

"A wonderful idiosyncratic South Bank building which also houses a small theatre"; "if you're on the meal 'n' ticket deal it's a no-brainer, but otherwise look elsewhere, as the food is rather plain and ordinary". / SE1 1RU; www.menierchocolatefactory.com; @MenChocFactory; 10.45 pm; closed Mon & Sun D; set dinner £33 (FP).

The Mercer EC2 £60 **3** **2** **2**

34 Threadneedle St 7628 0001 9–2C

As "a City business restaurant" this former banking hall – with its "unspectacular but well-cooked" cuisine – can come as a "pleasant surprise"; it has enlarged in recent times, so must be doing something right! / EC2R 8AY; www.themercer.co.uk; 9.30 pm; closed Sat & Sun.

Merchants Tavern EC2 **NEW** £58 **4** **4** **4**

35-42 Charlotte Rd awaiting tel 12–1B

"A fantastic addition to the East End's finer dining scene" – this "exciting" newcomer, complete with "vast open kitchen", delivers "simple but inspiring" cooking, with "great attention to detail", and in a "gorgeous" setting too. / EC2A 3PD; www.merchantstavern.co.uk; @merchantstavern; 11 pm, Sun 9 pm; closed Mon; set weekday L £39 (FP).

Le Mercury N1 £30 **2** **3** **4**

140a Upper St 7354 4088 8–2D

A "useful" and "fun" Islington bistro veteran, long known for "quick", "simple" and "tasty" Gallic fare, at "bargain" prices. / N1 1QY; www.lemercury.co.uk; 12.30 am, Sun 11 pm.

Meson don Felipe SE1 £40 **2** **2** **4**

53 The Cut 7928 3237 9–4A

"So Spanish" – even critics of this rammed veteran tapas bar, near the Old Vic, applaud its "great, bustling atmosphere"; everyone likes the large list of wines and sherries, but the food divides opinion. / SE1 8LF; www.mesondonfelipe.com; 11 pm; closed Sun; no Amex; no booking after 8 pm.

Carom at Meza W1 £33 4 4 3
100 Wardour St 7314 4002 3–2D
"Is it a disco or a restaurant?"; this huge and "lively" Soho Indian may
have decor "like a singles' cocktail lounge", but the food
is "surprisingly good", and it's an ideal choice for a "night out in a big
group"! / W1F 0TN; www.meza-soho.co.uk; 11 pm; closed Sat L & Sun;
SRA-3 stars.

Meza SW17 NEW £15 4 4 3
34 Trinity Rd 0772 211 1299 10–2C
"The secret's out!"; with its "fresh and super-tasty Lebanese cuisine
at enticingly low prices", this "tiny", "crowded" and "jolly" Tooting
spot has made quite a name for itself. / SW17 7RE; 10 pm; closed
Mon L.

Michael Nadra £54 5 3 1
6-8 Elliott Rd, W4 8742 0766 7–2A
42 Gloucester Ave, NW1 7722 2800 8–2B
Michael Nadra's "memorably delicious" cuisine offers "tremendous
value for money", at both his Chiswick base and his year-old Camden
Town offshoot; both sites are "difficult" however, although the
"cramped" W4 site is higher rated than the "cave-like" one in NW1.
/ www.restaurant-michaelnadra.co.uk; @michaelnadra; W4 10 pm, Fri-Sat
10.30 pm, NW1 10.30 pm, Sun 9 pm; W4 closed Sun D.

Mien Tay £31 4 2 2
180 Lavender Hill, SW11 7350 0721 10–1C
122 Kingsland Rd, E2 7729 3043 12–1B
"Highly authentic" Vietnamese scoff impresses all who comment
on these "mad-chaotic" Battersea and Shoreditch greasy spoons; no-
one cares that the decor is a little "down-at-heel", or that service
is "fast and furious". / 11 pm, Fri & Sat 11.30 pm, Sun 10.30 pm;
cash only.

Mildreds W1 £41 4 3 4
45 Lexington St 7494 1634 3–2D
"A London institution" – this "perfect little Soho nook" continues
to dish up "excellent" veggie food "that converts even die-hard
carnivores". / W1F 9AN; www.mildreds.co.uk; 10.45 pm; closed Sun;
no Amex; no booking.

Mill Lane Bistro NW6 £47 3 3 2
77 Mill Ln 7794 5577 1–1B
"There is an enormously large selection of brunch places
in West Hampstead, but none comes close to this" – a "reliable
local", where the "superb French take on a cooked breakfast"
is particularly worth checking out. / NW6 1NB; www.milllanebistro.com;
@millanebistro; closed Mon & Sun D; no Amex; set weekday L £28 (FP).

Min Jiang
The Royal Garden Hotel W8 £75 5 3 5
2-24 Kensington High St 7361 1988 5–1A
"The best Peking duck ever, plus breathtaking views over Kensington
Gardens" – the potent recipe for success at this "exciting" 8th-floor
dining room – one of London's foremost Chinese restaurants, and all
the more remarkable for "breaking the rule that rooms with views are
always dire!" / W8 4PT; www.minjiang.co.uk; 10 pm.

Mint Leaf £55 3 2 3
Suffolk Pl, Haymarket, SW1   7930 9020   2–2C
Angel Ct, Lothbury, EC2   7600 0992   9–2C
These slick and ambitious designer Indians – in a basement near
Trafalgar Square, and in the City – are certainly a "step up from
most curry houses"; the level of survey feedback they inspire,
however, is now very modest compared to their glory days.
/ www.mintleafrestaurant.com; SW1 11 pm, Sun 10.30 pm; EC2 10.30 pm;
SW1 closed Sat & Sun L; EC2 closed Sat & Sun.

Miran Masala W14 £23 5 4 2
3 Hammersmith Rd   7602 4555   7–1D
"The fantastic flavours of real Pakistani cooking" are to be found
at this basic BYO café, bang opposite Olympia. / W14 8XJ;
www.miranmasala.com; 10.45 pm.

Mirch Masala £24 3 1 1
171-173 The Broadway, UB1   8867 9222   1–3A
1416 London Rd, SW16   8679 1828   10–2C
213 Upper Tooting Rd, SW17   8767 8638   10–2D
111-113 Commercial Rd, E1   7377 0155   12–2D
For "addictive" Pakistani curries, these "buzzy" south London BYO-
canteens are well-established "cheap and cheerful" champions;
ratings were hit, though, by the occasional 'off' report this year.
/ www.mirchmasalarestaurant.co.uk; midnight.

Mishkin's WC2 £43 1 2 3
25 Catherine St   7240 2078   4–3D
"The least successful of Russell Norman's creations", this "chilled"
Covent Garden diner offers "NY-Yiddish-inspired comfort food"
realised to a decidedly "mediocre" standard – "save your money,
and head for the Big Apple!" / WC2B 5JS; www.mishkins.co.uk;
@MishkinsWC2; 11.15 pm, Sun 10.15 pm.

The Modern Pantry EC1 £56 3 3 3
47-48 St Johns Sq   7553 9210   9–1A
"A fun and quirky" choice – Anna Hansen's "bright" and "airy"
Clerkenwell dining room provides "genuinely different" flavour
combinations that "can hit real highs", even on its popular brunch
menu; critics, however, just dismiss the food as "weird". / EC1V 4JJ;
www.themodernpantry.co.uk; @themodernpantry; 10.30 pm, Sun 10 pm;
SRA-3 stars.

Momo W1 £70 2 2 5
25 Heddon St   7434 4040   3–2C
"It can be too noisy", but the ultra-"buzzy" and glam souk-style vibe
seduces many visitors to this fashion-crowd party-Moroccan, on the
fringe of Mayfair; the (pricey) food is relatively uneventful. / W1B 4BH;
www.momoresto.com; @momoresto; 11.30 pm, Sun 11 pm.

Mon Plaisir WC2 £59 2 3 4
19-21 Monmouth St   7836 7243   4–2B
"Nothing really changed since our first visit in the '60s!" – Covent
Garden's "stalwart" Gallic bistro (in fact, much expanded over the
years) is a "romantic" old favourite, with top-value menus at lunch
and pre-theatre; the food? – "never surprising, always reliable".
/ WC2H 9DD; www.monplaisir.co.uk; 11 pm; closed Sun; set pre-theatre £31
(FP), set weekday L £35 (FP).

Mona Lisa SW10 £28 **3** **3** **3**
417 King's Rd 7376 5447 5–3B
A veteran World's End greasy spoon, known for its simple but "always-tasty" Italian dishes, and for the diversity of its 'dukes-to-dustmen' clientèle. / SW10 0LR; 11 pm, Sun 5.30 pm; closed Sun D; no Amex.

Monmouth Coffee Company £12 **5** **5** **4**
27 Monmouth St, WC2 7379 3516 4–2B
Arches Northside, Dockley Rd, SE16 7232 3010 9–4D
2 Park St, SE1 7940 9960 9–4C
The coffee is "sublime" and the "perfectly trained staff" help create a "harmonious" ambience at these cult cafés; in Borough Market, "the rustic, communal wooden tables are laden with moreish bread, butter and a selection of preserves – get stuck in!" / www.monmouthcoffee.co.uk; 6 pm-6.30 pm; SE16 12 pm; closed Sun; SE16 open Sat only; no Amex; no booking.

The Morgan Arms E3 £47 **4** **3** **4**
43 Morgan St 8980 6389 1–2D
A "very popular gastropub in Mile End's backstreets", serving up "lovely" food that's complemented by a "good selection of ales". / E3 5AA; www.morganarmsbo.com; @TheMorganArms; 10 pm, Sun 9 pm.

Morito EC1 £36 **4** **4** **4**
32 Exmouth Mkt 7278 7007 9–1A
Moro's "cramped" little sister is a "bustling" and "basic" sort of Farringdon destination, serving "epic" tapas with "speed and style"; "no booking is a pain, but I guess otherwise you'd never get in!" / EC1R 4QE; www.morito.co.uk; @moritotapas; 11 pm, Sun 4 pm; closed Sun D; no Amex; no booking for D.

Moro EC1 £60 **5** **4** **4**
34-36 Exmouth Mkt 7833 8336 9–1A
"Year-after-year, true to its mission!"; this "consistently superb" Exmouth Market favourite has incredibly staying power, maintaining its "outstandingly flavourful" Moorish/Hispanic food, "excellent Iberian wines" and "buzzy scene"; as ever, it's "too noisy". / EC1R 4QE; www.moro.co.uk; 10.30 pm; closed Sun D.

Motcombs SW1 £62 **2** **3** **3**
26 Motcomb St 7235 6382 5–1D
"Old-fashioned in the best way", say (generally older) fans of this "welcoming" dining room, below a Belgravia wine bar; even they may concede that the food is "not the best", but it is "reliable". / SW1X 8JU; www.motcombs.co.uk; 11 pm; closed Sun D.

Moti Mahal WC2 £61 **4** **4** **3**
45 Gt Queen St 7240 9329 4–2D
With its "unusual and exciting" cooking, and "charming" and "attentive" service too, this somewhat overlooked Covent Garden outpost of a Delhi-based group is well worth seeking out. / WC2B 5AA; www.motimahal-uk.com; @motimahal59; 10.45 pm; closed Sat L & Sun; set pre theatre £29 (FP).

Moxon's Fish Bar SW12 £27 5 4 3
7 Westbury Pde 8675 2468 10–2C
"Oceans of praise" lap around fishmonger Robin Moxon's new addition to the Clapham scene – a "tiny but perfectly run upmarket chippy", offering "outstanding traditional fish 'n' chips" and "interesting specials" too. / SW12 9DZ; www.moxonsfishbar.com; @moxonsfish; 10 pm; closed Mon, Tue L, Wed L, Thu L, Sat L & Sun; no Amex.

Mr Chow SW1 £85 3 3 2
151 Knightsbridge 7589 7347 5–1D
"Resting on its laurels" or "still consistently delivering"? – opinions may differ on this once-glamorous but "overcrowded" Knightsbridge Chinese; there's some agreement, though, that "the prices reflect the location". / SW1X 7PA; www.mrchow.com; 11.45 pm; closed Mon L.

Mr Kong WC2 £32 3 3 3
21 Lisle St 7437 7341 4–3A
"One of Chinatown's better restaurants", with "smiling" service and "reliable" cooking from a menu which features "many interesting and unusual dishes". / WC2H 7BA; www.mrkongrestaurant.com; 2.45 am, Sun 1.45 am.

Murano W1 £99 4 4 4
20-22 Queen St 7495 1127 3–3B
Angela Hartnett's "inspiring" Italian cooking (often "with a twist") is currently on a high, at this "delightful" and "well-spaced" Mayfair spot – an exceptional "all-rounder" that's "ideal for that special occasion", be it for business or pleasure. / W1J 5PP; www.muranolondon.com; @muranolondon; 11 pm; closed Sun; set weekday L £50 (FP).

Nando's £31 2 2 2
Branches throughout London
This peri-peri chicken chain "does what you expect" – "well-cooked chicken, delivered quickly and without fuss"; "it somehow feels less wrong than taking the little ones for a cheap burger!" / www.nandos.co.uk; 11.30 pm, Sun 10.30 pm; no Amex; no booking.

Napulé SW6 £40 4 4 3
585 Fulham Rd 7381 1122 5–4A
This Fulham Broadway outpost of the Made in Italy chain is "really good for a casual supper" – there's "a good vibe" and the pizza, in particular, is "superb". / SW6 5UA; www.madeinitalygroup.co.uk; 11.30 pm, Sun 10.30 pm; closed weekday L; no Amex.

The Narrow E14 £53 1 1 2
44 Narrow St 7592 7950 11–1B
"They shouldn't trade on the Ramsay name"; his Limehouse pub is not just "poor", but "well overpriced" too – "the only saving grace is the spectacular location, right on the banks of the Thames". / E14 8DP; www.gordonramsay.com; @thenarrow; 10.30 pm, Sun 10 pm.

The National Dining Rooms
National Gallery WC2 £53 1 1 2
Sainsbury Wing, Trafalgar Sq 7747 2525 2–2C
"A wasted opportunity" – such a shame about the "deplorable" service and lacklustre cooking at this spacious central dining room; "great views of Trafalgar Square from the window tables" are the only undoubted plus. / WC2N 5DN; www.thenationaldiningrooms.co.uk; 7 pm; Sat-Thu closed D, Fri open L & D; no Amex.

National Gallery Café
National Gallery WC2   £46   3 1 2
East Wing, Trafalgar Sq   7747 5942   4–4B
For a "convenient" central location, an older fan base tip the "comfortable banquettes" of this tranquil haunt, right on Trafalgar Square; "disengaged" service, though, leaves some reporters decidedly disenchanted. / WC2N 5DN; www.thenationaldiningrooms.co.uk; 11 pm, Sun 6 pm; closed Sun D; no Amex.

Natural Kitchen   £37   3 2 3
55 Baker St, W1   7935 0987   2–1A
77-78 Marylebone High St, W1   3012 2123   2–1A
7 Pepys St, EC3   7702 4038   9–3D
15-17 New Street Sq, Fetter Ln, EC4   7353 5787   9–2A
These "airy" deli-diners offer "a pleasant snacking experience", despite service that's prone to be "amateur" and "slow". / EC4 9 pm; EC3 4 pm; W1 8 pm, Sat & Sun 7 pm; EC4 & EC3 closed Sat & Sun.

Nautilus NW6   £43   4 4 1
27-29 Fortune Green Rd   7435 2532   1–1B
Ignore the "basic" decor ("no-fuss, no-frills Formica special"), and there are "unbeatable fish and chips" to be had at this West Hampstead veteran; "the lovely waitresses have been there as long as I have been going – 40 years!" / NW6 1DU; 10 pm; closed Sun; no Amex.

Navarro's W1   £43   2 2 4
67 Charlotte St   7637 7713   2–1C
A "delightful" tiled interior is the special feature of this veteran Fitzrovia bar, which serves "good solid tapas at an affordable price". / W1T 4PH; www.navarros.co.uk; @SpanishEchelon; 10 pm; closed Sun.

Nazmins SW18   £38   3 4 4
396-398 Garratt Ln   8944 1463   10–2B
A "superb neighbourhood place"; this Earlsfield spot is your "quintessential" Indian, offering "a good selection of curries and brilliant breads". / SW18 4HP; www.nazmins.com; @nazmins; 11.30 pm.

Needoo E1   £26   4 3 2
87 New Rd   7247 0648   12–2D
Just round the corner from the legendary Tayyabs, this East End Pakistani BYO is "altogether less stressful" than its famous rival, and offers "brilliant" scoff too. / E1 1HH; www.needoogrill.co.uk; 11.30 pm.

The New Angel W2 NEW   £82   4 4 3
39 Chepstow Pl   7221 7620   6–1B
TV chef John Burton-Race's Bayswater newcomer pleases early-days reporters, as it did us, with its "elegant" decor – in a bourgeois style you don't often see in London nowadays – and its "surprisingly generous" modern European cooking. / W2 4TS; www.thenewangel-nh.co.uk; @newangel_london.

New Mayflower W1   £40   4 3 2
68-70 Shaftesbury Ave   7734 9207   4–3A
"It's always reassuring to see so many Chinese customers"; "excellent into the small hours", this Chinatown stalwart serves up "consistently good" Cantonese fare; "service used to be a bit rough and gruff but is nowadays of a good standard". / W1D 6LY; www.newmayflowerlondon.com; 4 am; D only; no Amex.

New Street Grill EC2 £57 2 3 4
16a New St   3503 0785   9–2D

For business, this "well-spaced" warehouse conversion decked out "with lots of dark wood and leather" makes "a very good option in the wasteland round Liverpool Street"; "great steaks", but sceptics complain of "unexceptional" food at "relatively high" prices. / EC2M 4TR; www.newstreetgrill.co.uk; @newstreetgrill; 10.45 pm; closed Sat L & Sun D; SRA-3 stars.

New Tom's W11 NEW £54
226 Westbourne Grove   7243 3341   6–1B

Long mainly of note as a "lazy" weekend brunch destination, this Notting Hill deli-bistro was relaunched in 2014; it still has the same proprietor, though, as when it was just called 'Tom's' – Tom Conran, that is. / W11 2RH; www.newtoms.co.uk.

New World W1 £37 3 2 3
1 Gerrard Pl   7434 2508   4–3A

"The fun factor, with the circulating trolleys, is arguably better than the food itself" – perhaps why this gigantic Chinatown classic remains a particular hit with reporters for dim sum. / W1D 5PA; www.newworldlondon.com; 11.30 pm, Sun 11 pm.

Newman Street Tavern W1 £41 3 2 3
48 Newman St   3667 1445   3–1D

"Nice to find a good central gastropub"; this very popular Marylebone spot certainly fits the bill with its "thoughtful" but "uncomplicated" cooking, and its "laid-back" style. / W1T 1QQ; www.newmanstreettavern.co.uk; @NewmanStTavern; 10.30 pm; closed Sun D; SRA-2 stars.

1901
Andaz Hotel EC2 £65 1 1 3
40 Liverpool St   7618 7000   12–2B

"A preferred business breakfast choice, but at other times of day the cooking isn't strong enough to make a visit worthwhile" – this "airy" and undeniably impressive-looking chamber, by Liverpool Street, falls far below its potential. / EC2M 7QN; www.andazdining.com; 10 pm; closed Sat L & Sun; booking: max 20.

Nizuni W1 £47 4 4 2
22 Charlotte St   7580 7447   2–1C

"The freshest sushi, plus decent hot dishes" from a mixed Korean/Japanese menu – most reporters are "very impressed" with this café-style Fitzrovia spot. / W1T 2NB; www.nizuni.com; @nizuni; 10.45 pm; closed Sun L.

Nobu
Metropolitan Hotel W1 £90 4 2 2
19 Old Park Ln   7447 4747   3–4A

"It's certainly no longer London's hottest place", service remains "moody", and "the bill is always more than you expect"... but this once-path-breaking Mayfair dining room still offers "brilliant" Japanese fusion fare, and "great people-watching" too. / W1K 1LB; www.noburestaurants.com; @NobuOldParkLane; 10.15 pm, Fri & Sat 11 pm, Sun 10 pm.

Nobu Berkeley W1 £90 3 2 2
15 Berkeley St   7290 9222   3–3C
"Lovely sushi" and other "superb" Japanese-fusion dishes still win
praise for this "busy" Mayfair rendezvous, despite its "rushed" service
and "horrible" prices; really, though, this is a place you go "to see and
be seen". / W1J 8DY; www.noburestaurants.com; 11 pm, Sun 9.45 pm; closed
Sat L & Sun L.

The Noodle House WC2 NEW £39
117 Shaftsbury Ave   3725 5777   4–2B
"Slightly off the beaten track" (well, as much as you can be in Covent
Garden), this new offshoot of a pan-Asian chain is praised in early
reports (few), as an "enjoyable café" serving "great-tasting food".
/ WC2H 8AD; www.tnhlondon.com; @noodlehouseLDN; Mon-Tue 9.45 pm,
Wed-Sat 10.45 pm, Sun 8.45 pm.

Noor Jahan £39 4 4 4
2a, Bina Gdns, SW5   7373 6522   5–2B
26 Sussex Pl, W2   7402 2332   6–1D
"It never changes… thankfully"; this "excellent neighbourhood curry
house", in Earl's Court, is a "basic but classic" affair that's "always
reliable, and always packed"; W2 is good too – "not sophisticated,
but you couldn't ask for a better local cuzza!" / 11.30 pm, Sun 10 pm.

Nopi W1 £56 5 4 4
21-22 Warwick St   7494 9584   3–2D
"Wow-factor flavours" – "pungent and dramatic!" – make "every
mouthful amazing" at Yottam Ottolenghi's contemporary Middle
Eastern spot, just off Regent Street; it offers "small-plate dining at its
best", in an "informal", "cosy" and "beautiful" setting. / W1B 5NE;
www.nopi-restaurant.com; @ottolenghi; 10.15 pm, Sun 4 pm; closed Sun D.

Nordic Bakery £15 3 3 3
14a, Golden Sq, W1   3230 1077   3–2D
37b, New Cavendish St, W1   7935 3590   2–1A
48 Dorset St, W1   7487 5877   2–1A
Cinnamon buns which "never disappoint", and "fabulous" coffee too
– particular attractions which keep many reporters coming back
to these "restrained" ("austere") and "refreshingly different" cafés.
/ Golden Square 8 pm, Sat 7 pm, Sun 7 pm; Cavendish Street & Dorset Street
6 pm.

The Norfolk Arms WC1 £46 4 3 2
28 Leigh St   7388 3937   8–4C
"Looks like any old pub, except for the legs of jamón hanging in the
window" – this "Spanish-inspired" gastropub-cum-tapas bar,
near King's Cross, is something of a "hidden gem". / WC1H 9EP;
www.norfolkarms.co.uk; 10.15 pm.

North China W3 £41 4 4 3
305 Uxbridge Rd   8992 9183   7–1A
"A great family-run restaurant in Acton, which surpasses most places
in Chinatown"; the setting may be a touch "gloomy" for some tastes,
but the food is "lovely". / W3 9QU; www.northchina.co.uk; 11 pm, Fri & Sat
11.30 pm.

The North London Tavern NW6 £46 3 3 3
375 Kilburn High Rd 7625 6634 1–2B
A "homely" boozer, handily located near Kilburn's Tricycle Theatre, where the food is "definitely better than pub standard"; prices, though, "are moving up". / NW6 7QB; www.northlondontavern.co.uk; @NorthLondonTav; 10.30 pm, Sun 9.30 pm.

North Sea Fish WC1 £38 3 3 2
7-8 Leigh St 7387 5892 8–4C
"The fish is as fresh as the decor is tired", at this "old-fashioned-plush" Bloomsbury chippy; who cares if it sometimes feels "like an OAP daycare centre"? / WC1H 9EW; www.northseafishrestaurant.co.uk; Mon-Sat 10 pm, Sun 5.30 pm; closed Sun; no Amex.

The Northall
Corinthia Hotel SW1 £64 3 4 3
10a, Northumberland Ave 7321 3100 2–3C
The "smart" and "spacious" dining room of this new(ish) grand hotel, off Trafalgar Square, deserves to be more widely known – it's "a little pricey", but "on a good day, provides top ingredients, simply cooked!" / SW1A 2BD; www.thenorthall.co.uk; @CorinthiaLondon; 10.45 pm.

Northbank EC4 £54 3 3 3
1 Paul's Walk 7329 9299 9–3B
"A great location by the Millennium Bridge" is the particular attraction of this bar-restaurant facing Tate Modern; with its leather booths and "British comfort food in generous portions", it makes a good option for a business lunch. / EC4V 3QH; www.northbankrestaurant.co.uk; @NorthbankLondon; 10 pm; closed Sun.

Notes £18 2 4 4
31 St Martin's Ln, WC2 7240 0424 4–4C
36 Wellington St, WC2 7240 7899 4–3D
6a, Tileyard Studios, N7 7700 0710 8–2C
1 Ropemaker St, EC2 7628 5178 12–2A **NEW**
As "a welcome haven from the Trafalgar Square hubbub", the best-known branch of these atmospheric cafés (by the Coliseum) is well-worth seeking out; the "excellent" coffee, though, does outshine the "straightforward" snacks. / Wellington St Mon-Wed 10 pm, Thu-Fri 11 pm, Sun 6 pm; St Martin's Ln Mon-Wed 9 pm, Thu-Sat 10 pm, Sun 6 pm; N7 closed Sat-Sun.

Notting Hill Kitchen W11 £31 2 3 2
92 Kensington Park Rd 7313 9526 6–2B
Remarkably little feedback on this quite grand, year-old, Portuguese-run restaurant and tapas bar; fans vaunt its "interesting" menu and "attentive" service, but even they may note that it's "not cheap" for what it is. / W11 2PN; Rated on Editors' visit; www.nottinghillkitchen.co.uk; @NottingHillKTN; 10 pm; closed Mon L, Tue L, Wed L & Sun.

Noura £57 2 2 2
16 Hobart Pl, SW1 7235 9444 2–4B
17 Hobart Pl, SW1 7235 9696 2–4B
2 William St, SW1 7235 5900 5–1D
16 Curzon St, W1 7495 1050 3–4B
These swankily located Lebanese joints have their fans, but they inspire little survey feedback… which tends to support those who say they offer only "standard" food, and that service is "in need of improvement". / www.noura.co.uk; 11.30 pm, Sun 10 pm; 16 Hobart Place closed Sun.

Novikov (Asian restaurant) W1   £102   [1] [2] [3]
50A Berkeley St   7399 4330   3–3C
*"Eye-popping prices and arrogance" are coming to characterise the
once-promising pan-Asian section of this blingy Mayfair spot;
"if someone else is paying", though, it can still be fun for people-
watching – "minigarchs, massage therapists, shiny people, expense-
accounters…" / W1J 8HD; www.novikovrestaurant.co.uk; 11.15 pm.*

Novikov (Italian restaurant) W1   £101   [1] [1] [1]
50A Berkeley St   7399 4330   3–3C
*A "tasteless bling-fest" where the food is "surprisingly OK", but prices
are "insane" – the "noisy" Italian section of the eponymous Moscow
restaurateur's Eurotrash magnet, in the heart of Mayfair. / W1J 8HD;
www.novikovrestaurant.co.uk; 11.30 pm.*

Numero Uno SW11   £53   [3] [4] [4]
139 Northcote Rd   7978 5837   10–2C
*"A trusted friend for many years" – this "buzzy" neighbourhood
stalwart for "the between-the-Commons crowd" is "often packed",
thanks to its "hearty" and "consistent" Italian fare, and its "charming
and helpful" service. / SW11 6PX; 11.30 pm; no Amex.*

Nuovi Sapori SW6   £44   [3] [4] [3]
295 New King's Rd   7736 3363   10–1B
*A "good local Italian", down Fulham way; expect "basic but well-
prepared" cuisine and "very friendly service". / SW6 4RE; 11 pm;
closed Sun.*

Nusa Kitchen   £12   [4] [4] [2]
9 Old St, EC1   7253 3135   9–1B
2 Adam's Ct, EC2   7628 1149   9–2C
88 Cannon St, EC4   7621 9496   9–3C
*"Soup is dull unless it comes from Nusa!" – "Asian flavours are used
brilliantly", in the "strong-tasting" dishes on offer at these City and
Farringdon pit stops. / www.nusakitchen.co.uk; 4 pm; Sat & Sun; no booking.*

Oak   £51   [4] [4] [4]
243 Goldhawk Rd, W12   8741 7700   7–1B
137 Westbourne Park Rd, W2   7221 3355   6–1B
*"Incredible thin and crispy pizza" – especially at the "really buzzing"
Bayswater original – helps make these "airy" and "fun" west London
pub-conversions perennially popular hangouts; in W2, there's
a "vibey" bar upstairs too.*

Obika   £47   [2] [2] [1]
11 Charlotte St, W1   7637 7153   2–1C
19-20 Poland St, W1   3327 7070   3–1D
96 Draycott Ave, SW3   7581 5208   5–2C
35 Bank St, E14   7719 1532   11–1C
*Our mystification at the ongoing success of these 'Mozzarella bars'
continues, as they inspire very little survey feedback, and such
as there is divides equally between those who say they're "a bit of a
hidden gem", and those who say: "don't bother". / www.obika.co.uk;
10 pm - 11 pm; E14 Closed Sun.*

Oblix
The Shard SE1 £85 ② ② **5**
31 St Thomas St 7268 6700 9–4C
The views are "to die for", and many reporters are "pleasantly
surprised" to find that food and service can match up, at this 32nd-
floor South Bank eyrie; critics, though, find the food "mediocre",
and service "disinterested". / SE1 9RY; www.oblixrestaurant.com;
@OblixRestaurant; 11 pm.

Odette's NW1 £58 ③ ③ **4**
130 Regent's Park Rd 7586 8569 8–3B
Bryn Williams's famously "romantic" Primrose Hill "classic" has been
"on fine form" of late, attracting improved survey ratings for his
accomplished cuisine, and the "not too formal, but classy" ambience;
the "excellent" weekday lunch is a particular hit. / NW1 8XL;
www.odettesprimrosehill.com; @Odettes_rest; Sun-Thu 10 pm, Fri & Sat
10.30 pm; no Amex; set weekday L £31 (FP), set always available £37 (FP).

Ognisko Restaurant SW7 £52 ② ③ **4**
55 Prince's Gate, Exhibition Rd 7589 0101 5–1C
Recently "rejuvenated", a "lovely, grand and spacious" dining room,
complete with a "wonderful terrace", near the Science Museum;
it offers "Polish cuisine, well executed" (and some "excellent
cocktails" too). / SW7 2PN; www.ogniskorestaurant.co.uk; 11 pm; closed
Mon L; no trainers.

The Old Brewery SE10 £49 ② ③ **4**
The Pepys Building, Old Royal Naval College 3327 1280 1–3D
A "big, breezy and bustling" Greenwich venue in the "lovely" environs
of the Naval College, with a large sun-trap garden; its impressive
artisanal beers are complemented by "simple but filling" dishes.
/ SE10 9LW; www.oldbrewerygreenwich.com; @OldBrewery; 10 pm, Fri & Sat
10.30 pm; D only; no Amex.

The Old Bull & Bush NW3 £42 ③ ② **3**
North End Rd 8905 5456 8–1A
"A real gem" of an old inn, opposite Golders Hill Park... as long
as you don't mind the fact that your meal may take "an eternity"
to arrive. / NW3 7HE; www.thebullandbush.co.uk; 9.30 pm, Sat 10 pm,
Sun 9 pm.

Oliveto
Olivo Restaurants SW1 £66 **4** ② ②
49 Elizabeth St 7730 0074 2–4A
"Phenomenal" thin-crust pizza and other "utterly delightful"
Sardinian dishes make this "kid-friendly" Belgravian a real crowd-
pleaser (and it gets jammed at weekends); given the locale,
no surprise that prices can seem "pretty steep". / SW1W 9PP;
www.olivorestaurants.com; 11 pm, Sun 10.30 pm; booking: max 7 at D.

Olivo SW1 £57 **4** **4** ②
21 Eccleston St 7730 2505 2–4B
"Expensive but excellent" Belgravia's 'original' Olivo looks pretty
"tired" nowadays, and it gets pretty "noisy" too; "after all these
years", though, the Sardinian cuisine remains "fresh" and "authentic".
/ SW1 9LX; www.olivorestaurants.com; 10.30 pm; closed Sat L & Sun L.

Olivocarne SW1 £54 4 4 2
61 Elizabeth St 7730 7997 2–4A
Fans of this Italian meat-specialist in the heart of Belgravia say it is the "undiscovered gem of the Olivo group" – this may be something to do with the bizarre and decidedly "unatmospheric" decor. / SW1W 9PP; www.olivorestaurants.com; Mon-Sat 11 pm, Sun 10.30 pm .

Olivomare SW1 £61 5 3 2
10 Lower Belgrave St 7730 9022 2–4B
"Brilliant-quality fish" and "first-class" seafood win top marks for this Sardinian venture in Belgravia; fans say the "spartan" '60s sci-fi decor is "crazy" and "cool", but it can equally well be seen as "weird" and "noisy". / SW1W 0LJ; www.olivorestaurants.com; 11 pm, Sun 10.30 pm; booking: max 10.

Olley's SE24 £40 4 3 2
65-69 Norwood Rd 8671 8259 10–2D
A Brockwell Park institution, still celebrated for "excellent" fish 'n' chips; "managing to sustain its quality over the years is a great achievement – long may it stay the course!" / SE24 9AA; www.olleys.info; 10 pm, Sun 9.30 pm; no Amex; set weekday L £23 (FP); SRA-3 stars.

Olympic
Olympic Studios SW13 NEW £47 2 2 3
117-123 Church Rd 8912 5161 10–1A
"A popular addition to Barnes", this "casual" neighbourhood joint (plus "fantastic" cinema) is a great use of an Edwardian building where many of legendary '70s rock tracks were recorded; to fans, its "buzzy" new guise makes it the perfect local, but critics say it's too "loud", with "hit-and-miss" service. / SW13 9HL; www.olympiccinema.co.uk; @Olympic_Cinema; 10 pm.

Olympus Fish N3 £34 4 4 1
140-144 Ballards Ln 8371 8666 1–1B
"Take-away is particularly good value" – and "you can opt for grilled as well as battered" – at this "no-frills" but "friendly" Finchley chippy, which "does exactly what it says on the tin". / N3 2PA; 11 pm.

On The Bab EC1 NEW £36 4 3 4
305 Old St 7683 0361 12–1B
"Serving innovative and delicious Korean street food, and good cocktails too" ensures this "cheap and cheerful" Shoreditch newcomer is usually pretty "lively". / EC1V 9LA; www.onthebab.com; @onthebab; 10.30 pm, Sun 10 pm; no bookings.

One Canada Square E14 £61 2 3 1
1 Canada Sq 7559 5199 11–1C
Carved out from a corner of the marbled lobby of one of Canary Wharf's great towers, this brasserie yearling certainly has a handy location; perhaps inevitably, it can feel "like an airport lounge", and critics find the cuisine "fussy", and "pricey" too. / E14 5AB; www.onecanadasquarerestaurant.com; @OneCanadaSquare; 10.45 pm; closed Sun.

101 Thai Kitchen W6 £33 4 2 1
352 King St 8746 6888 7–2B
"Tastes like Thailand"; "fiery" dishes – including some "real novelties" on the specials board – make this obscure café near Stamford Brook worth seeking out; "don't go for the decor!" / W6 0RX; www.101thaikitchen.com; 10.30 pm, Fri & Sat 11 pm.

One Kensington W8 NEW £71 2 3 1
1 Kensington High St 7795 6533 5–1A
*Staff try hard ("almost too hard") at this potentially "classy"
Kensington newcomer* — CLOSED — *the food can seem
"overcomplicated", and its airy interior "still feels like the bank
it originally was"; "bring back Zaika!" / W8 5NP;
www.one-kensington.com; 10.30 pm; closed Mon L.*

1 Lombard Street EC3 £71 2 1 2
1 Lombard St 7929 6611 9–3C
*This heart-of-the-City "stalwart", in a former banking hall, is still often
hailed as "a good place to impress clients" (or for breakfast);
too often of late, however, it has struck reporters as "bland"
or "soulless" – "you probably wouldn't go if you weren't
on expenses!" / EC3V 9AA; www.1lombardstreet.com; 10 pm; closed
Sat & Sun; 6 max in main restaurant; set dinner £49 (FP).*

One-O-One
Sheraton Park Tower SW1 £94 5 3 1
101 Knightsbridge 7290 7101 5–1D
*"Still London's finest fish restaurant by a mile!"; this Knightsbridge
hotel dining room may have "all the ambience of Davy Jones's
locker", but Pascal Proyart's Breton-based cuisine is without peer.
/ SW1X 7RN; www.oneoonerestaurant.com; @oneoone; 10 pm; booking:
max 6; set weekday L £54 (FP), set dinner £63 (FP).*

The Only Running Footman W1 £60 2 2 2
5 Charles St 7499 2988 3–3B
*"Solid", "useful", "consistent" – the sort of epithets reporters apply
to the "traditional" dining possibilities at this "busy" boozer,
near Claridge's. / W1J 5DF; www.therunningfootmanmayfair.com;
@theorfootman; 10 pm.*

Opera Tavern WC2 £41 4 4 4
23 Catherine St 7836 3680 4–3D
*"Divine small plates of Iberico, pata negra ham and must-try mini-
burgers" – all among the "stylish" treats on offer at this "jammed",
"good-natured" and "fun" sibling to Salt Yard, in a handily central
Covent Garden pub-conversion. / WC2B 5JS; www.operatavern.co.uk;
@saltyardgroup; 11.15 pm; closed Sun D; SRA-2 stars.*

The Orange SW1 £57 3 3 4
37 Pimlico Rd 7881 9844 5–2D
*"Delicious thin-based pizzas" headline an "enticing" menu, at this
"bright", "airy" and "relaxing" gastropub, in the heart of Pimlico.
/ SW1W 8NE; www.theorange.co.uk; @TheOrangeSW1; 10 pm, Sun 9.30 pm;
SRA-3 stars.*

Orange Pekoe SW13 £26 3 4 4
3 White Hart Ln 8876 6070 10–1A
*"A favourite of Barnes ladies who lunch" – "everything
an independent tearoom-cum-coffee shop should be", it offers
an "excellent range of teas", plus "fabulous" coffee, cake and salads.
/ SW13 0PX; www.orangepekoeteas.com; 5 pm; L only.*

The Orange Tree N20 £44 123
7 Totteridge Ln   8343 7031   1–1B
"It's a beautiful pub in a great location, and wonderful on a sunny afternoon", but this popular Totteridge boozer "should be so much better" on the food front; problem? – "there is no competition". / N20 8NX; www.theorangetreetotteridge.co.uk; @orangetreepub; 9.45 pm, Fri & Sat 10.30 pm, Sun 9 pm.

Orchard WC1 £42 333
11 Sicilian Ave   7831 2715   2–1D
This snug Bloomsbury café – Vanilla Black's more informal sibling – is located in a pretty Italianate arcade with some exceptional al fresco table; "delicious" sarnies and cakes, plus "lovely" veggie fare. / WC1A 2QH; Mon-Fri 7.30 pm, Sat 6.45 pm; closed Sun.

Orpheus EC3 £42 431
26 Savage Gdns   7481 1931   9–3D
A "brilliant seafood place hidden away near Tower Hill" – this '70s "time warp" in a railway arch is a place where you should "ignore the decor", and focus on the "excellent choice of fresh fish". / EC3N 2AR; www.orpheusrestaurant.co.uk; L only, closed Sat & Sun.

Orrery W1 £75 344
55 Marylebone High St   7616 8000   2–1A
"Staff are impeccable, and so is the food", say fans of this "calm and considered" first-floor dining room, overlooking a Marylebone churchyard – a "really lovely space with lots of natural light"; even fans, though, can find it "expensive for what it is". / W1U 5RB; www.orreryrestaurant.co.uk; @orrery; 10.30 pm, Fri & Sat 11 pm; set Sun L £52 (FP); SRA-2 stars.

Orso WC2 £56 332
27 Wellington St   7240 5269   4–3D
"Unpretentious, and reasonably-priced for Covent Garden" – this "reliable" basement Italian restaurant may give little hint nowadays of its fashionable past, but it's a "friendly" sort of place, and still with a fan club among reporters, especially pre- or post-Royal Opera House. / WC2E 7DB; www.orsorestaurant.co.uk; @Orso_Restaurant; 11.30 pm; set weekday L £34 (FP), set always available £37 (FP), set pre-theatre £39 (FP).

Oslo Court NW8 £63 454
Charlbert St, off Prince Albert Rd   7722 8795   8–3A
"Back to the '70s"; this "faultless" Regent's Park spot may be a "throwback", but it's an "incredibly good" one, where "nearly every table has a birthday to celebrate"; pièce de résistance? – "the famed dessert trolley", the arrival of which is "the best entertainment in town". / NW8 7EN; 11 pm; closed Sun; no jeans or trainers.

Osteria Antica Bologna SW11 £41 333
23 Northcote Rd   7978 4771   10–2C
This "great local Italian", near Clapham Junction, has been serving up "genuine" Bolognese cuisine for over two decades, and is a handy "cheap and cheerful" destination. / SW11 1NG; www.osteria.co.uk; @OsteriaAntica; 10.30 pm, Sun 10 pm.

Osteria Basilico W11   £55   **3 3 4**
29 Kensington Park Rd   7727 9957   6–1A
*"A classy neighbourhood Italian" that's long been an "easy-going" and
"always-fun" linchpin of Notting Hill – "authentic and of consistently
high quality"; arrive early if you want a table on the ground floor.
/ W11 2EU; www.osteriabasilico.co.uk; 11.30 pm, Sun 10.15 pm; no booking,
Sat L.*

Osteria Dell'Angolo SW1   £57   **3 4 2**
47 Marsham St   3268 1077   2–4C
*A "very polished" Westminster corner Italian, whose "sharp" service
and "very reliable" cooking naturally equip it for business; shame the
atmosphere is so "subdued". / SW1P 3DR; www.osteriadellangolo.co.uk;
@Osteria_Angolo; 10.30 pm; closed Sat L & Sun.*

Ostuni NW6   £43   **2 3 3**
43-45 Lonsdale Rd   7624 8035   1–2B
*In a former Victorian workshop, in Queen's Park, a Puglian yearling
praised for its "lovely ambience" and its "non-typical" cuisine;
the menu is "limited", though, with results ranging from "delicious"
to "not yet quite right". / NW6 6RA; www.ostuniristorante.co.uk; 10 pm.*

Otto's WC1   £52   **4 5 4**
182 Grays Inn Rd   7713 0107   2–1D
*"Otto is quite a character", contributing much to the "pleasingly
eccentric" ambience of his "determinedly old-fashioned" Bloomsbury
two-year-old; the food is "the sort of French cuisine you thought had
died a death", so don't forget to order your canard à la presse
in advance – pure "theatre". / WC1X 8EW; www.ottos-restaurant.com;
10 pm; closed Sat L & Sun.*

Ottolenghi   £48   **5 3 3**
13 Motcomb St, SW1   7823 2707   5–1D
63 Ledbury Rd, W11   7727 1121   6–1B
1 Holland St, W8   7937 0003   5–1A
287 Upper St, N1   7288 1454   8–2D
*Yotam Ottolenghi's "visually stunning" Middle Eastern-inspired
creations – "unbelievable salads in such a variety" and
"the most delicious cakes imaginable" – make his "innovative" cafés
just the ticket for a life-enhancing brunch; shame, though, about
"the queues and the crowding". / www.ottolenghi.co.uk; N1 10.15 pm;
W8 & W11 8 pm, Sat 7 pm, Sun 6 pm; N1 closed Sun D; Holland
St takeaway only; W11 & SW1 no booking, N1 booking for D only.*

**Outlaw's Seafood and Grill
The Capital Hotel SW3**   £67   **4 4 2**
22-24 Basil St   7589 5171   5–1D
*Nathan Outlaw's "perfectly executed seafood" and "discreet" service
win many accolades for this accomplished small dining room
by Harrods, especially for the "very good-value set lunch" (or the
"BYO deal on Thursdays"); shame the ambience of this oddly-shaped
chamber is "a bit flat and formal". / SW3 1AT; www.capitalhotel.co.uk;
@hotelcapital; 10 pm; closed Sun; set weekday L £35 (FP).*

(Brasserie)
Oxo Tower SE1   £71   1 2 2
Barge House St   7803 3888   9–3A
*"Is it worth paying significantly more than West End prices, just for
the brilliant view?" – as ever, the brasserie of this South Bank
riverside landmark is too often "unimpressive on all levels". / SE1 9PH;
www.harveynichols.com/restaurants/oxo-tower-london; 11 pm, Sun 10 pm;
set pre theatre £51 (FP).*

(Restaurant)
Oxo Tower SE1   £86   1 1 2
Barge House St   7803 3888   9–3A
*"Ugh!"; this "lazy" tourist trap at the top of the eponymous South
Bank fixture remains "as awful as ever" – "take away the spectacular
view, and everything else is rubbish". / SE1 9PH;
www.harveynichols.com/restaurants; @OxoTowerWharf; 11 pm, Sun 10 pm.*

Ozer WC2   £48   2 3 2
36 Tavistock St   7240 3773   3–1C
*"Good-value tasty fare, pre- or post-theatre", and not bad for lunch
either – the Sofra chain's flagship is a handy standby, especially for
those who work at neighbouring Broadcasting House, serving a wide-
ranging Turkish/Middle Eastern menu. / WC2E 7PB; www.sofra.co.uk;
11 pm.*

Le P'tit Normand SW18   £42   3 4 3
185 Merton Rd   8871 0233   10–2B
*Although it is as "long-lasting" and "traditional" a Gallic bistro as you
could hope to find, this Southfields fixture "has been gradually
improving" in recent years; it offers "classic" dishes and "carefully
chosen" wines, all at "good-value" prices. / SW18 5EF;
www.leptitnormand.co.uk; 10 pm, Sun 3 pm; closed Mon, Tue L, Wed L,
Thu L & Sun D; set weekday L £30 (FP).*

Pachamama W1 NEW
18 Thayer St   7935 9393   2–1A
*Another addition to London's growing Peruvian dining scene –
this time in Marylebone – combining dishes and cocktails native
to Peru with British fare. / W1U 3JY; www.pachamamalondon.com;
@pachamama_ldn.*

The Paddyfield SW12   £28   3 3 2
4 Bedford Hill   8772 1145   10–2C
*"Fresh spring rolls, salads and really good noodles" impress most,
if not quite all, reporters on this Balham Thai/Vietnamese; the BYO
policy helps make it quite a "cheap" night out too. / SW12 9RG;
www.thepaddyfield.co.uk; 11 pm; D only; no credit cards.*

Il Pagliaccio SW6   £39   2 3 3
182-184 Wandsworth Bridge Rd   7371 5253   10–1B
*An "excellent neighbourhood pizza joint", in Sands End, that's both
family- and wallet-friendly; the odd culinary miss is "more than
forgiven, as the place is so much fun and full of life". / SW6 2UF;
www.paggs.co.uk; @pagliacciopizza; midnight; no Amex.*

Le Pain Quotidien   £38   2 2 3
Branches throughout London
*"Not cheap, but pleasant" – this "welcoming", "rustic"-style
international café-bakery chain is ideal for a "great healthy brunch"
or an "imaginative salad". / www.painquotidien.com; most branches close
between 7 pm-10 pm; no booking at some branches, especially at weekends.*

The Painted Heron SW10   £58   5 3 2
112 Cheyne Walk   7351 5232   5–3B
*A recent change of management has done nothing to diminish the
"intricate but unfussy" charms of this "fabulous modern Indian",
tucked-away off the Chelsea Embankment; "why does it never get the
plaudits it deserves?" / SW10 0DJ; www.thepaintedheron.com; Mon-Sat
10.30 pm, Sun 10 pm; no Amex.*

The Palmerston SE22   £52   3 3 2
91 Lordship Ln   8693 1629   1–4D
*"Precision and taste are evident in every dish", at this "jovial"
East Dulwich "haven" – "a massive notch above standard gastropub
fare". / SE22 8EP; www.thepalmerston.co.uk; @thepalmerston; 10 pm,
Sun 9.30 pm; no Amex; set weekday L £27 (FP).*

Palmyra TW9   £42   4 3 2
277 Sandycombe Rd   8948 7019   1–3A
*A small Kew Lebanese, offering "delicious" and "authentic" dishes –
from "tasty and succulent" meats ("and in generous portions")
to mezzes with "an original twist". / TW9 3LU;
www.palmyrarestaurant.co.uk; 11 pm; no Amex.*

The Palomar W1 NEW   £40   4 5 4
34 Rupert St   7439 8777   4–3A
*"Genuinely new and different", this "brilliant" modern Israeli opening
is "off to a flying start" with its "interesting fusion-style menu",
"buzzing" atmosphere and "infectiously enthusiastic" staff; handy
location too, three minutes' walk from Piccadilly Circus. / W1D 6DN;
www.thepalomar.co.uk.*

The Pantechnicon SW1   £57   3 3 4
10 Motcomb St   7730 6074   5–1D
*More a "bar-bistro" than a boozer, this "buzzing" Belgravian may
be no bargain, but it offers "a nice blend of 'quality' attributes" and
attracts "a good mix of customers"; for more grandeur and comfort,
head upstairs. / SW1X 8LA; www.thepantechnicon.com; @ThePantechnicon;
Weekdays 10 pm, Sun 9.30 pm; SRA-3 stars.*

Pappa Ciccia   £40   4 3 3
105 Munster Rd, SW6   7384 1884   10–1B
41 Fulham High St, SW6   7736 0900   10–1B
*"Simply delicious and authentic pizza" (in "huge portions") and
"friendly service" too makes these BYO Fulham spots "lovely" places
to live near – "I've moved, but I still wish this was on my doorstep!"
/ www.pappaciccia.com; 11 pm, Sat & Sun 11.30 pm; Munster Rd no credit
cards.*

Paradise by Way of Kensal Green W10   £47   3 4 5
19 Kilburn Ln   8969 0098   1–2B
*The decor at this "charming" Kensal Green fixture is "an object
lesson in shabby-chic glamour", and its "super-helpful and glamorous
staff" serve up lovely food of "gastropub+" aspiration; nowhere
is perfect though – "parking is tricky". / W10 4AE;
www.theparadise.co.uk; @weloveparadise; 10.30 pm, Fri & Sat 11 pm,
Sun 9 pm; closed weekday L; no Amex.*

Paradise Hampstead NW3 £31 4 5 4
49 South End Rd 7794 6314 8–2A
"The staff remember you, and make the effort", at this "old-fashioned" curry "stalwart", in South End Green — world-famous locally for its "excellent, if standard, array of dishes" and "terrific value". / NW3 2QB; www.paradisehampstead.co.uk; 10.45 pm.

El Parador NW1 £36 4 4 4
245 Eversholt St 7387 2789 8–3C
"Why go elsewhere?", say fans of this "cosy" Camden Town gem — "it's the loveliest family-run tapas place you could wish for", and the dishes are "always fresh and interesting". / NW1 1BA; www.elparadorlondon.com; 11 pm, Fri & Sat 11.30 pm, Sun 9.30 pm; closed Sat L & Sun L; no Amex.

Paramount
Centre Point WC1 £75 2 2 4
101-103 New Oxford St 7420 2900 4–1A
"Incredible views" and the ultra-central location should inspire adulation for Centre Point's 32nd-floor dining room; the verdict, though? — with its "substandard" food and slack service, it's only "almost worth it"; maybe just grab a cocktail? / WC1A 1DD; www.paramount.uk.net; @ParamountSoho; 11 pm, Sun 10 pm.

Parlour NW10 NEW £46 4 4 3
5 Regent St 8969 2184 1–2B
"A great find, in the backwaters of Kensal Rise" (by the better-known Paradise); Jesse Dunford Wood's "fun" and casual hangout serves "insanely great" retro scoff at "everyday prices". / NW10 5LG; www.parlourkensal.com; @ParlourUK; 11 pm.

Patara £55 3 3 3
15 Greek St, W1 7437 1071 4–2A
7 Maddox St, W1 7499 6008 3–2C
181 Fulham Rd, SW3 7351 5692 5–2C
9 Beauchamp Pl, SW3 7581 8820 5–1C
"Charming" service, "beautiful" decor and a wide choice of "refined" dishes win enduring popularity for this "old-favourite" Thai chain; "after so many years, there's nothing new on the menu" however, and sceptics find standards "nothing special" nowadays. / www.pataralondon.com; 10.30 pm; Greek St closed Sun L.

Paternoster Chop House EC4 £55 3 3 3
Warwick Ct, Paternoster Sq 7029 9400 9–2B
An "airy" (but "noisy") steakhouse, whose al fresco tables enjoy "great views of St Paul's"; it's attracted more praise of late for its "fast and efficient" service of "simple" but "expensive" dishes — just the ticket for City types. / EC4M 7DX; www.paternosterchophouse.co.uk; @paternoster1; 10.30 pm; closed Sat & Sun D; SRA-3 stars.

Patio W12 £36 3 5 5
5 Goldhawk Rd 8743 5194 7–1C
"A great find"; this "eccentric" Polish operation offers "extraordinary value"; the fare is "home-cooked", and comes in "huge portions", but it's the "cute" '50s decor and superb service from the owner — not to mention "loads of flavoured vodkas" — that really set it apart. / W12 8QQ; www.patiolondon.com; 11 pm, Sat & Sun 11.30 pm; closed Sat L & Sun L.

Pâtisserie Valerie   £27   112 2
Branches throughout London
Those who remember the "former glories" of this once-tiny chain see its current venture capital-backed growth as a "travesty"; others still find it an OK pit stop, though, for a coffee and croissant, or a teatime bun. / www.patisserie-valerie.co.uk; most branches close between 5 pm-8 pm; no booking except Old Compton St Sun-Thu.

Patogh W1   £24   322
8 Crawford Pl   7262 4015   6–1D
"A little corner of Iran"; this "dingy" grill, just off the Edgware Road, serves "tender and tasty" lamb kebabs plus "other varieties of singed flesh"; BYO. / W1H 5NE; 11 pm; no credit cards.

Patty and Bun   £21   423
54 James St, W1   7487 3188   3–1A
22-23 Liverpool St, EC2   7621 1331   9–2D NEW
"If they laced dishes with crack, they wouldn't be more addictive", say fans of the "ultimate dirty burgers" (and "superb" wings too) served by these "funky" pit stops, near Selfridges and now in the City; they're "seriously cramped" though, and the queues can be "unreal". / www.pattyandbun.co.uk.

Paul   £27   322
Branches throughout London
"The only place to get an authentic baguette sandwich" – France's biggest café-pâtisserie chain impresses with its "excellent-quality sweets and savouries", mostly to take away (but Covent Garden has its own dining room); service can be "tragically slow, and so French...". / www.paul-uk.com; most branches close between 7 pm-8.30 pm; no booking.

Pavilion W8 NEW   £62   343
96 Kensington High St   7262 0905   5–1A
Jon Hunt's (of Foxton's fame) "unusual" and ultra-plush marbled hall – attached to a swish Kensington business centre – has been quite a hit, and early reports applaud Adam Simmonds's "excellent" cuisine; on our visit, though, it seemed almost as much of a bar as a restaurant, perhaps most suited to a drink or brunch? / W8 4SG; www.kensingtonpavilion.com; closed Mon, Tue, Wed, Thu, Fri, Sat & Sun.

Pearl Liang W2   £47   322
8 Sheldon Sq   7289 7000   6–1C
This "popular" Paddington Basin basement – with modern, opium den styling – has carved quite a name for its "unusual" dim sum, and other "high-quality" dishes; ratings are not what they were, though, and critics say it's "no longer worth the trip". / W2 6EZ; www.pearlliang.co.uk; 11 pm; set weekday L £26 (FP).

The Peasant EC1   £47   334
240 St John St   7336 7726   8–3D
"A very good and old-established gastropub" (early-'90s), in Clerkenwell, which still wins plaudits for the "upmarket bistro" fare served in its upstairs dining room; the atmosphere is "convivial" ("noisy") too. / EC1V 4PH; www.thepeasant.co.uk; @ThePeasant; 10.45 pm, Sun 9.30 pm.

Peckham Bazaar SE15 NEW £45 3 3 3
119 Consort Rd 0787 510 7471 1–4D
"Interesting" Balkan cuisine (and some "interesting and fairly priced" wines too) help make this converted house a popular south London destination; menu highlight – "perfect BBQ". / SE15 3RU; www.peckhambazaar.com.

Peckham Refreshment Rooms SE15 NEW £36 3 3 3
12-16 Blenheim Grove 7639 1106 1–4D
A "jammed" yearling, serving an "interesting", "tapas-like" British menu from a regularly changing menu; "you teeter on uncomfortable high stools" though, so it's "not a place to linger". / SE15 4QL; www.peckhamrefreshment.com.

Pellicano SW3 £60 3 5 3
35 Ixworth Pl 7589 3718 5–2C
This "perennial favourite" Chelsea backstreet Italian has now shifted to a new "warm and welcoming" home, part of a small hotel, on the same street as always; remarkably, regulars say the food is "better than ever"! / SW3 3QX; www.pellicanorestaurant.co.uk; 11 pm, Sun 10.30 pm; set always available £38 (FP).

E Pellicci E2 £21 2 4 5
332 Bethnal Green Rd 7739 4873 12–1D
An "old-school east London caff", known for its "beautiful" (listed) Art Deco interior, and "warm welcome"; it does a "great breakfast", and "really cheap too". / E2 0AG; 4.15 pm; L only, closed Sun; no credit cards.

Penkul & Banks EC2 NEW £45 4 4 2
77 Curtain Rd 7729 2966 12–1B
On the former site of Beard to Tail, this new café-bar-restaurant promises 'eclectic modern European cuisine with an Asian twist' (read: tapas and sharing plates). / EC2A 3BS; Rated on Editors' visit.

Pentolina W14 £44 4 5 4
71 Blythe Rd 3010 0091 7–1D
"It popped up from nowhere, and is still going strong!" – this "cosy and romantic" backstreet Italian is "becoming a stalwart of the Brook Green/Hammersmith scene", thanks to its "classic Italian home-cooking", and "delightful" service too. / W14 0HP; www.pentolinarestaurant.co.uk; 10 pm; closed Mon & Sun; no Amex.

The Pepper Tree SW4 £27 4 4 3
19 Clapham Common S'side 7622 1758 10–2D
"A great cheap and cheerful eatery", near Clapham Common tube, where communal canteen-style tables "add to the atmosphere" – its "very good" Thai cuisine is "ideal for a quick bite when out and about". / SW4 7AB; www.thepeppertree.co.uk; 10.45 pm, Sun & Mon 10.15 pm; no Amex; no booking.

Pescatori £56 3 2 2
11 Dover St, W1 7493 2652 3–3C
57 Charlotte St, W1 7580 3289 2–1C
"Fish is done well", at these simple and low-key West End Italians; they may be "dull" but – viewed as a standby choice – they "could be worse". / www.pescatori.co.uk; 11 pm; closed Sat L & Sun.

Petersham Hotel TW10 £65 **3 5 5**
Nightingale Ln 8940 7471 1–4A
An "old-fashioned" and "genteel" Richmond dining room ("diners all look like UKIP supporters!"), which benefits from "superb Thames views" ("if you can get a window table") and "fantastic" service too; the food is good, if "rather unimaginative" – "ideal for entertaining elderly relations!" / TW10 6UZ; www.petershamhotel.co.uk; @ThePetersham; 9.45 pm, Sun 8.45 pm; set Sun L £57 (FP).

Petersham Nurseries TW10 £72 **2 1 4**
Church Ln, Off Petersham Rd 8940 5230 1–4A
"An earth-floored greenhouse with distressed antiques, and lush foliage" creates the "special and romantic" atmosphere at this quirky venue, near Richmond; it's never really recovered since Skye Gyngell left, though, and – with its "inept" service – can feel "like an overpriced garden centre café" nowadays. / TW10 7AG; www.petershamnurseries.com; L only, closed Mon.

La Petite Maison W1 £86 **4 3 4**
54 Brook's Mews 7495 4774 3–2B
"Bubbly and genuinely French in feel", but "flashy and expensive" too, this mews spot brings the authentic charms of the Côte d'Azur to the backwoods of Mayfair – these include "perfect sunny-days food", "snooty" service and Russian oligarchs aplenty. / W1K 4EG; www.lpmlondon.co.uk; @lpmlondon; 10.30 pm, Sun 9 pm.

Pétrus SW1 £92 **4 4 4**
1 Kinnerton St 7592 1609 5–1D
"An outstanding all-rounder" – Gordon Ramsay's Belgravia dining room may be a bit "corporate" in feel, but no one's complaining about its "wonderful culinary creativity", "legendary wine list" or "tip-top" service. / SW1X 8EA; www.gordonramsay.com/petrus; @petrus; 10.15 pm; closed Sun; no trainers; set weekday L £59 (FP).

Peyote W1 NEW £62 **3 3 2**
13 Cork St 7409 1300 3–3C
"London needed Peyote", say fans of this "upscale" new Mayfair Mexican, lauding its "exciting" and "absolutely delicious" cuisine; tables are "cramped", though, and critics find the food "not really that much better than Wahaca". / W1S 3NS; www.peyoteresaurant.com.

Pham Sushi EC1 £38 **5 4 1**
159 Whitecross St 7251 6336 12–2A
"Awesome" sushi and sashimi is the "main asset" of this small and basic restaurant near the Barbican; all at "incredible-value" prices too. / EC1Y 8JL; www.phamsushi.co.uk; @phamsushi; 9.45 pm; closed Sat L & Sun.

The Phene SW3 £42 **1 2 3**
9 Phene St 7352 9898 5–3C
It's "fun", it's "happening", and "in the garden, the sun always seem to shine", but this "charming" Chelsea pub can suffer from "stressed out" service and "very poor" food. / SW3 5NY; www.thephene.com; @ThePheneSW3; 10 pm.

Pho £37 3 3 3
163-165 Wardour St, W1   7434 3938   3–1D
3 Great Titchfield St, W1   7436 0111   3–1C
Westfield, Ariel Way, W12   07824 662320   7–1C
48 Brushfield St, E1   7377 6436   12–2B
86 St John St, EC1   7253 7624   9–1A
*As Vietnamese street food-inspired chains go, these "honest" outlets
are surprisingly "convivial"; as the chain grows apace, however,
the food is becoming more middle-of-the-road – "no fireworks,
but tasty" is a pretty typical verdict nowadays. / www.phocafe.co.uk;
EC1 10 pm, Fri & Sat 10.30 pm; W1 10.30 pm; W12 9 pm, Sat 7 pm,
Sun 6 pm; EC1 closed Sat L & Sun; W1 closed Sun; no Amex; no booking.*

Phoenix Palace NW1 £55 3 2 2
5-9 Glentworth St   7486 3515   2–1A
*This "bustling" and "un-anglicised" fixture, near Baker Street, serves
a "wide-ranging menu, and the best dishes are the most unusual
ones" – "go with Chinese friends to get the dishes not on the menu";
its "a favourite for dim sum" too – "arrive by noon, or be prepared
to queue". / NW1 5PG; www.phoenixpalace.co.uk; 11.15 pm, Sun 10.15 pm.*

Piccolino £52 2 2 2
21 Heddon St, W1   7287 4029   3–2C
11 Exchange Sq, EC2   7375 2568   12–2B
*A low-profile but "always reliable" Italian chain, whose decent value
and kid-friendliness wins it somewhat better ratings than many
better-known competitors. / www.piccolinorestaurants.co.uk; 11 pm,
Sun 10 pm; EC2 closed Sat & Sun.*

Picture W1 £33 3 5 2
110 Great Portland St   7637 7892   2–1B
*Run by an ex-Arbutus/Wild Honey team, this "enthusiastic" yearling,
a short walk from Broadcasting House, dishes up "thoroughly
tempting" – but "surprisingly inexpensive" – small plates, "with a
smile"; the setting is "relaxed", or a touch "uncomfortable", to taste.
/ W1W 6PQ; Rated on Editors' visit; www.picturerestaurant.co.uk; 10 pm;
closed Sun.*

PIED À TERRE W1 £99 5 5 3
34 Charlotte St   7636 1178   2–1C
*Marcus Eaves's "fabulous food, beautifully presented" maintains
David Moore's "plush" Fitzrovia fixture as one of the capital's
foremost foodie temples; the ambience can seem "stuffy" though
(going on "dull", if you sit at the front). / W1T 2NH;
www.pied-a-terre.co.uk; @davidpied; 10.45 pm; closed Sat L & Sun; booking:
max 7; set weekday L £52 (FP).*

Pig & Butcher N1 £49 4 3 3
80 Liverpool Rd   7226 8304   8–3D
*"Modern but hearty" cuisine, with the meaty emphasis the name
suggests, has helped make this Islington gastroboozer quite a hit;
"fabulous Sunday lunches" a highlight. / N1 0QD;
www.thepigandbutcher.co.uk; @pigandbutcher; 10.30 pm; Mon-Thu D only,
Fri-Sun open L & D.*

The Pig's Ear SW3 £54 2 2 3
35 Old Church St 7352 2908 5–3C
An Art Nouveau-themed Chelsea boozer, where you can eat "in the quiet upstairs dining room, or downstairs with a bit of buzz"; fans say it's "what a gastropub should be", but it can be "totally let down" by "limp and tasteless" cooking. / SW3 5BS; www.thepigsear.info; 10 pm, Sun 9 pm.

Pilpel £9 4 4 2
38 Brushfield Street, London, E1 7247 0146 12–2B
Old Spitalfields Mkt, E1 7375 2282 12–2B
146 Fleet St, EC4 7583 2030 9–2A
Paternoster Sq, EC4 7248 9281 9–2B
"Amazing falafel that tastes like it does in Jerusalem" – the "authentic" attraction of this "reliable" small chain. / www.pilpel.co.uk.

ping pong £33 2 2 3
29a James St, W1 7034 3100 3–1A
45 Gt Marlborough St, W1 7851 6969 3–2C
74-76 Westbourne Grove, W2 7313 9832 6–1B
Southbank Centre, SE1 7960 4160 2–3D
Bow Bells Hs, 1 Bread St, EC4 7651 0880 9–2B
As a "fun" standby, these stylish budget hangouts do have their fans; however, the "exotic cocktails" and "interesting tea selection" are a safer bet than the dim sum itself ("nothing special"), and service is sometimes "awful". / www.pingpongdimsum.com; @pingpongdimsum; 10 pm-11.30 pm; EC2 & EC4 closed Sat & Sun; booking: min 8.

El Pirata W1 £39 2 3 5
5-6 Down St 7491 3810 3–4B
This "super-bustling tapas bar" is a "fun" little dive that's well worth knowing about – the food may only be "satisfactory" but, by Mayfair standards, it's very affordable. / W1J 7AQ; www.elpirata.co.uk; @elpirataw1; 11.30 pm; closed Sat L & Sun; set weekday L £19 (FP).

El Pirata de Tapas W2 £42 3 3 2
115 Westbourne Grove 7727 5000 6–1B
A Bayswater bar where the "dark and romantic" decor is "ideal for a date"; it offers "delicious" and "very economical" modern tapas, as well as some "lovely" Spanish wines. / W2 4UP; www.elpiratadetapas.co.uk; @Pirate_de_Tapas; 11 pm, Sun 10 pm; Mon-Thu D only, Fri-Sun open L & D.

Pitt Cue Co W1 £25 5 4 4
1 Newburgh St 7287 5578 3–2D
"The best BBQ ever... and I grew up in the southern States"! – reporters "drool at the mere thought" of a visit to this "awesome little place", off Carnaby Street, with its its "genius" pulled pork, burnt tips, pickles and other carnivorous treats; no wonder the queue is "everlasting". / W1F 7RB; www.pittcue.co.uk; @PittCueCo; SRA-1 star.

Pizarro SE1 £48 3 4 4
194 Bermondsey St 7407 7339 9–4D
"Why travel to Spain?"; at this Bermondsey favourite, José P dishes up "daringly simple" tapas which pack "a real punch"; it's "an unpretentious dining room full of the buzz of happy diners", but this year's survey ratings weren't quite as ecstatic as last year's. / SE1 3TQ; www.josepizarro.com/restaurants/pizarro; @Jose_Pizarro; 11 pm, Sun 10 pm.

Pizza East £48 **4** **3** **4**
310 Portobello Rd, W10   8969 4500   6–1A
79 Highgate Rd, NW5   3310 2000   8–1B
56 Shoreditch High St, E1   7729 1888   12–1B
Permanent long queues attest to the success of this "happening"
chain, where the "unusual" dishes offer "a great twist on pizza";
beware, though – "it's like there's a sign on the door, saying 'No Entry
without beard, check shirt and Converses'". / www.pizzaeast.com;
@PizzaEast; E1 Sun-Wed 11 pm, Thu 12 am, Fri-Sat 1am; W10 Mon-Thu
11.30 pm, Fri-Sat 12 am, Sun 10.30 pm.

Pizza Metro SW11 £45 **4** **4** **3**
64 Battersea Rise   7228 3812   10–2C
"Good fun", "excellent pizza" and "amazing pasta" – not much
to fault at these local pioneers of pizza-by-the-metre, both at the
Battersea original, and the newer one in Notting Hill. / SW11 1EQ;
www.pizzametropizza.com; @pizzametropizza; 11 pm; no Amex.

Pizza Pilgrims £23 **4** **4** **4**
102 Berwick St, W1   0778 066 7258   3–2D
11-12 Dean St, W1   0778 066 7258   3–1D
Kingly Ct, Carnaby St, W1   7287 8964   3–2C
"The van was great", and now the Elliot brothers have translated
their pop-up into a duo of "funky" Soho outfits – the "fantastic" thin
crusts and "minimal but extremely authentic" selection of toppings
have mercifully survived the transition, so "the hordes pile in" –
"expect to queue".

PizzaExpress £39 **2** **2** **3**
Branches throughout London
"Still the best pizza on the high street"; turning 50 this year,
this "old faithful" remains the yardstick by which other multiples are
judged; "frequent updating" keeps the formula fresh, but there is one
constant – "they really get kids!". / www.pizzaexpress.co.uk;
11.30 pm-midnight; most City branches closed all or part of weekend;
no booking at most branches.

Pizzeria Oregano N1 £41 **4** **4** **3**
18-19 St Albans Pl   7288 1123   8–3D
On account of its "great pizza, and fabulous pasta too",
this unpretentious spot, just off Upper Street, remains quite the
"neighbourhood favourite". / N1 0NX; www.pizzaoregano.co.uk;
@PizzeriaOregano; 11 pm, Fri 11.30 pm, Sun 10.30 pm; closed weekday L.

Pizzeria Pappagone N4 £38 **3** **3** **4**
131 Stroud Green Rd   7263 2114   8–1D
"Multiple birthday parties nightly" help ensure this "buzzing" Stroud
Green Italian is "always packed"; "delicious pizzas, and a great range
of pastas and specials ensure you never get bored". / N4 3PX;
www.pizzeriapappagone.co.uk; midnight.

Pizzeria Rustica TW9 £39 **4** **4** **3**
32 The Quadrant   8332 6262   1–4A
"A great little find", and handy for Richmond station too – this "lively"
family-run spot wins high praise for its "tasty" stone-baked pizza.
/ TW9 1DN; www.pizzeriarustica.co.uk; 11 pm, Fri & Sat 11.30 pm,
Sun 10.30 pm.

PJ's Bar and Grill SW3 £51 2 3 4
52 Fulham Rd 7581 0025 5–2C
The "quintessential classic brunch place" for the Chelsea set; the food
may be nothing to write home about, but as a "fun and buzzy place
to be" it's "still very passable and enjoyable". / SW3 6HH;
www.pjsbarandgrill.co.uk; @PJsBARANDGRILL; 10.30 pm, Sun 10 pm.

Plateau E14 £62 1 3 3
Canada Pl 7715 7100 11–1C
"A dependable business lunch location", made distinctive by its
impressive elevated views over Canary Wharf; it's very much in the
"bland and boring" style which was has traditionally been the D&D
Group's hallmark, so let's hope the evolution sometimes apparent
elsewhere begins to manifest itself here! / E14 5ER;
www.plateau-restaurant.co.uk; @plateaulondon; 10.15 pm; closed Sat L & Sun;
set dinner £38 (FP); SRA-2 stars.

Plum + Spilt Milk
Great Northern Hotel N1 £46 2 3 3
King's Cross 3388 0800 8–3C
By railway station hotel standards, this "glamorous" and "moodily lit"
King's Cross dining space is certainly "a good option" and fans say
the setting is nothing short of "magical"; the food, though, is "fairly
routine". / N1C 4TB; www.gnhlondon.com; @PlumSpiltMilk; 11 pm,
Sun 10 pm.

Plum Valley W1 £46 4 2 3
20 Gerrard St 7494 4366 4–3A
"A quality restaurant amidst many mediocre choices", and one that's
"pretty swanky and fun" by Chinatown standards too; innovative dim
sum is a highlight. / W1D 6JQ; www.plumvalleylondon.com; 11.30 pm.

Pod £14 3 3 2
Branches throughout London
"Tasty" breakfasts, and "great, healthy and delicious" lunches –
the sort of fare which makes these City and West End pit stops a hit
with all who comment on them. / www.podfood.co.uk; 3 pm-4 pm,
WC2 7 pm, Sat 8 pm, Sun 5 pm; branches closed Sat & Sun,
St Martin's & City Rd closed Sun.

Poissonnerie de l'Avenue SW3 £69 4 3 2
82 Sloane Ave 7589 2457 5–2C
"Old-fashioned, but still superb"; this tightly packed Brompton Cross
"classic" has a loyal older following for its "high-quality fish, reverently
served". / SW3 3DZ; www.poissonneriedelavenue.co.uk; 11.30 pm,
Sun 10.30 pm; set weekday L £52 (FP).

La Polenteria W1 NEW £37 3 4 3
64 Old Compton St 7434 3617 4–3A
This basic new Soho bistro does indeed just serve polenta, albeit
in various styles – "an eclectic idea which deserves to get more
traction!" / W1D 4UQ; www.lapolenteria.com; @La_Polenteria; 11 pm.

POLLEN STREET SOCIAL W1 £84 4 4 3
8-10 Pollen St 7290 7600 3–2C
A "very slick" Mayfair hangout, where Jason Atherton's "flavour-
popping" menu includes many "stunning" dishes; its "light and
bright" interior and "vibrant" style, however, ensures that it's "not the
place for a romantic supper!" / W1S 1NQ; www.pollenstreetsocial.com;
@PollenStSocial; 10.45 pm; closed Sun; set weekday L £53 (FP).

Polpo
£37 2 3 5

41 Beak St, W1   7734 4479   3–2D
6 Maiden Ln, WC2   7836 8448   4–3D
126-128 Notting Hill Gate, W11   7229 3283   6–2B NEW
2-3 Cowcross St, EC1   7250 0034   9–1A

Service that's "too cool for school" (but still "so friendly") helps set the "urbane" tone at Russell Norman's "warm and cosy" NYC-style Venetian tapas bars; the wait for a table can be "tedious", though, especially as the food is "rather hit-and-miss" nowadays. / www.polpo.co.uk; W1 & EC1 11 pm; WC2 11 pm, Sun 10.30 pm; W1 & EC1 closed D Sun.

Pond N16 NEW

Stamford Works, 3 Gillett St   3772 6727   1–1C
Dalston says "aloha" to this restaurant that promises New Hawaiian cuisine; the initial press was encouraging. / N16 8JH; pond-dalston.com.

Le Pont de la Tour SE1
£72 2 2 3

36d Shad Thames   7403 8403   9–4D
It's hard to beat the "sensational" Tower Bridge views from the D&D Group's grand South Bank "icon"; for a date, or as a "smart and efficient business venue" it still has many fans, but foodwise it's "lost its passion", and is "far too expensive" nowadays. / SE1 2YE; www.lepontdelatour.co.uk; @lepontdelatour; 10.30 pm, Sun 9.30 pm; no trainers; set weekday L & dinner £42 (FP); SRA-1 star.

Popeseye
£52 3 4 2

108 Blythe Rd, W14   7610 4578   7–1C
277 Upper Richmond Rd, SW15   8788 7733   10–2A
"So the room is tired and I ended up smelling of the frying fat", but even so reporters (generally) applaud these "good-value" west London bistros, where "superlative steak and chips" is the only menu option. / www.popeseye.com; 10.30 pm; D only, closed Sun; no credit cards.

La Porchetta Pizzeria
£34 3 3 3

33 Boswell St, WC1   7242 2434   2–1D
141-142 Upper St, N1   7288 2488   8–2D
147 Stroud Green Rd, N4   7281 2892   8–1D
74-77 Chalk Farm Rd, NW1   7267 6822   8–2B
84-86 Rosebery Ave, EC1   7837 6060   9–1A
"Amazing pizza" plus a wide variety of other Italian dishes, all in very "good portions", are to be had at these "vibrant" north London fixtures – "a perfect standby for a quick, cheap and cheerful meal", and "very welcoming to kids" too. / www.laporchetta.net; last orders varies by branch; WC1 closed Sat L & Sun; N1,EC1 & NW1 closed Mon-Fri L; N4 closed weekday L; no Amex.

Portal EC1
£59 3 4 4

88 St John St   7253 6950   9–1B
"A fantastic ambassador" for Portuguese food ("which is generally underrated"), this Clerkenwell fixture also benefits from a "refined and beautiful" interior – "particularly the super-sized conservatory" – and an "eclectic and distinctive" list of wines and ports. / EC1M 4EH; www.portalrestaurant.com; @portalrestaurant; 10.15 pm; closed Sat L & Sun; SRA-3 stars.

La Porte des Indes W1 £63 3 3 4
32 Bryanston St 7224 0055 2–2A
*A deceptively large and unexpectedly lavishly-themed basement
("like being in the Tropics"), near Marble Arch; "it's a bit expensive",
but serves "interesting" French-colonial Indian food that's "just a little
bit different from the norm". / W1H 7EG; www.laportedesindes.com;
@LaPorteDesIndes; 11.30 pm, Sun 10.30 pm.*

Il Portico W8 £50 2 5 3
277 Kensington High St 7602 6262 7–1D
*A "nice old-fashioned trattoria" that's "always packed"; opinions differ
on the "home-cooking" – averaging out somewhere round
"more than adequate" – but it's the "family who run it with love and
care" who really make this a Kensington institution. / W8 6NA;
www.ilportico.co.uk; 10.45 pm; closed Sun.*

Portobello Ristorante W11 £48 3 4 4
7 Ladbroke Rd 7221 1373 6–2B
*Just off Notting Hill Gate, a "very cheerful" independent,
neighbourhood spot, with a lovely summer terrace; no-one minds the
"slightly haphazard" service, given "great pizza" (sold 'al metro') and
"other consistently good dishes". / W11 3PA; www.portobellolondon.co.uk;
10.30 pm, Sun 10.15 pm.*

The Portrait
National Portrait Gallery WC2 £53 2 2 4
St Martin's Pl 7312 2490 4–4B
*"Who can resist a date with Nelson?" – the "stunning view" from this
top-floor dining room in the heart of the West End is its particular
attraction; fans are "pleasantly surprised" by the cooking too, though
the less starry-eyed can find it "uninspiring". / WC2H 0HE;
http://www.npg.org.uk/visit/shop-eat-drink.php; Thu-Fri 8.30 pm; Sun-Wed
closed D.*

Potli W6 £38 4 3 4
319-321 King St 8741 4328 7–2B
*"Brilliant and always-buzzy", this "top-notch" Hammersmith Indian
offers many "spicy" and "delicious" dishes; of late, however, delivery
has perhaps been a touch more "uneven" than it was. / W6 9NH;
www.potli.co.uk; @Potlirestaurant; 10.30 pm, Fri & Sat 11.30 pm.*

La Poule au Pot SW1 £63 3 3 5
231 Ebury St 7730 7763 5–2D
*A date "can't fail", at this "so French" and "gorgeous" farmhouse-
style half-centenarian, whose "low light and dark corners" (and top
al fresco tables on sunny days) have long made it a classic romantic
choice; the "rustic cooking is "good... for '70s-style fare" and "if you
parler français, service is very good". / SW1W 8UT;
www.pouleaupot.co.uk; 11 pm, Sun 10 pm; set weekday L £42 (FP).*

Prawn On The Lawn N1 £27 4 5 3
220 St Paul's Rd 3302 8668 8–2D
*"The name may sound like the debris left behind after a picnic",
but this "cute" new restaurant and wine bar attracts rave reports for
its "amazingly fresh" seafood and its "crisp wines by the glass" too.
/ N1 2LY; prawnonthelawn.com; @PrawnOnTheLawn; Tue-Wed 9 pm, Thu-Sat
10 pm; closed Mon & Sun; no Amex.*

Pret A Manger   £15   2 4 2

Branches throughout London

"I went to one in Boston recently, and it was just as good as always!"
– as London-based success-stories go, this gold-standard sandwiches-
and-more chain has become "a legend"; it must help that it has
"the friendliest staff by a mile". / www.pret.com; generally 4 pm-6 pm;
closed Sun (except some West End branches); City branches closed Sat & Sun;
no Amex; no booking.

Primeur N5 NEW   £46

116 Petherton Rd   no tel   1–1C

A summer opening just too late to gather any survey feedback,
this Clissold Park spot is backed by a team whose experience includes
Brunswick House, Rita's and Wright Brothers – sounds as if should
be a handy addition to the area. / N5 2RT; www.primeurN5.co.uk;
@Primeur s1; no booking.

Princess Garden W1   £59   4 3 3

8-10 North Audley St   7493 3223   3–2A

"Amazingly good-value" dim sum is the highlight at this "elegant" and
"upmarket", if perhaps slightly "soulless", Mayfair Chinese; at other
times, it's a "totally reliable" option for "classic" Cantonese cooking.
/ W1K 6ZD; www.princessgardenofmayfair.com; 11 pm.

Princess of Shoreditch EC2   £47   3 4 3

76 Paul St   7729 9270   12–1B

"A slightly cramped room above what was a traditional corner
boozer" – the main dining option at this trendy and "still reliable"
Shoreditch stalwart. / EC2A 4NE; www.theprincessofshoreditch.com;
@princessofs; 10 pm, Sun 8 pm; no Amex.

Princess Victoria W12   £46   3 4 4

217 Uxbridge Rd   8749 5886   7–1B

"Large, light and airy", this huge tavern, in deepest Shepherd's Bush,
"has the real feel of a Victorian gin palace to it"; the food is of
consistent good quality, and there's an "excellent wine list" too.
/ W12 9DH; www.princessvictoria.co.uk; @pvwestlondon; 10.30 pm,
Sun 9.30 pm; no Amex.

Princi W1   £34   3 2 4

135 Wardour St   7478 8888   3–2D

"Love it, love it, love it!" – this "crazy and buzzy" ("packed to the
rafters") Milanese-inspired deli-coffee shop-pâtisserie is "perfect for
a quick bite in Soho"; "fantastic" pizza a highlight. / W1F 0UT;
www.princi.com; midnight, Sun 10 pm; no booking.

Prix Fixe W1   £38   3 4 4

39 Dean St   7734 5976   4–2A

It may be "slap bang in the middle of Soho", but this "little French
bistro" is well off the hipster trail; it's a "useful" and impressively
"consistent" operation however, and "keenly priced" too. / W1D 4PU;
www.prixfixe.net; @prixfixelondon; 11.30 pm.

Provender E11   £39   4 3 2

17 High St   8530 3050   1–1D

"A rose among the thorns of Wanstead High Street"; Max Renzland
has a long west London pedigree, but he's now behind this
"welcoming" Gallic bistro out East, where the set menus, in particular,
are hailed for their "very good value". / E11 2AA;
www.provenderlondon.co.uk; @ProvenderBistro; Sun 9 pm, Mon-Fri 10 pm.

The Providores W1 £68 **4** 2 2
109 Marylebone High St 7935 6175 2–1A
"Pacific Rim cooking at its best", and *"an NZ wine list that reaches
the bits other Kiwis can't reach"* still inspires positive reports on Peter
Gordon's tightly-packed first-floor Marylebone dining room... even if it
is *"beginning to get a bit long in the tooth"*. / W1U 4RX;
www.theprovidores.co.uk; 10.30 pm; SRA-2 stars.

**(Tapa Room)
The Providores W1** £54 **3** 2 **3**
109 Marylebone High St 7935 6175 2–1A
Peter Gordon's *"really interesting"* Pacific-fusion tapas have helped
this *"bustling"* Marylebone bar-diner make quite a name, especially
for a *"diverse and innovative brunch"*; its *"cramped"* premises
"rapidly gets too busy", though, and the food no longer seem
as special as once it did. / W1U 4RX; www.theprovidores.co.uk;
@theprovidores; 10.30 pm, Sun 10 pm.

Prufrock Coffee EC1 £13 **4** **3** **3**
23-25 Leather Ln 0785 224 3470 9–2A
"Coffee, made by people who really care about coffee" inspires high
praise for this *"quirky"* Holborn spot; the sandwiches and snacks are
"surprisingly good as well". / EC1N 7TE; www.prufrockcoffee.com;
@PrufrockCoffee; L only; no Amex.

Punjab WC2 £27 **3** **3** **3**
80 Neal St 7836 9787 4–2C
In Covent Garden, the *"UK's oldest North Indian restaurant"*
(they claim) maintains quite a fan club, who say the food is *"terrific"*;
not everyone is quite convinced, though, and on a bad day service can
seem *"rushed"* and *"pushy"*. / WC2H 9PA; www.punjab.co.uk; 11 pm,
Sun 10.30 pm.

Q Grill NW1 NEW £55 **3** **3** 2
29-33 Chalk Farm Rd 7267 2678 8–2B
"Be transported to the US", at this grand new barbecue restaurant,
near Camden Lock; curiously, for a place evidently striving so hard
to be *"über-trendy"*, though, it's the ambience which reporters find
the weakest link. / NW1 8AJ; www.q-grill.co.uk; @QGrillLondon; Sat 11 pm,
Sun 9.30 pm.

Quaglino's SW1 £65
16 Bury St 7930 6767 3–3D
For years, this guide pointed out that this once-glamorous St James's
brasserie was in ever more desperate need of refurbishment... and
its owners, the D&D Group, finally got round to completing precisely
that that in mid-2014; let's hope for major improvement – there was
certainly plenty of scope! / SW1Y 6AJ; www.quaglinos.co.uk; @quaglinos;
10.30 pm, Fri & Sat 11 pm; closed Sun; no trainers; set weekday L £38
(FP), set pre-theatre £43 (FP); SRA-2 stars.

The Quality Chop House EC1 £41 **4** **5** **4**
94 Farringdon Rd 7278 1452 9–1A
"Meat and two veg to perfection" (*"you can buy the meat from their
butcher next door"*) wins praise for Farringdon's revived *'working class
caterer'*, despite its *"authentically narrow"* bum-numbing benches;
"completely charming" service and *"excellent"* wines too. / EC1R 3EA;
www.thequalitychophouse.com; @QualityChop; 10.30 pm; closed Sun; SRA-2
stars.

Quantus W4 £38 3 5 4
38 Devonshire Rd 8994 0488 7–2A
*"Tucked away in the same street as the much better known
La Trompette", this Chiswick spot is "a local gem" that's worth
seeking out; service, led by "very welcoming" owner Leo,
has "real flair", and the food, with a South American bent, "can be
excellent". / W4 2HD; www.quantus-london.com; 10 pm; closed Mon L,
Tue L & Sun; set weekday L £35 (FP).*

Quattro Passi W1 NEW £154 2 2 2
34 Dover St 3096 1444 3–3C
*"Outstanding food... I felt I was eating at their sister restaurant
on the Amalfi Coast", says an early-days fan of this Mayfair
newcomer; prices, though – especially of wines – are "at nosebleed
level", and doubters just cannot persuade themselves they're justified.
/ W1S 4NG; www.quattropassi.co.uk; @quattropassiuk; 10.30 pm; closed
Sun D; set weekday L £98 (FP).*

Queen's Head W6 £39 2 2 4
13 Brook Grn 7603 3174 7–1C
*It's the vast green space at the rear and cute, ancient interior which
makes it quite an "event" to visit this Brook Green tavern; the food –
"not really very good" – is beside the point. / W6 7BL;
www.queensheadhammersmith.co.uk; 10 pm, Sun 9 pm.*

The Queens Arms SW1 £43 4 4 4
11 Warwick Way 7834 3313 2–4B
*A "lively" Pimlico gastroboozer where the food "seems to have
improved" of late – for more calm to enjoy it, head for the "airy and
light" dining room upstairs. / SW1V 1QT; www.thequeensarmspimlico.co.uk;
@thequeensarms; 11 pm, Sun 10.30 pm.*

Le Querce SE23 £40 4 4 2
66-68 Brockley Rise 8690 3761 1–4D
*"Divine homemade pasta" and "esoteric" ice creams and sorbets top
the bill at this "delightful and genuine" family-run Sardinian,
in Brockley Park; this year, though, did see the occasional "can't-see-
what-the-fuss-is-about" report. / SE23 1LN; www.lequerce.co.uk; 10 pm,
Sun 8.30 pm; closed Mon & Tue L.*

Quilon SW1 £69 4 3 2
41 Buckingham Gate 7821 1899 2–4B
*"Marvellous" Keralan cooking that's prepared "with a light touch"
puts this "sleek and sophisticated" dining room, near Buckingham
Palace, firmly on London's culinary map; the ambience, however,
remains determinedly "low-key". / SW1E 6AF; www.quilon.co.uk;
@TheQuilon; 10.45 pm, Sun 10.15 pm; set weekday L £47 (FP); SRA-2 stars.*

Quirinale SW1 £59 4 4 2
North Ct, 1 Gt Peter St 7222 7080 2–4C
*A "quiet" subterranean spot, hidden away in a Westminster
backstreet, dishing up "classy and consistent" Italian cuisine; thanks
to popularity with "MPs, civil servants and the quangocracy", it is
busiest at lunchtimes. / SW1P 3LL; www.quirinale.co.uk; @quirinaleresto;
10.30 pm; closed Sat & Sun.*

Quo Vadis W1 £56 **3** **4** **4**
26-29 Dean St 7437 9585 4–2A
The "hospitable" air of the Hart brothers' "charming" Soho old-timer
makes it a haven for those in search of a "good-value set lunch" or a
civilised pre-theatre meal; Jeremy Lee's "distinctive" British cuisine has
its fans too, but it can be "variable", or too "quirky" for some tastes.
/ W1D 3LL; www.quovadissoho.co.uk; 10.45 pm; closed Sun.

Rabbit SW3 **NEW**
172 King's Rd 3750 0172 5–3C
On the former site of Choys (RIP), the people behind The Shed
in Notting Hill bring this new nose-to-tail restaurant to the environs
of Chelsea Old Town Hall. / SW3 4UP; www.rabbit-restaurant.com.

Rabot 1745 SE1 **NEW** £71 **2** **3** **3**
2-4 Bedale St 7378 8226 9–4C
"It is NOT a gimmick!", say advocates of the "high standard
of cooking" at this "intriguing" newcomer, backed by the Hotel
Chocolat people, which features cocoa in most dishes (and which
is also of note for an atmospheric covered terrace overlooking
Borough Market); critics, though, just find the cooking rather
"mundane". / SE1 9AL; www.rabot1745.com; @rabot1745; closed Mon.

Racine SW3 £66 **2** **2** **2**
239 Brompton Rd 7584 4477 5–2C
"You feel like you're in Paris", say devotees of this Knightsbridge
fixture, who applaud its "seriously good bourgeois cooking" and "old-
school" style; sagging survey ratings, however, support those who feel
it's "going downhill" – "fairly average" nowadays, and "pricey" too.
/ SW3 2EP; www.racine-restaurant.com; @racine_kitchen; 10.30 pm,
Sun 10 pm; set weekday L & dinner £36 (FP).

Ragam W1 £27 **5** **4** **1**
57 Cleveland St 7636 9098 2–1B
"Whenever I go, I'm amazed I don't go more often!"; in 24 years,
the survey view of this "very small" and "tired"-looking outfit, in the
shadow of the Telecom Tower, has never really wavered – it's a total
"winner", serving "wondrous" South Indian dishes at "unbeatable"
prices. / W1T 4JN; www.ragam.co.uk; 10.45 pm; essential Fri & Sat.

Randall & Aubin W1 £55 **4** **4** **5**
16 Brewer St 7287 4447 3–2D
"Just right for Soho"; this "high energy" champagne and seafood bar
is a "fun" place in a very handy location; it's "always full". / W1F 0SG;
www.randallandaubin.com; @edbaineschef; 11 pm, Sat midnight, Sun 10 pm;
booking for L only; SRA-1 star.

Rani N3 £27 **3** **2** **2**
7 Long Ln 8349 4386 1–1B
A "long-established vegetarian" (and vegan) in Finchley, which offers
"great Gujarati home-cooking"; you don't really need to know what
to order, as the main attraction is the huge buffet. / N3 2PR;
www.raniuk.com; 10 pm; no Amex.

Ranoush   £47   **4 3 2**
338 King's Rd, SW3   7352 0044   5–3C
43 Edgware Rd, W2   7723 5929   6–1D
86 Kensington High St, W8   7938 2234   5–1A
*"Great Lebanese at good-value prices" – these budget offshoots
of the swanky Maroush chain make excellent pit stops; highlights
include juices, shawarma and mezze. / www.maroush.com; most branches
close between 1 am-3 am.*

Raoul's Café   £46   **2 2 3**
105-107 Talbot Rd, W11   7229 2400   6–1B
113-115 Hammersmith Grove, W6   8741 3692   7–1C
13 Clifton Rd, W9   7289 7313   8–4A
*"Spectacular" eggs top the bill at these laid-back west London cafés,
which are almost invariably tipped as "a safe bet for
breakfast or brunch", which they carry off "with panache"; other
meals inspire practically no feedback. / www.raoulsgourmet.com;
10.15 pm, W11 6.15 pm; booking after 5 pm only.*

Rasa   £38   **4 4 3**
6 Dering St, W1   7637 0222   3–2B
Holiday Inn Hotel, 1 Kings Cross, WC1   7833 9787   8–3D
55 Stoke Newington Church St, N16   7249 0344   1–1C
56 Stoke Newington Church St, N16   7249 1340   1–1C
*"Aromatic, spicy and delicious South Indian food at brilliant prices"
has won renown for this "consistently fabulous" and "charming" small
chain; fans still say "you've got to head to Stoke Newington for the
full effect", but W1 is actually higher rated these days.
/ www.rasarestaurants.com; 10.45 pm; WC1 & W1 closed Sun.*

Rasoi SW3   £104   **5 4 4**
10 Lincoln St   7225 1881   5–2D
*"The best Indian in London by a country mile"; Vineet Bhattia's
"elegant" Chelsea townhouse offers many "mind-blowing" dishes –
"outstanding, even amongst the elite places" – in a set of "intimate
and unstuffy" dining rooms; you spend a bomb of course, but it's
"worth it". / SW3 2TS; www.rasoirestaurant.co.uk; @GujaratiRasoi;
10.30 pm, Sun 10 pm; closed Mon & Sat L.*

Ravi Shankar NW1   £33   **4 3 2**
132-135 Drummond St   7388 6458   8–4C
*A veteran of the 'Little India' cluster, by Euston station; "it's certainly
cheap 'n' cheerful, but what it lacks in decor and style it makes up for
in dosas and thalis" – "there's so much choice, even carnivores don't
miss the meat!" / NW1 2HL; 10.30 pm; no Amex or Maestro.*

Raw Duck E8 **NEW**
197 Richmond Rd   8986 6534   1–2D
*Rising like a phoenix from the ashes after the original location was
demolished, this sibling to Soho restaurant Ducksoup has now
reopened; a review of this effectively new operation will have to wait
till next year. / E8 3NJ.*

The Real Greek £40 222
56 Paddington St, W1   7486 0466   2–1A
60-62 Long Acre, WC2   7240 2292   4–2D
Westfield, Ariel Way, W12   8743 9168   7–1C
1-2 Riverside Hs, Southwark Br Rd, SE1   7620 0162   9–3B
6 Horner Sq, E1   7375 1364   12–2B
Could it be that this Greek chain is finally sorting itself out? – it won more praise this year for the "predictable reliability" of its "tasty" mezze. / www.therealgreek.com; 10.45 pm; WC2 10.30 pm, E1 Sun 7 pm; EC1 closed Sun, N1 closed Sun-Mon; WC2 no booking.

Red Dog £41 323
37 Hoxton Sq, N1   3551 8014   12–1B
27-31 Bedford Rd, SW4   3714 2747   10–2D **NEW**
'Authentic Kansas City Bar-B-Q' is the promise at this Hoxton hangout, whose hickory-smoked meatilicious treats generally win the thumbs-up from reporters; a new Clapham branch opened shortly after the survey closed.

Red Fort W1 £65 332
77 Dean St   7437 2525   4–2A
"It's set the standard for Indian food for years", say fans of this Soho stalwart (which underwent a "faintly impersonal" modern revamp a few years ago); others are more cautious – "it was good on an 'offer', but would have seemed overpriced at full tariff". / W1D 3SH; www.redfort.co.uk; 11.15 pm, Sun 10.15 pm; closed Sat L & Sun L; set weekday L & pre-theatre £38 (FP).

The Red Pepper W9 £45 422
8 Formosa St   7266 2708   8–4A
"Still a great local favourite" – seating may be "cramped", and service "amateur", but this Maida Vale fixture still attracts a big following for its "excellent" pizzas. / W9 1EE; Sat 11 pm, Sun 10.30 pm; closed weekday L; no Amex.

Le Relais de Venise L'Entrecôte £43 323
120 Marylebone Ln, W1   7486 0878   2–1A
18-20 Mackenzie Walk, E14   3475 3331   11–1C
5 Throgmorton St, EC2   7638 6325   9–2C
"A fantastic concept!"; "you can have anything you like, so long as it's steak" – which comes "slathered in secret sauce", with salad and "awesome" fries – at these "crammed" and "efficient" Gallic bistros; "go early or late to avoid the queues". / www.relaisdevenise.com; W1 11 pm, Sun 10.30 pm; EC2 10 pm; EC2 closed Sat & Sun; no booking.

Reubens W1 £55 322
79 Baker St   7486 0035   2–1A
Scant feedback of late on this long-serving kosher deli-restaurant in Marylebone; fans insist it still serves "excellent salt beef", and "great chicken schnitzel" too. / W1U 6RG; www.reubensrestaurant.co.uk; 10 pm; closed Fri D & Sat; no Amex.

Rextail W1 **NEW** £80 122
13 Albermarle St   3301 1122   3–3C
"Not worth the money" – Arkady Novikov's new Mayfair basement brasserie-steakhouse takes huge flak from reporters for its "joyless" food and "silly" prices; the lunchtime prix-fixe, though, has its uses. / W1S 4HJ; www.rextail.co.uk; @Rextail_London.

The Rib Man N1 £12 5 3 4
KERB, King's Cross   no tel   8–3C
"Wow... just wow!" – eloquent feedback on the "ribs to die for",
"greatest pulled pork" and "mean range of hot sauces and rubs"
at Mark Gevaux's food stall at KERB, behind King's Cross. / N1;
www.theribman.co.uk; @theribman.

Rib Room
Jumeirah Carlton Tower Hotel SW1 £103 3 3 2
Cadogan Pl   7858 7250   5–1D
If only all hotel makeovers were as successful as the rejuvenation
of this "spacious" Belgravia dining room – "a high quality traditional
experience", now offering what fans say is "the best roast beef
in London", albeit at "huge" cost. / SW1X 9PY; www.jumeirah.com;
@RibRoomSW1; 10.45 pm, Sun 10.15 pm; set weekday L £66 (FP).

Riccardo's SW3 £43 2 2 2
126 Fulham Rd   7370 6656   5–3B
Critics of this Chelsea Italian small-plates veteran have "no idea why
it's so popular", citing "complacent" service and "bland and
underwhelming" realisation of its "simple" cuisine; supporters,
however, sense the beginnings of a return to old form. / SW3 6HU;
www.riccardos.it; @ricardoslondon; 11.30 pm.

Riding House Café W1 £55 2 2 4
43-51 Great Titchfield St   7927 0840   3–1C
Breakfast and brunch "NYC-style" – "hearty, delicious and creative"
– have helped generate a big buzz around this "vibey" Fitzrovia
brasserie; lunches and dinners, though, can underwhelm. / W1W 7PQ;
www.ridinghousecafe.co.uk; 11 pm, Sun 10.30 pm.

Rising Sun NW7 £44 3 4 3
137 Marsh Ln, Highwood Hill   8959 1357   1–1B
"The best Italian food for miles around" – a surprise find at this
"lovely", if sometimes "chaotic", family-run gastropub, in Mill Hill.
/ NW7 4EY; www.therisingsunmillhill.co.uk; @therisingsunpub; 9.30 pm,
Sun 8.30 pm; closed Mon L.

(Palm Court)
The Ritz W1 £44 3 4 5
150 Piccadilly   7493 8181   3–4C
Sure it's "overpriced", but the "institution" which is afternoon tea
at the Ritz wins impressively consistent survey approval – book well
ahead for an "amazing" experience! / W1C 9BR; www.theritzlondon.com;
9.30 pm; jacket & tie.

The Ritz Restaurant
The Ritz W1 £122 3 4 5
150 Piccadilly   7493 8181   3–4C
"Totally overwhelming" in its "magical" Louis XVI style, this chamber
overlooking Green Park is often acclaimed as "the most elegant dining
room in England"; "it doesn't always get the best food crits" but many
"marvellous" meals were reported this year... as you'd hope, given
the "daunting" prices. / W1J 9BR; www.theritzlondon.com; @theritzlondon;
10 pm; jacket & tie; set dinner & pre-theatre £80 (FP).

Riva SW13   £60   **3** **4** **2**
169 Church Rd   8748 0434   10–1A
"Either you love it, or hate it"; to foodies ("Heston and AA Gill were on the next table!"), Andreas Riva's Barnes Italian is a "smooth" classic with "wonderful" cooking… but to sceptics it's a "tired"-looking, "expensive" place where "regulars are favoured, and it shows". / SW13 9HR; 10.30 pm, Sun 9 pm; closed Sat L.

Rivea
Bulgari Hotel SW7 NEW   £68   **2** **4** **2**
171 Knightsbridge   7151 1025   5–1C
"Light and interesting food… just it feels like eating in a hotel lounge"; this Ducasse-branded newcomer, in a glitzy Knightsbridge basement, impresses most reporters with its French-Italian small-plate cuisine, but feedback is far from consistent – "promised much, delivered little", says one of the unconvinced. / SW7 1DW; www.bulgarihotels.com; 10.15 pm.

THE RIVER CAFÉ W6   £90   **3** **2** **3**
Thames Wharf, Rainville Rd   7386 4200   7–2C
It's "still the benchmark", say its many fans, but even some devotees discern a "drop in standards" of late at this world-famous Hammersmith Italian, and to its growing legions of critics it's an "overcrowded" and "impersonal" place, where "uneventful" dishes come at "merciless" prices. / W6 9HA; www.rivercafe.co.uk; @RiverCafeLondon; 9 pm, Sat 9.15 pm; closed Sun D.

Rivington Grill   £50   **2** **2** **3**
178 Greenwich High Rd, SE10   8293 9270   1–3D
28-30 Rivington St, EC2   7729 7053   12–1B
"Always busy and buzzy", these Shoreditch and Greenwich brasseries can be handy "for a lazy breakfast" or a burger; but could one not expect more of a Caprice group production? – "they're never terrible, but never as good as hoped either". / www.rivingtongrill.co.uk; 11 pm, Sun 10 pm; SE10 closed Mon, Tue L & Wed L.

Roast SE1   £69   **2** **2** **2**
Stoney St   0845 034 7300   9–4C
In its "fabulous" location, looking down on Borough Market, this "light and airy" British restaurant dishes up "hands down, the best breakfast"; thereafter, however, it "seems to be aimed at tourists and businessmen", and can seem "really overpriced for what it is". / SE1 1TL; www.roast-restaurant.com; 10.45 pm; closed Sun D; set weekday L & dinner £50 (FP); SRA-3 stars.

Rocca Di Papa   £43   **2** **2** **3**
73 Old Brompton Rd, SW7   7225 3413   5–2B
75-79 Dulwich Village, SE21   8299 6333   1–4D
"No fuss, just straightforward Italian food" – the reason to seek out these "busy, busy, busy" South Kensington and Dulwich Village spots, which major in "delicious thin-crust pizzas". / SW7 11.30 pm; SE21 11 pm.

Rochelle Canteen E2 £41 4 4 4
Arnold Circus 7729 5677 12–1C
*"Worth the effort!"; Melanie Arnold & Margot Henderson's "quirky"
and "incredibly hard-to-find" daytime venture, hidden away behind
the wall of a Victorian school in Shoreditch, attracts a dedicated
following with a "daily-changing" menu which makes much use
of "super-fresh produce". / E2 7ES; www.arnoldandhenderson.com; L only,
closed Sat & Sun; no Amex.*

Rocket £46 3 3 3
36-38 Kingsway, WC2 7242 8070 2–1D **NEW**
2 Churchill Pl, E14 3200 2022 11–1C
201 Bishopsgate, EC2 7377 8863 12–2B
6 Adams Ct, EC2 7628 0808 9–2C
*For "great pizza" and other "decent staples", these "bustling" diners
are worth knowing about as "reasonable-value" destinations in pricey
areas – tucked away in an alleyway off Bond Street, hidden in a
courtyard by Bank, and in Canary Wharf (with great views).
/ 10.30 pm,Sun 9.30 pm; W1 closed Sun; EC2 closed Sat & Sun;
SW15 Mon-Wed D only, Bishopsgate closed Sun D, E14.*

Roka £80 5 3 4
30 North Audley St, W1 7305 5644 3–2A **NEW**
37 Charlotte St, W1 7580 6464 2–1C
71-91 Aldwych, WC2 7580 6464 2–2D **NEW**
Unit 4, Park Pavilion, 40 Canada Sq, E14 7636 5228 11–1C
*"Forget Nobu – this is much better!"; "Zuma's little sisters" offer
"light-hearted and creative" Japanese-fusion dishes that "explode
on the palate", and "terrific" cocktails too; the Charlotte Street
original is the best, with the new Mayfair branch "not as convincing";
late-2014 sees a large new Aldwych branch. / www.rokarestaurant.com;
11.15 pm, Sun 10.30 pm; booking: max 8.*

The Rooftop Café
The Exchange SE1 **NEW** £44 3 4 5
28 London Bridge St 3102 3770 9–4C
*"A lovely hidden gem in the shadow of The Shard"; "it takes a bit
of finding", but this "bright" and "airy" café, on top of an office block,
rewards diners with great views and an "ever-changing, concise and
well-executed menu". / SE1 9SG; www.theexchange.so/rooftop;
@ExchangeLDN; closed Mon D, Tue D & Sun.*

Roots at N1 N1 £49 5 5 3
115 Hemingford Rd 7697 4488 8–3D
*A candlelit ex-pub, in Islington, which now functions as "an excellent
upmarket Indian", and one with "considerable charm" too; it serves
an "attractive", if "minimalist", menu of "brilliant" dishes –
"much better value than the big names". / N1 1BZ; www.rootsatn1.com;
@rootsatn1; 10 pm, Sun 9 pm; closed Mon, Tue–Sat D only, Sun open L & D.*

Rossopomodoro £39 222

50-52 Monmouth St, WC2   7240 9095   4–3B
214 Fulham Rd, SW10   7352 7677   5–3B
1 Rufus St, N1   7739 1899   12–1B
10 Jamestown Rd, NW1   7424 9900   8–3B
46 Garrett Ln, SW18   07931920377   10–2B
The "aggressive branch buildout" has done nothing for reporters'
esteem for this Neapolitan-based pizza chain; fans still praise its
"authentic" style, but overall it's difficult to escape the verdict of the
reporter who says it's now "like PizzaExpress without the
excitement". / www.rossopomodoro.co.uk; 11.30 pm; WC2 Sun 11.30 pm.

Roti Chai W1 £46 443

3 Portman Mews South   7408 0101   3–1A
"Inspired by Indian street food", an excellent two-year-old,
near Selfridges, which serves up dishes that are "precisely spiced",
"authentic" and "very good value"; both the café and more "formal"
basement come recommended. / W1H 6HS; www.rotichai.com; @rotichai;
10.30 pm.

Rotorino E8 NEW £48 223

432-434 Kingsland Rd   7249 9081   1–1D
This "chic" new easterly counterpoint to Stevie Parle's Dock Kitchen
has instantly been hailed as a "buzzy addition to Dalston"; reports
on the food, however, range all the way from "amazing"
to "embarrassing" – "microscopic" portions can give rise to particular
complaint. / E8 4AA; www.rotorino.com; @Rotorino.

**Rotunda Bar & Restaurant
Kings Place N1** £53 213

90 York Way   7014 2840   8–3C
The "great" canalside area is the crown jewel feature of this attractive
arts centre brasserie, near King's Cross; the steak, in particular,
can be "excellent" too, but "patchy" service has led to some
decidedly up-and-down reports this year. / N1 9AG;
www.rotundabarandrestaurant.co.uk; @rotundalondon; 10.30 pm,
Sun 6.30 pm.

**Roux at Parliament Square
RICS SW1** £78 342

12 Great George St   7334 3737   2–3C
"Mainly of interest to the parliamentary and business crowd",
the Rouxs' high-ceilinged dining room offers "elegant" cuisine of a
"high grade", with "charming and efficient" staff helping to offset the
somewhat "library-like" atmosphere. / SW1P 3AD;
www.rouxatparliamentsquare.co.uk; 10 pm; closed Sat & Sun.

**Roux at the Landau
The Langham W1** £97 333

1c Portland Pl   7965 0165   2–1B
The Roux brothers' "quiet and dignified" outpost, opposite
Broadcasting House, offers "outstanding food and service in a really
beautiful space", say its fans (and "superb value" too, if you go for
the set lunch); this year, however, there were also quite a few critics,
who found meals "below expectations". / W1B 1JA; www.thelandau.com;
@Langham_Hotel; 10 pm; closed Sat L & Sun; no trainers.

Rowley's SW1 £69 2 2 **3**

113 Jermyn St 7930 2707 3–3D

Original features – dating from the premises' days as the first Wall's butchers shop – "add to the charm" of a visit to this St James's "staple"; it's "possibly overpriced", but has won more praise of late for its "good chateaubriand and unlimited fries" ("brought around regularly, hot from the pan"). / SW1Y 6HJ; www.rowleys.co.uk; @rowleys_steak; 10.30 pm.

Royal Academy W1 £53 **1** 2 2

Burlington Hs, Piccadilly 7300 5608 3–3D

"It's a shame the advantage of its location is not built on" – this potentially "delightful" heart-of-the-West-End café could be a brilliant standby, but, despite a recent refurbishment, it remains "below par". / W1J 0BD; www.royalacademy.org.uk; 9 pm; L only, ex Fri open L & D; no booking at L.

Royal China £47 **4** 2 2

24-26 Baker St, W1 7487 4688 2–1A
805 Fulham Rd, SW6 7731 0081 10–1B
13 Queensway, W2 7221 2535 6–2C
30 Westferry Circus, E14 7719 0888 11–1B

"Fantastic, Hong Kong-quality dim sum" – many reporters would say "the best in town" – makes this "unwelcoming" Cantonese chain a London benchmark; the "garish" decor "may not be what you'd have at home, but fits the occasion brilliantly". / www.royalchinagroup.co.uk; 10.45 pm, Fri & Sat 11.15 pm, Sun 9.45 pm; no booking Sat & Sun L.

Royal China Club W1 £62 **4** **4** **3**

40-42 Baker St 7486 3898 2–1A

"Hong Kong comes to London", at the Royal China group's "top-class" Marylebone flagship; "superb dim sum" is a highlight of the sometimes "amazing" Cantonese cuisine. / W1U 7AJ; www.royalchinagroup.co.uk; 11 pm, Fri & Sat 11.30 pm, Sun 10.30 pm.

The Royal Exchange Grand Café
The Royal Exchange EC3 £55 2 2 **4**

The Royal Exchange Bank 7618 2480 9–2C

An "excellent location", in a huge and gracious covered courtyard, surrounded by luxury shops, helps make this heart-of-the-City seafood bar "perfect for business" – "the food is not really good enough to be any sort of distraction". / EC3V 3LR; www.royalexchange-grandcafe.co.uk; @rexlondon; 9.30 pm; closed Sat & Sun; SRA-1 star.

RSJ SE1 £48 **3** **4** 2

33 Coin St 7928 4554 9–4A

"The best Loire wine list in the world" has long been the special appeal of this remarkably consistent stalwart, near the National Theatre; it would win few prizes for interior design, but service is "efficient", and the food is "dependable" and "reasonably-priced". / SE1 9NR; www.rsj.uk.com; @RSJWaterloo; 11 pm; closed Sat L & Sun.

Rugoletta N2 NEW £38 **4** **4** 2

59 Church Ln 8815 1743 1–1B

"Beautiful Italian home-cooking" (with "outstanding" pizzas a highlight) – at "very reasonable" prices – has made quite a hit of this East Finchley spot; its new Barnet offshoot is "less cramped but just as good" (but not, unlike the original, BYO). / N2 8DR; www.larugoletta.com; 10.30 pm; closed Sun.

Rules WC2   £72   **3** **4** **5**

35 Maiden Ln   7836 5314   4–3D

*"For tourists, but not touristy"; with its "beautiful" antique interior,
London's oldest restaurant (Covent Garden, 1798) may be perennially
packed with visitors but – with its "true" English fare and "seamless"
service – it mercifully transcends its tourist-trap potential; game a
speciality. / WC2E 7LB; www.rules.co.uk; 11.30 pm, Sun 10.30 pm; no shorts;
set weekday L £49 (FP).*

Le Sacré-Coeur N1   £36   **2** **3** **4**

18 Theberton St   7354 2618   8–3D

*A venerable bistro in Islington which, say fans, "goes from strength
to strength"; not all reporters are quite so enamoured, but even they
usually concede it's at least a "decent neighbourhood restaurant".
/ N1 0QX; www.lesacrecoeur.co.uk; 11 pm, Sat 11.30 pm, Sun 10.30 pm;
set weekday L £23 (FP).*

Sacro Cuore NW10   £32   **4** **3** **4**

45 Chamberlayne Rd   8960 8558   1–2B

*"Faultless dough" and "well-sourced ingredients from Italy" add to the
"authenticity" of this diminutive two-year-old pizzeria, in Kensal Rise;
on the downside, it can be "too noisy". / NW10 3NB;
www.sacrocuore.co.uk/menu.html; @SacroCuorePizza; 10.30 pm; closed
weekday L; no Amex; need 4+ to book, Fri & Sat no bookings.*

Sagar   £38   **3** **2** **2**

17a Percy St, W1   7631 3319   3–2B
31 Catherine St, WC2   7836 6377   4–3D
157 King St, W6   8741 8563   7–2C

*"If you're looking for Indian street snacks" or "yummy dosas",
the branches of this unpretentious chain are generally "a delight",
"even for non-veggies"; "you don't go for the ambience".
/ www.sagarveg.co.uk; Sun-Thu 10.45 pm, Fri & Sat 11.30 pm.*

Sager & Wilde E2   £22   **3** **4** **4**

193 Hackney Rd   8127 7330   12–1C

*A Hoxton "oasis" – a "personal" operation, where an interesting wine
list, including some "beautiful" finds, is backed up by "a good small
selection of food". / E2 8JP; www.sagerandwilde.com; closed weekday L.*

Saigon Saigon W6   £41   **3** **4** **3**

313-317 King St   8748 6887   7–2B

*It may look "tired", but all reporters recommend this "pretty
authentic" Vietnamese on Hammersmith's main drag – "reasonable
value and great fun". / W6 9NH; www.saigon-saigon.co.uk;
@saigonsaigonuk; 11.30 pm, Sun & Mon 10 pm.*

St John EC1   £65   **4** **4** **2**

26 St John St   7251 0848   9–1B

*It's "not everyone's cup of tea", but Fergus Henderson's famous
advertisement for 'nose-to-tail' (offal-heavy) British eating still inspires
adulation; some fans also adore the spartan aesthetic of his
Smithfield ex-smokehouse, which others just find "uncomfortable".
/ EC1M 4AY; www.stjohngroup.uk.com; @SJRestaurant; 11 pm; closed
Sat L & Sun D.*

St John Bread & Wine E1   £55   **5** **3** **4**
94-96 Commercial St   7251 0848   12–2C
*"A new and fantastic experience every time"; with its menu
of "quirky" small-plate dishes (usually meaty) and "cheapish and
unusual wines", this "noisy" Shoreditch canteen is "always a joy";
indeed, the survey rates it more highly than its fabled Smithfield
parent. / E1 6LZ; www.stjohngroup.uk.com/spitalfields; @StJBW; 10.30 pm,
Sun 9.30 pm.*

St Johns N19   £48   **3** **3** **5**
91 Junction Rd   7272 1587   8–1C
*A "lovely" setting, in a huge former ballroom – plus the constant
"buzz of a full house" – helps make this Archway "neighbourhood
favourite" a very charming destination; the cooking is often
"first rate" too, although some reporters discern "a little more
variability" of late. / N19 5QU; www.stjohnstavern.com; @stjohnstavern;
11 pm, Sun 9.30 pm; Mon-Thu D only, Fri-Sun open L & D; no Amex; booking:
max 12.*

St Pancras Grand
St Pancras Int'l Station NW1   £53   **2** **2** **2**
The Concourse   7870 9900   8–3C
*"It's a railway café on a grand scale", but that's about the only plus
of this "beautiful" but "very patchy" brasserie… even if apologists
insist it's "much better than anything on offer at the Gare du Nord!"
/ NW1 2QP; www.searcys.co.uk; @SearcysBars; 10.30 pm.*

Sakana-tei W1   £35   **4** **4** **2**
11 Maddox St   7629 3000   3–2C
*"Just like Tokyo, the food is everything, the service takes an interest,
and the place is falling apart" – that's the deal at this Mayfair
basement. / W1S 2QF; 10 pm; closed Sun.*

Sake No Hana SW1   £69   **2** **1** **2**
23 St James's St   7925 8988   3–4C
*This landmark building in St James's may have a "very cool" dining
room, but this "pretentious" Japanese, with its sometimes "intrusive"
and "uppity" service, inspires little affection among reporters; "it only
survives thanks to its location". / SW1A 1HA; www.sakenohana.com;
@sakenonhana; 11 pm, Fri & Sat 11.30pm; closed Sun.*

Sakura W1   £33   **2** **2** **2**
23 Conduit St   7629 2961   3–2C
*"A good range of well prepared classic dishes" and
a "very convenient" location draw fans to this "reasonably-priced"
Mayfair spot. / W1S 2XS; www.sakuramayfair.com; 10 pm.*

Salaam Namaste WC1   £35   **3** **3** **2**
68 Millman St   7405 3697   2–1D
*"A real find for Bloomsbury!" – this "brightly decorated" Indian puts
"a slightly modern twist on the usual offerings", and offers "fresh and
spicy" fare that's "better than average". / WC1N 3EF;
www.salaam-namaste.co.uk; @SalaamNamasteUK; 11.30 pm, Sun 11 pm.*

Sale e Pepe SW1   £65   **2** **2** **3**
9-15 Pavilion Rd   7235 0098   5–1D
*"Not changed in 40 years" – this "noisy" trattoria, near Harrods may
be "expensive for ordinary Italian food", but "it still has that buzz,
and the staff are fun!" / SW1X 0HD; www.saleepepe.co.uk; 11.30 pm;
no shorts.*

Salloos SW1 £61 **4 4 2**
62-64 Kinnerton St 7235 4444 5–1D
It may look "drab", but this age-old Pakistani, in a Belgravia mews,
is a perennial "undiscovered gem", serving "melting lamb chops" and
other "wonderful" tandoori dishes; "it doesn't come cheap" –
what does, round here? – but "it's worth it, now and then".
/ SW1X 8ER; www.salloos.co.uk; 11 pm; closed Sun; need 5+ to book.

The Salt House NW8 £46 **2 1 2**
63 Abbey Rd 7328 6626 8–3A
Erratic reports of late from this large and "buzzy" St John's Wood
gastropub; for a sunny day, though, it does have some "delightful"
al fresco seating. / NW8 0AE; www.salthouseabbeyroad.com;
@thesalthousenw8; 11 pm, Fri & Sat midnight.

Salt Yard W1 £47 **3 4 3**
54 Goodge St 7637 0657 2–1B
"Unusual and excellent" Italian/Spanish tapas and "an original wine
list" have made a big name for this "buzzy" Fitzrovia fixture; the site
can seem a touch "claustrophobic", though, and the occasional critic
senses "a decrease in standards since the heady early days".
/ W1T 4NA; www.saltyard.co.uk; @SaltYardGroup; 10.45 pm; closed Sun;
SRA-2 stars.

Salvation In Noodles N1 NEW £33 **4 4 3**
122 Balls Pond Rd 7254 4534 1–1C
"Wow, I haven't had such great pho since I was in Vietnam!" – early
reports on this "infuriatingly hip" Dalston spot agree the food
is "authentic", and service is "friendly" too. / N1 4AE;
www.salvationinnoodles.co.uk; @SINDalston; 10.30 pm; closed weekday L.

Sam's Brasserie W4 £49 **3 4 4**
11 Barley Mow Pas 8987 0555 7–2A
"Tucked away down an alleyway", off Chiswick's main drag,
this versatile and atmospheric hangout is a "consistently good
neighbourhood brasserie", ideal for a "heavenly" family brunch,
but also useful for a business lunch or any sort of general get-
together. / W4 4PH; www.samsbrasserie.co.uk; @samsbrasserie; 10.30 pm,
Sun 10 pm; set weekday L £32 (FP); SRA-3 stars.

San Carlo Cicchetti W1 £47 **3 3 3**
215 Piccadilly 7494 9435 3–3D
Handily sited a few paces from Piccadilly Circus, a "bustling" Italian
tapas bar, offering "a good food selection and friendly service"; on the
downside its serried ranks of tables are "rather cramped". / W1J 9HN;
www.sancarlo.co.uk; @SanCarlo_Group; midnight.

San Daniele del Friuli N5 £43 **3 4 3**
72 Highbury Park 7226 1609 8–1D
"An excellent long-established local", in Highbury Park, that's
"very friendly and feels like being in Italy"; the cooking is never less
than "sound". / N5 2XE; www.sandanielehighbury.co.uk; 10.30 pm; closed
Mon L, Tue L, Wed L & Sun; no Amex.

San Lorenzo Fuoriporta SW19 £67 **2 2 2**
38 Wimbledon Hill Rd 8946 8463 10–2B
Mixed views on this stalwart '70s Italian; for fans, this is
"Wimbledon's top destination", but for doubters the cooking's "solid,
not inspirational", and it "trades on the loyalty of regulars".
/ SW19 7PA; www.sanlorenzosw19.squarespace.com; @fuoriporta; 10.40 pm.

The Sands End SW6　　　　　£52　　4 4 4
135 Stephendale Rd　7731 7823　10–1B
A "top-notch gastropub", in the eponymous section of Fulham,
that "impresses on all fronts" (not least with its "amazing homemade
Scotch eggs"); perhaps the main attraction, though, is a "great twenty
something crowd, who make the place swing". / SW6 2PR;
www.thesandsend.co.uk; @thesandsend; 11.30 pm, Thu-Sat midnight;
set weekday L £32 (FP).

Santa Lucia SW10　　　　　£42　　3 2 2
2 Hollywood Rd　7352 8484　5–3B
"Good pizzas, served with panache" – and "delicious" pasta too –
draw Chelsea locals to this "fun" (but "tightly-packed") backstreet
spot. / SW10 9HY; www.madeinitalygroup.co.uk; 11.30 pm, Sun 10.30 pm;
closed weekday L.

Santa Maria W5　　　　　£32　　5 3 3
15 St Mary's Rd　8579 1462　1–3A
"The best pizza this side of Naples" has made this "wonderfully
genuine" outfit world-famous in Ealing; one drawback, though –
"it's nigh on impossible to get a table". / W5 5RA;
www.santamariapizzeria.com; @SantaMariaPizza; 10.30 pm.

Santini SW1　　　　　£70　　2 3 4
29 Ebury St　7730 4094　2–4B
"Improved" of late, this stalwart swanky Belgravia Italian is a
"professional" operation – it's always been "on the pricey side",
though, and particularly popular "for business". / SW1W 0NZ;
www.santini-restaurant.com; 11 pm, Sun 10 pm; set pre theatre £46 (FP).

Santore EC1　　　　　£43　　4 4 2
59 Exmouth Mkt　7812 1488　9–1A
"A little bit of Italy"; this superb Exmouth Market spot majors
in Neapolitan pizza "to die for"; "lovely outside tables on a summer's
day" too. / EC1R 4QL; www.santorerestaurant.co.uk; 11 pm.

Sapori Sardi SW6　　　　　£48　　4 4 2
786 Fulham Rd　7731 0755　10–1B
The "most fabulous local"; the Sardinian cuisine "comes straight from
the heart" at this two-year-old Fulham spot, and it is not just "tasty"
but "extremely reasonably priced" too. / SW6 5SL; www.saporisardi.co.uk;
11 pm; no Amex.

Sarastro WC2　　　　　£50　　1 3 3
126 Drury Ln　7836 0101　2–2D
"Lots to look at while you dine" – and "fantastic entertainment" –
justify a trip to this flamboyant operatic-themed Covent Garden
haunt; without the opera, though, the whole experience would
be eminently "forgettable". / WC2B 5SU; www.sarastro-restaurant.com;
@SastroR; 10.30 pm, Sat 11 pm.

Sardo W1　　　　　£55　　3 3 2
45 Grafton Way　7387 2521　2–1B
"Unfussy and well-executed" Sardinian dishes make for
an "enjoyable" experience at this Fitzrovia fixture, where the interior
is "pleasant but often noisy". / W1T 5DQ; www.sardo-restaurant.com;
11 pm; closed Sat L & Sun.

Sarracino NW6 £42 `4` `3` `2`
186 Broadhurst Gdns 7372 5889 1–1B
*"No better pizza than this!" – served 'al metro' – wins praise from
reporters for this West Hampstead trattoria; apparently, "everyone
in the kitchen is from round Naples".* / NW6 3AY;
www.sarracinorestaurant.com; 11 pm; closed weekday L.

Sartoria W1 £59 `3` `3` `2`
20 Savile Row 7534 7000 3–2C
*"Spacious", "comfortable" and "efficient", this Mayfair Italian is a
popular business venue, offering some "very enjoyable" cooking;
impressive wine too, from the "thoroughly knowledgeable" sommelier.*
/ W1S 3PR; www.sartoria-restaurant.co.uk; @SartoriaRest; 10.45 pm; closed
Sat L & Sun; SRA-2 stars.

Satay House W2 £35 `3` `3` `2`
13 Sale Pl 7723 6763 6–1D
*An "authentically Malaysian" veteran in a Bayswater backwater,
offering a consistently "decent" level of cooking.* / W2 1PX;
www.satay-house.co.uk; 11 pm.

Sauterelle
Royal Exchange EC3 £72 `3` `3` `4`
Bank 7618 2483 9–2C
*"Tucked away on the mezzanine level of the Royal Exchange", this is
a D&D Group outpost that's "perfect for business"; "it has worked
hard to up its game" in recent times, and the modern French cuisine
can be very good.* / EC3V 3LR; www.sauterelle-restaurant.co.uk; 9.30 pm;
closed Sat & Sun; no trainers; SRA-1 star.

Savoir Faire WC1 £39 `3` `3` `2`
42 New Oxford St 7436 0707 4–1C
*A "welcoming" spot offering "homely French bistro cooking", in a
"perfect location near the British Museum"; it's "very reasonably
priced" too.* / WC1A 1EP; www.savoir.co.uk; 11 pm.

(Savoy Grill)
The Savoy Hotel WC2 £75 `2` `3` `3`
Strand 7592 1600 4–3D
*Once London's unchallenged power-dining scene, this "elegant" room,
now a Ramsay outpost, "still delivers the goods", say fans; there are
quite a few critics too, though, for whom the "fairly staid" British food
"never ends up more than OK", and – apart from the "great-value
set lunch" – is "expensive" too.* / WC2R 0EU;
www.gordonramsay.com/thesavoygrill; @savoygrill; 10.45 pm, Sun 10.15 pm;
jacket required; set pre-theatre £49 (FP), set weekday L £51 (FP).

Scalini SW3 £73 `3` `3` `3`
1-3 Walton St 7225 2301 5–2C
*"A long-established Italian that's always buzzing"; the food
is "consistent good", if "expensive"... but then it is just a few paces
from Harrods.* / SW3 2JD; www.scalinionline.com; 11.30 pm, Sun 11 pm;
no shorts.

Scandinavian Kitchen W1 £16 **4 5 3**
61 Great Titchfield St 7580 7161 2–1B
*With its "cleverly prepared" open sarnies, "tasty" meatballs, and the
"hilarious Scandi-themed pun of the day", this Fitzrovia haunt
is "guaranteed to lift the spirits"; want to try this at home? – select
from a "concise collection of Nordic food essentials" to take away.
/ W1W 7PP; www.scandikitchen.co.uk; @scanditwitchen; 7 pm, Sat 6 pm,
Sun 4 pm; L only; no Maestro; no booking.*

SCOTT'S W1 £80 **4 5 4**
20 Mount St 7495 7309 3–3A
*Richard Caring's "stunning" Mayfair glamour-magnet "will leave your
guest über-impressed" – it is "one of the slickest operations
in London", where the "confident" staff serve up "fresh
interpretations of classic fish dishes" with "ease and efficiency".
/ W1K 2HE; www.scotts-restaurant.com; 10.30 pm, Sun 10 pm; booking:
max 6.*

Sea Containers
Mondrian London SE1 **NEW**
20 Upper Ground 0808 234 9523 9–3A
*In the first non-US outpost of the trendy Mondrian hotel chain, on the
South Bank, a restaurant that's attracted positive early-days
commentary, especially for its design. / SE1 9PD;
www.mondrianlondon.com; @MondrianLDN.*

The Sea Cow SE22 £31 **3 3 3**
37 Lordship Ln 8693 3111 1–4D
*Modest feedback nowadays on this "upmarket" East Dulwich chippy,
where you squash onto benches, and fish is cooked to order –
all positive though! / SE22 8EW; www.theseacow.co.uk; @seacowcrew;
11 pm, Sun & Mon 10 pm; closed Mon L, Tue L & Wed L; no Amex.*

Seafresh SW1 £37 **3 3 1**
80-81 Wilton Rd 7828 0747 2–4B
*It's "not exactly romantic", but this "efficient" veteran Pimlico chippy
rewards investigation of its "wide range of fish" (and a few other
dishes too). / SW1V 1DL; www.seafresh-dining.com; 10.30 pm; closed Sun.*

The Sea Shell NW1 £43 **4 4 2**
49 Lisson Grove 7224 9000 8–4A
*"Top-quality fish (battered or grilled), excellent non-greasy chips and
extremely friendly service" – that's the deal at this famous
Marylebone chippy; since its "pleasant" makeover a couple of years
back, take-away is no longer necessary. / NW1 6UH;
www.seashellrestaurant.co.uk; @SeashellRestaur; 10.30 pm; closed Sun;
SRA-1 star.*

Season Kitchen N4 £38 **4 4 3**
53 Stroud Green Rd 7263 5500 8–1D
*A Finsbury Park spot that's "a real find", thanks to its "well thought-
through and frequently-changing menu", which does proper justice
to its advertised themes of seasonality and local sourcing; "fairly-
priced wines" too. / N4 3EF; www.seasonkitchen.co.uk; 10.30 pm, Sun 9 pm;
D only.*

Seven Park Place SW1 £91 **3 4 4**

7-8 Park Pl   7316 1600   3–4C

The "nooks and crannies" of this "quirky" but "sumptuous"
St James's room add to its possibilities as a business or romantic
venue; best to visit for the "good-value lunch", though – evening
prices for William Drabble's "high-quality" cuisine can be "alarming".
/ SW1A 1LP; www.stjameshotelandclub.com; @SevenParkPlace; 10 pm; closed
Mon & Sun; set weekday L £55 (FP).

Seven Stars WC2 £30 **3 2 4**

53 Carey St   7242 8521   2–2D

It's a "tight space", but fans love the "wonderful quirky charm" of this
ancient tavern, behind the Royal Courts of Justice, presided over
by larger-than-life landlady Roxy Beaujolais; the pub grub's really not
bad either. / WC2A 2JB; 9.30 pm.

1701
Bevis Marks Synagogue EC3 £68 **4 3 3**

Bevis Marks   7621 1701   9–2D

"London has never had kosher food like this!" – with its "traditional-
with-a-very-interesting-twist" menu, this year-old venture, in the
"lovely and historic" space next to the UK's oldest synagogue,
"surpasses expectations"; it's a "fine location for business lunches"
too. / EC3A 5DQ; www.restaurant1701.co.uk; @Restaurant1701; 10 pm;
closed Sat & Sun.

Shake Shack WC2 £23 **2 2 2**

23 The Mkt, Covent Garden   3598 1360   4–3D

"Stonking" burgers and "amazing shakes" convince some reporters
that top NYC restaurateur Danny Meyer's export to Covent Garden
is a real winner; the survey, however, doesn't rate the food much
better than Byron's. / WC2E 8RD;
www.shakeshack.com/location/london-covent-garden; @shakeshack; 11 pm,
Sun 10.30 pm.

Shampers W1 £49 **2 4 5**

4 Kingly St   7437 1692   3–2D

"The owners set an excellent tone of bonhomie", at this
"unchanging" wine bar veteran, just off Carnaby Street; it's "always
packed at lunchtime" with "surveyors and professional types", drawn
by the "simple but effective" cooking and a wine list with "some real
gems". / W1B 5PE; www.shampers.net; 10.45 pm; closed Sun.

Shanghai E8 £36 **3 2 4**

41 Kingsland High St   7254 2878   1–1C

"My Chinese friend travels from Essex to come here!"; "brilliant dim
sum" are the culinary highlight at this former pie 'n' eel shop
in Dalston – make sure you sit in the superb tiled section at the front.
/ E8 2JS; www.shanghaidalston.co.uk; 11 pm; no Amex.

Shanghai Blues WC1 £64 **4 2 4**

193-197 High Holborn   7404 1668   4–1D

"Perpetually dark", in a moody sort of way, this Holborn Chinese
is sometimes hailed as a "hidden gem" – it's a "consistently good"
lunchtime dim sum stop, and its jazz evenings can form the basis for
a "perfect night out". / WC1V 7BD; www.shanghaiblues.co.uk; 11 pm,
Sun 10.30 pm.

The Shed W8 £39 | 3 | 3 | 5 |
122 Palace Gardens Ter 7229 4024 6–2B
"You feel you are in the country" (almost!) at this "quirky" faux-rustic spot, by Notting Hill Gate; fans praise its "imaginative British tapas", but critics can find the experience "too self-consciously whimsical", given toppish prices and the "uncomfortable" seating. / W8 4RT; www.theshed-restaurant.com; @theshed_resto; 11 pm; closed Mon & Sun; SRA-3 stars.

J SHEEKEY WC2 £70 | 4 | 4 | 4 |
28-34 St Martin's Ct 7240 2565 4–3B
Deep in the heart of Theatreland, this "peerless" icon (est 1896) is yet again London's most talked-about destination; "straightforward, classical fish and seafood" (most famously, fish pie) is "slickly" served in a "cosseting", if "squeezed", ramble of "snug" and "classy" rooms. / WC2N 4AL; www.j-sheekey.co.uk; @CapriceHoldings; 11.30 pm, Sun 10.30 pm; booking: max 6; set weekday L & Sun L £49 (FP).

J Sheekey Oyster Bar WC2 £63 | 4 | 5 | 5 |
32-34 St Martin's Ct 7240 2565 4–3B
Expansion has done nothing to dim the charms of this "fabulous" bar attached to the Theatreland legend, where "simply outstanding fish dishes" are "efficiently" served perched at a stool around the glamorous and supremely "buzzy" bar. / WC2N 4AL; www.j-sheekey.co.uk; @CapriceHoldings; 11.30 pm, Sun 10.30 pm; booking: max 3.

Shilpa W6 £31 | 4 | 3 | 1 |
206 King St 8741 3127 7–2B
"Remarkably good" Keralan cuisine at "a quarter of the cost of more fashionable places" makes this Hammersmith caff a top pick on the "curry-crowded King Street drag" – "don't let the impressively drab setting put you off!" / W6 0RA; www.shilparestaurant.co.uk; 11 pm, Thu-Sat midnight.

The Shiori W2 £86 | 5 | 5 | 3 |
45 Moscow Rd 7221 9790 6–2C
"As good a Japanese meal as you can get in Kyoto!" – the Takagis' tiny and "peaceful" Bayswater yearling offers "beautifully refined" kaiseki and "perfect" service too; "you'll need to take out a small mortgage, but it'll be worth it". / W2 4AH; www.theshiori.com; @SHIORIoflondon; 8.30 pm; closed Mon & Sun.

The Ship SW18 £49 | 3 | 3 | 4 |
41 Jews Row 8870 9667 10–2B
"When the weather's good, the crowds descend" on this "busy" riverside boozer, by Wandsworth Bridge; it's a popular dining destination at any time, but the "inventive and hearty" barbecue is a particular summer attraction. / SW18 1TB; www.theship.co.uk; @shipwandsworth; 10 pm; no booking, Sun L.

Shoryu Ramen £27 | 3 | 2 | 3 |
9 Regent St, SW1 no tel 3–3D
3 Denman St, W1 no tel 3–2D
5 Kingly Ct, W1 no tel 3–2C NEW
"Fast, furious, and packed to the rafters!" – these "basic" and "very noisy" Japanese pit stops major in "wonderful broth and noodles" and "tasty hirata buns". / Regent St 11.30 pm, Sun 10.30 pm – Soho midnight, Sun 10.30 pm; no booking (except Kingly Ct).

Shrimpy's N1 £50 3 3 3
King's Cross Filling Station, Good's Way 8880 6111 8–3C
"Who knew a former petrol station could be turned into a cool 'beachfront' diner?" – this "fun" outfit, in the heart of redeveloping King's Cross, is just the place for an "epic soft-shell crab burger" or some other "funky" bite. / N1C 4UR; www.shrimpys.co.uk; @shrimpyloves; 11 pm.

Sichuan Folk E1 £44 4 3 2
32 Hanbury St 7247 4735 12–2C
Dishes will "blow your head off… in a good way" at this East End joint, praised by all for its "real Sichuanese food"; for the uninitiated, "the menu has photos that actually look like the plates served!" / E1 6QR; www.sichuan-folk.co.uk; 10.30 pm; no Amex.

The Sign of the Don EC4 £55 2 3 4
21 St Swithin's Ln 7626 2606 9–3C
The Don's new neighbour, is "a welcome extension of the original" and widely praised as a "great spot for City lunching", in "mid-price brasserie style"; the food, though, still has a little way to go to measure up to the original. / EC4N 8AD; www.thesignofthedon.com; @TheDonLondon.

Signor Sassi SW1 £67 2 3 3
14 Knightsbridge Grn 7584 2277 5–1D
This long-established Knightsbridge-crowd Italian still serves up some great pasta and the like; fans proclaim its "lovely" ambience too, cramped and noisy as the setting undoubtedly is. / SW1X 7QL; www.signorsassi.co.uk; 11.30 pm, Sun 10.30 pm.

Silk Road SE5 £24 5 2 1
49 Camberwell Church St 7703 4832 1–3C
"Just big bold flavours and great tasting food… so long as you like chilli, garlic and cumin!" – this "authentic" and "unusual" Xingjiang café, in Camberwell, is, for those of a culinarily adventurous disposition, "really worth the trip". / SE5 8TR; 10.30 pm; closed Sat L & Sun L; no credit cards.

Simply Fish NW1 £39 3 3 3
4 Inverness St 7482 2977 8–3B
For "high-quality" fish, regulars tip these "funky" Camden Town and Shoreditch canteens – you choose a fish, and specify the preparation style and accompaniments. / NW1 7HJ; www.simplyfishcamden.co.uk; @wearesimplyfish; 10 pm.

Simpson's Tavern EC3 £38 3 4 5
38 1/2 Ball Ct, Cornhill 7626 9985 9–2C
"Like going back in time"; this Dickensian City chophouse is currently on top form, with its "efficient" staff dishing up "good-value" scoff that's "like school dinners on a good day" (including some "gorgeous" puddings); popular for breakfast too. / EC3V 9DR; www.simpsonstavern.co.uk; @SimpsonsTavern; 3 pm; L only, closed Sat & Sun.

Simpsons-in-the-Strand WC2 £77 1 2 2
100 Strand 7836 9112 4–3D
"The home of an unbeatable Full English breakfast", it may be, but otherwise this "stately" temple to the Roast Beef god, by the Savoy, has decidedly "slipped in recent years" – nowadays, "it's just an expensive tourist trap". / WC2R 0EW; www.simpsonsinthestrand.co.uk; 10.45 pm, Sun 9 pm; no trainers.

Singapore Garden NW6 £46 4 3 2

83a Fairfax Rd 7624 8233 8–2A

"Always packed, even on a weekday, despite its out-of-the-way location" – thanks to its "fresh, tasty, and well-priced" Chinese/Malaysian/Singaporean fare, this "hardy veteran", hidden away in Swiss Cottage, remains one of north London's most popular spots. / NW6 4DY; www.singaporegarden.co.uk; @SingaporeGarden; 11 pm, Fri & Sat 11.30 pm.

64 Degrees
Artist Residence Hotel SW1 NEW

52 Cambridge St 3262 0501 2–4B

Around the publication date of this guide, a small-plates concept that's a smash hit in Brighton opens in the Smoke; might it bring a bit of a life to a dull part of Pimlico? – time will tell. / SW1V 4QQ; artistresidencelondon.co.uk.

(Gallery)
Sketch W1 £80 1 2 4

9 Conduit St 7659 4500 3–2C

As a "fun" young-fashionista hangout, this eclectically decorated Mayfair party scene – known for London's funkiest WCs – has certainly shown staying power, but it perennially takes flak for "rubbish" food, and at prices that are "beyond excessive" too. / W1S 2XG; www.sketch.uk.com; 11 pm; booking: max 10.

(Lecture Room)
Sketch W1 £120 2 2 3

9 Conduit St 7659 4500 3–2C

Inspired by Parisian über-chef Pierre Gagnaire, this "crazy" Mayfair dining room offers "experimental" ("weird") cooking that's often "incredible", but which "occasionally fails dramatically"; it's "way overpriced", naturally. / W1S 2XG; www.sketch.uk.com; @sketchlondon; 10.30 pm; closed Mon, Sat L & Sun; no trainers; booking: max 8; set weekday L £62 (FP).

(The Parlour)
Sketch W1 £82 2 2 4

9 Conduit St 7659 4533 3–2C

"OMG the cakes are amazing", but "the best thing is actually the decor", say fans of this cute and stylish Mayfair room, best liked for afternoon tea or breakfast; other food can be "very ordinary", though, and service likewise. / W1S 2XG; www.sketch.uk.com; 10 pm; no booking.

Skipjacks HA3 £40 4 4 2

268-270 Streatfield Rd 8204 7554 1–1A

"A bit more than just a chippy"; this "unpretentious" family-run Harrow veteran of three decades' standing is "a beacon in a desert", and serves "the best fish 'n' chips". / HA3 9BY; 10.30 pm; closed Sun; no Amex.

Skylon
South Bank Centre SE1 £59 1 2 3

Belvedere Rd 7654 7800 2–3D

"The view of the Thames is wonderful" and "the decor is straight out of Mad Men", so it's a shame that this "spectacular" South Bank chamber offers such "ordinary" food, and at very high prices too. / SE1 8XX; www.skylonrestaurant.co.uk; @skylonsouthbank; 10.30 pm; closed Sun D; no trainers; max 12; SRA-2 stars.

Skylon Grill SE1   £57   1 2 3
Belvedere Rd   7654 7800   2–3D
*The cheaper option at the D&D Group's massive South Bank dining
room fares no better with reporters than its neighbour, but it does
at least have the same "fantastic" view. / SE1 8XX;
www.skylon-restaurant.co.uk; @skylonsouthbank; 11 pm; closed Sun D; set pre
theatre £29 (FP).*

Smiths Brasserie E1   £53   3 3 4
22 Wapping High St   7488 3456   11–1A
*"Fabulous views of Tower Bridge and the Shard" add to the appeal
of this "Essex-chic" Wapping yearling (offshoot of an outfit in Ongar);
it wins consistent praise for its "excellent fish prepared to order",
but live music and big groups can make for a "noisy" experience.
/ E1W 1NJ; smithsrestaurant.com; 10 pm; closed Sun D.*

(Top Floor)
Smiths of Smithfield EC1   £72   2 2 2
67-77 Charterhouse St   7251 7950   9–1A
*"Steak, steak, steak... and lovely views of St Paul's" – the selling
points of this business-friendly rooftop dining room, overlooking the
City; as ever, though, it takes a fair degree of flak for being
"overpriced and underwhelming". / EC1M 6HJ;
www.smithsofsmithfield.co.uk; 10.45 pm; closed Sat L & Sun; booking: max 10.*

(Dining Room)
Smiths of Smithfield EC1   £53   2 2 2
67-77 Charterhouse St   7251 7950   9–1A
*"Reliable", "businesslike" and "always buzzy", the first-floor brasserie
of this Smithfield warehouse-complex has its fans; service rarely
sparkles, though, and the "expensive" meaty fare is often merely
"OK". / EC1M 6HJ; www.smithsofsmithfield.co.uk; @thisismiths; 10.45 pm;
closed Sat L & Sun; booking: max 12; set weekday L & dinner £34 (FP).*

(Ground Floor)
Smiths of Smithfield EC1   £33   2 2 4
67-77 Charterhouse St   7251 7950   9–1A
*"THE place to catch up the morning after the night before" –
"there's always a great buzz in the mornings", at this celebrated
Smithfield hangout. / EC1M 6HJ; www.smithsofsmithfield.co.uk; L only;
no bookings.*

The Smokehouse Islington N1   £46   3 4 3
63-69 Canonbury Rd   7354 1144   8–2D
*"A reliably great neighbourhood restaurant"; this "off-the-beaten-
track" Canonbury yearling is a "friendly" sort of place, where the
"hearty" gastropub-style food is "rich and incredibly yummy".
/ N1 2RG; www.smokehouseislington.co.uk; @smokehouseN1; 10.30 pm.*

Social Eating House W1   £60   4 4 5
58-59 Poland St   7993 3251   3–2D
*"An excellent addition to Atherton's empire" – thanks to its "big and
gutsy" dishes, Jason A's "no-frills" Soho yearling has shone ever
brighter since its debut; don't miss some "pretty amazing cocktails"
in the upstairs "speakeasy". / W1F 7NR; www.socialeatinghouse.com;
10 pm; closed Sun.*

Sofra £36 2 3 3
1 St Christopher's Pl, W1 7224 4080 3–1A
18 Shepherd St, W1 7493 3320 3–4B
36 Tavistock St, WC2 7240 3773 4–3D
"Always reliable", "always busy" – this Turkish chain remains a handy standby, thanks to its "tasty" mezze and "easy pricing"; the set lunch is a particularly good deal. / www.sofra.co.uk; 11 pm-midnight.

Soho Diner W1 £38 2 3 4
19 Old Compton St 7734 5656 4–2A
The former Soho Diner, rebranded but under unchanged ownership, now boasts a clubby new interior and more extensive French-American menu; it remains a very handy drop-in, and its long hours makes it "a rare find in the early hours". / W1D 5JJ; Rated on Editors' visit; www.sohodiner.com; SohoDinerLDN; 11.45 pm.

Soif SW11 £52 4 4 3
27 Battersea Rise 7223 1112 10–2C
"Wines for all tastes and pockets" are matched with "delicious and unpretentious French-provincial" dishes at this Terroirs-sibling in Battersea; it has "a good neighbourhood vibe" but "can get noisy when packed". / SW11 1HG; www.soif.co.uk; @soifSW11; 10 pm; closed Mon L, Tue L, Wed L.

Solly's NW11 £45 2 2 2
146-150 Golders Green Rd 8455 0004 1–1B
It's a feature of Golders Green life but this busy Israeli take-away (with upstairs restaurant) inspired little (and mediocre) feedback this year. / NW11 1HE; 10.30 pm; closed Fri D & Sat L; no Amex.

Sông Quê E2 £34 2 1 2
134 Kingsland Rd 7613 3222 12–1B
"It's a bit of a canteen, but you will be fed in the best possible way", and at "low prices" too, say fans of this "brusque" Vietnamese, in Shoreditch; sceptics, though, say standards are "slipping" and that its cooking is "not competitive with others in the strip". / E2 8DY; www.sonque.co.uk; 11 pm; no Amex.

Sonny's Kitchen SW13 £55 2 2 2
94 Church Rd 8748 0393 10–1A
"Everything's done properly, without show", say fans of this Barnes stalwart, which has long been applauded as "a great local restaurant"; nowadays, however, it's far too "hit and miss" – "with the Olympic now opened opposite, you'd have thought they'd have upped their game". / SW13 0DQ; www.sonnyskitchen.co.uk; Fri-Sat 11 pm, Sun 9.30 pm; set weekday L & dinner £34 (FP).

Sophie's Steakhouse £53 2 3 2
29-31 Wellington St, WC2 7836 8836 4–3D
311-313 Fulham Rd, SW10 7352 0088 5–3B
"Consistently attractive over the years", these Covent Garden and Fulham spots have quite a few fans for their "great choice of steaks"; critics, though, can find this a formula which offers "nothing distinctive". / www.sophiessteakhouse.com; SW10 11.45 pm, Sun 11.15 pm; WC2 12.45 am, Sun 11 pm; no booking.

Sotheby's Café W1 £60 343
34-35 New Bond St 7293 5077 3–2C
It's not just the "people-watching" possibilities which make the café off the foyer of the famous Mayfair auction house of interest; the small menu of luxurious snacks is "surprisingly good" too. / W1A 2AA; www.sothebys.com; L only, closed Sat & Sun; booking: max 8.

Source SW11 NEW £48 234
Unit 29, 35-37 Parkgate Rd 7350 0555 5–4C
This "casual" new venture on the site of Ransome's Dock (RIP) has many of the virtues of its predecessor, minus the legendary wine – a "friendly" place (with its own parking!), where the food is somewhere between "decent" (very much our own experience) and "dull". / SW11 4NP; www.sourcebattersea.com; closed Sun D.

Spianata & Co £11 443
Tooley St, SE1 8616 4662 9–4D
41 Brushfield St, E1 7655 4411 12–2B
20 Holborn Viaduct, EC1 7248 5947 9–2A
17 Blomfield St, EC2 7256 9103 9–2C
73 Watling St, EC4 7236 3666 9–2B
"Freshly baked flatbreads" with "gorgeous" fillings, "good snacks and salads" and "the best cappuccino in the City" win nothing but praise for this small Italian take-away chain. / www.spianata.com; 3.30 pm; EC3 11 pm; closed Sat & Sun; E1 closed Sat; no credit cards; no booking.

Spice Market
W Hotel London W1 £77 233
10 Wardour St 7758 1088 4–3A
"The main problem is that it's nowhere near as good as its NYC namesake"; there's little actually wrong with Jean-Georges Vongerichten's Leicester Square outpost, but his pan-Asian dining room continues to inspire remarkably little (and mixed) feedback. / W1D 6QF; www.spicemarketlondon.co.uk; @spicemarketLDN; 11 pm, Thu-Sat 11.30 pm; set weekday L & pre-theatre £44 (FP).

Spring
Somerset House WC2 NEW
Lancaster Pl 3011 0115 2–2D
Australian chef Skye Gyngell carved a major name when she was at Petersham Nurseries; perhaps she can repeat the trick with her new venue at Somerset House. / WC2R 1LA; springrestaurant.co.uk.

Spuntino W1 £41 235
61 Rupert St no tel 3–2D
Russell Norman's "unbelievably cool", "industrial-look" Soho bar (where you eat at the counter) "still does the best sliders", and other "lovely" 'dirty' dishes too; the bills, though, "can rack up quite quickly". / W1D 7PW; www.spuntino.co.uk; 11.30 pm, Sun 10.30 pm.

THE SQUARE W1 £113 443
6-10 Bruton St 7495 7100 3–2C
"Discreet, quiet and well-spaced", this Mayfair landmark has long been a top expense-account choice, thanks to Phil Howard's "brilliantly focussed" cuisine, and the "phenomenal" wine list; the experience can seem "a bit soulless", though, and it is of course "astronomically expensive". / W1J 6PU; www.squarerestaurant.com; @square_rest; 9.45 pm, Sat 10.15 pm, Sun 9.30 pm; closed Sun L; booking: max 8; set weekday L £55 (FP).

Sree Krishna SW17   £27   4 3 2
192-194 Tooting High St   8672 4250   10–2C
"Hasn't changed in years, and that's why we go!" – this Tooting
veteran, now in its fourth decade, still serves up some *"excellent
value"* South Indian fare (*"especially the dosas"*); Mon-Fri, you can
BYO. / SW17 0SF; www.sreekrishna.co.uk; @SreeKrishnaUk; 10.45 pm, Fri &
Sat 11.45 pm.

Star of India SW5   £54   4 2 –
154 Old Brompton Rd   7373 2901   5–2B
*The cooking at this long-established Earl's Court subcontinental has
been "on a peak" in recent times* – let's hope this carries on after the
major refurbishment carried out in the summer of 2014! / SW5 0BE;
www.starofindia.eu; 11.45 pm, Sun 11.15 pm.

Sticks'n'Sushi   £48   3 3 3
11 Henrietta St, WC2   3141 8800   4–3D
58 Wimbledon Hill Rd, SW19   3141 8800   10–2B
A stylish Danish-Japanese (!) hybrid, in Covent Garden and
Wimbledon, that offers an *"innovative twist on sushi"*; it may
be *"a bit pricey"* but it *"does what it does pretty well"*.
/ www.sticksnsushi.com; Sun - Tues 10 pm, Wed -Sat 11 pm.

Sticky Fingers W8   £43   2 2 2
1a Phillimore Gdns   7938 5338   5–1A
Diehard fans still see this veteran Kensington burger-joint (decked out
with Bill Wyman's Rolling Stones memorabilia) as *"a quirky antidote
to the homogenous chains"*; in spite of its new menu, though, critics
still feel it is in need of a *"serious overhaul"*. / W8 7QR;
www.stickyfingers.co.uk; 10.45 pm; set weekday L £19 (FP).

STK Steakhouse
ME by Meliá London WC2   £69   2 2 2
336-337 The Strand   7395 3450   4–3C
On the fringe of Covent Garden, an *"extremely loud"* and
"very expensive" steakhouse – it offers *"none of the fun sexiness
of the NYC original, nor the more casual excellence of Hawksmoor
or Goodman"*. / WC2R 1HA; www.stkhouse.com; @STKLondon; Mon-Wed
11 pm, Thu-Sat midnight, Sun 10 pm; D only.

Stock Pot   £27   2 2 2
38 Panton St, SW1   7839 5142   4–4A
54 James St, W1   7935 6034   3–1A
273 King's Rd, SW3   7823 3175   5–3C
No one has a bad word to say about these hardy '60s canteens,
whose huge range of basic scoff at bargain-basement prices has
nourished generations of students, shoppers and those who just can't
be bothered to cook. / SW1 11.30 pm, Wed-Sat midnight, Sun 11 pm SW3
10.15 pm, Sun 9.45 pm; no Amex.

Story SE1   £81   4 4 3
201 Tooley St   7183 2117   9–4D
"Mind-blowing and unique!" – Tom Sellers's *"Scandi-style"* dining
room, not far from Tower Bridge, offers multi-course meals that
most reports say are just *"out of this world"*; for the occasional critic,
though, it is all is a bit too *"post-modern/bonkers"*! / SE1 2UE;
www.restaurantstory.co.uk; @Rest_Story; 9.30 pm; closed Mon & Sun;
set weekday L £53 (FP).

Story Deli E2 £43 **5** **2** **3**
123 Bethnal Green Rd 0791 819 7352 12–2B
Still close to the Brick Lane action (although no longer in the Truman Brewery, where it was once located), this hip hangout is still "worth a visit" for its "really different" thin-crust pizza. / E2 7DG; www.storydeli.com; 10.30 pm; no credit cards.

Strada £42 **1** **2** **2**
Branches throughout London
These "family-friendy" pizza-and-pasta spots have been very "inconsistent" in recent years, and many long term fans can't help feeling they've "gone off"; can Hugh Osmond (who bought the chain in late-2014) sprinkle on them some of the magic he once helped instil at PizzaExpress? / www.strada.co.uk; 10.30 pm-11 pm; some booking restrictions apply.

Strand Dining Rooms WC2 NEW £64 **2** **4** **3**
1-3 Grand Buildings, Strand 7930 8855 2–2C
An ambitiously large all-day British brasserie, which opened near Trafalgar Square in the summer of 2014; it couldn't have a much handier location (especially for breakfast or tea), and service tries so hard, but our early-days lunchtime visits found food with no oomph at all. / WC2N 4JF; www.thestranddiningrooms.com; @StrandDining; 11 pm.

Street Kitchen EC2 £18 **3** **3** –
Broadgate Circle no tel 12–2B
For "good-quality take-away", many City worker bees tip this Silver Airstream, near Broadgate Circle, overseen by 'name' chefs Mark Jankel and Jun Tanaka. / EC2; www.streetkitchen.co.uk/home.shtml; @Streetkitchen; L only.

Sufi W12 £31 **3** **3** **4**
70 Askew Rd 8834 4888 7–1B
"The bread, made in front of you, is worth the trip alone", say fans of his welcoming Persian, in the depths of Shepherd's Bush – a "great-value" local. / W12 9BJ; www.sufirestaurant.com; @SUFIRESTAURANT; 11 pm.

Suk Saran SW19 £52 **4** **2** **1**
29 Wimbledon Hill Rd 8947 9199 10–2B
Part of a three-strong southwest London chain, this upmarket Wimbledon Town restaurant is a handy Thai option – good food, but service "can be slow and inattentive". / SW19 7NE; www.sukhogroup.com; 10.30 pm; booking: max 25; set weekday L £35 (FP).

Sukho Fine Thai Cuisine SW6 £53 **5** **4** **3**
855 Fulham Rd 7371 7600 10–1B
"The best Thai food in town" can come as a "surprise" find at this unassuming shop-conversion in deepest Fulham; "charming" service helps offset the "cramped" conditions, though, and it always feels "busy" and "buzzy". / SW6 5HJ; www.sukhogroup.co.uk; 11 pm; set weekday L £35 (FP).

The Summerhouse W9 £55 **3** **3** **5**
60 Blomfield Rd 7286 6752 8–4A
An "exceptional location", by the canal in Little Venice, makes this simply decorated spot a "superb" and "very romantic" summertime choice; "after a shaky start, the kitchen is turning out consistently good food", with fish the speciality. / W9 2PA; www.thesummerhouse.co.uk; 10.30 pm, Sun 10 pm; no Amex.

Sumosan W1 £78 3 2 2
26b Albemarle St 7495 5999 3–3C
"It's never had the pull of Nobu, Novikov or Zuma", but this moody-looking Japanese-fusion spot, in Mayfair, wins praise from its small fan club, particularly for sushi that's "fantastic, even if it's not cheap". / W1S 4HY; www.sumosan.com; @sumosan_; 11.30 pm, Sun 10.30 pm; closed Sat L & Sun L.

The Surprise SW3 £45 2 3 4
6 Christchurch Ter 7351 6954 5–3D
"Once a Sloaney watering hole", this "delightful" pub, near the Royal Hospital, has a bright new look nowadays, and serves an "ace tapas-sized menu" that's "great for sharing or filling up". / SW3 4AJ; www.geronimo-inns.co.uk/thesurprise; @TheSurpriseSW3; 10 pm, Sun 9 pm.

Sushisamba EC2 £78 3 3 5
Heron Tower, 110 Bishopsgate 3640 7330 9–2D
"A magical lift journey" wafts diners to this "memorable" 38th-39th-floor bar-terrace-restaurant, by Liverpool Street; it ain't no bargain, of course, but this is one of the very best rooms with a view, offering Japanese/South American fusion fare that's sometimes a "wow", and service much improved on the early days. / EC2N 4AY; www.sushisamba.com; Sun-Thu midnight, Fri & Sat 1 am; smart casual.

Sushi Tetsu EC1 £58 5 5 3
12 Jerusalem Pas 3217 0090 9–1A
"You are sat at the bar, one of only 7 people, face-to-face with the chef", at this "intense" Clerkenwell one-off, which is run by a "superb husband-and-wife team"; the sushi is "the best in the UK", so it's no surprise that "getting a table takes real commitment". / EC1V 4JP; www.sushitetsu.co.uk; @SushiTetsuUK; midnight; closed Mon & Sun.

Sushi-Say NW2 £44 5 4 2
33b Walm Ln 8459 7512 1–1A
The decor is "simple" and the Willesden Green location obscure, but this unassuming café is "always full" – it's one of the top Japanese restaurants in town, and serves "some of the best sushi ever!" / NW2 5SH; 10 pm, Sat 10.30 pm, Sun 9.30 pm; closed Mon, Tue, Wed L, Thu L & Fri L; no Amex.

The Swan W4 £46 4 4 5
119 Acton Ln 8994 8262 7–1A
"In the fabulous garden, it feels like you're on holiday", at this "spacious" and characterful pub, tucked-away on the Chiswick/Acton borders; service is "very warm and welcoming" too, and the Mediterranean cooking is "wonderful". / W4 5HH; www.theswanchiswick.co.uk; @SwanPubChiswick; 10 pm, Fri & Sat 10.30 pm, Sun 10 pm; closed weekday L.

The Swan at the Globe SE1 £58 3 3 4
21 New Globe Walk 7928 9444 9–3B
With "the most amazingly romantic view over the Thames and St Paul's", this first-floor South Bank venture makes "a great place for a celebratory occasion"; it offers quite a "limited" British menu, but the results generally hit the spot. / SE1 9DT; www.loveswan.co.uk; @swanabout; 9.45 pm, Sun 4.45 pm; closed Sun D.

Sweet Thursday N1 £34 3 3 3
95 Southgate Rd 7226 1727 1–2C
"A superb local pizza restaurant"; this retro-chic two-year-old, in De Beauvoir, offers "excellent" Neapolitan-style thin-crusts; the wine shop at the front "has some real gems" too. / N1 3JS; www.sweetthursday.co.uk; @Pizza_and_Pizza; 10 pm, Sat 10.30 pm, Sun 9 pm.

Sweetings EC4 £65 3 2 3
39 Queen Victoria St 7248 3062 9–3B
"The best of the old-school City restaurants"; this "unique" Victorian fish parlour has a "jovial" but "slightly haphazard" air that's "totally English", and its fish and seafood, if "not cheap", is "consistently good" too; arrive early for a table. / EC4N 4SA; www.sweetingsrestaurant.com; 3 pm; L only, closed Sat & Sun; no booking.

T.E.D N1 NEW
47-51 Caledonian Rd 3763 2080 8–3D
'Sustainability' always seems to have been a bit of a King's Cross speciality; Ted Grainger-Smith made quite a hit of a sustainable resturant with Acorn House (now RIP), so perhaps he can do the same again at this summer-2014 newcomer. / N1 9BU; www.tedrestaurants.co.uk; @TEDrestaurant.

Taberna Etrusca EC4 £50 3 3 3
9 -11 Bow Churchyard 7248 5552 9–2C
A "thoroughly enjoyable high-end City Italian", in "classic" style; thanks not least to its "reliable" cooking, it's "heaving at lunchtime" – in summer, the al fresco tables are particularly popular. / EC4M 9DQ; www.etruscarestaurants.com; 10 pm; closed Mon D, Sat & Sun.

The Table SE1 £46 2 2 2
83 Southwark St 7401 2760 9–4B
Over the road from Tate Modern, this "stylish indie café" – once an architects' practice office canteen – is "very popular for weekend brunch"; "you'll be rammed in on benches though, so it's a place to get caffeinated not relaxed". / SE1 0HX; www.thetablecafe.com; @thetablecafe; 10.30 pm; closed Mon D & Sun D; SRA-2 stars.

Taiwan Village SW6 £35 5 5 3
85 Lillie Rd 7381 2900 5–3A
"It might not have the posh decor you'd find in the West End", but this Fulham operation behind an "unlikely-looking shopfront" offers "superb" and "utterly reliable" Chinese dishes; "choose the 'leave it to the chef' menu – he really does know best". / SW6 1UD; www.taiwanvillage.com; 11.30 pm, Sun 10.30 pm; closed weekday L; booking: max 20.

Tajima Tei EC1 £36 3 3 3
9-11 Leather Ln 7404 9665 9–2A
A "hidden gem" of a Japanese, not far from Holborn Circus; it's well-known locally for its "good-value" set menu – including "very well-made sushi" – and consequently "jammed at lunchtimes". / EC1N 7ST; www.tajima-tei.co.uk; 10 pm; closed Sat & Sun; no booking, L.

Talad Thai SW15 £32 3 2 1
320 Upper Richmond Rd 8246 5791 10–2A
"It's a little bit like a transport caff", but this long-serving Thai canteen, attached to an Asian supermarket in Putney, serves "authentic" scoff at "great-value" prices. / SW15 6TL; www.taladthairestaurant.com; 10.30 pm, Sun 9.30 pm; no Amex.

Tamarind W1 £75 4 4 3
20 Queen St 7629 3561 3–3B
"High-end Indian food cooked to perfection" and *"incredibly helpful"*
staff help win rave reports for this *"extremely civilised"* and *"classy"*
Mayfair stalwart; if there is a reservation, it's the basement setting.
/ W1J 5PR; www.tamarindrestaurant.com; 10.45 pm, Sun 10.30 pm; closed
Sat L; booking: max 20; set weekday L £47 (FP).

Tandoori Nights SE22 £38 3 4 3
73 Lordship Ln 8299 4077 1–4D
A welcoming East Dulwich fixture, consistently applauded for Indian
food that's always *"decent"*, and which locals proclaim outstanding.
/ SE22 8EP; www.tandoorinightsdulwich.co.uk; 11.30 pm, Fri & Sat midnight;
closed weekday L & Sat L.

Tapas Brindisa £43 3 2 3
46 Broadwick St, W1 7534 1690 3–2D
18-20 Southwark St, SE1 7357 8880 9–4C
41-43 Atlantic Rd, SW9 7095 8655 10–2D
"Sociable, bustling, noisy, cramped" – this Borough Market tapas bar
can be *"a nightmare to get into"*, but perennially draws the crowds
with its *"authentic"* style and *"high-quality, if expensive"* dishes;
the Soho spin-off is hardly mentioned. / 10.45 pm, Sun 10 pm;
W1 booking: max 10.

Taqueria W11 £35 3 4 3
139-143 Westbourne Grove 7229 4734 6–1B
"A far remove from the usual Tex Mex" – this *"always buzzing"*
Notting Hill cantina offers an *"interesting"* menu majoring in tacos,
"admirably complemented" by some *"excellent"* tequila-based
cocktails. / W11 2RS; www.taqueria.co.uk; @TaqueriaUK; 11 pm, Fri & Sat
11.30 pm, Sun 10.30 pm; no Amex; no booking Fri-Sun.

Taro £35 2 3 2
10 Old Compton St, W1 7439 2275 4–2B
61 Brewer St, W1 7734 5826 3–2D
"Vast numbers of diners ensure the food is always super fresh",
at these *"cheap"* Soho canteens, *"efficiently run"* under *"the ever-
watchful eye of Mr Taro"*; critics find them too *"business-like"* but the
more common verdict is that they're *"great value"*.
/ www.tarorestaurants.co.uk; 10.30 pm, Sun 9.30 pm; no Amex.

Tartufo SW3 £57 5 4 3
11 Cadogan Gdns 7730 6383 5–2D
"A rare find"; Alexis Gauthier's *"restful"* and *"cleverly designed"*
yearling may be *"buried in a hard-to-find hotel basement, off Sloane
Square"*, but it makes a *"brilliant"* discovery, thanks to its *"friendly"*
style and *"refined"* Italian cuisine, and all at *"incredibly good-value
prices"* too. / SW3 2RJ; www.tartufolondon.co.uk; 10 pm; closed Mon & Sun.

Tas £37 2 3 3
22 Bloomsbury St, WC1 7637 4555 2–1C
33 The Cut, SE1 7928 2111 9–4A
76 Borough High St, SE1 7403 8557 9–4C
97-99 Isabella St, SE1 7620 6191 9–4A
37 Farringdon Rd, EC1 7430 9721 9–1A
"Stick to the mezze and you can feast cheaply" – always the
best advice, at these *"handy"* Turkish *"standbys"*, whose *"bustling"*
style add to their appeal; the original branch at The Cut has always
been a boon for those going to the Old Vic. / www.tasrestaurant.com;
11.30 pm, Sun 10.30 pm.

Tas Pide SE1 £34 **2** **3** **4**
20-22 New Globe Walk   7928 3300   9–3B
*Right by the Globe Theatre, this large but cosy Anatolian café is a
"reliable" spot, where "you can feast cheaply" on mezze and "tasty"
Turkish pizza ('pide'). / SE1 9DR; www.tasrestaurant.com/tas_pide;
11.30 pm, Sun 10.30 pm.*

(Whistler Restaurant)
Tate Britain SW1 £54 **2** **3** **5**
Millbank   7887 8825   2–4C
*"Welcome back!" – this "calm" dining room has emerged from
an 18-month restoration of its famous Whistler murals… "pretty
much the same as it was prior to the closure!"; as ever, the food
is only "OK", and the real draw is the "superlative" wine selection
at "sensible" prices. / SW1 4RG; www.tate.org.uk; L & afternoon tea only.*

(Restaurant, Level 6)
Tate Modern SE1 £48 **2** **2** **4**
Bankside   7887 8888   9–3B
*"Breathtaking" views of the City and St Paul's are the undoubted
reason to seek out this "canteen-like" space on the gallery's top floor
– the British cuisine ranges from "much better than expected"
to "awful". / SE1 9TG; www.tate.org.uk; @TateFood; 9 pm; Sun-Thu closed
D, Fri & Sat open L & D; SRA-2 stars.*

Taylor St Baristas £15 **4** **4** **3**
22 Brooks Mews, W1   7629 3163   3–2B
Unit 3 Westminster Hs, Kew Rd, TW9   07969 798650   1–4A
110 Clifton St, EC2   7929 2207   12–2B
Unit 3, 125 Old Broad St, EC2   7256 8668   9–2C
2 Botolph Alley, EC3   7283 1835   9–3C
*"They take coffee seriously", at this small Aussie chain; "surprisingly
good" sarnies and other snacks too. / EC2M 4TP; www.taylor-st.com;
All branches 5 pm; Old Broad ST, Clifton St, W1, E14 closed Sat & Sun;
New St closed Sat; TW9 closed Sun.*

Tayyabs E1 £28 **4** **2** **3**
83 Fieldgate St   7247 9543   9–2D
*"Notwithstanding the chaos, there's nothing to beat the lamb chops"
– this "amazing" East End Pakistani "madhouse" gets "crazily busy",
so "get their early, or queue for ages"; but has it expanded too far? –
now on three floors, it can feel like it is pushing out curries "on an
industrial scale". / E1 1JU; www.tayyabs.co.uk; @itayyabs; 11.30 pm.*

Telegraph SW15 £40 **3** **2** **4**
Telegraph Rd   8788 2011   10–2A
*"They bill themselves as the leading country pub in London, and I'd
say that's a pretty good description" – this "tucked away" Putney
Heath pub couldn't be much more leafily located, and its satisfactory
scoff makes it a happy weekend or sunny day destination.
/ SW15 3TU; www.thetelegraphputney.co.uk; 9 pm, Fri & Sat 9.30 pm.*

The 10 Cases WC2 £55 **2** **3** **3**
16 Endell St   7836 6801   4–2C
*"Limited but fascinating", the wine list is the "star" at this "convivial"
Covent Garden two-year-old, explaining why its "crowded" quarters
are so "busy, busy, busy"; "decent" food plays a supporting role.
/ WC2H 9BD; www.the10cases.co.uk; @10cases; 11 pm; closed Sun.*

10 Greek Street W1 £47 **5 5 3**
10 Greek St 7734 4677 4–2A
"Informal brilliance" has won a huge following for this *"well-priced"* (but *"cramped"*) Soho two-year-old, which offers *"outstanding"* dishes from an ever-changing menu, and *"great, well priced wines"* to go with them; only problem – no dinner reservations. / W1D 4DH; www.10greekstreet.com; @10GreekStreet; 11.30 pm; closed Sun.

Tendido Cero SW5 £46 **3 3 4**
174 Old Brompton Rd 7370 3685 5–2B
"Consistently delicious and inventive" tapas ensure this *"slick"* South Kensington bar is always *"buzzing with a sleek thirty-something clientele"*… who presumably don't mind prices critics find *"mind-boggling"*. / SW5 0BA; www.cambiodetercio.co.uk; @CambiodTercio; 11 pm.

Tendido Cuatro SW6 £42 **4 4 4**
108-110 New King's Rd 7371 5147 10–1B
Cambio de Tercio's *"lovely"*, if cramped, Fulham outpost serves up *"terrific tapas"*, and a *"good wine list"* too. / SW6 4LY; www.cambiodetercio.co.uk; @Cambiode Tercio; 11 pm, Sun 10.30 pm.

Tentazioni SE1 £55 **3 4 4**
2 Mill St 7394 5248 11–2A
"You feel squirrelled away", at this *"out-of-the-way"* but *"welcoming"* Italian, near Shad Thames; it's not well-known nowadays but still *"really rather good"*, offering an *"amazing range of game pastas"*, and some *"unusual meat dishes"* too. / SE1 2BD; www.tentazioni.co.uk; @TentazioniWorld; 10.45 pm, Sun 9 pm; closed Sat L; set weekday L £17 (FP).

The Terrace W8 NEW £57 **2 4 4**
33c Holland St 7937 3224 5–1A
Newly resurrected, this *"lovely"* Kensington local (with tiny, er, terrace) wins praise for its *"charming"* service and *"precise but simple"* cooking; for the prices, though, critics can find the food rather *"average"*. / W8 4LX; www.theterracehollandstreet.co.uk; 10.30 pm; closed Sun.

Terroirs WC2 £45 **3 2 3**
5 William IV St 7036 0660 4–4C
"A weird and wonderful wine list with some corkers" (and *"some like home brew!"*) is the undoubted star at this *"reassuring"* Gallic bistro, near Charing Cross; its *"strongly flavoured"* small plates inspire more diverse reactions than they used to, though, and service can sometimes be *"chaotic"*. / WC2N 4DW; www.terroirswinebar.com; @terroirswinebar; 11 pm; closed Sun.

Texture W1 £92 **3 4 3**
34 Portman St 7224 0028 2–2A
Agnar Sverrisson's cuisine shows some *"sophisticated Icelandic twists"*, and it is complemented by some notably good wines and (especially) champagnes, at this ambitious spot, near Selfridges; some reporters found the place rather *"overrated"* this year, though, and the high-ceilinged interior is rather *"noisy"*. / W1H 7BY; www.texture-restaurant.co.uk; 10.30 pm; closed Mon & Sun; set weekday L £56 (FP).

Thai Corner Café SE22　　　　£21　③③③
44 North Cross Rd　8299 4041　1–4D
"Very cramped, as so many people try to get in!" – this "cheap 'n'
cheerful" East Dulwich BYO is treasured by the locals for "basic Thai
scoff that's full of flavour". / SE22 9EU; www.thaicornercafe.co.uk;
10.30 pm; closed Mon L & Tue L; no credit cards.

Thai Square　　　　£41　②②②
166-170 Shaftesbury Ave, WC2　7836 7600　4–1B
229-230 Strand, WC2　7353 6980　2–2D
19 Exhibition Rd, SW7　7584 8359　5–2C
347-349 Upper St, N1　7704 2000　8–3D
136-138 Minories, EC3　7680 1111　9–3D
"Reliable and reasonably priced"… "dependable, but oh-so-average"
– the broad spectrum of opinion on the outlets of this Thai chain;
SW15 has "the best river views". / www.thaisquare.net; 10 pm-11.30 pm;
SW1 Fri & Sat 1 am; EC3, EC4 & St Annes Ct closed Sat & Sun, Strand
branches and Princess St closed Sun.

Thali SW5　　　　£44　④④②
166 Old Brompton Rd　7373 2626　5–2B
"Consistently great" North Indian dishes are the draw to this crisp-
looking Earl's Court venue – "not cheap", but a meal still costs
"way less than the super-Indians". / SW5 0BA; www.thali.uk.com;
11.30 pm, Sun 10.30 pm.

Theo Randall
InterContinental Hotel W1　　　　£88　③②②
1 Hamilton Pl　7318 8747　3–4A
In the past, Theo Randall's ace Italian cuisine has usually transcended
the "sterile and dull" interior of this windowless chamber, in a
"corporate" Hyde Park Corner hotel; of late, however, the food has
sometimes proved "not as stellar as expected", and service has been
a mite "unpredictable" too. / W1J 7QY; www.theorandall.com;
@theorandall; 11 pm; closed Sat L & Sun; set dinner £57 (FP).

34 W1　　　　£78　③③③
34 Grosvenor Sq　3350 3434　3–3A
"The cooking is plain but top-class", say fans of Richard Caring's
"posh" Mayfair grill-house, hailing "the best steaks… period"; critics,
though, feel it's only "OK", and say its "bloated" prices makes it one
for "hedgies and the offspring of oligarchs". / W1K 2HD;
www.34-restaurant.co.uk; 10.30 pm; set weekday L £50 (FP).

Thirty Six
Duke's Hotel SW1　　　　£85　②②①
35-36 Saint James's Pl　7491 4840　3–4C
Feedback for this hotel restaurant "tucked away in a St James
backstreet" is again modest and curiously mixed; fans enthuse of an
establishment that "truly shines", but critics bemoan the "dire"
atmosphere, and food that's "average at best for a place at this
level". / SW1A 1NY; www.dukeshotel.com; @dukeshotel; 9.30 pm; closed
Mon L & Sun D; set weekday L £50 (FP).

The Thomas Cubitt SW1   £51   3 3 4
44 Elizabeth St   7730 6060   2–4A
"Permanently thronged with Belgravia's young bloods",
this "glammed-up boozer" serves food in both its "charming" upstairs
room and on the "bustling" ground floor (where there are some
tightly-packed al fresco tables); "it's not cheap, but then it is SW1..."
/ SW1W 9PA; www.thethomascubitt.co.uk; 10 pm; booking only in restaurant;
SRA-3 stars.

3 South Place
South Place Hotel EC2   £60   2 3 3
3 South Pl   3503 0000   12–2A
"For breakfast and convenience, hard to beat!" – this ground-floor
brasserie of a D&D Group hotel, by Liverpool Street, makes a useful
standby at any time of day; for a more serious lunch or dinner option,
however, see 'Angler'. / EC2M 2AF; www.southplacehotel.com;
@southplacehotel; 10.30 pm; max 22.

tibits W1   £35   3 2 3
12-14 Heddon St   7758 4110   3–2C
A Swiss-run veggie, near Piccadilly Circus, where you pay by weight;
"the wide variety of wholesome yet comforting food" is "always fresh
and interesting"; beware, though – "the pick 'n' mix formula makes
it easy to get carried away!" / W1B 4DA; www.tibits.co.uk; 11.30 pm,
Sun 10 pm; no Amex; Only bookings for 8+.

Tinello SW1   £48   4 4 4
87 Pimlico Rd   7730 3663   5–2D
"Subtle and sophisticated" Tuscan dishes are served by "very caring"
staff at this "elegant" and "genuinely Italian" restaurant, not far from
Sloane Square, which is emerging as an "all-round" favourite for
many reporters. / SW1W 8PH; www.tinello.co.uk; @tinello_london;
10.30 pm; closed Sun.

Ting
Shangri-La Hotel at the Shard SE1   NEW £86   2 2 3
Shangri-La Hotel At The Shard   7234 8000   9–4C
"Gorgeous views" distinguish this 35th-floor hotel dining room, but it's
otherwise a remarkably "anonymous" venue, lacking any of the
sparkle you might expect from the illustrious Shangri-La chain;
afternoon teas, though, are "fantastic". / SE1 9RY; www.shangri-la.com;
11.30 pm.

Toasted SE22   £46   3 3 4
38 Lordship Ln   8693 9021   1–4D
"Another local gem" in the Caves de Pryène (Terroirs and so on)
empire – this East Dulwich yearling mixes a "brilliant selection
of small plates for sharing" with the wine importer's "lovely draught
wines at amazingly reasonable prices". / SE22 8HJ; toastdulwich.co.uk;
toastdulwich; 9.45 pm; closed Sun D.

Toff's N10   £40   4 3 2
38 Muswell Hill Broadway   8883 8656   1–1B
"The freshness and variety of the fish" distinguish this "always-busy",
"no-frills" Muswell Hill institution – north London's top chippy.
/ N10 3RT; www.toffsfish.co.uk; @toffsfish; 10 pm; closed Sun.

Tokyo Diner WC2 £26 ②②③
2 Newport Pl   7287 8777   4–3B
*It's "tatty" and "cramped", but this Chinatown "treasure" has a place
in fans' hearts for its "fast, cheap and healthy" bites. / WC2H 7JJ;
www.tokyodiner.com; 11.30 pm; no Amex; no booking, Fri & Sat.*

Tom's Kitchen £65 ②①①
Somerset House, 150 Strand, WC2   7845 4646   2–2D
27 Cale St, SW3   7349 0202   5–2C
11 Westferry Circus, E14   3011 1555   11–1C
1 Commodity Quay, E1   3011 5433   9–3D
*Save as "hustling and bustling" brunch venues (SW3 especially),
reporters rarely give solidly positive reports on Tom Aikens's growing
bistro chain – prices for the "very average" food can seem
"excruciating", and service can be "shambolic"; WC2 has
a "wonderful location overlooking the Thames". / 10 pm - 10.45 pm;
WC2 closed Sun D.*

Tommi's Burger Joint £18 ④②③
30 Thayer St, W1   7224 3828   3–1A
342 Kings Rd, SW3   7349 0691   5–3C
*It's a "meaty dream", exclaim fans of this "simple and
straightforward" – order-at-the-counter – Marylebone burger parlour
(for which you can expect to queue); good ratings for its new Chelsea
sibling too.*

Tonkotsu £32 ③③③
63 Dean St, W1   7437 0071   4–2A
Arch 334 1a Dunston St, E8   7254 2478   1–2D NEW
*You eat "with someone texting at your elbow" amidst the "controlled
chaos" of this "cramped" Soho ramen bar, which serves "consistently
good noodles to sooth the soul"; it now has a larger branch
in Haggerston too.*

Tortilla £18 ③②②
Branches throughout London
*Just as highly rated as, if less well-known than, Chipotle, these simple
outlets offer "a good choice of meats and plenty of interesting fillings"
at "competitive prices" – "perfect for some quick refuelling".
/ www.tortilla.co.uk; W1 & N1 11 pm, Sun 9 pm, SE1 & E14 9 pm,
EC3 7 pm, E14 Sun 7 pm; SE1 & EC3 closed Sat & Sun, N1 closed sun;
no Amex.*

Tosa W6 £42 ④②②
332 King St   8748 0002   7–2B
*"It's hard to stop ordering", at this "down-to-earth and authentic"
Hammersmith café, which is "always full of Japanese people";
it offers a "good selection of sushi and yakitori" (plus "some more
unusual dishes too, for a change"). / W6 0RR; www.tosauk.com;
10.30 pm.*

Toto's
Walton House SW1 NEW £79 ③⑤④
Lennox Gardens Mews   7589 0075   5–2C
*"Welcome back!" to this "light and airy" resurrected Knightsbridge
trattoria, and its "beautifully presented" dishes; oddly –
but successfully, it seems – the 'face' of the enterprise is none other
than Silvano Giraldin, former maître d' of the very Gallic Gavroche.
/ SW1 0DP; www.totosrestaurant.com; 11 pm, Sun 10.30 pm.*

Tozi SW1 £41 **3 4 3**
8 Gillingham St   7769 9771   2–4B
*"What a find in a 'dead' restaurant area!" – this "authentic" and
"enjoyable" cicchetti restaurant transcends its potentially anonymous
hotel location, near Victoria, and many reporters find they "just keep
going back". / SW1V 1HN; www.tozirestaurant.co.uk; @ToziRestaurant;
10 pm.*

Tramontana Brindisa EC2 £37 **3 2 3**
152-154 Curtain Rd   7749 9961   12–1B
*In Shoreditch, a fairly typical outlet of the Brindisa empire –
fans applaud "great small-plate food" (here with something of a
Catalan twist) and "excellent cocktails", but critics find some dishes
"slightly disappointing", and service so-so. / EC2A 3AT;
www.brindisatapaskitchens.com; @brindisa; Mon-Sat 11 pm, Sun 9 pm.*

The Tramshed EC2 £57 **2 2 4**
32 Rivington St   7749 0478   12–1B
*"An amazing interior with Damien Hirst's 'Cock and Bull' looming
overhead" sets the scene at Mark Hix's vast Shoreditch shed;
most reports extol the "basic" but "mouthwatering" formula
of chicken or steak 'n' chips, but a sizeable minority "just don't get
it". / EC2A 3LX; www.chickenandsteak.co.uk; @HIXrestaurants.*

Tredwell's WC2 **NEW**
4 Upper St Martin's Ln   3764 0840   4–3B
*From the Marcus Wareing group, a new multi-floor all-day operation,
at Seven Dials; early-days press reviews have been notably mixed.
/ WC2H 9NY; www.tredwells.com.*

Trinity SW4 £68 **4 5 3**
4 The Polygon   7622 1199   10–2D
*"Outstanding but unassuming", Adam Byatt's "superb" Clapham
HQ remains "the best in the area by a mile", thanks to its "seasonal
ingredients prepared with great flair", and "service that makes you
feel like a VIP". / SW4 0JG; www.trinityrestaurant.co.uk; @TrinityLondon;
9.45 pm; closed Mon L & Sun D; set weekday L £50 (FP), set Sun L £56 (FP).*

Trishna W1 £65 **4 3 2**
15-17 Blandford St   7935 5624   2–1A
*"Spellbinding" southwest Indian cuisine has made quite a name for
this "basic" ("lacking warmth or charm") Marylebone outpost of a
famous Mumbai fish restaurant; this year, however, standards have
sometimes seemed a little "inconsistent". / W1U 3DG;
www.trishnalondon.com; @TrishnaLondon; 10.45 pm; set weekday L £44 (FP).*

Les Trois Garçons E1 £70 **2 2 2**
1 Club Row   7613 1924   12–1C
*"Such fun and eccentric decor" has helped make quite a name for
this camp East End pub-conversion; its Gallic menu is no bargain,
though, and a number of reports of late are of an all-round
"mediocre" experience. / E1 6JX; www.lestroisgarcons.com;
@lestroisgarcons; 9.30 pm, Sat 10.30 pm; closed Mon L, Tue L, Wed L,
Sat L & Sun; need credit card to book; set weekday L £43 (FP).*

LA TROMPETTE W4 £67 **5 4 4**

5-7 Devonshire Rd   8747 1836   7–2A

"After a fall from grace post-refurb" (in 2013), this "fabulous" Chiswick "jewel" – sibling to the legendary Chez Bruce – "has recovered its zing"; ratings for its "glorious" Gallic cuisine ("just the right balance of classic and innovative"), "outstanding" wine and "immaculate" service are all impressive. / W4 2EU; www.latrompette.co.uk; @LaTrompetteUK; 10.30 pm, Sun 9.30 pm; set weekday L £48 (FP), set Sun L £53 (FP).

Troubadour SW5 £43 **2 3 4**

263-267 Old Brompton Rd   7370 1434   5–3A

"A piece of '60s history", and perhaps the last redoubt of bohemianism in the SWs! – this "quirky" Earl's Court café (and basement music venue) serves "decent" all-day nosh, including a "wide choice of breakfast dishes". / SW5 9JA; www.troubadour.co.uk; 11 pm.

Trullo N1 £51 **4 4 4**

300-302 St Paul's Rd   7226 2733   8–2D

Hailed as a "baby River Café" by its gigantic north London fan club, Jordan Trullo's "smart but relaxed" Highbury venture serves up an "outstanding" (and "often gutsy") menu, complemented by an "educational treasury" of a wine list; let's hope "creeping prices" don't spoil the fun! / N1 2LH; www.trullorestaurant.com; @Trullo_LDN; 10.30 pm; closed Sun D; no Amex; booking: max 12; set weekday L £37 (FP).

Truscott Arms W9 NEW £54 **3 3 4**

55 Shirland Rd   7266 9198   1–2B

With its "buzzing bar on the ground floor, upstairs dining room and dining conservatory", this Maida Vale gastropub wins all-round praise, including for its gourmet food at "neighbourhood prices". / W9 2JD; www.thetruscottarms.com; @TheTruscottArms; 9 pm; SRA-3 stars.

Tsunami £49 **5 2 2**

93 Charlotte St, W1   7637 0050   2–1C
5-7 Voltaire Rd, SW4   7978 1610   10–1D

"Black cod to die for" and other Asian-fusion wizardry still inspire raves for this Clapham destination (with Fitzrovia spin-off), which fans say is "as good as Nobu"… but half the cost; on the downside, "the decor has seen better days", and service is sometimes "terrible". / www.tsunamirestaurant.co.uk; @Tsunamirest; SW4 10.30 pm, Fri & Sat 11 pm, Sun 9.30 pm; W1 11 pm; SW4 closed Mon - Fri L; W1 closed Sat L and Sun; SW4 no Amex.

28-50 £53 **3 3 4**

15 Maddox St, W1   7495 1505   3–2C
15-17 Marylebone Ln, W1   7486 7922   3–1A
140 Fetter Ln, EC4   7242 8877   9–2A

"The food is fine, but the real story is the wine" – "interesting selections by the glass", and a "killer collector's list of old and rare bottles with modest mark-ups" are making a big hit of this growing bistro chain; it's often hailed as "a good choice for lunch". / www.2850.co.uk; EC4 9.30 pm; W1 Mon-Wed 10 pm, Thu-Sat 10.30 pm, Sun 9.30 pm; EC4 closed Sat-Sun.

21 Bateman Street W1 NEW £36 3 4 4
21 Bateman St 7287 6638 4–2A

A "welcome new one-room restaurant", in the heart of Soho, "buzzing with the sound of Greek voices", and offering "unparalleled value for money"; the "rather minimal" menu focusses on charcoal grill-cooked souvlaki "done to perfection". / W1D 3AL; www.21batemanstreet.co.uk; Mon-Thu 11.30 pm, Sat midnight, Sun 10.20 pm.

Two Brothers N3 £42 3 3 2
297-303 Regent's Park Rd 8346 0469 1–1B

"Really fresh fish and terrific chips" maintain the reputation of this ever-"popular" Finchley fixture as one of north London's premier chippys. / N3 1DP; www.twobrothers.co.uk; 10 pm, Sun 8 pm; closed Mon.

2 Veneti W1 £47 3 4 3
10 Wigmore St 7637 0789 3–1B

"Pleasant and helpful" service and "good-quality, traditional cooking" are mainstays of the simple formula which makes this "well-spaced" Venetian a useful destination in the "bereft area" round the Wigmore Hall, especially for business. / W1U 2RD; www.2veneti.com; @2Veneti; 10.30 pm, Sat 11 pm; closed Sat L & Sun.

Typing Room
Town Hall Hotel E2 NEW £85 5 4 4
Patriot Square 7871 0461 1–2D

"A superb replacement for Viajante (RIP)"; "amazing" tasting menus – with "wow" flavours, "fantastic" presentation, and "interesting wine pairings" – are quickly putting this Bethnal Green dining room firmly back on the map; service is notably "attentive" too. / E2 9NF; www.typingroom.com; @TypingRoom; 10.15 pm; closed Mon & Tue; set weekday L £52 (FP).

Umu W1 £105 2 1 2
14-16 Bruton Pl 7499 8881 3–2C

"Ouch! Make sure you ask your bank manager first…"; Marlon Abela's discreetly-located but "blingy" Mayfair Japanese offers some "lovely" Kyoto-style kaiseki, but it is losing its way, and the cost is "crazy". / W1J 6LX; www.umurestaurant.com; 10.30 pm; closed Sat L & Sun; no trainers; booking: max 14.

Uni SW1 NEW £46 4 4 3
18a, Ebury St 7730 9267 2–4B

A bright Belgravia newcomer, acclaimed in early-days survey reports for its "unusual and creative" Peruvian/Japanese cuisine; "superb sushi" a highlight. / SW1W 0LU; www.restaurantuni.com; @UNIRestaurant; 10 pm.

The Union Café W1 £45 2 3 2
96 Marylebone Ln 7486 4860 3–1A

A "reliable" and "no-nonsense" Marylebone fixture, where the food is "good value and always tasty", if arguably "a little uninspiring"; real plus point? – "no silly mark-ups on the wine!" / W1U 2QA; www.brinkleys.com; @BrinkleysR; 10.30 pm; closed Sun.

Union Street Café SE1 £49 2 2 2
Harling Hs, Union St 7592 7977 9–4B

"Striving too hard for some sort of industrial chic", Gordon Ramsay's "SoHo-style" Italian yearling, in Borough, is "a bit of a Curate's Egg" – too often, it seems a "pretentious" place where standards are "average" all-round. / SE1 0BS; www.gordonramsay.com/union-street-cafe; @unionstreetcafe; Mon-Fri 10 pm, Sat 9.45 pm, Sun 7.30 pm.

Upstairs SW2 £57 4 4 4
89b Acre Ln (door on Branksome Rd) 7733 8855 10–2D
Knock to enter this "fun" Brixton "hidden gem" – "a charming combination of Berlin-style secret venue and French family restaurant", where "gorgeous" cocktails help sustain the "romantic" vibe. / SW2 5TN; www.upstairslondon.com; @upstairsbrixton; 9.30 pm, Thu-Sat 10.30 pm; D only, closed Mon & Sun.

Le Vacherin W4 £62 3 3 3
76-77 South Pde 8742 2121 7–1A
"All the French classics" are realised to a "perfectly sound" standard at Malcolm John's "professional but laid-back" bistro, opposite Acton Green; it has the knack of "making a series of small surprises into a very satisfactory all-round experience". / W4 5LF; www.levacherin.co.uk; @Le_Vacherin; 10.15 pm, Fri & Sat 10.45 pm, Sun 9.45; closed Mon L; set always available £38 (FP).

Vanilla Black EC4 £64 3 3 3
17-18 Tooks Ct 7242 2622 9–2A
"I didn't believe veggie food could taste this good!"; this "delightful" restaurant, "tucked away" down a Midtown alleyway, inspires consistently positive reports on its "upmarket and imaginative", "if sometimes quirky", cuisine. / EC4A 1LB; www.vanillablack.co.uk; @vanillablack1; 10 pm; closed Sun.

Vapiano £25 3 2 3
19-21 Great Portland St, W1 7268 0080 3–1C
90B Southwark St, SE1 7593 2010 9–4B NEW
This (German-owned) Mediterranean self-serve canteen concept may be "a bit odd"… but most reporters find it "very useful" for "a quick, easy and tasty meal"; now in Soho too. / www.vapiano.co.uk.

Vasco & Piero's Pavilion W1 £58 4 4 3
15 Poland St 7437 8774 3–1D
"Very unshowy, and often overlooked", this "real old-fashioned Italian" offers "faultless" cooking, "very friendly" service and a "cosy" old-Soho atmosphere – all in all, a "memorable" combination. / W1F 8QE; www.vascosfood.com; @Vasco_and_Piero; 10.15 pm; closed Sat L & Sun.

Veeraswamy W1 £75 4 4 4
Victory Hs, 99-101 Regent St 7734 1401 3–3D
London's oldest Indian should be a tourist trap, yet it's anything but – yes it's "a bit expensive", but the "light and fragrant" cooking, "yummy cocktails" and "sumptuous" modern design make a visit "well worthwhile". / W1B 4RS; www.veeraswamy.com; 10.30 pm, Sun 10 pm; booking: max 14; set pre theatre £48 (FP).

Verden E5 NEW £42
181 Clarence Rd 8986 4723 1–1D
A chef of impeccable West End provenance (Scott's) has gone East, to Clapton, to help establish this new meat-, cheese- and wine-specialist bar; early feedback is euphoric, but too scant to justify a survey rating. / E5 8EE; www.verdene5.com; @VerdenE5; midnight; closed Mon.

El Vergel SE1 £33 4 3 4
132 Webber St 7401 2308 9–4B
"A great place for a quick lunchtime bite", or brunch – this Latino canteen, near Borough tube, is known for its "deliciously fresh" fare; "I'd think of moving to Southwark just to eat there every day!" / SE1 0QL; www.elvergel.co.uk; 2.45pm, Sat-Sun 3.45 pm; closed D, closed Sun; no Amex.

Il Vicolo SW1 £50 3 4 2
3-4 Crown Passage 7839 3960 3–4D
"Tucked away" in a St James's alleyway, this "cheery" Sicilian stalwart is particularly buoyed up by its "always lively" service, but the "traditional" fare is "consistently good" too. / SW1Y 6PP; www.vicolo.co.uk; 10 pm; closed Sat L & Sun.

The Victoria SW14 £49 3 4 3
10 West Temple 8876 4238 10–2A
Not far from Richmond Park, Paul Merrett's large hostelry – with a spacious conservatory and a "lovely garden in summer", complete with playground – makes a natural weekend destination; dependable food too, including a BBQ in summer. / SW14 7RT; www.thevictoria.net; @thevictoria_pub; 10 pm, Sat 10 pm; no Amex; set weekday L £38 (FP).

Viet Grill E2 £38 4 2 3
58 Kingsland Rd 7739 6686 12–1B
"The best place on the Viet-Town strip" – this "upmarket... for the area" Shoreditch café offers "very tasty and authentic dishes at reasonable prices". / E2 8DP; www.vietnamesekitchen.co.uk; @CayTreVietGrill; 11 pm, Fri & Sat 11.30 pm, Sun 10.30 pm.

Vijay NW6 £31 3 4 2
49 Willesden Ln 7328 1087 1–1B
"Real subtlety in the use of herbs as well as spices" – with "fair prices" too – wins a loyal fan base for this South Indian veteran, in Kilburn; they "could improve the decor" though. / NW6 7RF; www.vijayrestaurant.co.uk; 10.45 pm, Fri & Sat 11.45 pm.

Villa Bianca NW3 £60 2 2 3
1 Perrins Ct 7435 3131 8–2A
In a cute Hampstead lane, "one of the few remaining traditional Italian silver service restaurants"; while fans (perennially) claim that "it's raised its game again" of late, critics find the food "no more than competent", and "pricey" for what it is too. / NW3 1QS; www.villabiancanw3.com; 11.30 pm, Sun 10.30 pm.

Village East SE1 £55 3 2 3
171-173 Bermondsey St 7357 6082 9–4D
A "busy and buzzy" Bermondsey's local eatery, with open kitchen, which – after a recent revamp – is still quite a crowd-pleaser; it makes "a very lively place for a weekend breakfast". / SE1 3UW; www.villageeast.co.uk; @VillageEastSE1; 10 pm, Sun 9.30 pm.

Villandry £51 2 2 2
170 Gt Portland St W1 7631 3131 2–1B
11-12 Waterloo Pl SW1 7930 3305 3–3D NEW
So much missed potential – these "pricey" grand cafés, now with a smart St James's branch to complement the Marylebone original, could easily be the "excellent all-rounders" their fans suggest, but reports overall support those who say the food is "all over the place". / W1W 5QB; www.villandry.com; 10.30 pm; closed Sun D.

Villiers Coffee Co WC2 NEW £46
31a Villiers St 7925 2100 2–2D
A summer opening from the same family as the ever-popular Gordon's Wine Bar, just down the street; favourably reviewed in the press, it's potentially a very handy sort of all-day standby in a street that's improved immeasurably in recent years. / WC2N 6ND; @VilliersCoffee.

The Vincent Rooms
Westminster Kingsway College SW1 £32 ③③③
76 Vincent Sq 7802 8391 2–4C
"The students got through it, and so did we!" – the elegant dining room of this Westminster college can offer "delicious" food "even though it's cooked and served by catering students"; you have to accept "a few hairy moments", but "who knows, these may be great chefs of the future!" / SW1P 2PD; www.thevincentrooms.com; 7.15 pm; closed Mon D, Tue D, Fri D, Sat & Sun; no Amex.

VQ £47 ②③②
St Giles Hotel, Great Russell St, WC1 7300 3000 4–1A
325 Fulham Rd, SW10 7376 7224 5–3B
"Breakfast, at any time!" – the special feature of this long-established 24/7 Chelsea diner, which now has an offshoot in Bloomsbury. / www.vingtquatre.co.uk; open 24 hours.

Vinoteca £45 ②④④
15 Seymour Pl, W1 7724 7288 2–2A
55 Beak St, W1 3544 7411 3–2D
18 Devonshire Rd, W4 3701 8822 7–2A
7 St John St, EC1 7253 8786 9–1B
"Heaven for wine lovers"; these "cramped" bars are run by staff "with a real passion for inspiring their customers" with their "creative" and very "sensibly-priced" list; the "simple" bistro fare? – "sound but unexciting". / www.vinoteca.co.uk; 11 pm, Seymour Pl Sun 5 pm; EC1 Sun; Seymour Pl Sun D.

Vivat Bacchus £53 ②③②
4 Hay's Ln, SE1 7234 0891 9–4C
47 Farringdon St, EC4 7353 2648 9–2A
"Useful for a get-together after a day in the City", this "relaxed" spot is of special note for its "fantastic" South African wine list, and "amazing array" of cheeses, although its other "simple" fare is generally "dependable" too; the SE1 branch rarely elicits reports. / www.vivatbacchus.co.uk; 9.30 pm; EC4 closed Sat & Sun; SE1 closed Sat L & Sun.

Vivo N1 NEW £35 ④④④
57-58 Upper St 7424 5992 8–3D
"A fantastic addition to Islington" – offering light Italian dishes, "like a sort of poor man's Princi", this "excellent casual dining spot" has inspired only positive comments in its first year of operation; it even boasts a "roof terrace"! / N1 0NY; www.vivotaste.com; @vivo_taste; 11 pm, Fri & Sat 1am, Sun 10.30 pm.

Vrisaki N22 £36 ③③③
73 Middleton Rd 8889 8760 1–1C
"If you order mezze, the portions are huge" – you'll be pushed to finish – at this quirky old taverna and take-away, which makes an offbeat find in an unassuming Bounds Green street. / N22 8LZ; www.vrisaki.uk.com; @vrisaki; 11.30 pm, Sun 9 pm; closed Mon; no Amex.

Wagamama £38 2 3 2
Branches throughout London
This "crowd-pleasing" Asian noodle chain remains "a safe bet" for most reporters (and kids, in particular, undoubtedly "love it"); it's "fallen a long way from where it once was", though, and the food "while fresh, lacks the real taste of the East". / www.wagamama.com; 10 pm-11 pm; EC4 & EC2 closed Sat & Sun; no booking.

Wahaca £33 2 3 4
19-23 Charlotte St, W1   7323 2342   2–1C
80-82 Wardour St, W1   7734 0195   3–2D
66 Chandos Pl, WC2   7240 1883   4–4C
68-69 Upper St, N1   3697 7990   8–3D
Southbank Centre, SE1   7928 1876   2–3D
"Vibrant colours and flavours that tingle the taste buds" ensure this "sociable" Mexican street food chain remains a major hit; there are reporters, however, who "just don't get it"… and they are becoming more vocal. / www.wahaca.com; WC2 & W1 & E14 11 pm, Sun 10.30 pm; W12 11 pm, Sun 10 pm; no booking.

The Wallace
The Wallace Collection W1 £56 2 2 5
Hertford Hs, Manchester Sq   7563 9505   3–1A
This Marylebone museum café boasts a "stunning" setting in an "airy" atrium adjoining an 18th-century palazzo; with its "ordinary" cooking and "eccentric" service, though, it can seem a "wasted opportunity". / W1U 3BN; www.thewallacerestaurant.co.uk; Fri & Sat 9.15 pm; Sun-Thu closed D; no Amex.

Waterloo Bar & Kitchen SE1 £54 3 3 2
131 Waterloo Rd   7928 5086   9–4A
A handy standby for Waterloo commuters and Old Vic theatre-goers – a cavernous (and sometimes "noisy") spot where "engaging" staff dish up "tasty" bistro fare. / SE1 8UR; www.barandkitchen.co.uk; 10.30 pm.

The Waterway W9 £51 2 1 4
54 Formosa St   7266 3557   8–4A
Thanks to the "perfect canalside location", there's "always a buzz" at this "happening" spot, near Little Venice – sadly, this often seems to mean that the kitchen is "overloaded", and service "hard to get". / W9 2JU; www.thewaterway.co.uk; @thewaterway_; 10.30 pm, Sun 10 pm.

The Wells NW3 £49 3 2 4
30 Well Walk   7794 3785   8–1A
This "very consistent" Hampstead hostelry, handy for the Heath, is one of NW3's finest destinations; "it's the place to be if you have a dog, but even without a canine friend it's buzzy and fun". / NW3 1BX; www.thewellshampstead.co.uk; @WellsHampstead; 10 pm, Sun 9.30 pm.

The Wet Fish Café NW6 £47 3 3 3
242 West End Ln   7443 9222   1–1B
"A dream local, with flattering lighting and a well-considered soundtrack" – this former fishmongers' shop in West Hampstead "hits the spot" at any time, but especially for weekend brunch. / NW6 1LG; www.thewetfishcafe.co.uk; @thewetfishcafe; 10 pm; no Amex.

The Wharf TW11   £48   2 3 4
22 Manor Rd   8977 6333   1–4A
It's the "good riverside location", overlooking Teddington Lock, which makes this airy bar/brasserie, with large terrace, a special destination; locals say the cooking's OK too. / TW11 8BG; www.thewharfteddington.com; Mon-Sat 10 pm, Sun 8.30 pm; closed Mon L; set always available £32 (FP), set Sun L £38 (FP).

White Horse SW6   £51   2 2 4
1-3 Parsons Grn   7736 2115   10–1B
"A first-rate list of well-chosen beers" and "a great buzzy atmosphere", especially when it's sunny, are the prime attractions of Fulham's famous 'Sloaney Pony'; the food? – "perfectly competent pub grub". / SW6 4UL; www.whitehorsesw6.com; 10.30 pm; no Maestro.

White Rabbit N16   £27   4 3 3
15-16 Bradbury St   7682 0163   1–1C
"As clever as any food you will have in smarter postcodes... just with more beards"; this Dalston yearling offers a "beautifully textured" cuisine, and its "very unusual" small plates can be "out of this world". / N16 8JN; www.whiterabbitdalston.com; 9.30 pm; D only, closed Mon.

The White Swan EC4   £63   4 4 3
108 Fetter Ln   7242 9696   9–2A
"Very sound", "high-end gastropub-style food" makes this "excellent" Fleet Street pub a "reliably good choice for a business lunch"; the upstairs dining room "is fortunately well-insulated from the noisy bar below". / EC4A 1ES; www.thewhiteswanlondon.com; @thewhiteswanEC4; 10 pm; closed Sat & Sun.

Whits W8   £48   3 5 3
21 Abingdon Rd   7938 1122   5–1A
A "very friendly" welcome from the "brilliant" co-owner Eva helps make for a "special evening out" at this "cosy" Kensington side street bistro, which offers "elegant" Gallic dishes in paradoxically "large" portions. / W8 6AH; www.whits.co.uk; @Whitsrestaurant; 10 pm; D only, closed Mon & Sun.

Whyte & Brown W1 NEW   £37   3 4 4
Kingly Ct, Kingly St   3747 9820   3–2C
A "lovely" atmosphere – "both in the courtyard and inside" – helps make this "buzzy" Carnaby Street newcomer something of a surprise hit; fans say the chicken-centric menu is "a brilliant concept" too. / W1B 5PW; www.whyteandbrown.com; @whyteandbrown; Mon-Sat 10.45 pm, Sun 5.30 pm; closed Sun D.

Wild Honey W1   £68   3 3 3
12 St George St   7758 9160   3–2C
"Much improved" since the recent refurbishment, this "relaxed but classy" Mayfair spot is a "good but pricey" fixture, where the food is "reliably interesting", and whose "clubby, wood-panelled intimacy" suits business in particular. / W1S 2FB; www.wildhoneyrestaurant.co.uk; @whrestaurant; 10.30 pm; closed Sun.

Wiltons SW1   £100   3 4 4
55 Jermyn St   7629 9955   3–3C
"So wonderfully old-fashioned"; this "very professional" St James's
bastion of the Establishment (est 1742, but here only since 1984)
offers "perfect Dover sole" and other "first-rate" British seafood;
prices are certainly high, though – "best visit on someone else's
expenses". / SW1Y 6LX; www.wiltons.co.uk; @wiltons1742; 10.15 pm;
closed Sat & Sun; jacket required; set dinner £64 (FP).

The Windmill W1   £38   3 2 3
6-8 Mill St   7491 8050   3–2C
"Pie heaven!"; this "time-warped" Young's boozer, near Savile Row,
offers pastries with a "huge variety" of fillings, and at
"very reasonable prices" too. / W1S 2AZ; www.windmillmayfair.co.uk;
@tweetiepie_w1; 9.30 pm, Sat 4 pm; closed Sat & Sun; no Amex.

The Windsor Castle W8   £43   2 2 5
114 Campden Hill Rd   7243 8797   6–2B
Consistent but not exciting reports on the food at this old Kensington
coaching inn; who cares, though? – it's the delightful walled garden
and snug ancient interior that's always been the real attraction.
/ W8 7AR; www.thewindsorcastlekensington.co.uk; @windsorcastlew8; 10 pm,
Sun 9 pm.

The Wine Library EC3   £26   1 3 5
43 Trinity Sq   7481 0415   9–3D
A "one-off"; these ancient City cellars offer "a place for wine lovers
to explore and relax", and their "eclectic and expert array of wines"
(at cost plus a small mark-up) is the "star of the show" – the picnic-
style buffet is "just so you can say you had something to eat while you
drank"! / EC3N 4DJ; www.winelibrary.co.uk; 8 pm, Mon 6 pm; closed Mon D,
Sat & Sun.

Wishbone SW9   £18   3 2 2
Brixton Village, Coldharbour Ln   7274 0939   10–2D
"It has its detractors but if you go at a quiet time, it's easy to get
a table, and the chicken is really good", at this "fancy fried chicken
shack", in Brixton Market (part of the MEAT franchise). STOP PRESS
– since late summer 2014 now trading as CHICKENliquor. / SW9 8PR;
www.wishbonebrixton.co.uk; @wishbonebrixton; closed Mon.

Wolfe's WC2   £48   3 4 3
30 Gt Queen St   7831 4442   4–1D
Having ridden the burger craze (the '70s one), this stalwart Covent
Garden diner de luxe may be in a rather dated style, but it's
a "relaxing" sort of place with "consistent" standards; "great
lunchtime menu". / WC2B 5BB; www.wolfes-grill.net; @wolfesbargrill;
10 pm, Fri & Sat 10.30 pm, Sun 9 pm.

THE WOLSELEY W1   £59   3 4 5
160 Piccadilly   7499 6996   3–3C
For pure theatre and excitement, Corbin & King's "splendid", "celeb-
packed" London linchpin, by The Ritz, just can't be beat; its brasserie
fare is "solid" but "not the most exciting", although the (power)
"breakfast event" here is famously "the best in town". / W1J 9EB;
www.thewolseley.com; @TheWolseleyRest; midnight, Sun 11 pm; SRA-3 stars.

Wong Kei W1 £30
41-43 Wardour St 7437 8408 4–3A
*"New management, new staff, new air conditioning, new all-black
uniform and new manners!" – this Chinatown landmark reopened
under new management as our survey for the year was wrapping up;
a proper assessment of the new régime will have to wait till next year.
/ W1D 6PY; www.wongkeilondon.com; 11.30 pm, Fri & Sat 11.45 pm,
Sun 10.30 pm; no credit cards; no booking.*

Woodlands £41 3 3 2
37 Panton St, SW1 7839 7258 4–4A
77 Marylebone Ln, W1 7486 3862 2–1A
102 Heath St, NW3 7794 3080 8–1A
*These under-the-radar veggie stalwarts may look dull, but they serve
some "unusual and tasty" South Indian dishes.
/ www.woodlandsrestaurant.co.uk; 10 pm; NW3 no L Mon.*

Workshop Coffee EC1 £45 4 3 3
27 Clerkenwell Rd 7253 5754 9–1A
*"Yummy, casual and fun", this Oz-style café in Clerkenwell serves
"the best coffee, no question", and an "outstanding brunch" too.
/ EC1M 5RN; www.workshopcoffee.com; @WorkshopCoffee; 10 pm; closed
Mon D, Sat D & Sun D.*

Wright Brothers £53 4 3 3
13 Kingly St, W1 7434 3611 3–2D
11 Stoney St, SE1 7403 9554 9–4C
8 Lamb St, E1 7377 8706 9–2D
*"Oysters zinging with the taste of the sea" and other "phenomenal"
seafood has made a major hit of the "crowded" but "happy" Borough
Market original; its more spacious Soho and, now, Spitalfields spin-offs
are good too, if not quite so much fun. / 10.30 pm, Sun 9 pm; booking:
max 8.*

XO NW3 £47 2 2 2
29 Belsize Ln 7433 0888 8–2A
*"Nothing beats sitting in a booth with friends enjoying the wide range
of cocktails", say fans of this "solid" Belsize Park local; as a place
to eat, though, it can seem "stale" – "resting on its laurels, in the
absence of much local competition". / NW3 5AS;
www.rickerrestaurants.com; 10.30 pm.*

Yalla Yalla £35 3 3 4
1 Green's Ct, W1 7287 7663 3–2D
12 Winsley St, W1 7637 4748 3–1C
186 Shoreditch High St, E1 0772 584 1372 8–3C
*"Zingy bites served in a minuscule café besieged by irritating queues"
– the "crowded" original branch of this Lebanese street food chain,
in the sleaziest heart of Soho; other branches rarely inspire
commentary. / www.yalla-yalla.co.uk; Green's Court 11 pm, Sun 10 pm;
Winsley Street 11.30 pm, Sat 11 pm; W1 Sun.*

Yard Sale Pizza E5 NEW £31
105 Lower Clapton Rd 3602 9090 1–1D
*A popular pop-up goes permanent; this Clapton newcomer seeks
to make the pizza experience fun – successfully on the basis of an
early-days report. / E5 0NP; www.yardsalepizza.com; @yardsalepizza;
11 pm, Sun 10 pm; closed Mon.*

Yashin W8 £84 **5** **3** **2**
1a Argyll Rd   7938 1536   5–1A
With its "superb Japanese food" – "reserve a table upstairs (ground floor) to watch the dishes being expertly prepared" – this "top-notch", Manhattan-esque Kensington operation is generally hailed as "worth the cost", considerable as that is... / W8 7DB; www.yashinsushi.com; 10 pm.

Yashin Ocean House SW7 £82 **1** **1** **3**
117-119 Old Brompton Rd   7373 3990   5–2B
"Overpriced, overrated, weird and not wonderful" – you'd never guess that Yashin's South Kensington offshoot would inspire such a drubbing; fans do applaud its "wonderfully inventive" Japanese-fusion cuisine, but to foes "it's very unusual... but just not very nice!" / SW7 3RN; www.yashinocean.com; @YashinLondon.

Yauatcha W1 £72 **4** **2** **3**
Broadwick Hs, 15-17 Broadwick St   7494 8888   3–2D
It's "still serving outstanding dim sum", but this "slick" Soho basement operation is starting to slip; sometimes "slow" or "shirty" service doesn't help, and critics are beginning to feel it's "lost its edge foodwise" too. / W1F 0DL; www.yauatcha.com; @yauatcha; 11.15 pm, Sun 10.30 pm.

The Yellow House SE16 £44 **3** **4** **2**
126 Lower Rd   7231 8777   11–2A
"The best restaurant in Surrey Quays"; this "family-friendly" spot is of particular note for its "delicious" pizzas, and "the fudge cooked to the chef's mother's recipe" is "amazing" too. / SE16 2UE; www.theyellowhouse.eu; @theyellowhousejazz; 10.30 pm, Sun 9.30 pm; closed Mon, Tue–Sat closed L, Sun open L & D.

Yi-Ban E16 £45 **4** **3** **2**
London Regatta Ctr, Royal Albert Dock   7473 6699   11–1D
"Fantastic dim sum" draw a good following to this obscurely located waterside Chinese, in deepest Docklands – "a pity it's so far away from the rest of London", but a fab destination for (City Airport) plane-spotters! / E16 2QT; www.yi-ban.co.uk; 10.45 pm.

Yipin China N1 £42 **5** **2** **1**
70-72 Liverpool Rd   7354 3388   8–3D
"The most sublime Chinese food in the most unprepossessing of surroundings" – that's the trade-off at this "brightly lit and functional" Sichuanese two-year-old, in Islington; "you can eat strangely and wonderfully" but beware – "dishes marked 'mild' are very hot by Western standards!" / N1 0QD; www.yipinchina.co.uk; 11 pm.

Yming W1 £40 **4** **5** **3**
35-36 Greek St   7734 2721   4–2A
A "haven", an "oasis", "the best Chinese in Soho"... Christine Yau's "effortlessly pleasing" corner "stalwart" has been "consistent for years" – "maitre d' William is the host with the most", and "the food always hits the mark". / W1D 5DL; www.yminglondon.com; 11.45 pm; set weekday L & pre-theatre £25 (FP).

Yo Sushi £28 1 1 2
Branches throughout London
With its "sad plates of circulating sushi" and "second- or even third-rate" standards, this gimmicky chain gives "a poor and very overpriced representation of Japanese food"; even those who find the whole show "depressing", though, concede that "kids love it!"
/ www.yosushi.co.uk; 10.30 pm; no booking.

Yoisho W1 £45 3 2 2
33 Goodge St 7323 0477 2–1C
"There is nowhere more authentic", say supporters of this izakaya-style Fitzrovia stalwart; it's particularly known for its grills, although one former fan this year thought they'd become "nothing special".
/ W1T 2PS; 10.30 pm; D only, closed Sun; no Amex.

York & Albany NW1 £59 2 2 4
127-129 Parkway 7388 3344 8–3B
Vanishingly few reports of late on Gordon Ramsay's "cool"-looking and "spacious" operation, in a monumental old tavern near Regent's Park; it's for breakfast and business meetings that it mostly seems to shine. / NW1 7PS; www.gordonramsay.com; @yorkandalbany; 10.30 pm, Sun 8 pm.

Yoshino W1 £44 3 4 2
3 Piccadilly Pl 7287 6622 3–3D
"Hidden-away down an alley off Piccadilly", a "quality" Japanese operation all the more worth knowing about in such a central location; those who remember the old days, however, are inclined to regret that it's "not as good as it used to be". / W1J 0DB; www.yoshino.net; 10 pm; closed Sun.

Yum Yum N16 £40 3 2 4
187 Stoke Newington High St 7254 6751 1–1D
This large and rather "beautiful" Thai has long been one of Stoke Newington's key destinations for a meal plus a cocktail or two; it still attracts largely favourable reports. / N16 0LH; www.yumyum.co.uk; @yumyum; 10.30 pm, Fri & Sat 11.30 pm.

Zafferano SW1 £76 3 3 3
15 Lowndes St 7235 5800 5–1D
"A taste of upper-class Italy!"; this "comfortable" and "intimate" Belgravia classic "has had its ups and downs over the years", but continues to be a "perennial favourite" serving some "top-notch" dishes – even some who say "it used to be better" still feel it's "a treat". / SW1X 9EY; www.zafferanorestaurants.com; 11 pm, Sun 10.30 pm.

Zaffrani N1 £45 4 4 3
47 Cross St 7226 5522 8–3D
"Definitely not your typical curry house" – this "classy" Islington spot serves cuisine that's "lighter than traditional Indian fare". / N1 2BB; www.zaffrani-islington.co.uk; 10.30 pm.

Zayna W1 £50 4 3 2
25 New Quebec St 7723 2229 2–2A
"Excellent" judiciously spiced curries, mixing flavours Indian and Pakistani, win praise for this handy operation, near Marble Arch; the basement dining room is "far less atmospheric". / W1H 7SF; www.zaynarestaurant.co.uk; 11.15 pm, Fri & Sat 11.45 pm; closed weekday L.

Zero Degrees SE3 £43 3 2 2
29-31 Montpelier Vale 8852 5619 1–4D
A "great selection of pizzas" and "very-good-quality beer" make for
"an interesting combination" at this Blackheath microbrewery;
its critics feel there has been a slip in general standards of late,
though, with the premises feeling "less welcoming" after recent
expansion. / SE3 0TJ; www.zerodegrees.co.uk; @Zerodegreesbeer; midnight,
Sun 11.30 pm.

Zest
JW3 NW3 NEW £48 3 2 2
341-351 Finchley Rd 7433 8955 1–1B
"Rescuing Jewish cuisine from stodgy, Mittel-European associations",
this "dramatic", "high-ceilinged" space, on the Finchley Road, offers
"interesting", "Ottolenghi-style" salads and fish dishes; "service
is pleasant, but needs to sharpen up". / NW3 6ET; Sun-Thu 9.45 pm;
closed Fri & Sat.

Ziani's SW3 £55 3 3 3
45 Radnor Walk 7351 5297 5–3C
Peak times are "so noisy and cramped", but Chelsea locals still love
this "fun" and "friendly" Italian, which dishes up "home-cooking"
from its postage stamp-sized kitchen. / SW3 4BP; www.ziani.co.uk;
11 pm, Sun 10 pm.

Zizzi £47 2 2 2
Branches throughout London
"Unexceptional" and "unsophisticated" it undoubtedly is, but this
"pleasant" kid-friendly pizza-'n'-pasta chain is still generally rated
a "useful, if unspectacular, standby". / www.zizzi.co.uk; 11 pm.

Zoilo W1 £54 4 4 3
9 Duke St 7486 9699 3–1A
"Easy to miss, but an excellent find"; this small Argentinean yearling,
near Selfridges, "bombs your taste buds with hugely flavourful tapas"
– "get a seat at the counter downstairs where it's exciting see all the
activity in the open kitchen". / W1U 3EG; www.zoilo.co.uk;
@Zoilo_London; 10.30 pm; closed Sun.

Zucca SE1 £55 5 4 3
184 Bermondsey St 7378 6809 9–4D
"Unpretentious fine dining at its best!"; this "charming" Bermondsey
Italian is "such a 'wow'!" – even if the "crowded" and "canteen-like"
setting can be "very noisy", the "impassioned" cooking
is "outstanding" and "fairly priced" and "there's a real treat of a wine
list". / SE1 3TQ; www.zuccalondon.com; @ZuccaSam; 10 pm; closed
Mon & Sun D; no Amex.

Zuma SW7 £82 5 3 4
5 Raphael St 7584 1010 5–1C
"If you can cope with the fact that all the customers look like Tamara
Ecclestone", what's not to like about this "jaw-droppingly" pricey
Knightsbridge glamour-magnet? – the Japanese-fusion fare "may not
be classic gastronomy, but it's absolutely wonderful". / SW7 1DL;
www.zumarestaurant.com; 10.45 pm, Sun 10.15 pm; booking: max 8.

INDEXES

BREAKFAST
(with opening times)

Central
Al Duca (9)
Athenaeum (7)
The Attendant (8 am, Sat 10 am)
Aubaine: Heddon St W1 (8, Sat 10); Dover
St W1 (8 am); Oxford St W1 (9.30 am
Mon-Sat)
Baker & Spice: SW1 (7)
Balans: W1 (8)
Balthazar (7.30 Mon-Fri, 9 Sat & Sun)
Bar Italia (6.30)
Bentley's (Mon-Fri 7.30)
The Berners Tavern (7)
Bistro 1: Beak St W1 (Sun 11)
Black & Blue: Berners St W1 (9)
The Botanist (8, Sat & Sun 9)
La Bottega: Eccleston St SW1 (8, Sat 9);
Lower Sloane St SW1 (8, Sat 9, Sun 10)
Boulestin (7)
Boulevard (9)
Brasserie Max (7, Sun 8)
Browns (Albemarle) (7, Sun 7.30)
Café Bohème (8, Sat & Sun 9)
Café in the Crypt (Mon-Sat 8)
Caffè Vergnano: WC1 (6.30 am,
Sun 8.30 am); WC2 (8, Sun 11)
Cecconi's (7 am, Sat & Sun 8 am)
Christopher's (Sat & Sun 11.30)
The Cinnamon Club (Mon-Fri 7.30)
Colbert (8)
Comptoir Libanais: Wigmore
St W1 (8.30); Broadwick St W1 (8 am)
Cut (7am, Sat & Sun 7.30 am)
Daylesford Organic: SW1 (8, Sun 10);
W1 (9)
Dean Street Townhouse (Mon-Fri
7, Sat-Sun 8)
The Delaunay (7, Sat & Sun 11)
Diner: W1 (10, Sat & Sun 9);
WC2 (9.30 am)
Dishoom: WC2 (8, Sat & Sun 10)
Dorchester Grill (7, Sat & Sun 8)
Ed's Easy Diner: Sedley Pl,
14 Woodstock St W1 (Sat 9.30 am)
Fernandez & Wells: Beak St W1 (7.30,
sat& sun 9); Lexington St W1 (7 am);
St Anne's Ct W1 (8, sat 10); WC2 (8am, sat-
sun 9am)
Flat White (8, Sat & Sun 9)
Fleet River Bakery (7, Sat 9)
The Fountain (Fortnum's) (7.30,
Sun 11)
Franco's (7, Sat 8)
La Fromagerie Café (8, Sat 9, Sun 10)
Fuzzy's Grub: SW1 (7)
Gelupo (Sat & Sun 12)
The Goring Hotel (7, Sun 7.30)
Grazing Goat (7.30)
Hélène Darroze (Sat 11)
Holborn Dining Room (Mon - Fri
7, Sat & Sun 8)
Homage (7)
Hush: WC1 (8 am)
Indigo (6.30)
Inn the Park (8, Sat & Sun 9)
JW Steakhouse (6.30, Sat & Sun 7)
Kaffeine (7.30, Sat 8.30, Sun 9.30)
Kaspar's Seafood and Grill (7)

Kazan (Cafe): Wilton Rd SW1 (8 am,
Sun 9 am)
Konditor & Cook: WC1 (9.30);
W1 (9.30, Sun 10.30)
Kopapa (8.30, Sat & Sun 10)
Koya-Bar (Mon-Fri 8.30, Sat & Sun 9:30)
Ladurée: W1 (9); SW1 (Mon - Sat
9, Sun noon - 1.30)
Langan's Brasserie (7 Mon-Fri)
Lantana Cafe: W1 (8, Sat & Sun 9)
Maison Bertaux (8.30, Sun 9.15)
maze Grill (6.45)
Monmouth Coffee
Company: WC2 (8)
The National Dining Rooms (10)
National Gallery Café (8, Sat
& Sun 10)
Natural Kitchen: Marylebone High
St W1 (8, Sat 9, Sun 11)
Nopi (8, Sat & Sun 10)
Nordic Bakery: Dorset St W1 (8 am,
Sat-Sun 9); Golden Sq W1 (Mon-Fri 8, Sat 9,
Sun 11)
The Northall (6.30, Sat & Sun 7)
Noura: William St SW1 (8)
One-O-One (7)
The Only Running Footman (7.30,
Sat & Sun 9.30)
The Orange (8)
Ottolenghi: SW1 (8, Sun 9)
Ozer (8)
The Pantechnicon (Sat & Sun 9)
Paramount (7)
The Portrait (10)
Princi (8, Sun 8.30)
The Providores (9am)
Providores (Tapa Room) (9, Sat
& Sun 10)
Rib Room (7, Sun 8)
Riding House Café (7.30, Sat & Sun
9)
The Ritz Restaurant (7, Sun 8)
Roux at the Landau (7)
Royal Academy (10)
Scandinavian Kitchen (8, Sat
& Sun 10)
Simpsons-in-the-Strand (Mon-Fri
7.30)
The Sketch (Parlour) (Mon-Fri
8, Sat 10)
Sophie's Steakhouse: all
branches (Sat & Sun 11)
Sotheby's Café (9.30)
Spice Market (7, Sat & Sun 8)
Stock Pot: SW1 (9.30)
Strand Dining Rooms (7, Sat
& Sun 8)
Tate Britain (Rex Whistler) (Sat-
Sun 10)
Taylor St Baristas: W1 (8 am)
Thirty Six (7)
tibits (9, Sun 11.30)
Tom's Kitchen: WC2 (Sat & Sun 10)
Villandry (Sat 8 am, Sun 9 am)
The Wallace (10)
Wolfe's (9)
The Wolseley (7, Sat & Sun 8)
Yalla Yalla: Green's Ct W1 (Sat-Sun 10)

West
Adams Café (7.30 am)
Angelus (10)

BUSINESS

St John
Sauterelle
1701
Smiths (Top Floor)
Smiths (Dining Rm)
Sweetings
Taberna Etrusca
28-50: *EC4*
Vivat Bacchus: *all branches*
The White Swan

BYO

(Bring your own wine at no
or low – less than £3 – corkage.
Note for £5-£15 per bottle,
you can normally negotiate
to take your own wine to many,
if not most, places.)

Central
Cyprus Mangal
Food for Thought
Golden Hind
India Club
Patogh
Ragam

West
Adams Café
Alounak: *all branches*
Café 209
Chelsea Bun Diner
Faanoos: *all branches*
Fez Mangal
Fitou's Thai Restaurant
Miran Masala
Mirch Masala: *all branches*
Pappa Ciccia: *Munster Rd SW6*

North
Ali Baba
Chutneys
Diwana Bhel-Poori House
Huong-Viet
Jai Krishna
Rugoletta
Toff's
Vijay

South
Apollo Banana Leaf
Cah-Chi: *all branches*
Faanoos: *all branches*
Hot Stuff
Kaosarn: *SW9*
Lahore Karahi
Lahore Kebab House: *all branches*
Mien Tay: *all branches*
Mirch Masala: *all branches*
The Paddyfield
Sree Krishna
Thai Corner Café

East
Lahore Kebab House: *all branches*
Little Georgia Café: *E2*

Mangal 1
Mien Tay: *all branches*
Mirch Masala: *all branches*
Needoo
Rochelle Canteen
Tayyabs

CHILDREN

(h – high or special chairs
m – children's menu
p – children's portions
e – weekend entertainments
o – other facilities)

Central
A Wong *(h)*
Abeno: *WC2 (h); WC1 (hm)*
About Thyme *(hp)*
Al Duca *(hp)*
Al Hamra *(hp)*
Al Sultan *(hp)*
Alloro *(hp)*
Alyn Williams *(hp)*
Ametsa *(h)*
The Ape & Bird *(hm)*
aqua kyoto *(h)*
aqua nueva *(p)*
Arbutus *(hp)*
Asadal *(h)*
Assunta Madre *(h)*
L'Atelier de Joel Robuchon *(hp)*
Athenaeum *(m)*
The Attendant *(h)*
Aubaine: *Heddon St W1, Dover St W1 (h)*
L'Autre Pied *(hp)*
Axis *(hmp)*
Babbo *(hp)*
Balans: *W1 (hm)*
The Balcon *(hmp)*
Balthazar *(hmp)*
Bank Westminster *(hp)*
Bar Boulud *(hp)*
Bar Italia *(hp)*
Il Baretto *(hp)*
Barrica *(p)*
Bar Shu *(h)*
Beiteddine *(p)*
Belgo Centraal: *Earlham*
  St WC2 (hm); Kingsway WC2 (m)
Bellamy's *(hp)*
Benares *(h)*
Benito's Hat: *Goodge St W1 (hp)*
Bentley's *(h)*
Bibimbap Soho *(h)*
The Blind Pig *(h)*
Bocca Di Lupo *(ehp)*
Bodean's: *W1 (ehm)*
La Bodega Negra *(hp)*
Bone Daddies *(hp)*
Bonnie Gull *(hp)*
The Botanist *(h)*
Boudin Blanc *(hp)*
Boulestin *(mp)*
Boulevard *(hm)*
Brasserie Chavot *(hp)*
Brasserie Max *(hmp)*
Brasserie Zédel *(hp)*

The Modern Pantry *(hp)*
The Morgan Arms *(hp)*
Morito *(h)*
Moro *(h)*
The Narrow *(hp)*
Needoo *(h)*
New Street Grill *(ehm)*
1901 *(hp)*
Northbank *(h)*
Nusa Kitchen: *EC1, EC2 (p)*
On The Bab *(e)*
One Canada Square *(ehm)*
1 Lombard Street *(p)*
Paternoster Chop House *(hp)*
The Peasant *(hp)*
E Pellicci *(hp)*
Pho: *all east branches (hp)*
Piccolino: *EC2 (hp)*
Pizza East: *E1 (hp)*
Plateau *(hmp)*
La Porchetta Pizzeria: *all branches (hp)*
Portal *(hp)*
Princess of Shoreditch *(p)*
Provender *(hm)*
The Quality Chop House *(hp)*
Relais de Venise
    L'Entrecôte: *EC2 (hp)*
Rivington Grill: *EC2 (hp)*
Rocket: *Adams Ct EC2 (hp)*
Royal China: *all branches (h)*
Sager & WIlde *(h)*
St John *(h)*
St John Bread & Wine *(hp)*
Sauterelle *(p)*
1701 *(hp)*
Shanghai *(h)*
Sichuan Folk *(h)*
Simpson's Tavern *(m)*
Smiths (Top Floor) *(hp)*
Smiths (Dining Rm) *(hp)*
Smiths (Ground Floor) *(hp)*
Sông Quê *(h)*
Story Deli *(hp)*
Sweetings *(p)*
Taberna Etrusca *(h)*
Tas: *EC1 (h)*
Tayyabs *(h)*
3 South Place *(ehm)*
Typing Room *(p)*
Viet Grill *(hop)*
Vinoteca: *EC1 (p)*
The White Swan *(p)*
Yi-Ban *(h)*

ENTERTAINMENT
(Check times before you go)

Central
Bentley's
    (pianist, Thu-Sat)
Blanchette
    (DJ every second Sun)
Boisdale
    (jazz, soul, blues, Mon-Sat)
Café in the Crypt
    (jazz, Wed night)
Le Caprice
    (jazz brunch, Sat & last Sun D of each month)
Ciao Bella
    (pianist, nightly)
Crazy Bear
    (DJ, Sat)
Criterion
    (live music, Wed)
The Diamond Jub' Salon
    (Fortnum's)
    (Pianist daily)
Hakkasan: *Hanway Pl W1*
    (DJ, nightly)
Ham Yard Restaurant
    (theatre, movies)
Hard Rock Café
    (regular live music)
Ishtar
    (live music, Tue-Sat; belly dancer, Fri & Sat)
Joe Allen
    (pianist, Mon-Fri & Sun L)
Kettners
    (pianist, Tue-Sat)
Levant
    (belly dancer, nightly)
Maroush: *W1*
    (music & dancing, nightly)
Mint Leaf: *SW1*
    (DJ, Fri D)
Momo
    (live music on various days)
The Northall
    (Jazz on Sun Brunch)
Notes: *Wellington St WC2*
    (jazz, most Wed and Thu evenings)
Noura: *W1*
    (belly dancer, Fri & Sat)
Quaglino's
    (live music, Fri & Sat)
Quattro Passi
    (member's club)
Red Fort
    (DJ, Fri & Sat)
The Ritz Restaurant
    (live music, Sat)
Roka: *Charlotte St W1*
    (DJ, Thu-Sat)
Royal Academy
    (jazz, Fri)
Sarastro
    (opera, Sun, Mon D, Thu D and other Motown and Latin nights)
Shanghai Blues
    (jazz, Fri & Sat)
Simpsons-in-the-Strand
    (pianist, nightly)
Sketch (Gallery)
    (DJ, Thu-Sat)
STK Steakhouse
    (dj, Tue-Sat from 8.00 pm)
Tom's Kitchen: *WC2*
    (DJ, Fri)
The Windmill
    (live music, Mon)

West
The Andover Arms
    (jazz, first Thu of each month, opera last Thu)
Babylon
    (nightclub, Fri & Sat; magician, Sun; jazz, Tue)
Beach Blanket Babylon: *all branches*
    (DJ, Fri & Sat)
Belvedere
    (pianist, nightly Sat & Sun all day)
Big Easy: *SW3*
    (live music, nightly)

LATE
*(open to midnight or later;
may be earlier Sunday)*

tibits
Tinello
Tom's Kitchen: WC2
Toto's
Trishna
Tsunami: W1
Vapiano: W1
Villandry
Vinoteca Seymour Place: Seymour Pl W1
The Wallace
Wolfe's
Yalla Yalla: Green's Ct W1

West
The Abingdon
The Admiral Codrington
Al-Waha
Anarkali
Angelus
The Anglesea Arms
The Anglesea Arms
Annie's: all branches
The Atlas*
Aubaine: SW3
Babylon
Baker & Spice: SW3
Balans: W12, W4
Beach Blanket Babylon: W11
Beirut Express: SW7
Belvedere
Best Mangal: SW6, North End Rd W14
Bibendum Oyster Bar
Big Easy: SW3
Bird in Hand
Black & Blue: W8
Bluebird
Bombay Palace
La Bouchée
La Brasserie
Brinkley's
Bumpkin: SW3, SW7
Cambio de Tercio
Canta Napoli: W4
Capote Y Toros
The Carpenter's Arms*
Casa Brindisa
Casa Malevo
Charlotte's Place
Chelsea Bun Diner
Cibo
Le Colombier
The Cow
Cumberland Arms
The Dartmouth Castle
Daylesford Organic: W11
La Delizia Limbara
Duke of Sussex
Durbar
E&O
Edera
Eelbrook*
Electric Diner
The Enterprise
Essenza
La Famiglia*
Fat Boy's: all west branches
Fire & Stone: W12

First Floor
Foxtrot Oscar
Gallery Mess
The Gate: W6
Geales: W8
Haché: SW10
The Hampshire Hog*
The Havelock Tavern
The Henry Root
Hereford Road
Hole in the Wall*
Indian Zing
Joe's Brasserie
Julie's
Karma
Kateh
Kensington Square Kitchen
The Kensington Wine Rooms
Khan's
Kurobuta
The Ladbroke Arms
Made in Italy: SW3
The Mall Tavern
The Malt House
Manicomio: all branches
Maxela
Mazi
Mediterraneo
Medlar
Mona Lisa
Noor Jahan: W2
The Oak W12: all branches
Polish Club
Osteria Basilico
Il Pagliaccio
Pappa Ciccia: Fulham High St SW6
Paradise by Way of Kensal Green
Pellicano
Pentolina
The Phene
Poissonnerie de l'Avenue
Il Portico
Princess Victoria
Queen's Head*
Raoul's Café & Deli: W11*; W9
The Real Greek: W12
The Red Pepper
Riccardo's
The River Café
Rocca Di Papa: SW7
Royal China: SW6
Saigon Saigon
The Sands End
Santa Lucia
Santa Maria
The Shed
The Summerhouse*
The Swan*
Tartufo
Tendido Cero
Tendido Cuatro
The Terrace*
Thali
Tosa
La Trompette
Troubadour

PRIVATE ROOMS
* particularly recommended

Ibérica: *E14 (50)*
The Jugged Hare *(40)*
Lahore Kebab House: *E1 (50)*
Little Georgia Café: *E2 (50)*
Lutyens *(20,8,6,12)*
Manicomio: *all branches (30)*
The Mercer *(4,10,20,40,40,120)*
Merchants Tavern *(20)*
Mien Tay: *E2 (40)*
Mint Leaf: *all branches (60)*
The Modern Pantry *(12,22)*
The Narrow *(20)*
Needoo *(45)*
New Street Grill *(40)*
Northbank *(30)*
One Canada Square *(32)*
1 Lombard Street *(45)*
Orpheus *(18)*
Paternoster Chop House *(13)*
The Peasant *(18)*
Piccolino: *EC2 (24)*
Pizza East: *E1 (18)*
Plateau *(20,30)*
Portal *(9,14)*
Rivington Grill: *EC2 (25)*
Rocket: *Adams Ct EC2 (25)*
Royal China: *E14 (12,12,12)*
The Royal Exchange Grand
   Café *(26)*
St John *(18)*
Sauterelle *(26)*
Shanghai *(40,50)*
Sichuan Folk *(15)*
Simpson's Tavern *(40-100)*
Smiths (Dining Rm) *(36)*
Sushisamba *(63,160,230)*
Taberna Etrusca *(30)*
Tajima Tei *(16,6,4)*
Tas: *EC1 (50)*
Tayyabs *(35)*
3 South Place *(16-200)*
Les Trois Garçons *(10)*
28-50: *EC4 (14,6)*
Viet Grill *(100)*
Vinoteca: *EC1 (30)*
Vivat Bacchus: *EC4 (45)*
Workshop Coffee *(45)*
Yi-Ban *(30)*

ROMANTIC

Central
Andrew Edmunds
L'Artiste Musclé
L'Atelier de Joel Robuchon
Aurora
Bam-Bou
The Berners Tavern
Bob Bob Ricard
Boudin Blanc
Café Bohème
Le Caprice
Cecconi's
Chor Bizarre
Clos Maggiore
Corrigan's Mayfair
Coya

Crazy Bear
Dean Street Townhouse
The Delaunay
Les Deux Salons
Elena's L'Etoile
L'Escargot
Galvin at Windows
Gauthier Soho
Le Gavroche
Gay Hussar
Gordon's Wine Bar
Hakkasan: *Hanway Pl W1*
Honey & Co
Hush: *W1*
The Ivy
Kettners
Langan's Brasserie
Levant
Locanda Locatelli
Marcus
Momo
Mon Plaisir
Orrery
La Petite Maison
Pied à Terre
Polpo: *W1*
La Porte des Indes
La Poule au Pot
Ritz (Palm Court)
The Ritz Restaurant
Roux at the Landau
Rules
Sarastro
Scott's
Seven Park Place
J Sheekey
J Sheekey Oyster Bar
Toto's
The Wolseley
Zafferano

West
Albertine
Angelus
Annie's: *all branches*
Assaggi
Babylon
Beach Blanket Babylon: *all branches*
Belvedere
Bibendum
La Bouchée
Brinkley's
Charlotte's Place
Cheyne Walk Brasserie
Chutney Mary
Clarke's
Le Colombier
Daphne's
The Dock Kitchen
E&O
Eight Over Eight
La Famiglia
Ffiona's
First Floor
The Five Fields
Julie's
Launceston Place

ROOMS WITH A VIEW

CUISINES

An asterisk (*) after an entry
indicates exceptional or very
good cooking

AMERICAN
Central
The Avenue (SW1)
Big Easy (WC2)
Bodean's (W1)
Bubbledogs (W1)
Christopher's (WC2)
Hard Rock Café (W1)
Hubbard & Bell (WC1)
Jackson & Rye (W1)
Jamie's Diner (W1)
Joe Allen (WC2)
The Lockhart (W1)
Mishkin's (WC2)
Pitt Cue Co (W1)*
Soho Diner (W1)
Spuntino (W1)
The Chiltern Firehouse (W1)

West
Big Easy (SW3)
Bodean's (SW6)
Dirty Bones (W8)
Electric Diner (W11)
Lucky Seven (W2)
Sticky Fingers (W8)

North
Chicken Shop (NW5)
Karpo (NW1)
Pond (N16)
Q Grill (NW1)
Red Dog Saloon (N1)
Shrimpy's (N1)

South
Bodean's (SW4)
Chicken Shop (SW17)
Oblix (SE1)
Red Dog South (SW4)
Wishbone (SW9)

East
Bodean's (EC3)
Chicken Shop & Dirty
  Burger (E1)
The Hoxton Grill (EC2)

AUSTRALIAN
Central
Lantana Cafe (W1)

West
Granger & Co (W11)

East
Granger & Co (EC1)
Lantana Cafe (EC1)

BELGIAN
Central
Belgo (WC2)

North
Belgo Noord (NW1)

BRITISH, MODERN
Central
Alyn Williams (W1)*
Andrew Edmunds (W1)
The Angel & Crown (WC2)
The Ape & Bird (WC2)
Arbutus (W1)*
Athenaeum (W1)
Aurora (W1)
Axis (WC2)
Balthazar (WC2)
Bank Westminster (SW1)
Barnyard (W1)
Bellamy's (W1)
The Berners Tavern (W1)
The Blind Pig (W1)*
Bob Bob Ricard (W1)
The Botanist (SW1)
Brasserie Max (WC2)
Le Caprice (SW1)
Coopers Restaurant & Bar (WC2)
Criterion (W1)
Daylesford Organic (SW1,W1)
Dean Street Townhouse (W1)
Le Deuxième (WC2)
Dorchester Grill (W1)
Ducksoup (W1)
Ebury Rest' & Wine Bar (SW1)
Fera at Claridge's (W1)*
The Fifth Floor Restaurant (SW1)
Gordon's Wine Bar (WC2)
The Goring Hotel (SW1)
Grazing Goat (W1)
Ham Yard Restaurant (W1)
Hardy's Brasserie (W1)
Heddon Street Kitchen (W1)
Hix (W1)
Homage (WC2)
Hush (W1,WC1)
Indigo (WC2)
Inn the Park (SW1)
The Ivy (WC2)
Kettners (W1)
Langan's Brasserie (W1)
Little Social (W1)
Natural Kitchen (W1)
Newman Street Tavern (W1)
The Norfolk Arms (WC1)*
The Northall (SW1)
The Only Running Footman (W1)
The Orange (SW1)
Ozer (WC2)
The Pantechnicon (SW1)
Paramount (WC1)
Picture (W1)
Pollen Street Social (W1)*
The Portrait (WC2)
Quaglino's (W1)
The Queens Arms (SW1)*
Quo Vadis (W1)
Randall & Aubin (W1)*
Roux at Parliament Square (SW1)
Roux at the Landau (W1)
Seven Park Place (SW1)

Seven Stars (WC2)
1707 (W1)
Shampers (W1)
64 Degrees (SW1)
Social Eating House (W1)*
Sotheby's Café (W1)
Spring (WC2)
Tate Britain (Rex Whistler) (SW1)
10 Greek Street (W1)*
Thirty Six (SW1)
The Thomas Cubitt (SW1)
Tom's Kitchen (WC2)
Tredwell's (WC2)
The Union Café (W1)
Villandry (W1)
The Vincent Rooms (SW1)
Vinoteca (W1)
VQ (WC1)
Whyte & Brown (W1)
Wild Honey (W1)
The Wolseley (W1)

West

The Abingdon (W8)
The Anglesea Arms (W6)*
The Anglesea Arms (SW7)
Babylon (W8)
Beach Blanket Babylon (W11)
Belvedere (W8)
Bluebird (SW3)
The Brackenbury (W6)*
Brinkley's (SW10)
The Builders Arms (SW3)
Bush Dining Hall (W12)
The Cadogan Arms (SW3)
The Carpenter's Arms (W6)
City Barge (W4)*
Clarke's (W8)
The Cow (W2)
The Dartmouth Castle (W6)
Daylesford Organic (W11)
The Dock Kitchen (W10)
Duke of Sussex (W4)
The Enterprise (SW3)
First Floor (W11)
The Five Fields (SW3)*
The Frontline Club (W2)
Harwood Arms (SW6)*
The Havelock Tavern (W14)
Hedone (W4)*
The Henry Root (SW10)
High Road Brasserie (W4)
Hole in the Wall (W4)
Joe's Brasserie (SW6)
Julie's (W11)
Kensington Place (W8)*
Kensington Square Kitchen (W8)
Kitchen W8 (W8)*
The Ladbroke Arms (W11)
Launceston Place (W8)
The Ledbury (W11)*
The Magazine Restaurant (W2)
The Mall Tavern (W8)
Marianne (W2)*
Medlar (SW10)*
New Tom's (W11)

Paradise by Way of Kensal
   Green (W10)
Pavilion (W8)
The Phene (SW3)
Princess Victoria (W12)
Queen's Head (W6)
Rabbit (SW3)
Sam's Brasserie (W4)
The Sands End (SW6)*
The Shed (W8)
The Terrace (W8)
Tom's Kitchen (SW3)
Truscott Arms (W9)
VQ (SW10)
Vinoteca (W4)
The Waterway (W9)
White Horse (SW6)
Whits (W8)

North

The Albion (N1)
Bald Faced Stag (N2)
Bradley's (NW3)
The Bull (N6)
Caravan King's Cross (N1)
The Clissold Arms (N2)
The Drapers Arms (N1)
The Duke of Cambridge (N1)
The Engineer (NW1)
The Fellow (N1)
Frederick's (N1)
Grain Store (N1)
The Haven (N20)
The Horseshoe (NW3)
The Junction Tavern (NW5)
Juniper Dining (N5)
Landmark (Winter Gdn) (NW1)
LeCoq (N1)*
Made In Camden (NW1)
Mango Room (NW1)
Market (NW1)*
The North London Tavern (NW6)
Odette's (NW1)
The Old Bull & Bush (NW3)
Parlour (NW10)*
Pig & Butcher (N1)*
Plum + Spilt Milk (N1)
Rising Sun (NW7)
Rotunda Bar & Restaurant (N1)
St Pancras Grand (NW1)
Season Kitchen (N4)*
T.E.D (N1)
The Wells (NW3)
The Wet Fish Cafe (NW6)
White Rabbit (N16)*

South

Abbeville Kitchen (SW4)
Albion (SE1)
Aqua Shard (SE1)
The Bingham (TW10)
Bistro Union (SW4)
Blueprint Café (SE1)
The Bolingbroke (SW11)
The Brown Dog (SW13)
Brunswick House Cafe (SW8)
The Camberwell Arms (SE5)*

Cannizaro House (SW19)
Cantina Vinopolis (SE1)
Chapters (SE3)
Chez Bruce (SW17)*
Claude's Kitchen (SW6)*
The Crooked Well (SE5)
The Dairy (SW4)*
The Dartmouth Arms (SE23)
The Depot (SW14)
Earl Spencer (SW18)
Edwins (SE1)
Elliot's Cafe (SE1)*
Emile's (SW15)*
Entrée (SW11)*
40 Maltby Street (SE1)*
Franklins (SE22)
Garrison (SE1)
The Glasshouse (TW9)*
Inside (SE10)*
Lamberts (SW12)*
The Lido Cafe (SE24)
Linnea (TW9)*
Magdalen (SE1)*
Menier Chocolate Factory (SE1)
The Old Brewery (SE10)
Olympic Café (SW13)
Oxo Tower (Rest') (SE1)
The Palmerston (SE22)
Peckham Refreshment
   Rms (SE15)
Petersham Hotel (TW10)
Petersham Nurseries (TW10)
Le Pont de la Tour (SE1)
Rivington Grill (SE10)
RSJ (SE1)
Sea Containers (SE1)
Skylon (SE1)
Skylon Grill (SE1)
Sonny's Kitchen (SW13)
Source (SW11)
Story (SE1)*
The Swan at the Globe (SE1)
The Table (SE1)
Tate Modern (Level 7) (SE1)
The Dysart Petersham (TW10)*
Trinity (SW4)*
Union Street Café (SE1)
The Victoria (SW14)
Waterloo Bar & Kitchen (SE1)
The Wharf (TW11)

East

The Anthologist (EC2)
Balans (E20)
Beach Blanket Babylon (E1)
Bevis Marks (E1)
Bird (E2)*
Bird of Smithfield (EC1)
Bistrotheque (E2)
Blackfoot (EC1)
The Boundary (E2)
Bread Street Kitchen (EC4)
Caravan (EC1)
The Chancery (EC4)
Chiswell Street Dining Rms (EC1)
City Social (EC2)*
The Clove Club (EC1)*

The Don (EC4)
Duck & Waffle (EC2)
Eat 17 (E17)
The Empress (E9)
Foxlow (EC1)
Gin Joint (EC2)
The Gun (E14)
High Timber (EC4)
Hilliard (EC4)*
Hixter (EC2)
Hoi Polloi (E1)
The Jugged Hare (EC1)
Lyle's (E1)*
The Mercer (EC2)
Merchants Tavern (EC2)*
The Modern Pantry (EC1)
The Morgan Arms (E3)*
The Narrow (E14)
1901 (EC2)
Northbank (EC4)
Notes (EC2)
One Canada Square (E14)
1 Lombard Street (EC3)
The Peasant (EC1)
Princess of Shoreditch (EC2)
Raw Duck (E8)
Rivington Grill (EC2)
Rochelle Canteen (E2)*
Sager & Wilde (E2)
The Sign of the Don (EC4)
Smiths Brasserie (E1)
Smiths (Ground Floor) (EC1)
Street Kitchen (EC2)
3 South Place (EC2)
Tom's Kitchen (E1, E14)
Vinoteca (EC1)
The White Swan (EC4)*

BRITISH, TRADITIONAL
Central
Boisdale (SW1)
Browns (Albemarle) (W1)
Corrigan's Mayfair (W1)
Dinner (SW1)
The Fountain (Fortnum's) (W1)
Fuzzy's Grub (SW1)
Great Queen Street (WC2)
Green's (SW1)
The Guinea Grill (W1)
Hardy's Brasserie (W1)
Holborn Dining Room (WC1)
The Keeper's House (W1)
The Lady Ottoline (WC1)
The National Dining
   Rooms (WC2)
Rib Room (SW1)
Rules (WC2)
Savoy Grill (WC2)
Scott's (W1)*
Simpsons-in-the-Strand (WC2)
Strand Dining Rooms (WC2)
Wiltons (SW1)
The Windmill (W1)

West
The Brown Cow (SW6)*
Bumpkin (SW3, SW7, W11)

Ffiona's (W8)
The Hampshire Hog (W6)
Hereford Road (W2)
Maggie Jones's (W8)
The Malt House (SW6)*
The Surprise (SW3)

North
Bull & Last (NW5)*
Gilbert Scott (NW1)
Kentish Canteen (NW5)
St Johns (N19)

South
The Anchor & Hope (SE1)*
Butlers Wharf Chop House (SE1)
Canteen (SE1)
Canton Arms (SW8)
Fox & Grapes (SW19)
The Lord Northbrook (SE12)
Roast (SE1)

East
Albion (E2)
Bumpkin (E20)
Canteen (E1, E14)
The Fox and Anchor (EC1)
Fuzzy's Grub (EC4)
George & Vulture (EC3)
Hix Oyster & Chop House (EC1)
Paternoster Chop House (EC4)
E Pellicci (E2)
The Quality Chop House (EC1)*
St John (EC1)*
St John Bread & Wine (E1)*
Simpson's Tavern (EC3)
Sweetings (EC4)

EAST & CENT. EUROPEAN
Central
The Delaunay (WC2)
Gay Hussar (W1)
The Wolseley (W1)

North
Kipferl (N1)

FISH & SEAFOOD
Central
Belgo Centraal (WC2)
Bellamy's (W1)
Bentley's (W1)
Bonnie Gull (W1)*
Bubba Gump Shrimp
    Company (W1)
Burger & Lobster (W1)
Fishworks (W1)
Green's (SW1)
Kaspar's Seafood and Grill (WC2)
Loch Fyne (WC2)
Olivomare (SW1)*
One-O-One (SW1)*
The Pantechnicon (SW1)
Pescatori (W1)
Quaglino's (SW1)
Randall & Aubin (W1)*
Rib Room (SW1)

Royal China Club (W1)*
Scott's (W1)*
J Sheekey (WC2)*
J Sheekey Oyster Bar (WC2)*
Wiltons (SW1)
Wright Brothers (W1)*

West
Bibendum Oyster Bar (SW3)
Big Easy (SW3)
Le Café Anglais (W2)
Chez Patrick (W8)
The Cow (W2)
Geales (W8)
Kensington Place (W8)*
Mandarin Kitchen (W2)*
Outlaw's Seafood and
    Grill (SW3)*
Poissonnerie de l'Avenue (SW3)*
The Summerhouse (W9)

North
Belgo Noord (NW1)
Bradley's (NW3)
Carob Tree (NW5)*
Olympus Fish (N3)*
Prawn On The Lawn (N1)*
Simply Fish (NW1)
Toff's (N10)*

South
Applebee's Cafe (SE1)
Cornish Tiger (SW11)*
fish! (SE1)
Gastro (SW4)
The Lobster House (SW18)
Lobster Pot (SE11)*
Le Querce (SE23)*
Wright Brothers (SE1)*

East
Angler (EC2)
Bonnie Gull Seafood Cafe (EC1)*
Burger & Lobster (EC1)
Chamberlain's (EC3)
Fish Central (EC1)
Fish Market (EC2)
Forman's (E3)*
The Grapes (E14)
Hix Oyster & Chop House (EC1)
Loch Fyne (EC3)
Orpheus (EC3)*
The Royal Exchange Grand
    Café (EC3)
Sweetings (EC4)
Wright Brothers (E1)*

FRENCH
Central
Alain Ducasse (W1)
Antidote (W1)*
L'Artiste Musclé (W1)
L'Atelier de Joel Robuchon (WC2)
Aubaine (W1)
L'Autre Pied (W1)*
The Balcon (SW1)
Bar Boulud (SW1)

Bellamy's *(W1)*
Blanchette *(W1)*
Boudin Blanc *(W1)*
Boulestin *(SW1)*
Boulevard *(WC2)*
Brasserie Chavot *(W1)*
Brasserie Zédel *(W1)*
Café Bohème *(W1)*
Café des Amis *(WC2)*
Chabrot Bistrot d'Amis *(SW1)*
Le Cigalon *(WC2)*
Clos Maggiore *(WC2)**
Colbert *(SW1)*
Compagnie des Vins S. *(WC2)**
Les Deux Salons *(WC2)*
Elena's L'Etoile *(W1)*
L'Escargot *(W1)*
Galvin at Windows *(W1)*
Galvin Bistrot de Luxe *(W1)*
Le Garrick *(WC2)*
Gauthier Soho *(W1)**
Le Gavroche *(W1)**
Green Man & French
   Horn *(WC2)*
The Greenhouse *(W1)**
Hélène Darroze *(W1)*
Hibiscus *(W1)*
Koffmann's *(SW1)**
Marcus *(SW1)*
maze *(W1)*
Mon Plaisir *(WC2)*
Orrery *(W1)*
Otto's *(WC1)**
La Petite Maison *(W1)**
Pétrus *(SW1)**
Pied à Terre *(W1)**
La Poule au Pot *(SW1)*
Prix Fixe *(W1)*
Randall & Aubin *(W1)**
Le Relais de Venise
   L'Entrecôte *(W1)*
The Ritz Restaurant *(W1)*
Savoir Faire *(WC1)*
Savoy Grill *(WC2)*
Sketch (Lecture Rm) *(W1)*
Sketch (Gallery) *(W1)*
The Square *(W1)**
Terroirs *(WC2)*
28-50 *(W1)*
Villandry *(W1)*
The Wallace *(W1)*

West

Albertine *(W12)*
Angelus *(W2)*
Aubaine *(SW3, W8)*
Belvedere *(W8)*
Bibendum *(SW3)*
La Bouchée *(SW7)*
La Brasserie *(SW3)*
Le Café Anglais *(W2)*
Charlotte's Bistro *(W4)*
Charlotte's Place *(W5)*
Cheyne Walk Brasserie *(SW3)*
Chez Patrick *(W8)*
Le Colombier *(SW3)*
L'Etranger *(SW7)*

Garnier *(SW5)*
Gordon Ramsay *(SW3)*
Les Gourmets Des Ternes *(W9)*
The Pig's Ear *(SW3)*
Poissonnerie de l'Avenue *(SW3)**
Quantus *(W4)*
Racine *(SW3)*
La Trompette *(W4)**
Le Vacherin *(W4)*
Whits *(W8)*

North

L'Absinthe *(NW1)*
The Almeida *(N1)*
Les Associés *(N8)*
L'Aventure *(NW8)**
Bistro Aix *(N8)**
Blue Legume *(N1, N16, N8)*
Bradley's *(NW3)*
La Cage Imaginaire *(NW3)*
Le Coq *(N1)*
Le Mercury *(N1)*
Michael Nadra *(NW1)**
Mill Lane Bistro *(NW6)*
Oslo Court *(NW8)**
Le Sacré-Coeur *(N1)*
The Wells *(NW3)*

South

Augustine Kitchen *(SW11)**
Bellevue Rendez-Vous *(SW17)*
Brasserie Toulouse-Lautrec *(SE11)*
Brula *(TW1)**
La Buvette *(TW9)*
Casse-Croute *(SE1)**
Gastro *(SW4)*
Gazette *(SW11, SW12, SW15)*
The Lawn Bistro *(SW19)*
Lobster Pot *(SE11)**
Ma Cuisine *(TW9)*
Le P'tit Normand *(SW18)*
Soif *(SW11)**
Toasted *(SE22)*
Upstairs *(SW2)**

East

Bistrot Bruno Loubet *(EC1)*
Bleeding Heart *(EC1)*
Brawn *(E2)**
Café du Marché *(EC1)*
Café Pistou *(EC1)*
Cellar Gascon *(EC1)*
Chabrot Bistrot des Halles *(EC1)*
Club Gascon *(EC1)**
Comptoir Gascon *(EC1)*
Coq d'Argent *(EC2)*
The Don *(EC4)*
Galvin La Chapelle *(E1)**
Lutyens *(EC4)*
Plateau *(E14)*
Provender *(E11)**
Relais de Venise L'Entrecôte *(E14, EC2)*
The Royal Exchange Grand
   Café *(EC3)*
Sauterelle *(EC3)*
Les Trois Garçons *(E1)*

28-50 *(EC4)*

FUSION
Central
Bubbledogs Kitchen Table *(W1)**
Kopapa *(WC2)*
Providores (Tapa Room) *(W1)*
Uni *(SW1)**

West
E&O *(W11)*
Eight Over Eight *(SW3)*
L'Étranger *(SW7)*

North
XO *(NW3)*

South
Champor-Champor *(SE1)*
Tsunami *(SW4)**
Village East *(SE1)*

East
Caravan *(EC1)*
Penkul & Banks *(EC2)**

GAME
Central
Boisdale *(SW1)*
Rules *(WC2)*
Wiltons *(SW1)*

West
Harwood Arms *(SW6)**

North
San Daniele del Friuli *(N5)*

GREEK
Central
Ergon *(W1)**
Real Greek *(W1,WC2)*
21 Bateman Street *(W1)*

West
Halepi *(W2)*
Mazi *(W8)*
The Real Greek *(W12)*

North
Carob Tree *(NW5)**
Lemonia *(NW1)*
Vrisaki *(N22)*

South
Real Greek *(SE1)*

East
Kolossi Grill *(EC1)*
Real Greek *(E1)*

HUNGARIAN
Central
Gay Hussar *(W1)*

INTERNATIONAL
Central
Balans *(W1)*
Boulevard *(WC2)*
Café in the Crypt *(WC2)*
Canvas *(SW1)*
Colony Grill Room *(W1)*
Cork & Bottle *(WC2)*
Ember Yard *(W1)*
Fischer's *(W1)*
Gordon's Wine Bar *(WC2)*
Grumbles *(SW1)*
Carom at Meza *(W1)**
Motcombs *(SW1)*
National Gallery Café *(WC2)*
The Providores *(W1)**
Rextail *(W1)*
Rocket *(WC2)*
Sarastro *(WC2)*
Stock Pot *(SW1,W1)*
The 10 Cases *(WC2)*
Terroirs *(WC2)*

West
The Andover Arms *(W6)*
Annie's *(W4)*
Balans *(W12,W4,W8)*
Chelsea Bun Diner *(SW10)*
Eelbrook *(SW6)*
Foxtrot Oscar *(SW3)*
Gallery Mess *(SW3)*
The Kensington Wine
  Rooms *(W8)*
Margaux *(SW5)*
Michael Nadra *(W4)**
Mona Lisa *(SW10)*
The New Angel *(W2)**
One Kensington *(W8)*
Rivea *(SW7)*
Stock Pot *(SW3)*
Troubadour *(SW5)*
The Windsor Castle *(W8)*

North
Banners *(N8)*
8 Hoxton Square *(N1)*
The Haven *(N20)*
The Old Bull & Bush *(NW3)*
The Orange Tree *(N20)*
Primeur *(N5)*

South
Annie's *(SW13)*
Brigade *(SE1)*
Hudsons *(SW15)*
Joanna's *(SE19)*
The Light House *(SW19)*
London House *(SW11)**
Rabot 1745 *(SE1)*
The Rooftop Cafe *(SE1)*
The Ship *(SW18)*
Telegraph *(SW15)*
The Clink *(SW2)*
Ting *(SE1)*
Vivat Bacchus *(SE1)*
The Wharf *(TW11)*
The Yellow House *(SE16)*

East
LMNT *(E8)*
Les Trois Garçons *(E1)*
Typing Room *(E2)*
Verden *(E5)*
Vivat Bacchus *(EC4)*
The Wine Library *(EC3)*

IRISH
East
Lutyens *(EC4)*

ITALIAN
Central
Al Duca *(SW1)*
Alloro *(W1)*
Amico Bio *(WC1)*
Assunta Madre *(W1)*
Babbo *(W1)*
Il Baretto *(W1)*
Bocca Di Lupo *(W1)*
La Bottega *(SW1,WC2)*
Briciole *(W1)*
C London *(W1)*
Caffè Caldesi *(W1)*
Caffé Vergnano *(WC2)*
Caraffini *(SW1)*
Cecconi's *(W1)*
Ciao Bella *(WC1)*
Como Lario *(SW1)*
Il Convivio *(SW1)*
Da Mario *(WC2)*
Polpo *(WC2)*
Dehesa *(W1)*
Delfino *(W1)*
Franco's *(SW1)*
La Genova *(W1)*
Gustoso *(SW1)*
Latium *(W1)*
Locanda Locatelli *(W1)*
Made in Italy *(W1)*
Mele e Pere *(W1)*
Murano *(W1)*
Novikov (Italian restaurant) *(W1)*
Obika *(W1)*
Oliveto *(SW1)*
Olivo *(SW1)*
Olivocarne *(SW1)*
Olivomare *(SW1)*
Opera Tavern *(WC2)*
Orso *(WC2)*
Osteria Dell'Angolo *(SW1)*
Ottolenghi *(SW1)*
Pescatori *(W1)*
Piccolino *(W1)*
La Polenteria *(W1)*
Polpo *(W1)*
La Porchetta Pizzeria *(WC1)*
Princi *(W1)*
Quattro Passi *(W1)*
Quirinale *(SW1)*
Café Murano *(SW1)*
Rossopomodoro *(WC2)*
Sale e Pepe *(SW1)*
Salt Yard *(W1)*
San Carlo Cicchetti *(W1)*
Santini *(SW1)*

Sardo *(W1)*
Sartoria *(W1)*
Signor Sassi *(SW1)*
Theo Randall *(W1)*
Tinello *(SW1)*
Toto's *(SW1)*
Tozi *(SW1)*
2 Veneti *(W1)*
Vapiano *(W1)*
Vasco & Piero's Pavilion *(W1)*
Il Vicolo *(SW1)*
Zafferano *(SW1)*

West
Aglio e Olio *(SW10)*
L'Amorosa *(W6)*
Assaggi *(W2)*
Bird in Hand *(W14)*
La Bottega *(SW7)*
Buona Sera *(SW3)*
Canta Napoli *(W4)*
Cibo *(W14)*
Da Mario *(SW7)*
Daphne's *(SW3)*
La Delizia Limbara *(SW3)*
Edera *(W11)*
Essenza *(W11)*
La Famiglia *(SW10)*
Frantoio *(SW10)*
Locanda Ottomezzo *(W8)*
Lucio *(SW3)*
Made in Italy *(SW3)*
Manicomio *(SW3)*
Mediterraneo *(W11)*
Mona Lisa *(SW10)*
Napulé *(SW6)*
Nuovi Sapori *(SW6)*
The Oak W12 *(W12,W2)*
Obika *(SW3)*
Osteria Basilico *(W11)*
Ottolenghi *(W11,W8)*
Il Pagliaccio *(SW6)*
Pappa Ciccia *(SW6)*
Pellicano *(SW3)*
Pentolina *(W14)*
Polpo *(W1)*
Il Portico *(W8)*
Portobello Ristorante *(W11)*
The Red Pepper *(W9)*
Riccardo's *(SW3)*
The River Café *(W6)*
Rossopomodoro *(SW10)*
Santa Lucia *(SW10)*
Scalini *(SW3)*
Tartufo *(SW3)*
Ziani's *(SW3)*

North
Artigiano *(NW3)*
L'Artista *(NW11)*
Il Bacio *(N16, N5)*
La Collina *(NW1)*
Fabrizio *(N19)*
Fifteen *(N1)*
500 *(N19)*
Ostuni *(NW6)*
Ottolenghi *(N1)*

Pizzeria Oregano (N1)*
Pizzeria Pappagone (N4)
La Porchetta Pizzeria (N1, N4, NW1)
Rugoletta (N2)*
The Salt House (NW8)
San Daniele del Friuli (N5)
Sarracino (NW6)*
Trullo (N1)*
Villa Bianca (NW3)
Vivo (N1)*
York & Albany (NW1)

South
A Cena (TW1)
Al Forno (SW15, SW19)
Antico (SE1)*
Antipasto & Pasta (SW11)
Artusi (SE15)*
La Barca (SE1)
Bibo (SW15)*
Al Boccon di'vino (TW9)*
Buona Sera (SW11)
Canta Napoli (TW11)
Donna Margherita (SW11)*
Enoteca Turi (SW15)*
Lorenzo (SE19)
Numero Uno (SW11)
Osteria Antica Bologna (SW11)
Pizza Metro (SW11)*
Le Querce (SE23)*
Riva (SW13)
San Lorenzo Fuoriporta (SW19)
Sapori Sardi (SW6)*
The Table (SE1)
Tentazioni (SE1)
Vapiano (SE1)
Zucca (SE1)*

East
Amico Bio (EC1)
L'Anima (EC2)
L' Anima Cafe (EC2)
Apulia (EC1)
Il Bordello (E1)*
Coco Di Mama (EC4)*
Fabrizio (EC1)*
La Figa (E14)
Lardo (E8)
Manicomio (EC2)
Obika (E14)
E Pellicci (E2)
Piccolino (EC2)
Polpo (EC1)
La Porchetta Pizzeria (EC1)
Rotorino (E8)
Santore (EC1)*
Taberna Etrusca (EC4)

MEDITERRANEAN
Central
About Thyme (SW1)
Bistro 1 (W1, WC2)
Dabbous (W1)*
Hummus Bros (W1, WC1)
Massimo (SW1)
Nopi (W1)*

The Norfolk Arms (WC1)*
Riding House Café (W1)

West
The Atlas (SW6)*
Cumberland Arms (W14)*
Locanda Ottomezzo (W8)
Made in Italy (SW3)
Mediterraneo (W11)
Raoul's Cafe (W9)
Raoul's Café & Deli (W11, W6)
The Swan (W4)*
Troubadour (SW5)

North
Blue Legume (N16)
The Little Bay (NW6)

South
Cantina Vinopolis (SE1)
Fish in a Tie (SW11)
The Fox & Hounds (SW11)*
The Little Bay (SW11)
Oxo Tower (Brass') (SE1)
Peckham Bazaar (SE15)
The Wharf (TW11)

East
The Eagle (EC1)*
Hummus Bros (EC1, EC2)
The Little Bay (EC1)
Morito (EC1)*
Portal (EC1)
Rocket (E14, EC2)
Vinoteca (EC1)

ORGANIC
Central
Daylesford Organic (SW1, W1)

West
Daylesford Organic (W11)

North
The Duke of Cambridge (N1)

East
Smiths (Dining Rm) (EC1)

POLISH
West
Daquise (SW7)
Polish Club (SW7)
Patio (W12)

South
Baltic (SE1)

PORTUGUESE
West
Lisboa Pâtisserie (W10)*

East
Eyre Brothers (EC2)*
The Gun (E14)
Portal (EC1)

RUSSIAN
Central
Bob Bob Ricard (W1)

SCANDINAVIAN
Central
Nordic Bakery (W1)
Scandinavian Kitchen (W1)*
Texture (W1)

SCOTTISH
Central
Boisdale (SW1)

East
Boisdale of Canary Wharf (E14)

SPANISH
Central
Ametsa (SW1)
aqua nueva (W1)
Barrafina (W1,WC2)*
Barrica (W1)*
Bilbao Berria (SW1)
Cigala (WC1)
Copita (W1)
Dehesa (W1)*
Donostia (W1)*
Drakes Tabanco (W1)
Fino (W1)*
Goya (SW1)
Ibérica (W1)
Navarro's (W1)
Opera Tavern (WC2)*
El Pirata (W1)
Salt Yard (W1)
Tapas Brindisa Soho (W1)

West
Cambio de Tercio (SW5)*
Capote Y Toros (SW5)*
Casa Brindisa (SW7)
Duke of Sussex (W4)
Notting Hill Kitchen (W11)
El Pirata de Tapas (W2)
Tendido Cero (SW5)
Tendido Cuatro (SW6)*

North
Bar Esteban (N8)*
La Bota (N8)
Café del Parc (N19)*
Camino (N1)
El Parador (NW1)*

South
Alquimia (SW15)
Angels & Gypsies (SE5)
Boqueria (SW2)*
don Fernando's (TW9)
José (SE1)*
Lola Rojo (SW11)
Meson don Felipe (SE1)
Pizarro (SE1)
Tapas Brindisa (SE1, SW9)

East
Bravas (E1)*
Eyre Brothers (EC2)*
Ibérica (E14, EC1)
Morito (EC1)*
Moro (EC1)*
Tramontana Brindisa (EC2)

STEAKS & GRILLS
Central
Black & Blue (W1)
Bodean's (W1)
Christopher's (WC2)
Cut (W1)
Flat Iron (W1,WC2)*
Gaucho (W1)
Goodman (W1)
The Guinea Grill (W1)
Hawksmoor (W1,WC2)*
JW Steakhouse (W1)
MASH Steakhouse (W1)
maze Grill (W1)
Carom at Meza (W1)*
Le Relais de Venise
    L'Entrecôte (W1)
Rib Room (SW1)
Rowley's (SW1)
Sophie's Steakhouse (WC2)
STK Steakhouse (WC2)
34 (W1)
Wolfe's (WC2)

West
The Admiral Codrington (SW3)
Black & Blue (W8)
Bodean's (SW6)
Casa Malevo (W2)*
Gaucho (SW3)
Haché (SW10)
Hawksmoor
    Knightsbridge (SW3)*
Kings Road Steakhouse (SW3)
Maxela (SW7)*
PJ's Bar and Grill (SW3)
Popeseye (W14)
Sophie's Steakhouse (SW10)

North
Haché (NW1)
The Smokehouse Islington (N1)

South
Archduke Wine Bar (SE1)
Black & Blue (SE1)
Bodean's (SW4)
Buenos Aires Café (SE10, SE3)
Butcher & Grill (SW11)
Cattle Grid (SW12)
Cornish Tiger (SW11)*
Gaucho (SE1)
Popeseye (SW15)

East
Barbecoa (EC4)
Buen Ayre (E8)*
Clutch (E2)*
Gaucho (EC1)

Goodman *(E14)*
Goodman City *(EC2)*
Hawksmoor *(E1, EC2)**
Hill & Szrok *(E8)*
Hix Oyster & Chop House *(EC1)*
M *(EC2)*
New Street Grill *(EC2)*
Relais de Venise L'Entrecôte *(E14, EC2)*
Simpson's Tavern *(EC3)*
Smiths (Top Floor) *(EC1)*
Smiths (Dining Rm) *(EC1)*
Smiths (Ground Floor) *(EC1)*
The Tramshed *(EC2)*

VEGETARIAN
Central
Amico Bio *(WC1)*
Chettinad *(W1)*
Food for Thought *(WC2)**
Hummus Bros *(W1,WC1)*
Malabar Junction *(WC1)*
Masala Zone *(W1)*
Mildreds *(W1)**
Orchard *(WC1)*
Ragam *(W1)**
Rasa Maricham *(WC1)**
Sagar *(W1)*
tibits *(W1)*
Woodlands *(SW1,W1)*

West
The Gate *(W6)*
Masala Zone *(SW5,W2)*
Sagar *(W6)*

North
Chutneys *(NW1)*
Diwana Bhel-Poori House *(NW1)*
Jai Krishna *(N4)**
Manna *(NW3)*
Masala Zone *(N1)*
Rani *(N3)*
Rasa *(N16)**
Vijay *(NW6)*
Woodlands *(NW3)*

South
Blue Elephant *(SW6)*
Ganapati *(SE15)**
Le Pont de la Tour *(SE1)*
Sree Krishna *(SW17)**

East
Amico Bio *(EC1)*
The Gate *(EC1)*
Hummus Bros *(EC2)*
Vanilla Black *(EC4)*

AFTERNOON TEA
Central
Athenaeum *(W1)*
The Diamond Jub' Salon (Fortnum's) *(W1)*
The Fountain (Fortnum's) *(W1)*
La Fromagerie Café *(W1)*
Ladurée *(SW1,W1,WC2)*

Maison Bertaux *(W1)**
Notes *(WC2)*
Ritz (Palm Court) *(W1)*
Royal Academy *(W1)*
The Sketch (Parlour) *(W1)*
Villandry *(W1)*
The Wallace *(W1)*
The Wolseley *(W1)*
Yauatcha *(W1)**

North
Kenwood (Brew House) *(NW3)*
Landmark (Winter Gdn) *(NW1)*

South
Cannizaro House *(SW19)*
San Lorenzo Fuoriporta *(SW19)*

East
Ladurée *(EC3)*

BURGERS, ETC
Central
Bar Boulud *(SW1)*
Beast *(W1)*
Black & Blue *(W1)*
Bobo Social *(W1)*
Burger & Lobster *(SW1,W1)*
Diner *(W1,WC2)*
Dub Jam *(WC2)**
Ed's Easy Diner *(W1)*
Five Guys *(WC2)*
Goodman *(W1)*
Hard Rock Café *(W1)*
Hawksmoor *(W1,WC2)**
Honest Burgers *(W1)**
Joe Allen *(WC2)*
Kettners *(W1)*
MEATLiquor *(W1)*
MEATmarket *(WC2)**
Opera Tavern *(WC2)**
Patty and Bun *(W1)**
Shake Shack *(WC2)*
Tommi's Burger Joint *(W1)**
Wolfe's *(WC2)*

West
The Admiral Codrington *(SW3)*
Big Easy *(SW3)*
Black & Blue *(W8)*
Diner *(SW7)*
Haché *(SW10)*
Honest Burgers *(W11)**
Lucky Seven *(W2)*
Sticky Fingers *(W8)*
Tommi's Burger Joint *(SW3)**
Troubadour *(SW5)*

North
The Diner *(NW1)*
Dirty Burger *(NW5)**
Duke's Brew & Que *(N1)*
Ed's Easy Diner *(NW1)*
Haché *(NW1)*
Harry Morgan's *(NW8)*
Honest Burgers *(NW1)**
Meat Mission *(N1)**

253

Red Dog Saloon (N1)
The Rib Man (N1)*

South
Black & Blue (SE1)
Cattle Grid (SW12)
Dip & Flip (SW11)*
Dirty Burger (SW8)*
Ed's Easy Diner (SW18)
Haché (SW4)
Honest Burgers (SW17, SW9)*
The Old Brewery (SE10)
Village East (SE1)

East
Big Apple Hot Dogs (EC1)*
Burger & Lobster (EC1, EC4)
Comptoir Gascon (EC1)
The Diner (EC2)
Goodman (E14)
Goodman City (EC2)
Haché (EC2)
Hawksmoor (E1, EC2)*
Patty and Bun (EC2)*
Smiths (Dining Rm) (EC1)

FISH & CHIPS
Central
Golden Hind (W1)
North Sea Fish (WC1)
Seafresh (SW1)

West
Geales (W8)
Geales Chelsea Green (SW3)
Kerbisher & Malt (W5, W6)

North
The Fish & Chip Shop (N1)*
Nautilus (NW6)*
The Sea Shell (NW1)*
Skipjacks (HA3)*
Toff's (N10)*
Two Brothers (N3)

South
Brady's (SW18)
Fish Club (SW11, SW4)*
Kerbisher & Malt (SW14, SW4)
Masters Super Fish (SE1)*
Moxon's Fish Bar (SW12)*
Olley's (SE24)*
The Sea Cow (SE22)

East
Ark Fish (E18)*
Faulkner's (E8)*

ICE CREAM
Central
Gelupo (W1)*

PIZZA
Central
Il Baretto (W1)
Bianco43 (WC2)
Bocconcino (W1)

Delfino (W1)
Fire & Stone (WC2)
Homeslice (WC2)*
Kettners (W1)
Made in Italy (W1)
Oliveto (SW1)*
The Orange (SW1)
Piccolino (W1)
Pizza Pilgrims (W1)*
La Porchetta Pizzeria (WC1)
Princi (W1)
Rossopomodoro (WC2)

West
Basilico (SW6)*
Bird in Hand (W14)
Buona Sera (SW3)
Canta Napoli (W4)
Da Mario (SW7)
La Delizia Limbara (SW3)*
Fire & Stone (W12)
Franco Manca (W4)*
Made in Italy (SW3)
The Oak W12 (W12, W2)*
Osteria Basilico (W11)
Il Pagliaccio (SW6)
Pappa Ciccia (SW6)
Pizza East Portobello (W10)*
Portobello Ristorante (W11)
The Red Pepper (W9)*
Rocca Di Papa (SW7)
Rossopomodoro (SW10)
Santa Lucia (SW10)
Santa Maria (W5)*

North
Il Bacio (N16, N5)
Basilico (N1, N8, NW3)*
Fabrizio (N19)
Pizza East (NW5)*
Pizzeria Oregano (N1)*
Pizzeria Pappagone (N4)
La Porchetta Pizzeria (N1, N4, NW1)
Rossopomodoro (N1, NW1)
Sacro Cuore (NW10)*
Sweet Thursday (N1)

South
Al Forno (SW15, SW19)
Basilico (SW11)*
Bianco43 (SE10, SE3)
Buona Sera (SW11)
Donna Margherita (SW11)*
Eco (SW4)
Franco Manca (SW11, SW12, SW9)*
Gourmet Pizza Company (SE1)
The Gowlett (SE15)*
Lorenzo (SE19)
Pizza Metro (SW11)*
Pizzeria Rustica (TW9)*
Rocca Di Papa (SE21)
Rossopomodoro (SW18)
San Lorenzo Fuoriporta (SW19)
The Yellow House (SE16)
Zero Degrees (SE3)

East
Il Bordello *(E1)**
La Figa *(E14)*
Franco Manca *(E20)**
GB Pizza *(EC1)**
Piccolino *(EC2)*
Pizza East *(E1)**
La Porchetta Pizzeria *(EC1)*
Rocket *(E14, EC2)*
Story Deli *(E2)**
Yard Sale Pizza *(E5)*

SANDWICHES, CAKES, ETC
Central
The Attendant *(W1)**
Baker & Spice *(SW1)*
Bar Italia *(W1)*
Caffé Vergnano *(WC1)*
Fernandez & Wells *(W1, WC2)*
Flat White *(W1)**
Fleet River Bakery *(WC2)*
La Fromagerie Café *(W1)*
Fuzzy's Grub *(SW1)*
Kaffeine *(W1)*
Konditor & Cook *(W1, WC1)*
Ladurée *(SW1, W1)*
Maison Bertaux *(W1)**
Monmouth Coffee
   Company *(WC2)**
Natural Kitchen *(W1)*
Nordic Bakery *(W1)*
Notes *(WC2)*
Royal Academy *(W1)*
Scandinavian Kitchen *(W1)**
The Sketch (Parlour) *(W1)*
Taylor St Baristas *(W1)**
Villiers Coffee Co *(WC2)*

West
Baker & Spice *(SW3, W9)*
Lisboa Pâtisserie *(W10)**

North
Ginger & White *(NW3)*
Greenberry Cafe *(NW1)*
Kenwood (Brew House) *(NW3)*
Notes *(N7)*

South
Caffé Vergnano *(SE1)*
Fulham Wine Rooms *(SW6)*
Konditor & Cook *(SE1)*
Monmouth Coffee
   Company *(SE1, SE16)**
Orange Pekoe *(SW13)*
Spianata & Co *(SE1)**
Taylor St Baristas *(TW9)**

East
Brick Lane Beigel Bake *(E1)**
Caffé Vergnano *(EC4)*
Department of Coffee *(EC1)*
Dose *(EC1)**
Fuzzy's Grub *(EC2, EC3, EC4)*
Konditor & Cook *(EC3)*
Look Mum No Hands! *(EC1)*
Natural Kitchen *(EC4)*

Nusa Kitchen *(EC1, EC2)**
Prufrock Coffee *(EC1)**
Spianata & Co *(E1, EC1, EC2, EC4)**
Taylor St Baristas *(EC2, EC3)**
Workshop Coffee *(EC1)**

SALADS
Central
Kaffeine *(W1)*
Natural Kitchen *(W1)*

West
Beirut Express *(SW7, W2)**

East
Natural Kitchen *(EC3, EC4)*

ARGENTINIAN
Central
Gaucho *(W1)*
Zoilo *(W1)**

West
Casa Malevo *(W2)**
Gaucho *(SW3)*
Quantus *(W4)*

South
Buenos Aires Café *(SE10, SE3)*
Gaucho *(SE1)*

East
Buen Ayre *(E8)**
Gaucho *(EC1)*

BRAZILIAN
East
Sushisamba *(EC2)*

MEXICAN/TEXMEX
Central
Benito's Hat *(W1, WC2)*
La Bodega Negra *(W1)*
Cantina Laredo *(WC2)**
Chilango *(WC2)*
Chipotle *(W1, WC2)*
Lupita *(WC2)*
Peyote *(W1)*
Wahaca *(W1, WC2)*

West
Taqueria *(W11)*

North
Benito's Hat *(N1)*
Chilango *(N1)*
Chipotle *(N1)*
Wahaca *(N1)*

South
Wahaca *(SE1)*

East
Benito's Hat *(EC1)*
Chilango *(E1, EC2, EC4)*
Daddy Donkey *(EC1)**
DF Mexico *(E1)*

PERUVIAN
Central
Ceviche *(W1)**
Coya *(W1)**
Lima *(W1)**
Lima Floral *(WC2)*
Pachamama *(W1)*

East
Andina *(E2)**
Sushisamba *(EC2)*

SOUTH AMERICAN
West
Quantus *(W4)*

South
El Vergel *(SE1)**

AFRO-CARIBBEAN
Central
Jamaica Patty Co. *(WC2)*

North
Mango Room *(NW1)*

MOROCCAN
West
Adams Café *(W12)*

NORTH AFRICAN
Central
Momo *(W1)*

West
Azou *(W6)**

SOUTH AFRICAN
Central
Bunnychow *(W1)*

East
Bunnychow *(E1)*

TUNISIAN
West
Adams Café *(W12)*

EGYPTIAN
North
Ali Baba *(NW1)*

ISRAELI
Central
Gaby's *(WC2)*
The Palomar *(W1)**

North
Solly's *(NW11)*

KOSHER
Central
Reubens *(W1)*

North
Kaifeng *(NW4)*
Solly's *(NW11)*

Zest *(NW3)*

East
Bevis Marks *(E1)*
Brick Lane Beigel Bake *(E1)**

LEBANESE
Central
Al Hamra *(W1)*
Al Sultan *(W1)*
Beiteddine *(SW1)*
Comptoir Libanais *(W1)*
Fairuz *(W1)**
Levant *(W1)*
Maroush *(W1)**
Noura *(SW1,W1)*
Yalla Yalla *(W1)*

West
Al-Waha *(W2)*
Beirut Express *(SW7,W2)**
Chez Abir *(W14)**
Comptoir Libanais *(SW7,W12)*
Maroush *(W2)**
Maroush *(SW3)**
Ranoush *(SW3,W2,W8)**

South
Arabica Bar and Kitchen *(SE1)*
Meza *(SW17)**
Palmyra *(TW9)**

East
Comptoir Libanais *(E20)*
Yalla Yalla *(E1)*

MIDDLE EASTERN
Central
Honey & Co *(W1)**
Patogh *(W1)*

North
Solly's *(NW11)*

East
Morito *(EC1)**
Nusa Kitchen *(EC4)**
Pilpel *(E1, EC4)**
1701 *(EC3)**

PERSIAN
West
Alounak *(W14,W2)*
Faanoos *(W4)*
Kateh *(W9)**
Sufi *(W12)*

North
Gilak *(N19)*

South
Faanoos *(SW14)*

SYRIAN
West
Abu Zaad *(W12)*

TURKISH
Central
Cyprus Mangal *(SW1)**
Ishtar *(W1)*
Kazan *(SW1)*
Sofra *(W1,WC2)*
Tas *(WC1)*

West
Best Mangal *(SW6,W14)**
Fez Mangal *(W11)**

North
Antepliler *(N1, N4)*
Gallipoli *(N1)*
Gem *(N1)*
Izgara *(N3)*
Mangal II *(N16)*

South
Ev Restaurant, Bar & Deli *(SE1)*
Tas Pide *(SE1)*

East
Haz *(E1, EC2, EC3)*
Mangal I *(E8)**
Tas *(EC1)*

AFGHANI
North
Afghan Kitchen *(N1)**

BURMESE
West
Mandalay *(W2)*

CHINESE
Central
A Wong *(SW1)**
Ba Shan *(W1)**
Baozi Inn *(WC2)*
Bar Shu *(W1)**
The Bright Courtyard *(W1)*
Chilli Cool *(WC1)**
China Tang *(W1)*
Er Mei *(WC2)**
The Four Seasons *(W1)**
Golden Dragon *(W1)*
The Grand Imperial *(SW1)*
Hakkasan Mayfair *(W1)**
Harbour City *(W1)*
Hunan *(SW1)**
Joy King Lau *(WC2)*
Kai Mayfair *(W1)**
Ken Lo's Memories *(SW1)*
Mr Chow *(SW1)*
Mr Kong *(WC2)*
New Mayflower *(W1)**
New World *(W1)*
Plum Valley *(W1)**
Princess Garden *(W1)**
Royal China *(W1)**
Royal China Club *(W1)**
Shanghai Blues *(WC1)**
Wong Kei *(W1)*
Yauatcha *(W1)**
Yming *(W1)**

West
The Four Seasons *(W2)**
Gold Mine *(W2)*
Good Earth *(SW3)*
Mandarin Kitchen *(W2)**
Min Jiang *(W8)**
North China *(W3)**
Pearl Liang *(W2)*
Royal China *(SW6,W2)**
Taiwan Village *(SW6)**

North
Good Earth *(NW7)*
Green Cottage *(NW3)*
Gung-Ho *(NW6)*
Kaifeng *(NW4)*
Phoenix Palace *(NW1)*
Singapore Garden *(NW6)**
Yipin China *(N1)**

South
Dalchini *(SW19)*
Dragon Castle *(SE17)*
Four Regions *(TW9)*
Good Earth *(SW17)*
Hutong *(SE1)*
Silk Road *(SE5)**

East
Chinese Cricket Club *(EC4)**
Gourmet San *(E2)**
HKK *(EC2)**
Lotus Chinese Floating
   Restaurant *(E14)*
Royal China *(E14)**
Shanghai *(E8)*
Sichuan Folk *(E1)**
Yi-Ban *(E16)**

CHINESE, DIM SUM
Central
The Bright Courtyard *(W1)*
dim T *(W1)*
Golden Dragon *(W1)*
The Grand Imperial *(SW1)*
Hakkasan Mayfair *(W1)**
Harbour City *(W1)*
Joy King Lau *(WC2)*
Leong's Legends *(W1)*
New World *(W1)*
ping pong *(W1)*
Princess Garden *(W1)**
Royal China *(W1)**
Royal China Club *(W1)**
Shanghai Blues *(WC1)**
Yauatcha *(W1)**

West
Bo Lang *(SW3)*
Min Jiang *(W8)**
Pearl Liang *(W2)*
ping pong *(W2)*
Royal China *(SW6,W2)**

North
dim T *(N6, NW3)*
Phoenix Palace *(NW1)*

South
dim T (SE1)
Dragon Castle (SE17)
ping pong (SE1)

East
Lotus Chinese Floating
  Restaurant (E14)
ping pong (EC4)
Royal China (E14)*
Shanghai (E8)
Yi-Ban (E16)*

GEORGIAN
Central
Marani (W1)

North
Little Georgia Café (N1)

East
Little Georgia Café (E2)

INDIAN
Central
Amaya (SW1)*
Benares (W1)
Chettinad (W1)
Chor Bizarre (W1)*
The Cinnamon Club (SW1)
Cinnamon Soho (W1)*
Dishoom (WC2)*
Gaylord (W1)
Gymkhana (W1)*
Imli Street (W1)
India Club (WC2)
Malabar Junction (WC1)
Masala Zone (W1,WC2)
Mint Leaf (SW1)
Moti Mahal (WC2)*
La Porte des Indes (W1)
Punjab (WC2)
Ragam (W1)*
Red Fort (W1)
Roti Chai (W1)*
Sagar (W1,WC2)
Salaam Namaste (WC1)
Salloos (SW1)*
Tamarind (W1)*
Trishna (W1)*
Veeraswamy (W1)*
Woodlands (SW1,W1)
Zayna (W1)*

West
Anarkali (W6)
Bombay Brasserie (SW7)*
Bombay Palace (W2)*
Brilliant (UB2)
Chakra (W11)
Chutney Mary (SW10)*
Durbar (W2)
Gifto's (UB1)
The Greedy Buddha (SW6)
Indian Zing (W6)*
Karma (W14)*
Khan's (W2)*

Madhu's (UB1)*
Malabar (W8)*
Masala Zone (SW5,W2)
Miran Masala (W14)*
Mirch Masala (UB1)
Noor Jahan (SW5,W2)*
The Painted Heron (SW10)*
Potli (W6)*
Rasoi (SW3)*
Sagar (W6)
Star of India (SW5)*
Thali (SW5)*

North
Chutneys (NW1)
Delhi Grill (N1)*
Dishoom (N1)*
Diwana Bhel-Poori House (NW1)
Eriki (NW3)*
Great Nepalese (NW1)
Guglee (NW3, NW6)
Indian Rasoi (N2)*
Jai Krishna (N4)*
Kadiri's (NW10)*
Masala Zone (N1)
Paradise Hampstead (NW3)*
Rani (N3)
Ravi Shankar (NW1)*
Roots at N1 (N1)*
Vijay (NW6)
Woodlands (NW3)
Zaffrani (N1)*

South
Apollo Banana Leaf (SW17)*
Babur (SE23)*
Bengal Clipper (SE1)
Chutney (SW18)*
Dalchini (SW19)
Everest Inn (SE3)*
Ganapati (SE15)*
Holy Cow (SW11)*
Hot Stuff (SW8)
Indian Moment (SW11)
Indian Ocean (SW17)*
Indian Zilla (SW13)*
Kennington Tandoori (SE11)*
Lahore Karahi (SW17)*
Lahore Kebab House (SW16)*
Ma Goa (SW15)*
Mango Food of India (SE1)
Mirch Masala (SW16, SW17)
Nazmins (SW18)
Sree Krishna (SW17)*
Tandoori Nights (SE22)

East
Café Spice Namaste (E1)*
Cinnamon Kitchen (EC2)*
Dishoom (E2)*
Lahore Kebab House (E1)*
Mint Leaf (EC2)
Mirch Masala (E1)
Needoo (E1)*
Tayyabs (E1)*

INDIAN, SOUTHERN
Central
India Club *(WC2)*
Malabar Junction *(WC1)*
Quilon *(SW1)*
Ragam *(W1)*
Rasa Maricham *(WC1)**
Rasa Samudra *(W1)**
Sagar *(W1,WC2)*
Woodlands *(SW1,W1)*

West
Sagar *(W6)*
Shilpa *(W6)*

North
Chutneys *(NW1)*
Rani *(N3)*
Rasa *(N16)**
Vijay *(NW6)*
Woodlands *(NW3)*

South
Ganapati *(SE15)**
Sree Krishna *(SW17)**

JAPANESE
Central
Abeno *(WC1,WC2)*
aqua kyoto *(W1)*
Atari-Ya *(W1)**
Bone Daddies *(W1)*
Chisou *(W1)**
Chotto Matte *(W1)**
Defune *(W1)*
Dinings *(W1)**
Eat Tokyo *(WC1,WC2)**
Flesh and Buns *(WC2)*
Hazuki *(WC2)*
Ippudo London *(WC2)*
Kiku *(W1)**
Kikuchi *(W1)**
Koya *(W1)**
Koya-Bar *(W1)**
Kulu Kulu *(W1,WC2)*
Matsuri *(SW1)*
Nizuni *(W1)**
Nobu *(W1)**
Nobu Berkeley *(W1)*
Roka *(W1,WC2)**
Sakana-tei *(W1)**
Sake No Hana *(SW1)*
Sakura *(W1)*
Shoryu Ramen *(SW1,W1)*
Sticks'n'Sushi *(WC2)*
Sumosan *(W1)*
Taro *(W1)*
Tokyo Diner *(WC2)*
Tonkotsu *(W1)*
Tsunami *(W1)**
Umu *(W1)*
Yoisho *(W1)*
Yoshino *(W1)*

West
Atari-Ya *(W5)**
Chisou *(SW3,W4)**

Eat Tokyo *(W6,W8)**
Inaho *(W2)**
Kiraku *(W5)**
Kulu Kulu *(SW7)*
Kurobuta *(W2)**
Maguro *(W9)**
The Shiori *(W2)**
Tosa *(W6)**
Yashin *(W8)**
Yashin Ocean House *(SW7)*
Zuma *(SW7)**

North
Akari *(N1)**
Asakusa *(NW1)**
Atari-Ya *(NW4, NW6)**
Bento Cafe *(NW1)**
Dotori *(N4)**
Eat Tokyo *(NW11)**
Jin Kichi *(NW3)**
Sushi-Say *(NW2)**

South
Fujiyama *(SW9)**
Hashi *(SW20)**
Matsuba *(TW9)**
Sticks'n'Sushi *(SW19)*
Tsunami *(SW4)**

East
City Miyama *(EC4)*
K10 *(EC2)**
Pham Sushi *(EC1)**
Roka *(E14)**
Sushisamba *(EC2)*
Sushi Tetsu *(EC1)**
Tajima Tei *(EC1)*
Tonkotsu East *(E8)*

KOREAN
Central
Asadal *(WC1)*
Bibimbap Soho *(W1)*
Kimchee *(WC1)**
Koba *(W1)*

North
Dotori *(N4)**

South
Cah-Chi *(SW18, SW20)**

East
On The Bab *(EC1)**

MALAYSIAN
Central
C&R Cafe *(W1)**
Spice Market *(W1)*

West
Satay House *(W2)*

North
Singapore Garden *(NW6)**

South
Champor-Champor (SE1)

PAKISTANI
Central
Salloos (SW1)*

West
Miran Masala (W14)*
Mirch Masala (UB1)

South
Lahore Karahi (SW17)*
Lahore Kebab House (SW16)*
Mirch Masala (SW16, SW17)

East
Lahore Kebab House (E1)*
Mirch Masala (E1)
Needoo (E1)*
Tayyabs (E1)*

PAN-ASIAN
Central
Banana Tree Canteen (W1)
Buddha-Bar London (SW1)
dim T (SW1,W1)
East Street (W1)
Hare & Tortoise (WC1)
Inamo (SW1,W1)
The Noodle House (WC2)
Novikov (Asian restaurant) (W1)
Spice Market (W1)

West
Banana Tree Canteen (W2,W9)
E&O (W11)
Eight Over Eight (SW3)
Hare & Tortoise (W14,W5)

North
dim T (N6, NW3)
Gilgamesh (NW1)
XO (NW3)

South
The Banana Tree Canteen (SW11)
dim T (SE1)
Hare & Tortoise (SW15)

East
Banana Tree Canteen (EC1)
Hare & Tortoise (EC4)

THAI
Central
Busaba Eathai (SW1,W1,WC2)
C&R Cafe (W1)*
Crazy Bear (W1)
Mango Tree (SW1)
Patara (W1)
Spice Market (W1)
Thai Square (WC2)

West
Addie's Thai Café (SW5)
Bangkok (SW7)

C&R Cafe (W2)*
Café 209 (SW6)
Churchill Arms (W8)
Esarn Kheaw (W12)*
Fat Boy's (W4,W5)
Fitou's Thai Restaurant (W10)*
101 Thai Kitchen (W6)*
Patara (SW3)
Sukho Fine Thai Cuisine (SW6)*
Thai Square (SW7)

North
Isarn (N1)*
Thai Square (N1)
Yum Yum (N16)

South
The Begging Bowl (SE15)*
Blue Elephant (SW6)
Fat Boy's (SW14,TW1,TW8)
Kaosarn (SW11, SW9)*
The Paddyfield (SW12)
The Pepper Tree (SW4)*
Suk Saran (SW19)*
Talad Thai (SW15)
Thai Corner Café (SE22)

East
Busaba Eathai (EC1)
Elephant Royale (E14)
Thai Square City (EC3)

VIETNAMESE
Central
Bam-Bou (W1)
Cây Tre (W1)
House of Ho (W1)*
Pho (W1)

West
Pho (W12)
Saigon Saigon (W6)

North
Huong-Viet (N1)
Salvation In Noodles (N1)*

South
Cafe East (SE16)*
Mien Tay (SW11)*
The Paddyfield (SW12)

East
Cây Tre (EC1)
City Càphê (EC2)*
Mien Tay (E2)*
Pho (E1, EC1)
Sông Quê (E2)
Viet Grill (E2)*

AREA OVERVIEWS

CENTRAL

Soho, Covent Garden & Bloomsbury
(Parts of W1, all WC2 and WC1)

£80+			
L'Atelier de Joel Robuchon	French		3 3 3
MASH Steakhouse	Steaks & grills		3 3 2
Roka	Japanese		5 3 4

£70+			
Christopher's	American		3 2 3
Brasserie Max	British, Modern		3 4 3
Homage	"		1 1 2
The Ivy	"		2 3 3
Paramount	"		2 2 4
Rules	British, Traditional		3 4 5
Savoy Grill	"		2 3 3
Simpsons-in-the-Strand	"		1 2 2
Kaspar's Seafood and Grill	Fish & seafood		3 3 3
J Sheekey	"		4 4 4
Yauatcha	Chinese		4 2 3
aqua kyoto	Japanese		2 2 2
Spice Market	Pan-Asian		2 3 3

£60+			
Axis	British, Modern		2 2 3
Balthazar	"		1 2 4
Bob Bob Ricard	"		3 4 5
Hix	"		2 2 2
Indigo	"		2 3 3
Kettners	"		2 2 3
Social Eating House	"		4 4 5
Tom's Kitchen	"		2 1 1
Strand Dining Rooms	British, Traditional		2 4 3
J Sheekey Oyster Bar	Fish & seafood		4 5 5
Clos Maggiore	French		4 5 5
L'Escargot	"		– – –
Gauthier Soho	"		5 5 4
Bocca Di Lupo	Italian		5 4 4
aqua nueva	Spanish		2 2 2
Hawksmoor	Steaks & grills		4 4 3
STK Steakhouse	"		2 2 2
Ladurée	Afternoon tea		2 2 2
Shanghai Blues	Chinese		4 2 4
Moti Mahal	Indian		4 4 3
Red Fort	"		3 3 2

£50+			
Big Easy	American		2 2 2
Jamie's Diner	"		2 1 2
Joe Allen	"		1 2 4
Arbutus	British, Modern		4 4 2
Aurora	"		3 3 4
Coopers	"		3 3 3

Dean Street Townhouse	"	3 3 4
Le Deuxième	"	2 2 1
Ducksoup	"	2 2 3
Ham Yard Restaurant	"	2 2 2
Hush	"	2 2 3
The Portrait	"	2 2 4
Quo Vadis	"	3 4 4
Holborn Dining Room	British, Traditional	2 2 3
The Lady Ottoline	"	2 2 3
The National Dining Rms	"	1 1 2
The Delaunay	East & Cent. Euro	3 4 5
Wright Brothers	Fish & seafood	4 3 3
Antidote	French	5 4 3
Café des Amis	"	1 2 2
Compagnie des Vins S.	"	4 2 2
Les Deux Salons	"	1 2 2
Mon Plaisir	"	2 3 4
Otto's	"	4 5 4
Randall & Aubin	"	4 4 5
Kopapa	Fusion	2 2 2
Ember Yard	International	3 3 3
Sarastro	"	1 3 3
The 10 Cases	"	2 3 3
Mele e Pere	Italian	2 2 2
Orso	"	3 3 2
Vasco & Piero's Pavilion	"	4 4 3
Nopi	Mediterranean	5 4 4
Sophie's Steakhouse	Steaks & grills	2 3 2
Cantina Laredo	Mexican/TexMex	4 4 3
Lima Floral	Peruvian	– – –
Bar Shu	Chinese	4 1 2
Chotto Matte	Japanese	4 2 4
Flesh and Buns	"	3 2 2
Patara	Thai	3 3 3
House of Ho	Vietnamese	4 3 2
£40+ Bodean's	American	2 2 2
Jackson & Rye	"	1 1 2
Mishkin's	"	1 2 3
Spuntino	"	2 3 5
Belgo	Belgian	2 4 3
Andrew Edmunds	British, Modern	3 4 5
The Angel & Crown	"	2 2 3
The Ape & Bird	"	– – –
The Norfolk Arms	"	4 3 2
Shampers	"	2 4 5
10 Greek Street	"	5 5 3
Vinoteca	"	2 4 4
VQ	"	2 3 2
Great Queen Street	British, Traditional	3 3 3
Loch Fyne	Fish & seafood	2 2 2
Café Bohème	French	2 3 4

Le Cigalon	"		3 3 3
Le Garrick	"		2 2 3
Green Man & French Horn	"		3 4 4
Terroirs	"		3 2 3
Real Greek	Greek		2 2 2
Gay Hussar	Hungarian		2 3 4
Balans	International		2 4 3
Boulevard	"		2 3 3
Cork & Bottle	"		2 3 4
National Gallery Café	"		3 1 2
Rocket	"		3 3 3
Ciao Bella	Italian		2 4 3
Da Mario	"		2 2 3
Dehesa	"		4 3 4
Made in Italy	"		3 3 4
Obika	"		2 2 1
San Carlo Cicchetti	"		3 3 3
Barrafina	Spanish		5 5 5
Cigala	"		3 3 2
Copita	"		3 2 4
Opera Tavern	"		4 4 4
Tapas Brindisa Soho	"		3 2 3
Mildreds	Vegetarian		4 3 4
Orchard	"		3 3 3
Burger & Lobster	Burgers, etc		3 2 3
Wolfe's	"		3 4 3
Bianco43	Pizza		3 2 2
Fire & Stone	"		2 2 2
Villiers Coffee Co	Sandwiches, cakes, etc		– – –
La Bodega Negra	Mexican/TexMex		2 3 4
Ceviche	Peruvian		4 3 3
The Palomar	Israeli		4 5 4
Ba Shan	Chinese		4 1 2
Harbour City	"		2 1 1
New Mayflower	"		4 3 2
Plum Valley	"		4 2 3
Yming	"		4 5 3
Cinnamon Soho	Indian		4 3 2
Dishoom	"		4 3 4
Malabar Junction	"		3 2 3
Abeno	Japanese		3 3 2
Hazuki	"		2 2 2
Sticks'n'Sushi	"		3 3 3
Asadal	Korean		3 2 2
Inamo	Pan-Asian		2 2 2
Thai Square	Thai		2 2 2
£35+			
Soho Diner	American		2 3 4
The Blind Pig	British, Modern		4 4 4
Whyte & Brown	"		3 4 4
Blanchette	French		3 5 4
Brasserie Zédel	"		2 4 5

Prix Fixe	"	3	4	4
Savoir Faire	"	3	3	2
21 Bateman Street	Greek	3	4	4
Polpo	Italian	2	3	5
La Polenteria	"	3	4	3
Amico Bio	Vegetarian	2	2	2
Honest Burgers	Burgers, etc	4	4	4
North Sea Fish	Fish & chips	3	3	2
Rossopomodoro	Pizza	2	2	2
Lupita	Mexican/TexMex	3	2	3
Gaby's	Israeli	3	3	2
Yalla Yalla	Lebanese	3	3	4
Sofra	Turkish	2	3	3
Tas	"	2	3	3
Er Mei	Chinese	4	4	3
Joy King Lau	"	3	2	2
New World	"	3	2	3
Leong's Legends	Chinese, Dim sum	3	2	3
Imli Street	Indian	3	4	4
Sagar	"	3	2	2
Salaam Namaste	"	3	3	2
Rasa Maricham	Indian, Southern	4	4	3
Koya	Japanese	4	4	3
Taro	"	2	3	2
Kimchee	Korean	4	2	3
Banana Tree Canteen	Pan-Asian	2	2	2
The Noodle House	"	–	–	–
Busaba Eathai	Thai	2	2	4
Cây Tre	Vietnamese	3	3	3
Pho	"	3	3	3

£30+ Seven Stars	British, Modern	3	2	4
Café in the Crypt	International	2	2	3
Gordon's Wine Bar	"	2	3	5
Carom at Meza	"	4	4	3
Caffé Vergnano	Italian	3	3	3
La Porchetta Pizzeria	"	3	3	3
Princi	"	3	2	4
Diner	Burgers, etc	1	3	3
Ed's Easy Diner	"	1	2	3
MEATmarket	"	4	2	2
Caffé Vergnano	Sandwiches, cakes, etc	3	3	3
Fernandez & Wells	"	3	2	4
Wahaca	Mexican/TexMex	2	3	4
Chilli Cool	Chinese	4	1	1
The Four Seasons	"	4	1	1
Golden Dragon	"	3	2	2
Mr Kong	"	3	3	3
Wong Kei	"	–	–	–
ping pong	Chinese, Dim sum	2	2	3
Masala Zone	Indian	3	4	3
Koya-Bar	Japanese	4	4	4

	Kulu Kulu	"	3	1	1
	Tonkotsu	"	3	3	3
	Bibimbap Soho	Korean	3	3	3
	Hare & Tortoise	Pan-Asian	3	2	3
	C&R Cafe	Thai	4	2	2
£25+	Pitt Cue Co	American	5	4	4
	Bar Italia	Sandwiches, cakes, etc	3	4	5
	Konditor & Cook	"	3	4	2
	Benito's Hat	Mexican/TexMex	3	4	2
	Comptoir Libanais	Lebanese	2	2	2
	India Club	Indian	3	2	1
	Punjab	"	3	3	3
	Shoryu Ramen	Japanese	3	2	3
	Tokyo Diner	"	2	2	3
£20+	Bistro 1	Mediterranean	2	4	4
	Flat Iron	Steaks & grills	4	5	4
	Food for Thought	Vegetarian	4	4	2
	Dub Jam	Burgers, etc	4	4	3
	Shake Shack	"	2	2	2
	Homeslice	Pizza	5	3	2
	Pizza Pilgrims	"	4	4	4
	Fleet River Bakery	Sandwiches, cakes, etc	3	2	3
	Bone Daddies	Japanese	3	4	4
	Eat Tokyo	"	4	2	2
£15+	La Bottega	Italian	3	4	4
	Hummus Bros	Mediterranean	3	3	2
	Nordic Bakery	Scandinavian	3	3	3
	Maison Bertaux	Afternoon tea	4	2	3
	Notes	Sandwiches, cakes, etc	2	4	4
	Chilango	Mexican/TexMex	3	2	2
	Chipotle	"	3	3	2
	Baozi Inn	Chinese	3	2	2
£10+	Five Guys	Burgers, etc	3	2	2
	Gelupo	Ice cream	5	2	3
	Flat White	Sandwiches, cakes, etc	4	4	4
	Monmouth Coffee Co	"	5	5	4
	Jamaica Patty Co.	Afro-Caribbean	3	2	2
	Bunnychow	South African	–	–	–

Mayfair & St James's (Parts of W1 and SW1)

£150+	Quattro Passi	Italian	2	2	2
£140+	Fera at Claridge's	British, Modern	4	5	5

Price	Restaurant	Cuisine	Ratings
£130+	Le Gavroche	French	5 5 5
£120+	Alain Ducasse	French	2 3 2
	The Greenhouse	"	4 4 4
	Hélène Darroze	"	2 3 4
	Hibiscus	"	3 3 2
	The Ritz Restaurant	"	3 4 5
	Sketch (Lecture Rm)	"	2 2 3
£110+	The Square	French	4 4 3
	Cut	Steaks & grills	2 2 2
£100+	Wiltons	British, Traditional	3 4 4
	C London	Italian	1 1 2
	Novikov (Italian restaurant)	"	1 1 1
	Umu	Japanese	2 1 2
	Novikov (Asian restaurant)	Pan-Asian	1 2 3
£90+	Dorchester Grill	British, Modern	2 3 1
	Seven Park Place	"	3 4 4
	Galvin at Windows	French	2 3 5
	Murano	Italian	4 4 4
	Kai Mayfair	Chinese	4 4 2
	Benares	Indian	3 3 3
	Nobu, Park Ln	Japanese	4 2 2
	Nobu, Berkeley St	"	3 2 2
£80+	Alyn Williams	British, Modern	4 4 2
	Athenaeum	"	3 3 3
	Pollen Street Social	"	4 4 3
	Thirty Six	"	2 2 1
	Browns (Albemarle)	British, Traditional	2 3 3
	Corrigan's Mayfair	"	2 2 2
	Bentley's	Fish & seafood	3 3 3
	Scott's	"	4 5 4
	maze	French	2 2 2
	La Petite Maison	"	4 3 4
	Sketch (Gallery)	"	1 2 4
	Assunta Madre	Italian	3 2 2
	Theo Randall	"	3 2 2
	Rextail	International	1 2 2
	The Sketch (Parlour)	Sandwiches, cakes, etc	2 2 4
	Hakkasan Mayfair	Chinese	4 2 4
	Matsuri	Japanese	3 3 1
	Roka	"	5 3 4
£70+	Le Caprice	British, Modern	3 4 4
	Little Social	"	3 3 3
	Green's	British, Traditional	3 4 4
	Babbo	Italian	2 2 2
	Cecconi's	"	2 2 4

			Rating		
	Franco's	"	3	4	3
	Gaucho	Steaks & grills	2	1	1
	JW Steakhouse	"	2	2	2
	maze Grill	"	1	1	1
	34	"	3	3	3
	Coya	Peruvian	4	2	3
	Momo	North African	2	2	5
	China Tang	Chinese	2	2	3
	Tamarind	Indian	4	4	3
	Veeraswamy	"	4	4	4
	Sumosan	Japanese	3	2	2
£60+	Bellamy's	British, Modern	3	4	4
	The Berners Tavern	"	3	3	5
	Criterion	"	2	2	5
	Langan's Brasserie	"	2	2	4
	The Only Running Footman	"	2	2	2
	Quaglino's	"	–	–	–
	Sotheby's Café	"	3	4	3
	Wild Honey	"	3	3	3
	The Fountain (Fortnum's)	British, Traditional	2	3	2
	The Keeper's House	"	3	2	3
	Boulestin	French	2	2	2
	Brasserie Chavot	"	3	3	3
	Alloro	Italian	2	4	2
	La Genova	"	2	2	2
	Goodman	Steaks & grills	3	3	3
	The Guinea Grill	"	3	3	3
	Hawksmoor	"	4	4	3
	Rowley's	"	2	2	3
	Ladurée	Afternoon tea	2	2	2
	Peyote	Mexican/TexMex	3	3	2
	Marani	Georgian	3	3	2
	Chor Bizarre	Indian	4	4	3
	Gymkhana	"	5	4	4
	Sake No Hana	Japanese	2	1	2
£50+	The Avenue	American	1	3	3
	Hush	British, Modern	2	2	3
	Inn the Park	"	2	2	4
	The Wolseley	"	3	4	5
	Fishworks	Fish & seafood	3	2	2
	Pescatori	"	3	2	2
	Aubaine	French	1	1	1
	Boudin Blanc	"	2	2	3
	28-50	"	3	3	4
	Piccolino	Italian	2	2	2
	Café Murano	"	4	4	4
	Sartoria	"	3	3	2
	Il Vicolo	"	3	4	2
	Diamond Jub' Salon)	Afternoon tea	3	5	5
	Delfino	Pizza	3	2	2

	Royal Academy	*Sandwiches, cakes, etc*	1	2	2
	Al Hamra	*Lebanese*	3	2	2
	Noura	*"*	2	2	2
	Princess Garden	*Chinese*	4	3	3
	Mint Leaf	*Indian*	3	2	3
	Chisou	*Japanese*	4	2	2
	Kiku	*"*	5	4	2
	Patara	*Thai*	3	3	3
£40+	Hard Rock Café	*American*	3	2	4
	1707	*British, Modern*	3	4	3
	L'Artiste Musclé	*French*	2	2	4
	Al Duca	*Italian*	2	2	2
	Ritz (Palm Court)	*Afternoon tea*	3	4	5
	Burger & Lobster	*Burgers, etc*	3	2	3
	Al Sultan	*Lebanese*	3	2	1
	Woodlands	*Indian*	3	3	2
	Yoshino	*Japanese*	3	4	2
	Inamo	*Pan-Asian*	2	2	2
£35+	The Windmill	*British, Traditional*	3	2	3
	El Pirata	*Spanish*	2	3	5
	tibits	*Vegetarian*	3	2	3
	Sofra	*Turkish*	2	3	3
	Rasa Samudra	*Indian, Southern*	4	4	3
	Sakana-tei	*Japanese*	4	4	2
	Busaba Eathai	*Thai*	2	2	4
£30+	Ed's Easy Diner	*Burgers, etc*	1	2	3
	Sakura	*Japanese*	2	2	2
£25+	Stock Pot	*International*	2	2	2
	Shoryu Ramen	*Japanese*	3	2	3
£15+	La Bottega	*Italian*	3	4	4
	Taylor St Baristas	*Sandwiches, cakes, etc*	4	4	3
£10+	Fuzzy's Grub	*Sandwiches, cakes, etc*	3	2	2

Fitzrovia & Marylebone (Part of W1)

£110+	Beast	*Burgers, etc*	3	2	3
£90+	Roux at the Landau	*British, Modern*	3	3	3
	Pied à Terre	*French*	5	5	3
	Bubbledogs (Kitchen Table @)	*Fusion*	4	5	4
	Texture	*Scandinavian*	3	4	3
£80+	The Chiltern Firehouse	*American*	2	2	5

	L'Autre Pied	*French*	4 4 2
	Hakkasan	*Chinese*	4 2 4
	Roka	*Japanese*	5 3 4
£70+	Orrery	*French*	3 4 4
	Locanda Locatelli	*Italian*	3 3 4
	Gaucho	*Steaks & grills*	2 1 1
£60+	Galvin Bistrot de Luxe	*French*	3 4 4
	The Providores	*International*	4 2 2
	Il Baretto	*Italian*	2 2 2
	Dabbous	*Mediterranean*	4 3 2
	Royal China Club	*Chinese*	4 4 3
	La Porte des Indes	*Indian*	3 3 4
	Trishna	*"*	4 3 2
	Defune	*Japanese*	3 2 1
	Crazy Bear	*Thai*	2 2 4
£50+	The Lockhart	*American*	2 2 2
	Grazing Goat	*British, Modern*	3 2 3
	Fishworks	*Fish & seafood*	3 2 2
	Pescatori	*"*	3 2 2
	Aubaine	*French*	1 1 1
	Elena's L'Etoile	*"*	1 1 1
	28-50	*"*	3 3 4
	Villandry	*"*	2 2 2
	The Wallace	*"*	2 2 5
	Providores (Tapa Room)	*Fusion*	3 2 3
	Fischer's	*International*	2 3 3
	Caffè Caldesi	*Italian*	3 4 2
	Latium	*"*	4 5 3
	Sardo	*"*	3 3 2
	Riding House Café	*Mediterranean*	2 2 4
	Fino	*Spanish*	4 4 4
	Black & Blue	*Steaks & grills*	2 2 2
	Zoilo	*Argentinian*	4 4 3
	Lima	*Peruvian*	4 2 2
	Reubens	*Kosher*	3 2 2
	Fairuz	*Lebanese*	4 3 3
	Levant	*"*	2 2 3
	The Bright Courtyard	*Chinese*	3 4 2
	Gaylord	*Indian*	3 3 2
	Zayna	*"*	4 3 2
	Dinings	*Japanese*	5 4 1
	Kikuchi	*"*	5 2 1
	Bam-Bou	*Vietnamese*	3 3 5
£40+	Barnyard	*British, Modern*	3 3 2
	Daylesford Organic	*"*	2 2 4
	Hardy's Brasserie	*"*	2 2 4
	Newman Street Tavern	*"*	3 2 3
	Ozer	*"*	2 3 2

Restaurant	Cuisine			
The Union Café	"	2	3	2
Vinoteca Seymour Place	"	2	4	4
Bonnie Gull	Fish & seafood	5	4	4
Ergon	Greek	4	4	3
Real Greek	"	2	2	2
Briciole	Italian	3	3	4
Made in Italy	"	3	3	4
Obika	"	2	2	1
2 Veneti	"	3	4	3
Barrica	Spanish	4	3	4
Donostia	"	5	4	4
Drakes Tabanco	"	3	4	3
Ibérica	"	3	2	3
Navarro's	"	2	2	4
Salt Yard	"	3	4	3
Le Relais de Venise	Steaks & grills	3	2	3
Maroush	Lebanese	4	2	2
Ishtar	Turkish	3	4	3
Royal China	Chinese	4	2	2
Roti Chai	Indian	4	4	3
Woodlands	"	3	3	2
Nizuni	Japanese	4	4	2
Tsunami	"	5	2	2
Yoisho	"	3	2	2
Koba	Korean	3	2	3

£35+				
Lantana Cafe	Australian	3	3	4
Natural Kitchen	British, Modern	3	2	3
MEATLiquor	Burgers, etc	3	2	3
La Fromagerie Café	Sandwiches, cakes, etc	3	2	4
Natural Kitchen	Salads	3	2	3
Yalla Yalla	Lebanese	3	3	4
Sofra	Turkish	2	3	3
Sagar	Indian	3	2	2
dim T	Pan-Asian	2	2	3
East Street	"	3	3	4
Pho	Vietnamese	3	3	3

£30+				
Bubbledogs	American	2	3	4
Picture	British, Modern	3	5	2
Wahaca	Mexican/TexMex	2	3	4
Honey & Co	Middle Eastern	4	4	3
ping pong	Chinese, Dim sum	2	2	3
Chettinad	Indian	3	4	3
Atari-Ya	Japanese	5	2	1

£25+				
Stock Pot	International	2	2	2
Vapiano	Italian	3	2	3
Golden Hind	Fish & chips	3	4	2
Benito's Hat	Mexican/TexMex	3	4	2
Comptoir Libanais	Lebanese	2	2	2
Ragam	Indian	5	4	1

| £20+ | Patty and Bun | Burgers, etc | 4 2 3 |
| | Patogh | Middle Eastern | 3 2 2 |

£15+	Nordic Bakery	Scandinavian	3 3 3
	Scandinavian Kitchen	"	4 5 3
	Tommi's Burger Joint	Burgers, etc	4 2 3
	Nordic Bakery	Sandwiches, cakes, etc	3 3 3
	Chipotle	Mexican/TexMex	3 3 2

| £10+ | The Attendant | Sandwiches, cakes, etc | 4 4 4 |
| | Kaffeine | " | 3 4 5 |

Belgravia, Pimlico, Victoria & Westminster (SW1, except St James's)

| £110+ | Marcus | French | 3 3 3 |

| £100+ | Dinner | British, Traditional | 3 3 3 |
| | Rib Room | Steaks & grills | 3 3 2 |

| £90+ | One-O-One | Fish & seafood | 5 3 1 |
| | Pétrus | French | 4 4 4 |

£80+	The Goring Hotel	British, Modern	3 5 5
	Koffmann's	French	5 5 3
	Ametsa	Spanish	2 3 1
	Mr Chow	Chinese	3 3 2

£70+	Roux at Parliament Square	British, Modern	3 4 2
	Santini	Italian	2 3 4
	Toto's	"	3 5 4
	Zafferano	"	3 3 3
	Massimo	Mediterranean	2 4 4
	Amaya	Indian	5 4 3
	The Cinnamon Club	"	3 3 4
	Buddha-Bar London	Pan-Asian	1 2 3

£60+	Bank Westminster	British, Modern	3 2 2
	The Botanist	"	1 1 1
	The Fifth Floor Restaurant	"	3 3 3
	The Northall	"	3 4 3
	Olivomare	Fish & seafood	5 3 2
	Bar Boulud	French	3 3 4
	Colbert	"	1 2 3
	La Poule au Pot	"	3 3 5
	Motcombs	International	2 3 3
	Sale e Pepe	Italian	2 2 3
	Signor Sassi	"	2 3 3
	Boisdale	Scottish	3 3 4

	Ladurée	*Afternoon tea*	2	2	2
	Oliveto	*Pizza*	4	2	2
	The Grand Imperial	*Chinese*	3	2	2
	Hunan	"	5	3	1
	Ken Lo's Memories	"	3	4	3
	Quilon	*Indian, Southern*	4	3	2
	Salloos	*Pakistani*	4	4	2
£50+	Ebury Rest' & Wine Bar	*British, Modern*	2	2	3
	The Orange	"	3	3	4
	The Pantechnicon	"	3	3	4
	Tate Britain (Rex Whistler)	"	2	3	5
	The Thomas Cubitt	"	3	3	4
	The Balcon	*French*	2	2	3
	Chabrot Bistrot d'Amis	"	3	4	3
	Caraffini	*Italian*	2	5	3
	Il Convivio	"	4	4	3
	Olivo	"	4	4	2
	Olivocarne	"	4	4	2
	Osteria Dell'Angolo	"	3	4	2
	Quirinale	"	4	4	2
	About Thyme	*Mediterranean*	3	4	2
	Beiteddine	*Lebanese*	3	3	2
	Noura	"	2	2	2
	Mango Tree	*Thai*	1	1	2
£40+	Daylesford Organic	*British, Modern*	2	2	4
	The Queens Arms	"	4	4	4
	Uni	*Fusion*	4	4	3
	Grumbles	*International*	2	3	3
	Como Lario	*Italian*	2	2	3
	Gustoso	"	3	5	3
	Ottolenghi	"	5	3	3
	Tinello	"	4	4	4
	Tozi	"	3	4	3
	Bilbao Berria	*Spanish*	3	4	3
	Goya	"	2	3	2
	Burger & Lobster	*Burgers, etc*	3	2	3
	Baker & Spice	*Sandwiches, cakes, etc*	2	2	2
	Kazan	*Turkish*	3	3	3
£35+	Seafresh	*Fish & chips*	3	3	1
	dim T	*Pan-Asian*	2	2	3
£30+	The Vincent Rooms	*British, Modern*	3	3	3
	Cyprus Mangal	*Turkish*	4	3	1
	A Wong	*Chinese*	4	3	3
£15+	La Bottega	*Italian*	3	4	4

WEST

Chelsea, South Kensington, Kensington, Earl's Court & Fulham (SW3, SW5, SW6, SW7, SW10 & W8)

Price	Name	Cuisine	Ratings
£120+	Gordon Ramsay	*French*	3 4 3
£100+	Rasoi	*Indian*	5 4 4
£80+	Bibendum	*French*	2 3 4
	Yashin	*Japanese*	5 3 2
	Yashin Ocean House	*"*	1 1 3
	Zuma	*"*	5 3 4
£70+	Babylon	*British, Modern*	2 4 4
	The Five Fields	*"*	5 5 4
	Launceston Place	*"*	3 4 4
	Cheyne Walk Bras'	*French*	3 3 3
	L'Etranger	*"*	3 4 2
	One Kensington	*International*	2 3 1
	Scalini	*Italian*	3 3 3
	Gaucho	*Steaks & grills*	2 1 1
	Min Jiang	*Chinese*	5 3 5
£60+	The Abingdon	*British, Modern*	3 3 4
	Bluebird	*"*	1 2 3
	Clarke's	*"*	3 3 2
	Kitchen W8	*"*	5 4 3
	Medlar	*"*	5 4 3
	Pavilion	*"*	3 4 3
	Tom's Kitchen	*"*	2 1 1
	Bibendum Oyster Bar	*Fish & seafood*	2 4 3
	Outlaw's Seafood and Grill	*"*	4 4 2
	Poissonnerie de l'Av.	*"*	4 3 2
	Belvedere	*French*	2 2 4
	Racine	*"*	2 2 2
	Margaux	*International*	3 3 3
	Rivea	*"*	2 4 2
	Daphne's	*Italian*	– – –
	La Famiglia	*"*	2 2 2
	Lucio	*"*	2 2 2
	Manicomio	*"*	3 2 3
	Pellicano	*"*	3 5 3
	Locanda Ottomezzo	*Mediterranean*	3 4 3
	Cambio de Tercio	*Spanish*	4 3 4
	Hawksmoor Knightsbridge	*Steaks & grills*	4 4 3
	Bo Lang	*Chinese, Dim sum*	2 3 3
£50+	Big Easy	*American*	2 2 2
	Brinkley's	*British, Modern*	3 3 4

The Enterprise	"	2	3	3
Harwood Arms	"	4	3	3
The Henry Root	"	2	2	3
Kensington Place	"	4	5	3
The Sands End	"	4	4	4
The Terrace	"	2	4	4
White Horse	"	2	2	4
Bumpkin	British, Traditional	3	2	2
Ffiona's	"	2	3	3
Maggie Jones's	"	2	3	5
The Malt House	"	4	4	3
Aubaine	French	1	1	1
La Brasserie	"	2	2	4
Le Colombier	"	3	4	4
Garnier	"	3	4	2
The Pig's Ear	"	2	2	3
Mazi	Greek	3	2	2
Foxtrot Oscar	International	2	2	2
Gallery Mess	"	2	2	2
The Kensington Wine Rms	"	2	2	3
Frantoio	Italian	2	2	3
Il Portico	"	2	5	3
Tartufo	"	5	4	3
Ziani's	"	3	3	3
Polish Club	Polish	2	3	4
The Admiral Codrington	Steaks & grills	2	2	2
Black & Blue	"	2	2	2
Kings Road Steakhouse	"	2	1	1
PJ's Bar and Grill	"	2	3	4
Sophie's Steakhouse	"	2	3	2
Good Earth	Chinese	3	3	2
Bombay Brasserie	Indian	4	4	4
Chutney Mary	"	4	5	4
The Painted Heron	"	5	3	2
Star of India	"	4	2	–
Chisou	Japanese	4	2	2
Eight Over Eight	Pan-Asian	3	3	3
Patara	Thai	3	3	3
Sukho Fine Thai Cuisine	"	5	4	3
£40+ Bodean's	American	2	2	2
Sticky Fingers	"	2	2	2
The Anglesea Arms	British, Modern	2	2	4
The Builders Arms	"	3	3	4
The Cadogan Arms	"	3	3	1
Joe's Brasserie	"	2	4	3
The Mall Tavern	"	2	2	3
The Phene	"	1	2	3
VQ	"	2	3	2
Whits	"	3	5	3
The Brown Cow	British, Traditional	4	4	4
The Surprise	"	2	3	4
La Bouchée	French	2	2	4

			Rating
Chez Patrick	"	3 5 4
Balans	International	2 4 3
Troubadour	"	2 3 4
The Windsor Castle	"	2 2 5
Aglio e Olio	Italian	3 3 2
Da Mario	"	2 3 3
Made in Italy	"	3 3 4
Napulé	"	4 4 3
Nuovi Sapori	"	3 4 3
Obika	"	2 2 1
Ottolenghi	"	5 3 3
Pappa Ciccia	"	4 3 3
Riccardo's	"	2 2 2
The Atlas	Mediterranean	4 4 4
Daquise	Polish	2 3 2
Capote Y Toros	Spanish	4 3 4
Casa Brindisa	"	2 2 2
Tendido Cero	"	3 3 4
Tendido Cuatro	"	4 4 4
Maxela	Steaks & grills	4 3 3
Geales	Fish & chips	2 1 2
La Delizia Limbara	Pizza	4 4 3
Rocca Di Papa	"	2 2 3
Santa Lucia	"	3 2 2
Baker & Spice	Sandwiches, cakes, etc	2 2 2
Beirut Express	Lebanese	4 2 2
Maroush	"	4 2 2
Ranoush	"	4 3 2
Royal China	Chinese	4 2 2
Malabar	Indian	4 4 2
Thali	"	4 4 2
Bangkok	Thai	3 2 2
Thai Square	"	2 2 2
£35+		
Dirty Bones	American	– – –
The Shed	British, Modern	3 3 5
Buona Sera	Italian	2 3 3
Il Pagliaccio	"	2 3 3
Haché	Steaks & grills	3 3 4
Basilico	Pizza	4 4 1
Rossopomodoro	"	2 2 2
Best Mangal	Turkish	4 4 3
Taiwan Village	Chinese	5 5 3
Noor Jahan	Indian	4 4 4
Churchill Arms	Thai	3 3 5
£30+		
Kensington Square Kitchen	British, Modern	3 4 4
Chelsea Bun Diner	International	3 2 3
Diner	Burgers, etc	1 3 3
The Greedy Buddha	Indian	3 2 2
Masala Zone	"	3 4 3
Kulu Kulu	Japanese	3 1 1

	Addie's Thai Café	*Thai*	3 3 2
£25+	Mona Lisa	*International*	3 3 3
	Stock Pot	*"*	2 2 2
	Comptoir Libanais	*Lebanese*	2 2 2
£20+	Eat Tokyo	*Japanese*	4 2 2
	Café 209	*Thai*	2 3 5
£15+	La Bottega	*Italian*	3 4 4
	Tommi's Burger Joint	*Burgers, etc*	4 2 3

Notting Hill, Holland Park, Bayswater, North Kensington & Maida Vale (W2, W9, W10, W11)

£130+	The Ledbury	*British, Modern*	5 5 4
£90+	Marianne	*British, Modern*	4 4 3
£80+	The New Angel	*International*	4 4 3
	The Shiori	*Japanese*	5 5 3
£70+	Angelus	*French*	3 5 4
	Assaggi	*Italian*	4 4 2
£60+	Beach Blanket Babylon	*British, Modern*	1 2 3
	Julie's	*"*	1 1 5
	Edera	*Italian*	3 4 3
	Chakra	*Indian*	2 1 1
	E&O	*Pan-Asian*	3 2 3
£50+	The Cow	*British, Modern*	3 4 4
	The Dock Kitchen	*"*	3 4 5
	The Frontline Club	*"*	3 3 3
	The Ladbroke Arms	*"*	3 1 4
	The Magazine Restaurant	*"*	2 3 5
	New Tom's	*"*	– – –
	Truscott Arms	*"*	3 3 4
	The Waterway	*"*	2 1 4
	Bumpkin	*British, Traditional*	3 2 2
	The Summerhouse	*Fish & seafood*	3 3 5
	Le Café Anglais	*French*	3 3 4
	Les Gourmets Des Ternes	*"*	– – –
	Essenza	*Italian*	3 3 3
	Mediterraneo	*"*	3 3 3
	The Oak	*"*	4 4 4
	Osteria Basilico	*"*	3 3 4
	Casa Malevo	*Argentinian*	4 3 3
	Bombay Palace	*Indian*	5 2 1

	Kurobuta	*Japanese*	4 2 3
£40+	Electric Diner	*American*	2 4 4
	Lucky Seven	"	3 3 3
	Granger & Co	*Australian*	2 3 4
	Daylesford Organic	*British, Modern*	2 2 4
	First Floor	"	3 2 5
	Paradise, Kensal Green	"	3 4 5
	Hereford Road	*British, Traditional*	3 3 2
	Halepi	*Greek*	3 4 2
	Ottolenghi	*Italian*	5 3 3
	Portobello Ristorante	"	3 4 4
	Raoul's Cafe	*Mediterranean*	2 2 3
	El Pirata de Tapas	*Spanish*	3 3 2
	Pizza East Portobello	*Pizza*	4 3 4
	The Red Pepper	"	4 2 2
	Baker & Spice	*Sandwiches, cakes, etc*	2 2 2
	Al-Waha	*Lebanese*	3 2 1
	Beirut Express	"	4 2 2
	Maroush	"	4 2 2
	Ranoush	"	4 3 2
	Kateh	*Persian*	5 4 3
	Mandarin Kitchen	*Chinese*	4 1 1
	Pearl Liang	"	3 2 2
	Royal China	"	4 2 2
	Inaho	*Japanese*	4 3 2
£35+	Polpo	*Italian*	2 3 5
	Honest Burgers	*Burgers, etc*	4 4 4
	Taqueria	*Mexican/TexMex*	3 4 3
	Noor Jahan	*Indian*	4 4 4
	Maguro	*Japanese*	4 4 3
	Satay House	*Malaysian*	3 3 2
	Banana Tree Canteen	*Pan-Asian*	2 2 2
£30+	Notting Hill Kitchen	*Spanish*	2 3 2
	Alounak	*Persian*	3 2 3
	The Four Seasons	*Chinese*	4 1 1
	Gold Mine	"	3 2 1
	ping pong	*Chinese, Dim sum*	2 2 3
	Durbar	*Indian*	3 3 3
	Masala Zone	"	3 4 3
	C&R Cafe	*Thai*	4 2 2
£25+	Mandalay	*Burmese*	3 3 1
	Fitou's Thai Restaurant	*Thai*	4 3 2
£20+	Fez Mangal	*Turkish*	5 4 3
	Khan's	*Indian*	4 2 2
£5+	Lisboa Pâtisserie	*Sandwiches, cakes, etc*	4 4 2

Hammersmith, Shepherd's Bush, Olympia, Chiswick, Brentford & Ealing (W4, W5, W6, W12, W13, W14, TW8)

£90+	The River Café	*Italian*	3	2	3
£80+	Hedone	*British, Modern*	5	4	3
£60+	La Trompette	*French*	5	4	4
	Le Vacherin	"	3	3	3
£50+	The Anglesea Arms	*British, Modern*	4	2	4
	The Brackenbury	"	4	3	2
	High Road Brasserie	"	2	2	3
	The Hampshire Hog	*British, Traditional*	2	2	3
	Charlotte's Bistro	*French*	3	4	3
	Charlotte's Place	"	3	4	3
	Michael Nadra	*International*	5	3	1
	Cibo	*Italian*	4	5	3
	The Oak W12	"	4	4	4
	Popeseye	*Steaks & grills*	3	4	2
	Chisou	*Japanese*	4	2	2
£40+	Bush Dining Hall	*British, Modern*	1	2	3
	The Carpenter's Arms	"	3	3	4
	City Barge	"	4	4	5
	The Dartmouth Castle	"	3	4	3
	Duke of Sussex	"	3	2	4
	The Havelock Tavern	"	3	2	3
	Hole in the Wall	"	2	3	3
	Princess Victoria	"	3	4	4
	Sam's Brasserie	"	3	4	4
	Vinoteca	"	2	4	4
	The Real Greek	*Greek*	2	2	2
	The Andover Arms	*International*	2	4	4
	Annie's	"	2	3	4
	Balans	"	2	4	3
	L'Amorosa	*Italian*	–	–	–
	Pentolina	"	4	5	4
	Cumberland Arms	*Mediterranean*	4	4	3
	Raoul's Café & Deli	"	2	2	3
	The Swan	"	4	4	5
	The Gate	*Vegetarian*	3	2	2
	Bird in Hand	*Pizza*	3	4	4
	Fire & Stone	"	2	2	2
	Azou	*North African*	4	4	4
	North China	*Chinese*	4	4	3
	Indian Zing	*Indian*	5	4	3
	Karma	"	4	4	2
	Tosa	*Japanese*	4	2	2
	Saigon Saigon	*Vietnamese*	3	4	3

£35+	Queen's Head	British, Modern	2 2 4
	Canta Napoli	Italian	3 3 2
	Patio	Polish	3 5 5
	Quantus	South American	3 5 4
	Best Mangal	Turkish	4 4 3
	Brilliant	Indian	3 3 3
	Madhu's	"	4 3 3
	Potli	"	4 3 4
	Sagar	"	3 2 2
	Kiraku	Japanese	5 3 2
	Fat Boy's	Thai	2 3 3
	Pho	Vietnamese	3 3 3
£30+	Albertine	French	2 4 4
	Santa Maria	Pizza	5 3 3
	Adams Café	Moroccan	2 5 4
	Chez Abir	Lebanese	4 3 2
	Alounak	Persian	3 2 3
	Sufi	"	3 3 4
	Anarkali	Indian	3 3 2
	Shilpa	Indian, Southern	4 3 1
	Atari-Ya	Japanese	5 2 1
	Hare & Tortoise	Pan-Asian	3 2 3
	Esarn Kheaw	Thai	4 3 1
	101 Thai Kitchen	"	4 2 1
£25+	Comptoir Libanais	Lebanese	2 2 2
	Faanoos	Persian	3 2 4
£20+	Franco Manca	Pizza	4 3 3
	Abu Zaad	Syrian	3 3 2
	Eat Tokyo	Japanese	4 2 2
	Miran Masala	Pakistani	5 4 2
	Mirch Masala	"	3 1 1
£15+	Kerbisher & Malt	Fish & chips	3 3 2
	Gifto's	Indian	3 2 2

NORTH

Hampstead, West Hampstead, St John's Wood, Regent's Park, Kilburn & Camden Town (NW postcodes)

£80+	Landmark (Winter Gdn)	British, Modern	2	3	4
£70+	Gilgamesh	Pan-Asian	2	2	3
£60+	Bull & Last	British, Traditional	4	3	3
	Gilbert Scott	"	2	2	4
	L'Aventure	French	4	5	5
	Oslo Court	"	4	5	4
	Villa Bianca	Italian	2	2	3
	Kaifeng	Chinese	3	2	2
£50+	Q Grill	American	3	3	2
	Bradley's	British, Modern	2	2	2
	The Engineer	"	2	2	3
	Market	"	4	3	2
	Odette's	"	3	3	4
	St Pancras Grand	"	2	2	2
	Michael Nadra	French	5	3	1
	La Collina	Italian	4	3	2
	York & Albany	"	2	2	4
	Manna	Vegetarian	2	3	2
	Good Earth	Chinese	3	3	2
	Phoenix Palace	"	3	2	2
£40+	Karpo	American	3	2	1
	Belgo Noord	Belgian	2	4	3
	The Horseshoe	British, Modern	3	2	3
	The Junction Tavern	"	3	4	4
	The North London Tavern	"	3	3	3
	The Old Bull & Bush	"	3	2	3
	Parlour	"	4	4	3
	Rising Sun	"	3	4	3
	The Wells	"	3	2	4
	The Wet Fish Cafe	"	3	3	3
	Kentish Canteen	British, Traditional	2	4	3
	L'Absinthe	French	2	3	2
	La Cage Imaginaire	"	3	3	4
	Mill Lane Bistro	"	3	3	2
	Lemonia	Greek	2	3	4
	Artigiano	Italian	3	3	3
	Ostuni	"	2	3	3
	The Salt House	"	2	1	2
	Sarracino	"	4	3	2
	Harry Morgan's	Burgers, etc	2	2	2
	Nautilus	Fish & chips	4	4	1

			Ratings		
	The Sea Shell	"	4	4	2
	Skipjacks	"	4	4	2
	Pizza East	Pizza	4	3	4
	Greenberry Cafe	Sandwiches, cakes, etc	3	3	3
	Mango Room	Afro-Caribbean	3	3	2
	Solly's	Israeli	2	2	2
	Zest	Kosher	3	2	2
	Green Cottage	Chinese	3	1	1
	Gung-Ho	"	3	4	2
	Eriki	Indian	4	3	2
	Woodlands	"	3	3	2
	Jin Kichi	Japanese	5	4	3
	Sushi-Say	"	5	4	2
	Singapore Garden	Malaysian	4	3	2
	XO	Pan-Asian	2	2	2
£35+	Made In Camden	British, Modern	3	3	3
	Simply Fish	Fish & seafood	3	3	3
	L'Artista	Italian	2	4	4
	El Parador	Spanish	4	4	4
	Haché	Steaks & grills	3	3	4
	Honest Burgers	Burgers, etc	4	4	4
	Basilico	Pizza	4	4	1
	Rossopomodoro	"	2	2	2
	Asakusa	Japanese	5	2	2
	Bento Cafe	"	4	4	2
	dim T	Pan-Asian	2	2	3
£30+	Chicken Shop	American	3	4	4
	Carob Tree	Greek	4	5	4
	La Porchetta Pizzeria	Italian	3	3	3
	The Little Bay	Mediterranean	2	3	4
	The Diner	Burgers, etc	1	3	3
	Ed's Easy Diner	"	1	2	3
	Sacro Cuore	Pizza	4	3	4
	Kenwood (Brew House)	Sandwiches, cakes, etc	2	2	5
	Chutneys	Indian	2	2	2
	Diwana B-P House	"	3	2	1
	Great Nepalese	"	3	4	2
	Guglee	"	3	4	4
	Paradise Hampstead	"	4	5	4
	Ravi Shankar	"	4	3	2
	Vijay	"	3	4	2
	Atari-Ya	Japanese	5	2	1
£20+	Ali Baba	Egyptian	3	2	2
	Kadiri's	Indian	4	3	2
	Eat Tokyo	Japanese	4	2	2
£15+	Ginger & White	Sandwiches, cakes, etc	3	3	4

£10+	Dirty Burger	Burgers, etc	4	4	4

Hoxton, Islington, Highgate, Crouch End, Stoke Newington, Finsbury Park, Muswell Hill & Finchley (N postcodes)

£60+	Frederick's	British, Modern	2	3	4
	Fifteen Restaurant	Italian	1	1	1

£50+	Shrimpy's	American	3	3	3
	The Duke of Cambridge	British, Modern	2	3	3
	Grain Store	"	3	2	3
	The Haven	"	2	2	2
	Rotunda Bar & Restaurant	"	2	1	3
	The Almeida	French	2	2	2
	Bistro Aix	"	4	3	3
	Trullo	Italian	4	4	4

£40+	Red Dog Saloon	American	3	2	3
	The Albion	British, Modern	2	2	4
	Bald Faced Stag	"	3	3	3
	The Bull	"	2	2	4
	Caravan King's Cross	"	3	2	4
	The Clissold Arms	"	3	4	4
	The Drapers Arms	"	3	2	3
	The Fellow	"	3	3	3
	Juniper Dining	"	3	3	2
	LeCoq	"	4	4	4
	Pig & Butcher	"	4	3	3
	Plum + Spilt Milk	"	2	3	3
	St Johns	British, Traditional	3	3	5
	Kipferl	East & Cent. Euro	3	3	3
	Les Associés	French	3	4	2
	Blue Legume	"	2	2	3
	Le Coq	"	3	4	3
	Banners	International	3	4	5
	8 Hoxton Square	"	3	3	2
	The Orange Tree	"	1	2	3
	Primeur	"	–	–	–
	500	Italian	3	4	2
	Ottolenghi	"	5	3	3
	Pizzeria Oregano	"	4	4	3
	San Daniele	"	3	4	3
	Camino	Spanish	2	3	3
	The Smokehouse Islington	Steaks & grills	3	4	3
	Duke's Brew & Que	Burgers, etc	3	2	3
	The Fish & Chip Shop	Fish & chips	4	4	4
	Toff's	"	4	3	2
	Two Brothers	"	3	3	2
	Il Bacio	Pizza	3	2	2
	Yipin China	Chinese	5	2	1

	Dishoom	*Indian*	4	3	4
	Roots at N1	"	5	5	3
	Zaffrani	"	4	4	3
	Isarn	*Thai*	4	3	2
	Thai Square	"	2	2	2
	Yum Yum	"	3	2	4
£35+	Season Kitchen	*British, Modern*	4	4	3
	Le Sacré-Coeur	*French*	2	3	4
	Vrisaki	*Greek*	3	3	3
	Pizzeria Pappagone	*Italian*	3	3	4
	Rugoletta	"	4	4	2
	Vivo	"	4	4	4
	Bar Esteban	*Spanish*	5	3	3
	Café del Parc	"	4	4	4
	Basilico	*Pizza*	4	4	1
	Rossopomodoro	"	2	2	2
	Gilak	*Persian*	3	3	2
	Antepliler	*Turkish*	3	2	2
	Gallipoli	"	3	4	3
	Mangal II	"	3	3	2
	Little Georgia Café	*Georgian*	3	2	3
	Indian Rasoi	*Indian*	4	4	3
	Rasa	*Indian, Southern*	4	4	3
	Akari	*Japanese*	4	2	3
	dim T	*Pan-Asian*	2	2	3
	Huong-Viet	*Vietnamese*	3	2	2
£30+	Olympus Fish	*Fish & seafood*	4	4	1
	Le Mercury	*French*	2	3	4
	La Porchetta Pizzeria	*Italian*	3	3	3
	La Bota	*Spanish*	3	4	3
	Meat Mission	*Burgers, etc*	4	3	3
	Fabrizio	*Pizza*	3	4	2
	Sweet Thursday	"	3	3	3
	Wahaca	*Mexican/TexMex*	2	3	4
	Gem	*Turkish*	3	4	4
	Izgara	"	3	2	1
	Delhi Grill	*Indian*	4	3	3
	Masala Zone	"	3	4	3
	Salvation In Noodles	*Vietnamese*	4	4	3
£25+	White Rabbit	*British, Modern*	4	3	3
	Prawn On The Lawn	*Fish & seafood*	4	5	3
	Benito's Hat	*Mexican/TexMex*	3	4	2
	Afghan Kitchen	*Afghani*	4	2	1
	Rani	*Indian*	3	2	2
	Dotori	*Korean*	4	2	2
£15+	Notes	*Sandwiches, cakes, etc*	2	4	4
	Chilango	*Mexican/TexMex*	3	2	2
	Chipotle	"	3	3	2

	Jai Krishna	*Indian*	4 3 2
£10+	The Rib Man	*Burgers, etc*	5 3 4

SOUTH

South Bank (SE1)

£80+			
	Oblix	American	2 2 5
	Aqua Shard	British, Modern	1 1 4
	Oxo Tower (Rest')	"	1 1 2
	Story	"	4 4 3
	Ting	International	2 2 3

£70+			
	Le Pont de la Tour	British, Modern	2 2 3
	Rabot 1745	International	2 3 3
	Oxo Tower (Brass')	Mediterranean	1 2 2
	Gaucho	Steaks & grills	2 1 1
	Hutong	Chinese	2 2 4

£60+			
	Butlers W'f Chop-house	British, Traditional	2 2 2
	Roast	"	2 2 2
	La Barca	Italian	2 2 2

£50+			
	Cantina Vinopolis	British, Modern	2 2 2
	Elliot's Cafe	"	4 3 3
	Magdalen	"	4 4 3
	Menier Chocolate Factory	"	1 2 3
	Skylon	"	1 2 3
	Skylon Grill	"	1 2 3
	The Swan at the Globe	"	3 3 4
	Waterloo Bar & Kitchen	"	3 3 2
	fish!	Fish & seafood	2 2 2
	Wright Brothers	"	4 3 3
	Village East	Fusion	3 2 3
	Vivat Bacchus	International	2 3 2
	Tentazioni	Italian	3 4 4
	Zucca	"	5 4 3
	Baltic	Polish	3 2 3
	Archduke Wine Bar	Steaks & grills	2 2 2
	Black & Blue	"	2 2 2

£40+			
	Albion	British, Modern	2 2 2
	Blueprint Café	"	3 2 5
	Edwins	"	3 3 4
	40 Maltby Street	"	4 4 4
	Garrison	"	3 3 3
	RSJ	"	3 4 2
	The Table	"	2 2 2
	Tate Modern (Level 7)	"	2 2 4
	Union Street Café	"	2 2 2
	The Anchor & Hope	British, Traditional	5 3 3
	Canteen	"	1 1 1
	Applebee's Cafe	Fish & seafood	3 2 2
	Champor-Champor	Fusion	3 2 3

	Real Greek	*Greek*	2 2 2
	Brigade	*International*	3 2 3
	The Rooftop Cafe	"	3 4 5
	Antico	*Italian*	4 4 3
	José	*Spanish*	5 4 5
	Meson don Felipe	"	2 2 4
	Pizarro	"	3 4 4
	Tapas Brindisa	"	3 2 3
	Arabica Bar and Kitchen	*Lebanese*	3 4 3
	Bengal Clipper	*Indian*	3 3 3
	Mango Food of India	"	3 2 2
£35+	Casse-Croute	*French*	4 4 5
	Ev Restaurant, Bar & Deli	*Turkish*	2 3 3
	dim T	*Pan-Asian*	2 2 3
£30+	Masters Super Fish	*Fish & chips*	4 1 1
	Gourmet Pizza Co.	*Pizza*	2 2 3
	Caffé Vergnano	*Sandwiches, cakes, etc*	3 3 3
	Wahaca	*Mexican/TexMex*	2 3 4
	El Vergel	*South American*	4 3 4
	Tas Pide	*Turkish*	2 3 4
	ping pong	*Chinese, Dim sum*	2 2 3
£25+	Vapiano	*Italian*	3 2 3
	Konditor & Cook	*Sandwiches, cakes, etc*	3 4 2
£10+	Monmouth Coffee Co	*Sandwiches, cakes, etc*	5 5 4
	Spianata & Co	"	4 4 3

Greenwich, Lewisham, Dulwich & Blackheath
(All SE postcodes, except SE1)

£60+	Lobster Pot	*Fish & seafood*	4 3 2
£50+	The Camberwell Arms	*British, Modern*	4 4 4
	Chapters	"	2 3 2
	The Palmerston	"	3 3 2
	Rivington Grill	"	2 2 3
	Buenos Aires Café	*Argentinian*	3 3 3
	Babur	*Indian*	5 4 3
£40+	The Crooked Well	*British, Modern*	3 4 4
	Franklins	"	3 3 3
	Inside	"	4 4 1
	The Lido Cafe	"	2 2 3
	The Old Brewery	"	2 3 4
	Brasserie Toulouse-Lautrec	*French*	3 4 3
	Toasted	"	3 3 4
	Joanna's	*International*	3 4 4

	The Yellow House	"	3	4	2
	Artusi	Italian	4	3	2
	Lorenzo	"	3	4	3
	Le Querce	"	4	4	2
	Peckham Bazaar	Mediterranean	3	3	3
	Angels & Gypsies	Spanish	2	2	3
	Olley's	Fish & chips	4	3	2
	Bianco43	Pizza	3	2	2
	Rocca Di Papa	"	2	2	3
	Zero Degrees	"	3	2	2
	Ganapati	Indian	5	4	4
	Kennington Tandoori	"	4	4	3
£35+	The Dartmouth Arms	British, Modern	2	2	3
	Peckham Refreshment Rms	"	3	3	3
	The Lord Northbrook	British, Traditional	3	4	4
	Dragon Castle	Chinese	3	1	1
	Everest Inn	Indian	4	4	4
	Tandoori Nights	"	3	4	3
	The Begging Bowl	Thai	5	4	5
£30+	The Sea Cow	Fish & chips	3	3	3
	The Gowlett	Pizza	4	3	4
£20+	Silk Road	Chinese	5	2	1
	Thai Corner Café	Thai	3	3	3
	Cafe East	Vietnamese	4	2	2
£10+	Monmouth Coffee Company	Sandwiches, cakes, etc	5	5	4

Battersea, Brixton, Clapham, Wandsworth Barnes, Putney & Wimbledon
(All SW postcodes south of the river)

£60+	Cannizaro House	British, Modern	2	3	4
	Chez Bruce	"	5	5	4
	Trinity	"	4	5	3
	The Lawn Bistro	French	2	2	2
	Riva	Italian	3	4	2
	San Lorenzo Fuoriporta	"	2	2	2
£50+	Abbeville Kitchen	British, Modern	3	4	2
	The Brown Dog	"	3	3	3
	Entrée	"	4	4	3
	Sonny's Kitchen	"	2	2	2
	Fox & Grapes	British, Traditional	2	2	2
	The Lobster House	Fish & seafood	2	2	3
	Soif	French	4	4	3
	Upstairs	"	4	4	4
	The Light House	International	2	3	3

	London House	"	4 5 4
	Bibo	*Italian*	4 3 3
	Enoteca Turi	"	4 4 3
	Numero Uno	"	3 4 4
	Alquimia	*Spanish*	3 4 2
	Popeseye	*Steaks & grills*	3 4 2
	Fulham Wine Rooms	*Sandwiches, cakes, etc*	2 3 4
	Good Earth	*Chinese*	3 3 2
	Suk Saran	*Thai*	4 2 1
£40+	Bodean's	*American*	2 2 2
	Red Dog South	"	3 2 3
	Bistro Union	*British, Modern*	2 2 3
	The Bolingbroke	"	3 2 3
	Brunswick House Cafe	"	2 2 5
	Claude's Kitchen	"	4 4 4
	The Dairy	"	5 4 4
	The Depot	"	2 3 5
	Earl Spencer	"	3 2 3
	Emile's	"	4 4 2
	Lamberts	"	5 5 4
	Olympic Café	"	2 2 3
	Source	"	2 3 4
	The Victoria	"	3 4 3
	Canton Arms	*British, Traditional*	3 3 4
	Augustine Kitchen	*French*	4 4 1
	Bellevue Rendez-Vous	"	3 3 3
	Gastro	"	2 1 5
	Le P'tit Normand	"	3 4 3
	Annie's	*International*	2 3 4
	Hudsons	"	2 2 3
	The Ship	"	3 3 4
	Telegraph	"	3 2 4
	Antipasto & Pasta	*Italian*	3 4 2
	Donna Margherita	"	4 3 3
	Ost. Antica Bologna	"	3 3 3
	Pizza Metro	"	4 4 3
	Sapori Sardi	"	4 4 2
	The Fox & Hounds	*Mediterranean*	4 4 4
	Lola Rojo	*Spanish*	3 2 3
	Tapas Brindisa	"	3 2 3
	Butcher & Grill	*Steaks & grills*	2 2 3
	Cattle Grid	"	3 2 3
	Cornish Tiger	"	4 4 3
	Indian Zilla	*Indian*	5 5 3
	Ma Goa	"	4 4 2
	Sticks'n'Sushi	*Japanese*	3 3 3
	Tsunami	"	5 2 2
	Blue Elephant	*Thai*	3 2 3
£35+	Gazette	*French*	2 2 4
	Buona Sera	*Italian*	2 3 3

	Fish in a Tie	*Mediterranean*	3	4	4
	Haché	*Burgers, etc*	3	3	4
	Honest Burgers	"	4	4	4
	Fish Club	*Fish & chips*	4	4	2
	Al Forno	*Pizza*	2	4	4
	Basilico	"	4	4	1
	Eco	"	3	3	4
	Rossopomodoro	"	2	2	2
	Dalchini	*Chinese*	3	4	2
	Indian Moment	*Indian*	3	4	3
	Nazmins	"	3	4	4
	Hashi	*Japanese*	4	4	3
	Cah-Chi	*Korean*	4	3	2
	The Banana Tree Canteen	*Pan-Asian*	2	2	2
	Fat Boy's	*Thai*	2	3	3
£30+	Chicken Shop	*American*	3	4	4
	The Clink	*International*	2	3	5
	The Little Bay	*Mediterranean*	2	3	4
	Boqueria	*Spanish*	4	4	4
	Ed's Easy Diner	*Burgers, etc*	1	2	3
	Brady's	*Fish & chips*	3	3	3
	Chutney	*Indian*	4	4	2
	Indian Ocean	"	4	4	3
	Hare & Tortoise	*Pan-Asian*	3	2	3
	Talad Thai	*Thai*	3	2	1
	Mien Tay	*Vietnamese*	4	2	2
£25+	Dip & Flip	*Burgers, etc*	4	3	2
	Moxon's Fish Bar	*Fish & chips*	5	4	3
	Orange Pekoe	*Sandwiches, cakes, etc*	3	4	4
	Faanoos	*Persian*	3	2	4
	Holy Cow	*Indian*	4	3	3
	Sree Krishna	"	4	3	2
	Fujiyama	*Japanese*	4	3	2
	Lahore Kebab House	*Pakistani*	5	2	2
	Kaosarn	*Thai*	4	3	4
	The Pepper Tree	"	4	4	3
	The Paddyfield	*Vietnamese*	3	3	2
£20+	Franco Manca	*Pizza*	4	3	3
	Apollo Banana Leaf	*Indian*	5	1	1
	Hot Stuff	"	3	3	2
	Lahore Karahi	*Pakistani*	4	2	2
	Mirch Masala SW17	"	3	1	1
£15+	Wishbone	*American*	3	2	2
	Kerbisher & Malt	*Fish & chips*	3	3	2
	Meza	*Lebanese*	4	4	3
£10+	Dirty Burger	*Burgers, etc*	4	4	4

Outer western suburbs
Kew, Richmond, Twickenham, Teddington

£80+	The Bingham	*British, Modern*	3 3 4
£70+	Petersham Nurseries	*British, Modern*	2 1 4
£60+	The Glasshouse	*British, Modern*	5 5 3
	Petersham Hotel	*"*	3 5 5
	The Dysart Petersham	*"*	4 4 2
	Al Boccon di'vino	*Italian*	4 3 5
£50+	A Cena	*Italian*	3 3 3
£40+	Linnea	*British, Modern*	5 4 3
	The Wharf	*"*	2 3 4
	Brula	*French*	4 4 4
	La Buvette	*"*	3 3 4
	Ma Cuisine	*"*	3 4 3
	don Fernando's	*Spanish*	2 3 2
	Palmyra	*Lebanese*	4 3 2
	Four Regions	*Chinese*	3 3 2
	Matsuba	*Japanese*	4 3 2
£35+	Canta Napoli	*Italian*	3 3 2
	Pizzeria Rustica	*Pizza*	4 4 3
	Fat Boy's	*Thai*	2 3 3
£15+	Taylor St Baristas	*Sandwiches, cakes, etc*	4 4 3

EAST

Smithfield & Farringdon (EC1)

£70+			
The Clove Club	British, Modern		4 4 4
Club Gascon	French		4 3 3
Gaucho	Steaks & grills		2 1 1
Smiths (Top Floor)	"		2 2 2

£60+			
Bird of Smithfield	British, Modern		2 2 3
Chiswell Street Dining Rms	"		2 2 2
The Jugged Hare	"		3 3 3
St John	British, Traditional		4 4 2
Bonnie Gull Seafood Cafe	Fish & seafood		4 3 3
Bleeding Heart	French		3 3 5
Moro	Spanish		5 4 4

£50+			
The Modern Pantry	British, Modern		3 3 3
Bistrot Bruno Loubet	French		3 3 3
Café du Marché	"		3 4 5
Fabrizio	Italian		4 4 2
Portal	Portuguese		3 4 4
Hix	Steaks & grills		3 2 2
Smiths (Dining Rm)	"		2 2 2
Sushi Tetsu	Japanese		5 5 3

£40+			
Granger & Co	Australian		2 3 4
Blackfoot	British, Modern		3 3 2
Caravan	"		3 2 4
Foxlow	"		3 3 3
The Peasant	"		3 3 4
Vinoteca	"		2 4 4
The Fox and Anchor	British, Traditional		3 3 5
The Quality Chop House	"		4 5 4
Chabrot Bistrot des Halles	French		2 2 2
Comptoir Gascon	"		3 3 4
Santore	Italian		4 4 2
Ibérica	Spanish		3 2 3
The Gate	Vegetarian		3 2 2
Burger & Lobster	Burgers, etc		3 2 3
Workshop Coffee	Sandwiches, cakes, etc		4 3 3

£35+			
Lantana Cafe	Australian		3 3 4
Cellar Gascon	French		3 3 3
Apulia	Italian		3 3 1
Polpo	"		2 3 5
Morito	Spanish		4 4 4
Amico Bio	Vegetarian		2 2 2
Tas	Turkish		2 3 3
Pham Sushi	Japanese		5 4 1
Tajima Tei	"		3 3 3

	On The Bab	*Korean*	4 3 4
	Banana Tree Canteen	*Pan-Asian*	2 2 2
	Busaba Eathai	*Thai*	2 2 4
	Cây Tre	*Vietnamese*	3 3 3
	Pho	"	3 3 3
£30+	Smiths (Ground Floor)	*British, Modern*	2 2 4
	Fish Central	*Fish & seafood*	3 3 2
	Kolossi Grill	*Greek*	3 4 4
	La Porchetta Pizzeria	*Italian*	3 3 3
	The Eagle	*Mediterranean*	4 3 4
	The Little Bay	"	2 3 4
	Look Mum No Hands!	*Sandwiches, cakes, etc*	3 3 4
£25+	GB Pizza	*Pizza*	4 4 3
	Benito's Hat	*Mexican/TexMex*	3 4 2
£15+	Hummus Bros	*Mediterranean*	3 3 2
	Department of Coffee	*Sandwiches, cakes, etc*	3 3 4
	Daddy Donkey	*Mexican/TexMex*	4 3 2
£10+	Big Apple Hot Dogs	*Burgers, etc*	4 4 –
	Dose	*Sandwiches, cakes, etc*	4 4 2
	Nusa Kitchen	"	4 4 2
	Prufrock Coffee	"	4 3 3
	Spianata & Co	"	4 4 3

The City (EC2, EC3, EC4)

£80+	Hixter	*British, Modern*	3 3 3
£70+	City Social	*British, Modern*	4 5 4
	1 Lombard Street	"	2 1 2
	Angler	*Fish & seafood*	3 3 4
	Chamberlain's	"	3 3 2
	Coq d'Argent	*French*	2 2 3
	Lutyens	"	2 2 2
	Sauterelle	"	3 3 4
	L'Anima	*Italian*	3 3 3
	HKK	*Chinese*	5 5 3
	Sushisamba	*Japanese*	3 3 5
£60+	Bread Street Kitchen	*British, Modern*	2 3 2
	The Don	"	3 4 3
	Duck & Waffle	"	2 2 5
	The Mercer	"	3 2 2
	1901	"	1 1 3
	3 South Place	"	2 3 3
	The White Swan	"	4 4 3

	Sweetings	*Fish & seafood*	3 2 3
	Manicomio	*Italian*	3 2 3
	Barbecoa	*Steaks & grills*	2 2 3
	Goodman City	*"*	3 3 3
	Hawksmoor	*"*	4 4 3
	Vanilla Black	*Vegetarian*	3 3 3
	Ladurée	*Afternoon tea*	2 2 2
	1701	*Middle Eastern*	4 3 3
£50+	The Hoxton Grill	*American*	2 2 4
	The Chancery	*British, Modern*	3 4 2
	Gin Joint	*"*	2 3 3
	High Timber	*"*	3 4 4
	Merchants Tavern	*"*	4 4 4
	Northbank	*"*	3 3 3
	Rivington Grill	*"*	2 2 3
	The Sign of the Don	*"*	2 3 4
	Paternoster Chop House	*British, Traditional*	3 3 3
	Fish Market	*Fish & seafood*	3 4 3
	The Royal Exchange	*French*	2 2 4
	28-50	*"*	3 3 4
	Vivat Bacchus	*International*	2 3 2
	Piccolino	*Italian*	2 2 2
	Taberna Etrusca	*"*	3 3 3
	Eyre Brothers	*Spanish*	4 3 4
	New Street Grill	*Steaks & grills*	2 3 4
	The Tramshed	*"*	2 2 4
	Chinese Cricket Club	*Chinese*	4 2 1
	Cinnamon Kitchen	*Indian*	4 4 3
	Mint Leaf	*"*	3 2 3
	City Miyama	*Japanese*	3 3 1
£40+	Bodean's	*American*	2 2 2
	The Anthologist	*British, Modern*	3 4 3
	Princess of Shoreditch	*"*	3 4 3
	George & Vulture	*British, Traditional*	2 3 5
	Loch Fyne	*Fish & seafood*	2 2 2
	Orpheus	*"*	4 3 1
	Penkul & Banks	*Fusion*	4 4 2
	L' Anima Cafe	*Italian*	3 4 3
	Rocket	*Mediterranean*	3 3 3
	Relais de Venise L'Entrecôte	*Steaks & grills*	3 2 3
	Burger & Lobster	*Burgers, etc*	3 2 3
	Thai Square City	*Thai*	2 2 2
£35+	Simpson's Tavern	*British, Traditional*	3 4 5
	Tramontana Brindisa	*Spanish*	3 2 3
	Haché	*Burgers, etc*	3 3 4
	Natural Kitchen	*Salads*	3 2 3
	Haz	*Turkish*	2 3 3
	K10	*Japanese*	4 3 2

£30+	The Diner	*Burgers, etc*	1 3 3
	Caffé Vergnano	*Sandwiches, cakes, etc*	3 3 3
	ping pong	*Chinese, Dim sum*	2 2 3
	Hare & Tortoise	*Pan-Asian*	3 2 3
£25+	Hilliard	*British, Modern*	4 2 2
	The Wine Library	*International*	1 3 5
	Konditor & Cook	*Sandwiches, cakes, etc*	3 4 2
£20+	Patty and Bun	*Burgers, etc*	4 2 3
£15+	Notes	*British, Modern*	2 4 4
	Street Kitchen	*"*	3 3 –
	Hummus Bros	*Mediterranean*	3 3 2
	Taylor St Baristas	*Sandwiches, cakes, etc*	4 4 3
	Chilango	*Mexican/TexMex*	3 2 2
£10+	Coco Di Mama	*Italian*	4 3 2
	Fuzzy's Grub	*Sandwiches, cakes, etc*	3 2 2
	Nusa Kitchen	*"*	4 4 2
	Spianata & Co	*"*	4 4 3
	Nusa Kitchen	*Middle Eastern*	4 4 2
	City Càphê	*Vietnamese*	4 3 2
£5+	Pilpel	*Middle Eastern*	4 4 2

East End & Docklands (All E postcodes)

£80+	Typing Room	*International*	5 4 4
	Roka	*Japanese*	5 3 4
£70+	Galvin La Chapelle	*French*	4 4 5
	Les Trois Garçons	*"*	2 2 2
£60+	Beach Blanket Babylon	*British, Modern*	1 2 3
	The Boundary	*"*	2 2 2
	Lyle's	*"*	4 4 2
	One Canada Square	*"*	2 3 1
	Tom's Kitchen	*"*	2 1 1
	Plateau	*French*	1 3 3
	Boisdale of Canary Wharf	*Scottish*	3 4 3
	Goodman	*Steaks & grills*	3 3 3
	Hawksmoor	*"*	4 4 3
	Bevis Marks	*Kosher*	2 2 2
£50+	Bistrotheque	*British, Modern*	3 2 4
	The Gun	*"*	3 3 5
	Hoi Polloi	*"*	2 3 3
	The Narrow	*"*	1 1 2

Smiths Brasserie	"	3	3	4
Bumpkin	British, Traditional	3	2	2
St John Bread & Wine	"	5	3	4
Forman's	Fish & seafood	4	3	3
Wright Brothers	"	4	3	3
Il Bordello	Italian	4	5	4
Buen Ayre	Argentinian	4	2	2
Café Spice Namaste	Indian	4	4	3
Elephant Royale	Thai	2	2	2

£40+					
Balans	British, Modern	2	4	3
The Empress	"	3	4	3
The Morgan Arms	"	4	3	4
Rochelle Canteen	"	4	4	4
Albion	British, Traditional	2	2	2
Canteen	"	1	1	1
The Grapes	Fish & seafood	1	2	5
Brawn	French	5	3	4
Real Greek	Greek	2	2	2
Verden	International	–	–	–
La Figa	Italian	3	3	3
Obika	"	2	2	1
Rotorino	"	2	2	3
Rocket	Mediterranean	3	3	3
Bravas	Spanish	4	3	4
Ibérica	"	3	2	3
Hill & Szrok	Steaks & grills	–	–	–
Relais de Venise L'Entrecôte	"	3	2	3
Ark Fish	Fish & chips	5	4	2
Pizza East	Pizza	4	3	4
Story Deli	"	5	2	3
Lotus	Chinese	3	2	2
Royal China	"	4	2	2
Sichuan Folk	"	4	3	2
Yi-Ban	"	4	3	2
Dishoom	Indian	4	3	4

£35+	Chicken Shop & Dirty Burger		American		
		–	–	–
Eat 17	British, Modern	3	4	5
Provender	French	4	3	2
LMNT	International	2	3	5
Lardo	Italian	3	2	4
Andina	Peruvian	4	3	4
Yalla Yalla	Lebanese	3	3	4
Haz	Turkish	2	3	3
Shanghai	Chinese	3	2	4
Little Georgia Café	Georgian	3	2	3
Pho	Vietnamese	3	3	3
Viet Grill	"	4	2	3

£30+	Bird	British, Modern	4	4	3

FSA Ratings: from **1** (Poor) to **5** (Exceptional)

	Clutch	*Steaks & grills*	4	4	4
	Faulkner's	*Fish & chips*	4	3	2
	Yard Sale Pizza	*Pizza*	–	–	–
	DF Mexico	*Mexican/TexMex*	3	3	4
	Mangal I	*Turkish*	5	3	2
	Tonkotsu East	*Japanese*	3	3	3
	Mien Tay	*Vietnamese*	4	2	2
	Sông Quê	*"*	2	1	2
£25+	Comptoir Libanais	*Lebanese*	2	2	2
	Gourmet San	*Chinese*	4	2	1
	Lahore Kebab House	*Pakistani*	5	2	2
	Needoo	*"*	4	3	2
	Tayyabs	*"*	4	2	3
£20+	Sager & Wilde	*British, Modern*	3	4	4
	E Pellicci	*Italian*	2	4	5
	Franco Manca	*Pizza*	4	3	3
	Mirch Masala	*Pakistani*	3	1	1
£15+	Chilango	*Mexican/TexMex*	3	2	2
£10+	Spianata & Co	*Sandwiches, cakes, etc*	4	4	3
	Bunnychow	*South African*	–	–	–
£5+	Brick Lane Beigel Bake	*Sandwiches, cakes, etc*	5	3	1
	Pilpel	*Middle Eastern*	4	4	2

MAPS

MAP I – LONDON OVERVIEW

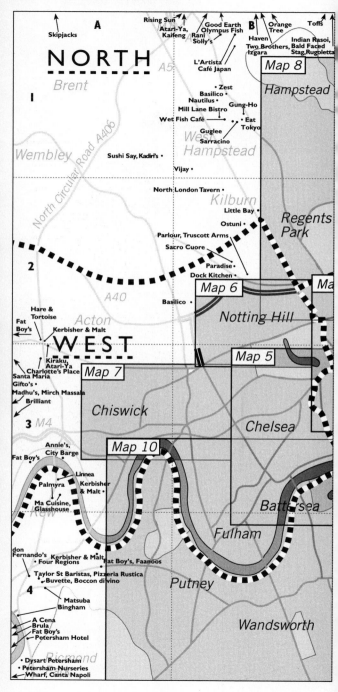

MAP 1 – LONDON OVERVIEW

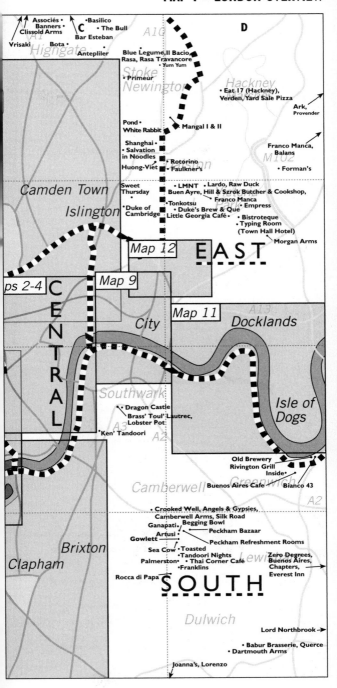

MAP 2 – WEST END OVERVIEW

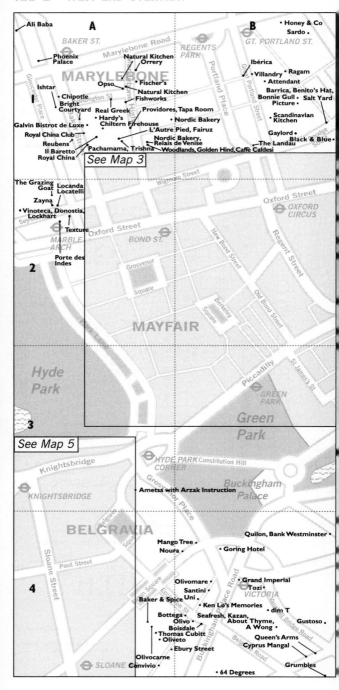

A

BAKER ST.

Ali Baba

Marylebone Road

REGENTS PARK

B

Honey & Co
Sardo

GT. PORTLAND ST.

Phoenix Palace

Natural Kitchen
Orrery

MARYLEBONE

Ishtar

Opso
Fischer's

Natural Kitchen
Fishworks

Ibérica
Villandry · Ragam
· Attendant

Chipotle
Bright
Courtyard

Barrica, Benito's Hat,
Bonnie Gull · Salt Yard
Picture ·

Real Greek
Hardy's
Chiltern Firehouse

Providores, Tapa Room

Galvin Bistrot de Luxe ·

Nordic Bakery

Scandinavian
Kitchen

Royal China Club

L'Autre Pied, Fairuz

Reubens
Il Baretto
Royal China

Nordic Bakery,
Relais de Venise

Gaylord ·

The Landau
Black & Blue

Pachamama, Trishna

Woodlands, Golden Hind, Caffè Caldesi

See Map 3

The Grazing
Goat

Locanda
Locatelli

Wigmore Street

Oxford Street

Zayna

OXFORD
CIRCUS

· Vinoteca, Donostia,
Lockhart

Texture

Oxford Street

BOND ST.

New Bond Street

Regent Street

MARBLE
ARCH

Grosvenor

2

Porte des
Indes

Square

Berkeley

MAYFAIR

Square

Old Bond Street

Hyde
Park

Park Lane

Piccadilly

St James's St.

3

GREEN
PARK

Green
Park

See Map 5

Knightsbridge

HYDE PARK Constitution Hill
CORNER

KNIGHTSBRIDGE

Buckingham
Palace

BELGRAVIA

Ametsa with Arzak Instruction

Sloane Street

Pont Street

Quilon, Bank Westminster ·

Mango Tree ·
Noura ·

· Goring Hotel

4

Olivomare ·
Santini ·
Uni

· Grand Imperial
Tozi

VICTORIA

Baker & Spice

Ken Lo's Memories ·

· dim T

Bottega
Olivo
Boisdale
· Thomas Cubitt
· Oliveto

Seafresh, Kazan,
About Thyme,
A Wong ·

Gustoso ·

Queen's Arms
Cyprus Mangal

· Ebury Street

SLOANE

Olivocarne
Convivio

Grumbles

· 64 Degrees

MAP 2 – WEST END OVERVIEW

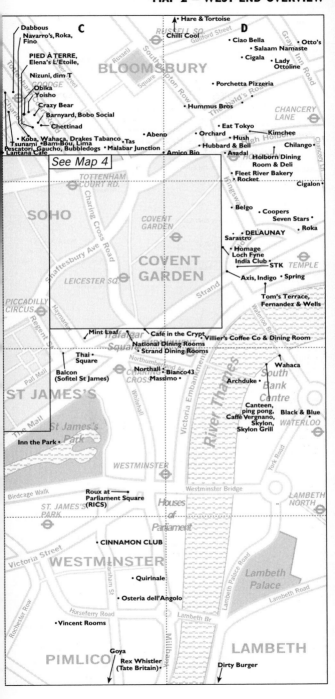

C

D

↑ Hare & Tortoise

Chilli Cool

• Ciao Bella • Otto's
• Salaam Namaste
• Cigala • Lady
Ottoline

• Dabbous
Navarro's, Roka,
Fino
PIED À TERRE,
Elena's L'Etoile,
Nizuni, dim T

BLOOMSBURY

• Porchetta Pizzeria

• Obika
• Yoisho
Crazy Bear
• Barnyard, Bobo Social
Chettinad

• Hummus Bros

CHANCERY
LANE

• Koba, Wahaca, Drakes Tabanco,
Tsunami, •Bam-Bou, Lima
Pescatori, Gaucho, Bubbledogs
Lantana Cafe

• Abeno

• Eat Tokyo
• Orchard •Kimchee
• Hush
• Hubbard & Bell Chilango
• Asadal

• Tas
•Malabar Junction
Amico Bio

Holborn Dining
Room & Deli
Fleet River Bakery
• Rocket
Cigalon •

See Map 4

**TOTTENHAM
COURT RD.**

• Belgo
Coopers
Seven Stars •
Roka

SOHO

**COVENT
GARDEN**

• DELAUNAY
Sarastro
• Homage
Loch Fyne
India Club •STK TEMPLE
Axis, Indigo • Spring

**COVENT
GARDEN**

LEICESTER SQ.

Strand

Tom's Terrace,
Fernandez & Wells

**PICCADILLY
CIRCUS**

Mint Leaf • Café in the Crypt
National Dining Rooms Villier's Coffee Co & Dining Room
• Strand Dining Rooms

Thai
Square •

Balcon
(Sofitel St James)

Northall •
• Bianco43
Massimo •

Wahaca
South
Bank
Centre

Archduke •

ST JAMES'S

Inn the Park •

**St James's
Park**

Canteen,
ping pong,
Caffè Vergnano, Black & Blue
Skylon, WATERLOO
Skylon Grill

WESTMINSTER

River Thames

**WESTMINSTER
BRIDGE**

LAMBETH
NORTH

Roux at
Parliament Square
(RICS)

**ST. JAMES'S
PARK**

Houses
of
Parliament

• CINNAMON CLUB

WESTMINSTER

Lambeth
Palace

• Quirinale

• Osteria dell'Angolo

• Vincent Rooms

PIMLICO

Goya
Rex Whistler
(Tate Britain)•

LAMBETH

Dirty Burger •

MAP 3 – MAYFAIR, ST JAMES'S & WEST SOHO

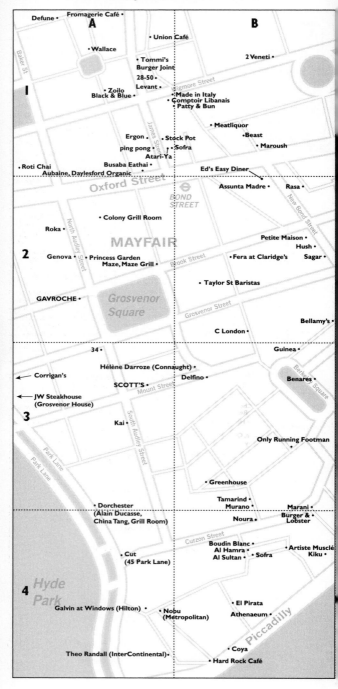

MAP 3 – MAYFAIR, ST JAMES'S & WEST SOHO

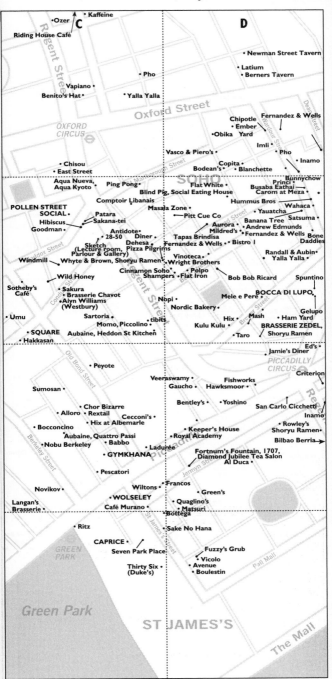

MAP 4 – EAST SOHO, CHINATOWN & COVENT GARDEN

MAP 4 – EAST SOHO, CHINATOWN & COVENT GARDEN

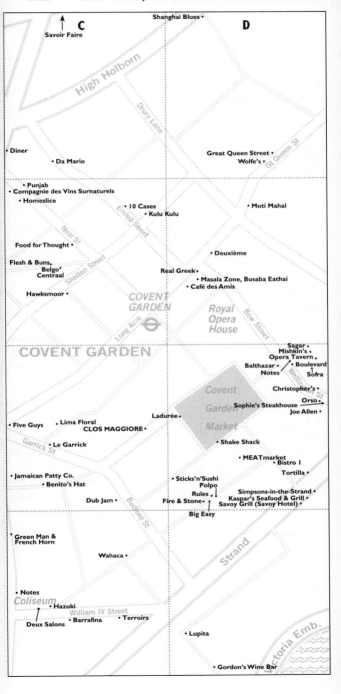

C D

Shanghai Blues •

Savoir Faire

High Holborn

Drury Lane

• Diner

• Da Mario

Great Queen Street •
Wolfe's •

Gt Queen St

• Punjab
• Compagnie des Vins Surnaturels
• Homeslice

Neal St

Endell Street

• 10 Cases
• Kulu Kulu

• Moti Mahal

Food for Thought •

Shelton Street

• Deuxième

Flesh & Buns,
Belgo•
Centraal

Real Greek •

• Masala Zone, Busaba Eathai
• Café des Amis

Hawksmoor •

COVENT
GARDEN

Long Acre

Royal
Opera
House

Bow Street

COVENT GARDEN

Sagar •
Mishkin's •
Opera Tavern •
Balthazar •
Notes •

Wellington St

• Boulevard
• Sofra

Christopher's •
Sophie's Steakhouse •

• Orso •
Joe Allen •

• Five Guys

• Lima Floral
CLOS MAGGIORE •

Ladurée •

Covent
Garden
Market

Garrick St

• Le Garrick

• Shake Shack

• MEATmarket
• Bistro 1
Tortilla •

• Jamaican Patty Co.
• Benito's Hat

Dub Jam •

Bedford St

• Sticks'n'Sushi
Polpo
Rules •
Fire & Stone •

Big Easy

Simpsons-in-the-Strand
Kaspar's Seafood & Grill •
Savoy Grill (Savoy Hotel) •

Green Man &
French Horn

Wahaca •

Strand

• Notes
Coliseum

• Hazuki

William IV Street

Deux Salons • Barrafina • Terroirs •

• Lupita

Victoria Emb.

• Gordon's Wine Bar

MAP 5 – KNIGHTSBRIDGE, CHELSEA & SOUTH KENSINGTON

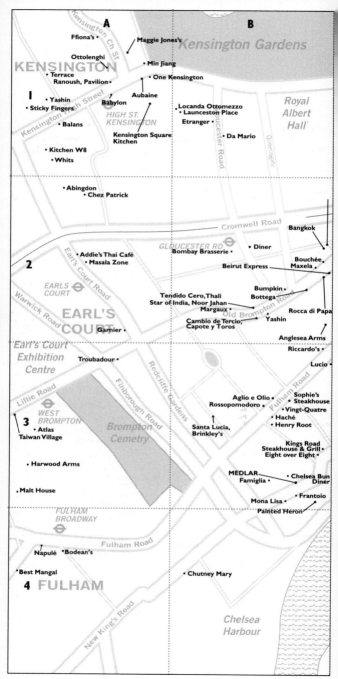

A

Ffiona's •

Maggie Jones's •

Kensington Gardens

Ottolenghi •

• Min Jiang

KENSINGTON

• Terrace

Ranoush, Pavilion •

• One Kensington

B

Royal Albert Hall

I

• Yashin

• Sticky Fingers

Aubaine •

Babylon •

Royal Albert Hall

• Balans

HIGH ST. KENSINGTON

• Locanda Ottomezzo

• Launceston Place

Etranger •

• Kitchen W8

Kensington Square Kitchen

• Da Mario

• Whits

• Abingdon

• Chez Patrick

Cromwell Road

Bangkok

GLOUCESTER RD

• Diner

Bombay Brasserie •

Bouchée •

Maxela •

2

• Addie's Thai Café

• Masala Zone

Beirut Express •

EARLS COURT

Bumpkin •

Bottega •

Tendido Cero, Thali

Star of India, Noor Jahan

Margaux •

EARL'S COURT

Rocca di Papa •

Cambio de Tercio,

Capote y Toros

• Yashin

Warwick Road

Garnier •

Anglesea Arms

Riccardo's •

Earl's Court Exhibition Centre

Troubadour •

Lucio •

Redcliffe Gardens

Aglio e Olio •

Rossopomodoro •

• Sophie's

• Steakhouse

Lillie Road

WEST BROMPTON

• Vingt-Quatre

• Atlas

Taiwan Village

Brompton Cemetery

Santa Lucia,

Brinkley's

• Haché

• Henry Root

3

• Harwood Arms

Kings Road

Steakhouse & Grill

Eight over Eight •

• Malt House

MEDLAR

Famiglia

• Chelsea Bun

Diner

Mona Lisa •

• Frantoio

Painted Heron

FULHAM BROADWAY

Fulham Road

Napulé •

• Bodean's

• Best Mangal

4 FULHAM

• Chutney Mary

New King's Road

Chelsea Harbour

MAP 5 – KNIGHTSBRIDGE, CHELSEA & SOUTH KENSINGTON

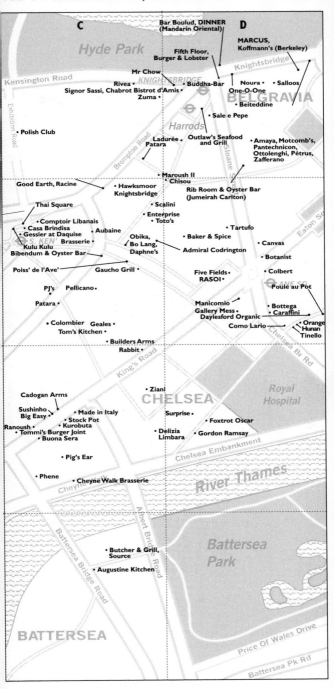

Hyde Park

C

Bar Boulud, DINNER
(Mandarin Oriental)

D

MARCUS,
Koffmann's (Berkeley)

Fifth Floor,
Burger & Lobster

Knightsbridge

Kensington Road

KNIGHTSBRIDGE

Mr Chow

Rivea •

Buddha-Bar •

Noura •

One-O-One

• Salloos

BELGRAVIA

Signor Sassi, Chabrot Bistrot d'Amis •

Zuma •

• Beiteddine

• Sale e Pepe

• Polish Club

Harrods

Brompton Road

Ladurée
Patara

Outlaw's Seafood
and Grill

Amaya, Motcomb's,
Pantechnicon,
Ottolenghi, Pétrus,
Zafferano

Good Earth, Racine

• Hawksmoor
Knightsbridge

Maroush II

Chisou

Rib Room & Oyster Bar
(Jumeirah Carlton)

Thai Square

• Scalini

• Enterprise

• Toto's

• Comptoir Libanais

• Casa Brindisa
• Gessler at Daquise   • Aubaine
Kulu Kulu   Brasserie

Bibendum & Oyster Bar

Obika,
Bo Lang,
Daphne's

• Tartufo

• Baker & Spice

Admiral Codrington

• Canvas

• Botanist

Poiss' de l'Ave'   Gaucho Grill •

Five Fields •
RASOI •

• Colbert

Poule au Pot

PJ's   Pellicano •

Patara •

Manicomio •
Gallery Mess
Daylesford Organic

Como Lario

• Bottega
• Caraffini

Orange

• Colombier   Geales •
Tom's Kitchen •

• Builders Arms

Rabbit •

King's Road

Hunan
Tinello

• Ziani

CHELSEA

Royal
Hospital

Cadogan Arms

Sushinho
Big Easy

• Made in Italy
• Stock Pot
• Kurobuta

Surprise •

• Foxtrot Oscar

Ranoush •
• Tommi's Burger Joint
• Buona Sera

• Delizia
Limbara

• Gordon Ramsay

Chelsea Embankment

• Pig's Ear

Chelsea Bridge Road

River Thames

• Phene   • Cheyne Walk Brasserie

Cheyne

Battersea Bridge Road

• Butcher & Grill,
Source

Albert Bridge Road

Battersea
Park

• Augustine Kitchen

BATTERSEA

Price Of Wales Drive

Battersea Pk Rd

MAP 6 – NOTTING HILL & BAYSWATER

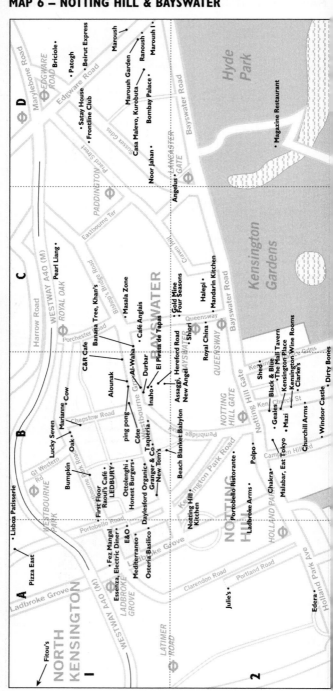

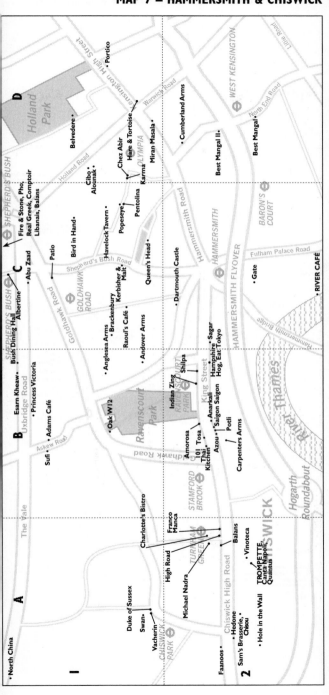

MAP 7 – HAMMERSMITH & CHISWICK

MAP 8 – HAMPSTEAD, CAMDEN TOWN & ISLINGTON

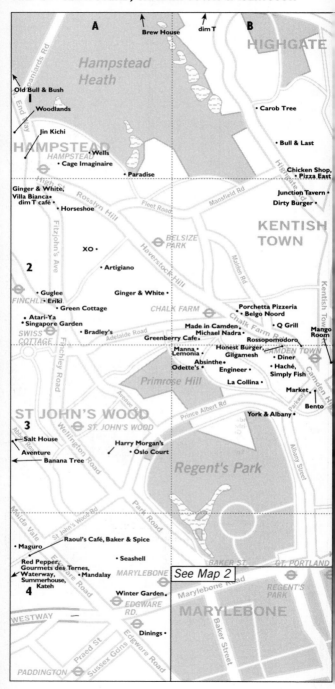

A

Brew House

dim T

B

HIGHGATE

Hampstead Heath

Old Bull & Bush

1

Woodlands

Jin Kichi

HAMPSTEAD

HAMPSTEAD • Wells

• Cage Imaginaire

• Paradise

• Carob Tree

• Bull & Last

Chicken Shop, • Pizza East

Ginger & White, Villa Bianca, dim T café

• Horseshoe

Rosslyn Hill

Fleet Road

Mansfield Road

Junction Tavern •

Dirty Burger •

KENTISH TOWN

Fitzjohn's Ave

2

XO •

BELSIZE PARK

Haverstock Hill

Maiden Rd

Kentish Town Rd

• Artigiano

• Guglee
FINCHLEY • Eriki
• Green Cottage

Ginger & White •

CHALK FARM

Porchetta Pizzeria
• Belgo Noord

• Q Grill

Mango Room

• Atari-Ya
Singapore Garden

Chalk Farm Rd

Made in Camden, •
Michael Nadra •

Rossopomodoro •

• Bradley's

Greenberry Cafe •

CAMDEN TOWN

SWISS COTTAGE

Finchley Road

Adelaide Road

Manna •
Lemonia •

Honest Burger,
Gilgamesh

• Diner

• Haché,
Simply Fish

Absinthe •

Odette's •

Engineer •

La Collina •

Market •

Camden High St

Bento •

Primrose Hill

Avenue Road

Prince Albert Rd

York & Albany •

Albany Street

ST JOHN'S WOOD

3

ST. JOHN'S WOOD

Wellington Road

Salt House

Aventure

Banana Tree

Harry Morgan's

• Oslo Court

Regent's Park

Park Road

Maida Vale

Raoul's Café, Baker & Spice

• Maguro

• Seashell

BAKER ST.

GT. PORTLAND

Red Pepper,
Gourmets des Ternes,
Waterway,
Summerhouse,
4 Kateh

Edgware Road

• Mandalay

MARYLEBONE

See Map 2

Marylebone Road

REGENT'S PARK

Winter Garden •

EDGWARE RD.

MARYLEBONE

Baker Street

WESTWAY

• Dinings

PADDINGTON

Praed St

Sussex Gdns

Sussex Gardens Rd

MAP 8 – HAMPSTEAD, CAMDEN TOWN & ISLINGTON

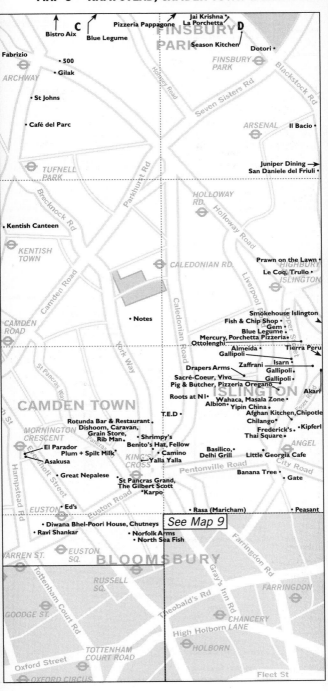

Bistro Aix **C**
Blue Legume
Pizzeria Pappagone
Jai Krishna •
La Porchetta •
D
Season Kitchen
Dotori •

• Fabrizio
• 500
FINSBURY PARK
FINSBURY PARK

• Gilak
ARCHWAY

• St Johns
ARSENAL
Il Bacio •

• Café del Parc

Juniper Dining →
San Daniele del Friuli •

TUFNELL PARK

HOLLOWAY RD.

• Kentish Canteen

KENTISH TOWN

CALEDONIAN RD.
Prawn on the Lawn •
Le Coq, Trullo •
HIGHBURY ISLINGTON

CAMDEN ROAD
• Notes
Smokehouse Islington
Fish & Chip Shop •
• Gem
Blue Legume •
Mercury, Porchetta Pizzeria•
Ottolenghi•
Almeida •
Gallipoli •
Tierra Peru •
Zaffrani •
Isarn •
Drapers Arms •
Gallipoli •
Sacré-Coeur, Vivo
Gallipoli •
Pig & Butcher, Pizzeria Oregano •
ISLINGTON
Akar
Roots at N1•
Wahaca, Masala Zone •
Albion• Yipin China •
Afghan Kitchen, Chipotle

CAMDEN TOWN
T.E.D •
Chilango•
Frederick's •
• Kipferl
Thai Square •
ANGEL
Rotunda Bar & Restaurant •
Dishoom, Caravan,
Grain Store,
Rib Man
Shrimpy's •
Benito's Hat, Fellow
Basilico,
Delhi Grill
• Little Georgia Cafe
MORNINGTON CRESCENT
El Parador
Plum + Spilt Milk
• Camino
Yalla Yalla
KING'S CROSS
Banana Tree
• Gate
Asakusa
• Great Nepalese
St Pancras Grand,
The Gilbert Scott
Karpo
Pentonville Road
EUSTON
• Ed's
Euston Road
• Rasa (Maricham)
• Peasant

See Map 9

• Diwana Bhel-Poori House, Chutneys
• Ravi Shankar
• Norfolk Arms
• North Sea Fish
WARREN ST.
EUSTON SQ.
BLOOMSBURY

RUSSELL SQ.
FARRINGDON

GOODGE ST.
CHANCERY LANE

TOTTENHAM COURT ROAD
HOLBORN

Oxford Street
OXFORD CIRCUS
Fleet St

MAP 9 – THE CITY

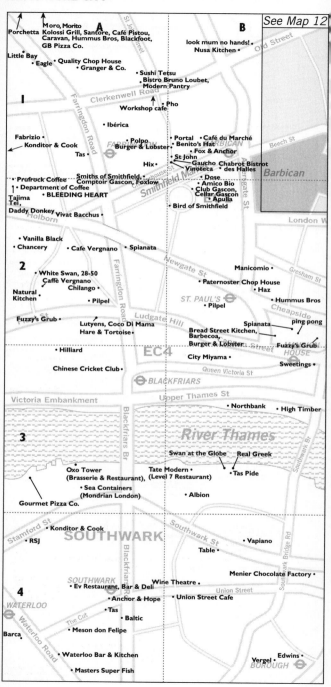

See Map 12

Porchetta

Moro, Morito
Kolossi Grill, Santore, Café Pistou,
Caravan, Hummus Bros, Blackfoot,
GB Pizza Co.

Little Bay
• Eagle

look mum no hands! •
Nusa Kitchen

A

B

Old Street

• Quality Chop House
• Granger & Co.

• Sushi Tetsu
• Bistro Bruno Loubet,
Modern Pantry

Clerkenwell Road

I

Fabrizio •
Konditor & Cook

Workshop cafe

• Ibérica

• Pho

Beech St

• Polpo
Burger & Lobster

• Portal • Café du Marché
• Benito's Hat

Barbican

Tas •

Hix •

• Fox & Anchor
St John
Gaucho Chabrot Bistrot
Vinoteca • des Halles

• Prufrock Coffee
↑ • Department of Coffee
Tajima **• BLEEDING HEART**
Tei,
Daddy Donkey Vivat Bacchus •

Smiths of Smithfield
Comptoir Gascon, Foxlow

• Dose
• Amico Bio
• Club Gascon,
Cellar Gascon • Apulia

London W

Holborn

• Bird of Smithfield

• Vanilla Black
• Chancery

• Cafe Vergnano • Spianata

Newgate St

Gresham St

2

• White Swan, 28-50
Caffè Vergnano
Chilango

Natural
Kitchen

• Pilpel

• Manicomio

• Paternoster Chop House
• Haz

ST. PAUL'S
• Pilpel

• Hummus Bros

Cheapside

Fuzzy's Grub •

Lutyens, Coco Di Mama
Hare & Tortoise

Spianata
ping pong

Ludgate Hill

Bread Street Kitchen,
Barbecoa,
Burger & Lobster

Fuzzy's Grub •

EC4

• Hilliard

City Miyama •

Sweetings •

Chinese Cricket Club •

BLACKFRIARS

Queen Victoria St

Victoria Embankment

Upper Thames St

• Northbank

• High Timber

3

River Thames

Swan at the Globe   Real Greek

Oxo Tower
(Brasserie & Restaurant),

Tate Modern •
(Level 7 Restaurant)

• Tas Pide

• Sea Containers
(Mondrian London)

Gourmet Pizza Co.

• Albion

Stamford St

• Konditor & Cook

SOUTHWARK

Southwark St

• RSJ

• Vapiano

Table •

Menier Chocolate Factory •

SOUTHWARK

WATERLOO

Wine Theatre •

• Ev Restaurant, Bar & Deli

• Union Street Cafe

Union Street

4

• Anchor & Hope

• Tas

Barca •

• Baltic

• Meson don Felipe

• Waterloo Bar & Kitchen

Vergel •   Edwins •

• Masters Super Fish

BOROUGH

MAP 9 – THE CITY

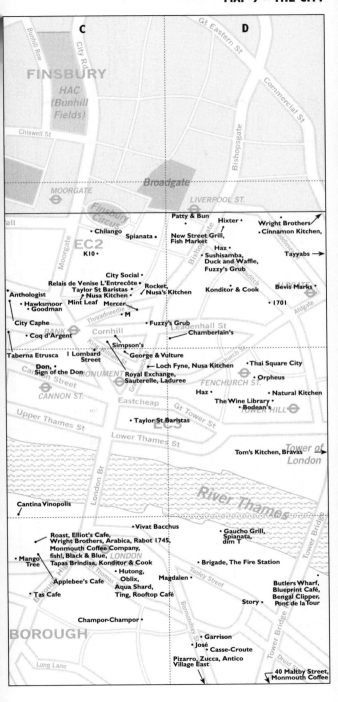

MAP 10 – SOUTH LONDON (& FULHAM)

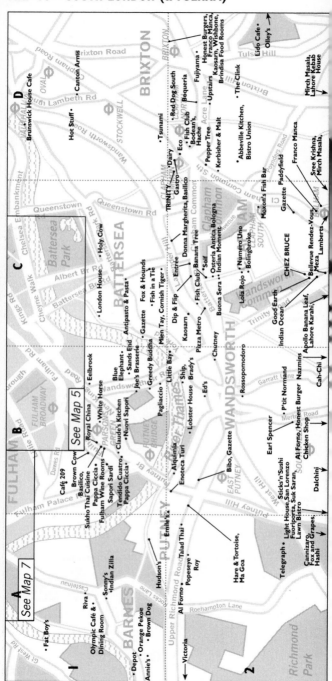

MAP 11 – EAST END & DOCKLANDS

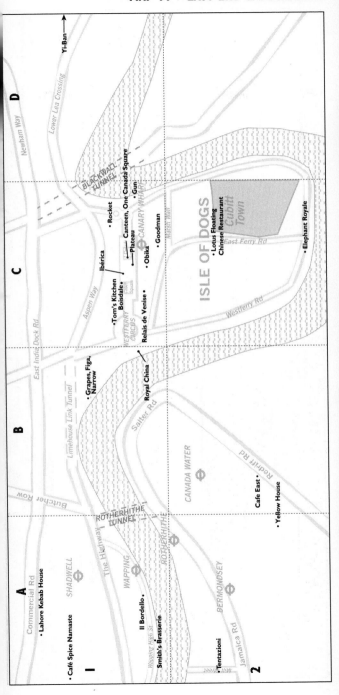

MAP 12 – SHOREDITCH & BETHNAL GREEN

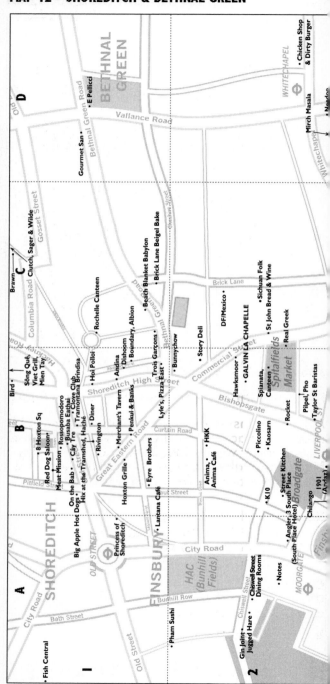

BETHNAL GREEN

SHOREDITCH

FINSBURY

WHITECHAPEL

Spitalfields Market

A   B   C   D

1   2

Columbia Road
Vallance Road
Bethnal Green Road
Gosset Street
Old
Hackney Road
Brick Lane
Commercial St
Bishopsgate
Curtain Road
Great Eastern Road
Shoreditch High Street
Old Street
Pitfield
City Road
Bunhill Row
Bath Street
Chiswell Street
Whitechapel

• Fish Central
• Pham Sushi
Gin Joint • Jugged Hare •
Chiswell Street Dining Rooms •
• Notes
Princess of Shoreditch •
• Lantana Café
Red Dog Saloon •
• 8 Hoxton Sq
Meat Mission •
Big Apple Hot Dogs •
On the Bab •
Hix at the Tramshed, Haché •
Cây Tre • Busaba Eathai •
Rossopomodoro •
Clove Club •
Tramontana Brindisa
• Diner
• Rivington
Merchant's Tavern •
Hoxton Grille •
Penkul & Banks •
Eyre Brothers •
Anima, • Anima Café
• HKK
• K10
• Piccolino
• Kaosarn
Street Kitchen •
Angler, 3 South Place
(South Place Hotel)
Chilango •
1901 (Andaz) •
Broadgate
Rocket •
Taylor St Baristas •
Pilpel, Pho •
• Real Greek
Splanata, Canteen •
St John Bread & Wine •
• Sichuan Folk
GALVIN LA CHAPELLE
Hawksmoor •
DF/Mexico •
• Story Deli
Bunnychow •
Troisgros Garçons •
Lyle's, Pizza East •
Hoi Polloi •
Andina •
• Dishoom
• Boundary, Albion
Rochelle Canteen •
Bird •
Sông Quê, Viet Grill, Mien Tây
Gourmet San •
Brawn •
Clutch, Sager & Wilde •
• E Pellici
Beach Blanket Babylon •
Brick Lane Beigel Bake •
• Mirch Masala
Chicken Shop & Dirty Burger •
Liverpool St
Moorgate
Finsbury